Voicing Memory

NEW WORLD STUDIES

A. James Arnold, *Editor*

J. Michael Dash, David T. Haberly, and Roberto Márquez, *Associate Editors*

Antonio Benítez-Rojo, Joan Dayan, Dell H. Hymes, Vera M. Kutzinski, Candace Slater, and Iris M. Zavala, *Advisory Editors*

Voicing Memory

History and Subjectivity in French Caribbean Literature

Nick Nesbitt

New World Studies
A. James Arnold, Editor

University of Virginia Press
Charlottesville and London

The University of Virginia Press
© 2003 by the Rector and Visitors of the University of Virginia
All rights reserved

First published 2003

9 8 7 6 5 4 3 2

Library of Congress Cataloging-in-Publication Data
Nesbitt, Nick, 1969–
    Voicing memory : history and subjectivity in French Caribbean
literature / Nick Nesbitt.
       p. cm. — (New World studies)
    Includes bibliographical references and index.
    ISBN 0-8139-2150-3 (cloth : alk. paper) — ISBN 0-8139-2151-1 (pbk. :
alk. paper)
    1. Caribbean literature (French)—History and criticism. I. Title.
II. Series.
    PQ3940 .N47 2003
    840.9'729—dc21
                                                        2002009071

In connection with the banknote reproduction on p. 10, please note the following warning from the Institut d'émission des départements d'outre-mer à la Guadeloupe: "La contrefaçon ou la falsification des billets de banque et la mise en circulation des billets contrefaits ou falsifiés sont punis par les articles 442-1 et 442-2 du Code Pénal de peines pouvant aller jusqu'à trente ans de réclusion criminelle et trois millions de francs d'amende."

*To Frank and Dorothy D. Nesbitt
and in memory of Albert Drucker*

Contents

List of Illustrations		ix
Preface		xi
List of Abbreviations		xix
Introduction: Aesthetic Construction and Postcolonial Subjectivity *A Genealogy of Antillean Historical Experience*		1
1	The Vicissitudes of Memory *Representations of Louis Delgrès*	49
2	Antinomies of Double Consciousness in Aimé Césaire's *Cahier d'un retour au pays natal*	76
3	Aimé Césaire, *Présence africaine,* and Black Atlantic Historical Experience	95
4	Cannibalizing Hegel *Decolonization and European Theory in* La tragédie du roi Christophe	118
5	Dreaming of the Masters *Jazz and Memory in Daniel Maximin's* L'Isolé soleil *and* L'Ile et une nuit	145

6 History, Totality and Other Modernist Projects
  *Global Consciousness in the Writings of
  Edouard Glissant*   170

7 Voicing Memory
  Maryse Condé, Edwidge Danticat   192

  Postscript   213

  Notes   215

  Bibliography   237

  Index   253

Illustrations

1. French Antillean five-thousand-franc note, circa 1957 — 10
2. Haitian *wanga* — 41
3. Memorial plaque to Louis Delgrès — 65
4. Delgrès memorial commemoration, 2001 — 73
5. Vera Mukhina's *Worker and Farmgirl* at the 1937 Paris Exposition Internationale — 87
6. Closing passage from Shostakovich's Fourth Symphony, 1936 — 94
7. *Présence africaine* title page, 1947 — 103
8. *Présence africaine* title page, 1955 — 107

Preface

> Now it is over. What meaning can you see? It is as if it had not come to be, And yet it circulates as if it were.
>
> —Goethe, *Faust*

HISTORICAL EXPERIENCE is a by-product of human imperialism. The violent and destructive encounter between the known and the unknown, the mastered and the unmastered, wrenches beings from an immersion in cyclical time to experience the new. This historicizing dimension of imperialism operates not only in its most obvious geo-political guise, from Herodotus's *History* to the expansion and epic memorialization of the thirteenth-century Maninka state in West Africa, or Columbus's day-by-day accounts of his voyages to the Americas. Imperialism is fundamental to the human experience of modernity, from the infinite expansion of scientific knowledge into unknown realms, to the tentacular creation of billions of human consumers of mass-marketed products. This world, our world, functions following the model of what Edward Said has called "the major, . . . determining political horizon of modern Western culture, namely, imperialism" (60).

Who "we" might be, where "our" world is located, and whether, as Said implies, this general "imperialist" structure applies only or primarily to "the West" and its politics, I leave as open questions; in any case, I have never encountered a culture that did not share some of the exhilarating and terrifying dimensions of imperialism taken in this larger sense, along with an accompanying measure of historical awareness. Nor have I encountered a culture that did not, at some level, contest its various implications in imperialism and the traumas of historical change. In order to grasp more clearly this underlying imperial logic of historical experience, this book turns not to those areas in which these various modes of imperialist expansion have long reigned supreme and taken on the air of eternal, unquestioned inevitability, but to the margins and zones of conflict and shock where historical consciousness first awakens, at the horizons of imperialism, where this global phenomenon reveals itself most clearly as historical, political, cultural, and theoretical contradiction.

In the centuries following the Renaissance, European civilization expanded across the planet to encounter other lands and civilizations in voyages of discovery and conquest that constituted new societies dedicated to universal freedom, societies that were paradoxically instituted through the violent domination of preexisting terrains and peoples. In the Americas, the emissaries of European expansion decimated native populations, enslaved and imported millions, and instituted colonial regimes of domination and control at the very historical moment that the concepts of freedom, equality, and noncoercive community overthrew late feudalist European regimes that had functioned via the systematic denial of universal humanity. Even in its concept, the European Enlightenment was inherently and fundamentally contradictory; it implied at once the universality of human rights and the possibility of perpetual peace, while the concretization of its ideals necessarily implied the destruction of existing worlds. European imperialist expansion wrought terrifying brutality upon those it encountered, transporting along with the Declaration of the Rights of Man a violence hidden away in the bowels of the vessels of discovery like the plague-infested rats of Nosferatu, sailing into the harbors of the Americas to destroy and rebuild those lands beyond recognition.

In 1791 in Haiti, hundreds of thousands of enslaved laborers drew the full consequences of the French Enlightenment and Revolution and asserted their equal rights as human beings; by 1804, after years of violent warfare had decimated the island, this revolution overthrew the world order of the previous century to institute the world's first black republic. For all its momentous implications, the Haitian Revolution remained largely quarantined within the confines of a single Caribbean island, the young nation working through its own dialectic of terror and enlightenment as slavery and colonialism lived on elsewhere throughout the nineteenth century. It would be over a century before a second Antillean revolution would occur in the years following the first world war, when the victims of racism and colonization, to state things emphatically, again seized the arms of their oppressors in an uprising that transformed the political and economic face of the planet, bringing an end to European colonialism.

The astounding fact of this revolution as it occurred in France's colonies, however, was that it proceeded—with important exceptions—not through the redeployment of absolute terror, violence, and destruction, but via a reconstruction in human understanding and experience. This was a transformation whose weapons were the humanist arms of imagination, communication, and insight: poetry, literature, theater, philosophy, and polemical tracts. Its generating force arose from the radical productivity of human consciousness and understanding. The dynamic creativity of these colonized subjects sparked the historical movement to transform a eurocentric worldview and power structure; they argued for the determinate universality of human rights by means of the particular, unique experience of the subjects of French colonialism. These artists' portrayals of their communities and their own self-experience, "mere" acts of aesthetic representation, initiated one of the most profound redistributions of political power in the twentieth century. Their revolt destroyed the mythology of a timeless colonial world to initiate a dynamic, often contradictory historical experience. This book tells the story of that revolution in consciousness as it unfolded across the twentieth century, to echo on, as yet incomplete, in our present.

The Toussaint Louverture of this cultural revolution was the Martinican poet and statesman Aimé Césaire. Césaire's 1939 poem, *Cahier d'un retour au pays natal* ("Notebook of a Return to My Native Land"), instigated the decolonization movement in the French-speaking world on the plane of cultural representation and self-understanding, operating alongside and slightly ahead of a range of historical, economic, and political factors. Just as the earlier architects of the Haitian Revolution had applied the standards of the French Enlightenment to the actual conditions of slavery and the plantation, Césaire, along with writers such as Frantz Fanon, René Ménil, and Edouard Glissant, transformed the tools they appropriated in Paris in the 1930s, 1940s, and 1950s—including the dialectical philosophy of Hegel, Frobenius's defense of traditional African societies, Marx's critique of human alienation, and the poetic models of Rimbaud, Lautréamont, and surrealism—redirecting these sources to critique and undermine colonial violence and to transform the colonized subjects it had produced.

René Ménil has affirmed unequivocally a penetrating insight into the function of modernity on the part of the colonized. "Since," wrote Ménil in 1959, "of all peoples, the colonized are those who bear most harshly the weight of modern history . . . , isn't it up to them to reveal, more than all others, the reality of this world?" (23). These authors' voracious intellects absorbed the entirety of knowledge available to them, accepting no boundaries to the limits of their inquiry. "The appetite for knowledge that drives these distant regions in their newly achieved self-consciousness," wrote Edouard Glissant in his 1958 novel *La Lézarde*, "is unimaginable" (19). In stark contrast to the mechanical rejection of European authors such as Hegel or Sartre in much recent postcolonial criticism, Césaire has described the wide-eyed excitement he felt upon discovering Hegel's *Phenomenology of Spirit* following the second world war: "When the French translation of the *Phenomenology* first came out, I showed it to [Léopold] Senghor, and said to him 'Listen to what Hegel says, Léopold: to arrive at the Universal, one must immerse oneself in the Particular!'"[1] Césaire's brief reminiscence confirms the relevance of the genealogy of Antillean thought this study undertakes: these Antillean authors, as Said has argued for Fanon in particular, "[are] unintelligible without grasping that [their] work is a response to theoretical elaborations produced by the culture of oppression and colonial enslavement. The whole of [their] *oeuvre* [strives to . . .] admit the non-European to the whole range of human experience" (268, 275). This book makes no claim to be the *only* form such a genealogy might take; many others, focusing more fully on African or pan-American, literary or poetic sources, have been and remain to be elaborated. Yet the French Caribbean writers considered below are—with the exception of Edwidge Danticat—all products of Parisian training in the *Sciences humaines* between 1930 and 1980. From Frobenius to Lévi-Strauss, Hegel to Marx, and Kojève to Sartre, this study is an attempt to elucidate the contents and implications of this inheritance for French Antillean culture.

The chapters that follow argue that the writings of Césaire and four of the authors who build upon his work—Edouard Glissant, Daniel Maximin, Maryse Condé, and Edwidge Danticat—have transformed colonial subjectivity, reconstructing a historical awareness lost amid the repressive violence of slavery, the plantation system, and the colonial control of historical discourse. I argue that this act of recovery occurs through an aesthetic construction of historical experience. French Antillean literature mediates historiographic and poetic voices within aesthetic objects; these texts retain the concrete material of history without abandoning the possibility of social transformation to a value-free scientific "objectivity." Antillean writers construct a living history through the critical force of the aesthetic imagination in their attempt to represent, in the past, present, and future, a postcolonial, noncoercive, nonalienated society.

The introductory chapter on Antillean historical experience describes the erasure of communal memory and its replacement by the mnemonic commodity, unfolding this course of events specific to Antillean culture in relation to the larger processes of historical alienation at work in Western modernity. I argue that Antillean writers' response to this erasure has been to construct a series of aesthetic sites that recover historical facticity while cultivating fragile individual, subjective experience. Chapter 1 traces the transformations of Antillean historical experience in light of a specific event: Louis Delgrès's 1802 rebellion in Guadeloupe. I describe how a mosaic of textual traces has constructed and altered historical perception of this highly contested event. These documents demonstrate the intimate link between the rebellion's horizon of visibility and Guadeloupe's historical development from colony to French overseas department.

Three central chapters trace the historical trajectory of the fundamental figure of Caribbean modernism, Aimé Césaire. Chapter 2 examines the contradictory nature of Aimé Césaire's Promethean *Cahier d'un retour au pays natal*. I analyze its thematic content and formal structure to show how it adroitly stages an unresolved conflict between negritude's promise of historical autonomy and the dissolution of the subject within the aura of mythological nature. The following chapter traces an increasing confrontation with history and society in the postwar writings of Césaire and his colleagues in diasporic forums such as the journal *Présence africaine*. The chapter depicts the constellation of voices whose contestation initiated the historical process of decolonization, tracing Césaire's progressive domination of this novel field of Francophone anti- and postcolonial cultural production.

Chapter 4 addresses the appropriation and reconstruction of a series of philosophies of history in the literature of decolonization, from the dialectical historiography of Hegel, Marx, and Kojève to that of the West African Yoruba in works such as Césaire's *La Tragédie du roi Christophe* (The tragedy of King Christopher). I conclude that these texts ultimately remain enclosed within the sacrificial logic they hope to critique, a logic that calls for the infinite postponement and sublimation of individual self-realization in deference to a totalitarian postcolonial state. Nonetheless, I show how such texts—as historicized aesthetic objects—performatively transcend such discursive limitations to produce historical experience, concretizing the project of cultural and political nation-building in the French Caribbean.

The chapter on Daniel Maximin's novels *L'Isolé soleil* (Lone sun) and *L'Ile et une nuit* (The island and a night) argues that jazz is central to their articulation of Antillean historical experience. I describe jazz as more than a mere theme in these novels, to show how it constructs a black Atlantic historiography that Maximin then appropriates in his recuperation of African diasporic history. The chapter describes the interpenetration of musical and poetic discourses within the aesthetic, vernacular historiography of the black Atlantic world.

Chapter 6 addresses the notion of historical totality in Edouard Glissant's work; I argue that the whole of Glissant's work, for all its surface transformations, is structured by the attempt both to represent a fractured Antillean historical experience and to surmount that rupture through the cultivation of a locally based, globally informed project of relational, ecological consciousness that would initiate a truly postcolonial Antillean experience.

The book's research into Antillean historical consciousness culminates in a call for an ethics responsive to the historical destruction of human possibility. Aesthetic representation offers the possibility of imagining a future beyond the instrumentality that has so far qualified the process of enlightenment. Maryse Condé's often-pessimistic, dystopic historical vision points to a critical transformation of Caribbean historical alienation via the force of the aesthetic, as it confronts its readers with the violence and dependency that have been a constant throughout Caribbean history. I close the book with a discussion of the work of Edwidge Danticat, whose novels and stories address Antillean history through the contradictory images of guilt and hope. Danticat's lyrical voice, I argue, reinvests Antillean historical experience with a powerful aesthetic semblance of the life so often eradicated by the violence of history.

AS I WRITE these words at the opening of the twenty-first century, the institutionalized colonialism that so uniquely characterized the French overseas departments seems finally to be on the point of transformation. Amid a flurry of propositions for statutory reform (Emeri et al.), regional politicians are calling for the creation of autonomous "régions d'outre-mer," and Martinican intellectuals have proposed a "project" to create the "first ecological country in the world" (Chamoiseau et al. 2).[2] For the first time even Jacques Chirac, the inheritor of de Gaulle's neocolonialist legacy, has proclaimed the end of French Universalism: "Our uniform legal statutes have seen their day.... Each overseas collective must henceforth, if it wishes, evolve toward a differentiated status, what one might call a custom-made status."[3] How far these changes might address what the Martinican author Patrick Chamoiseau has called "the anesthesia (under a democratic guise) of . . . a people adrift in welfare and dependency" remains to be seen.[4]

The increasing integration of this region into what Antonio Negri and Michael Hardt have called the "empire" of postmodernity, however, makes it all the more necessary to reflect upon this suddenly repudiated "departmentalization" and the historical and cultural dynamics of the

French Antilles. An intensive mediation of Western modernity and colonial and neocolonial locality characterized French Caribbean historical experience in the twentieth century. This modernity continues to structure Antillean "postmodernity," if such a thing may be said to exist, today. This inseparability, even mediated identity, with modernity holds true, I think, for the most stimulating accounts of postmodernity and postcoloniality;[5] in response, therefore, we can choose to examine and rework the legacy of modernity in the French Caribbean as a living presence, or merely let its symptoms and unfulfilled promises echo on, unrecognized, in a transformed world.

MANY MORE exceptional people have contributed to this project than I can hope to remember here. Thanks to Susan Rubin Suleiman, who first led me to ponder the relation between memory and society and who offered guidance, incisive reading, and mentorship at Harvard University. Tom Conley selflessly gave time, energy, inspiration, and friendship to this project, from the smallest details of wording and idea to his challenge to balance body and spirit in games of handball at the Boston Y. Maryse Condé, Edouard Glissant, Aimé Césaire, and Daniel Maximin graciously agreed to answer my questions about their work, history, philosophy, music, and writing in the French Caribbean. Henry Louis Gates Jr., Maryse Condé, Jann Mattlock, Doris Summer, Dwight Andrews, and Chris Bongie provided much help in reading and sustaining my work in Cambridge, while in France, Régis Antoine and Daniel Delas graciously took time to discuss the project. Juliette Dickstein, Paulette Smith, Serigne and Diaga Seck, Seth Graebner, Christopher Dunn, Andy Zeisler, Edwidge Danticat, and above all Kareen Obydol supported and inspired this project with their genial and insightful comments and kind friendship.

A fellowship offered early on from Harvard's Graduate Society brought me to the *archives départementales* in Bisdary, Guadeloupe, where Christian Frolleau facilitated my research, while Gérard Lafleur, Jacques Adelaïde-Merlande, Josette Faloppe, Alain Buffon, and the other members of the Société d'histoire de la Guadeloupe generously took time to discuss and support my work. Jim Arnold expressed interest in this work when it was hardly more than a grad student's ruminations, and his encouragement sustained me over these years of revisions. At Virginia, Cathie Brettschneider, David Sewell, and Paula Wadlington generously devoted their attention to this manuscript. Larry Porter offered critical insight, close reading, and wholehearted encouragement and friendship as I wrote and revised this material. His attention brought a measure of clarity and coherence to a wide-ranging project. The support and critique of Abiola Irele, Carroll Coates, Chris Bongie, Lydie Moudileno, Micheline Rice-Maximin, and Bernadette Cailler helped strengthen the arguments I put forward in this book. A research grant from Miami University allowed me to finish the final revisions of my manuscript in Paris and Martinique. My friends and colleagues in the Department of French and Italian at Miami University have challenged me to think through the philosophical and ethical implications of *Voicing Memory*. Jonathan Strauss and Jim Creech in particular provided models for theoretical insight, graceful writing, and ethical conviction that I have striven to emulate. Finally, I wish to thank in particular Jean-Godefroy Bidima and Donald Moerdijk; our exchanges over the years inform every dimension of this work. Donald's *esprit libre* and vast intellectual compass, as well as his boundless hospitality and friendship in Paris and Oléron, contributed in countless ways to the spirit and letter of this text.

EARLIER VERSIONS of material appearing in this volume were published in the *Journal of Haitian Studies, Littéréalité, Le Bulletin de la Société d'histoire de la Guadeloupe, Telos,* and the edited volume *Maryse Condé: Une nomade inconvenante.* A version of chapter 2 originally appeared in *Mosaic: a journal for the interdisciplinary study of literature,* vol. 33, no. 3 (Sept. 2000): 107–28; I am grateful for permission to reprint.

Abbreviations

(Refer to the bibliography for complete publication information on the editions used.)

Works by Edouard Glissant

CC	*La case du commandeur*
DA	*Discours antillais*
IP	*L'intention poétique*
IPD	*Introduction à une poétique du divers*
M	*Malemort*
PR	*Poétique de la relation*
SC	*Soleil de la conscience*
TM	*Tout-monde*
TTM	*Traité du tout-monde*

Works by Daniel Maximin

IS	*L'Isolé soleil*
IN	*L'Ile et une nuit*

Introduction: Aesthetic Construction and Postcolonial Subjectivity
A Genealogy of Antillean Historical Experience

> The past carries with it a secret index by which it is referred to redemption.
> —Walter Benjamin

> "Arbeit macht frei"
> —Exhortation posted on the entrance to the Auschwitz death camp

WHEN FRANCE, like other European nations, dismembered its colonial empire after the second world war, this process of "decolonization" promised to carry newly born countries such as Guinea, Senegal, and Côte-d'Ivoire into an era of independence and self-sufficiency. Instead, to varying degrees, these hopes soon foundered amid neocolonial economic dependency, the political repression of isolated one-party states, and recurrent coup d'états. The young "socialist" countries most dedicated to these ideals created disciplinary societies that in hindsight merely prepared for the arrival of the transnational corporations.[1] Today, as the nation-state disappears amid globalization, the unrealized goals of decolonization may seem to be the residue of an outdated, forgotten project, the hopeless expression of 1960s idealism. While the ideals of independence and autonomy were the call to arms for a generation of anticolonial intellectuals, they now seem like distant relics in media reports of the latest African coup d'état—hollow, outdated jargon in a postcolonial, postcommunist, postindustrial, postmodern age.

And yet to condemn such ideals unreflectingly as the mere catchwords of a superseded historical moment is, in a sense, to blame the ideological victims of the miscarriage of decolonization. The promise of decolonization to found noncoercive, nonexploitative societies in the developing world echoes beyond the moment of its historical default in the 1960s to live on to accuse a twenty-first century in which genocide and torture continue unabated. The project of decolonization, prematurely abandoned, resists relegation to a distant, putatively mastered past and instead returns, zombie-like, to condemn the cynical verdict of a history and a globalized economy that failed to concretize its ideals. The outdatedness of such ideals is itself a symptom, the sign of a failure we would rather forget.

Today, unmediated flows of information commodities, from infomercials and market data to techno-wars and natural catastrophes, stream across global networks. Daily life is increasingly reduced to the negotiation of the eternally present availability of archival servers and web pages. Andreas Huyssen has described this postmodern experience as an erasure of temporal distance amid an all-encompassing, exponentially expanding electronic archive:

> The more memory we store on data banks, the more the past is sucked into the orbit of the present, ready to be called up on the screen. A sense of historical continuity, or, for that matter, discontinuity, both of which depend on a before and an after, gives way to the simultaneity of all times and spaces readily accessible in the present. . . . As such simultaneity wipes out the alterity of past and present, here and there, it tends to lose its anchor in referentiality, in the real, and the present falls victim to its magical power of simulation and image projection. Real difference, real otherness in historical time or in geographic distance can no longer even be perceived. (253)

Somewhere beneath this flow of data and news, however, lies a sedimented events-unconscious, where the memory of yet-to-be-completed projects such as decolonization lies deposited, waiting to be reanimated. Such ideals might remind us that our recent history is definitively marked by the recurrent obliteration of communal memory. This obliteration occurred in a strong sense via the repeated perpetration of racial and ethnic genocide. It has also transpired as a weakening of historical sensibility accompanying the postmodern prepackaging and estrangement of experience.

And yet, if the promise of industrial society was that with technological advances no one would go hungry, the panoptic information age announces that we will register every act of inhumanity and have instant access to every response to cruelty yet imagined. This is the dilemma of history informing this book: the postmodern ubiquity of historical information constantly threatens to overwhelm our critical capacity both to understand and to act upon its implications. Flows of mnemonic capital increase exponentially, while unceasing violence reveals our incapacity to learn from the past. In place of an understanding of the past that would inform and transform the present, historical experience steadily recedes amid the hypermediated, twenty-four-hour-a-day global spectacle, and we survive by deflecting the shock of human suffering as we reduce the memory of this suffering to the ritualistic evocation of the mere date (9/11 . . .) or site (Rwanda . . .) of its occurrence.

In seeking to expose and transcend this dereliction of memory, the pages that follow look to a region in which for four centuries the problem of memory has been experienced in acute form, as if in distillation. The disappearance of communal memory so typical of recent history, familiar in the writings of critics of postmodernism such as Fredric Jameson and Andreas Huyssen, was in fact prefigured in the Americas in the complementary events of the Middle Passage and the Plantation. For if the former deprived survivors of collective memory as Africans of diverse origins were suddenly thrown together in the holds of slave ships, the violence of the plantation system deprived slaves of shared cultural and linguistic heritages by breaking up ethnic, linguistic, and familial groups to undermine resistance to its domination. In so doing, the plantation system drove memory underground, where it hid in its least-visible, subterranean forms. This destruction and entombment of memory occurred throughout the New World plantation societies.

In the French Antillean islands of Guadeloupe and Martinique, however, a peculiar and largely unique series of historical circumstances have created a singular postmodern variant of colonialism. In a region that since 1945 has seemingly defied the historical trend of decolonization to become ever more closely tied to its French colonizers, the problem of memory and history has itself become intimately coupled with questions of globalization and issues of political and economic dependency. In this region, the contradictions of modernity have radically transformed both material existence and the constitution of Antillean experience itself to a degree Richard Price makes apparent in *The Convict and the Colonel:* "Colonized for more than five centuries, quintessentially Western, Caribbean peoples face the challenge of somehow recasting the modernist paradigm of progress, unashamedly triumphalist and Eurocentric. How at the same time to appropriate and subvert the central ideas associated with modernity?" (166). In the expansionist phase of colonialism, France brought to the Antilles both the slave labor required for the global extension of instrumental reason[2] and the critical tools of the Enlightenment that might attack it. While the critique of exploitation at the heart of decolonization received perhaps its most original and developed formulation among Antillean thinkers, the region's dependency upon the French metropolis short-circuited the practical implementation of this critique.

The sheer violence, first of slavery and then of colonialism and neocolonialist globalism, remains the driving impulse behind the French Antillean questioning of memory and history. Thanks to this historical specificity, the interrogation of memory on these small islands has been so acute that it may illuminate the more general dilemmas of modernity and memory structuring recent historical experience. Indeed, one project of this book is to investigate whether the critical and utopian dimensions of memory are not mere relics of a now-transcended modernism, as Huyssen has at times argued (6), but instead retain an urgency most visible precisely on the margins of global society. Amid their growing dependency on and imbrication within national (French) and now global capitalism, Antilleans have consistently offered a multifaceted critique of their self-estrangement and lack of autonomy. This Antillean historical dilemma demonstrates that the abandonment of the project of modernity is a luxury not all communities can afford (or may wish) to affirm.

For all its success, the imposition of an endemic dependency and institutionalized amnesia in the French overseas departments has, inevitably, encountered resistance.[3] Since the 1920s a vibrant literary and critical tradition has developed unique forms of social critique and aesthetic innovation to counter at every turn this endemic dependency and communal forgetfulness. This study is not an analytical description of French Caribbean historical novels.[4] Instead, the chapters that follow will examine what I have called Antillean "historical experience," or the imaginative capacity of individuals to act within yet think beyond the historically preformed society that complexly determines them. This introductory chapter theorizes the recovery of Antillean historical experience via the aesthetic production of poetry, theater, novels, and criticism. Indeed, recent criticism understands memory itself—as opposed to the academic, monumentalist, archival history Nietzsche first attacked in his essay "On the Advantage and Disadvantage of History for Life"—to be a representational construction of the past in the present and thus to some degree an inherently aesthetic process. In this view, the aesthetic is emphatically not the realm of mere ideological alienation subsumed under the guise of the "Anti-Aesthetic."[5]

The aesthetic construction effected in Antillean poetry, novels, and criticism provides a zone of indeterminacy in which to model a historically aware subject that evades an encompassing instrumental logic of commodification. In this region, access to historical experience—fundamental for the constitution of subjectivity understood since Locke's *Essay concerning Human Understanding* (1694) as the temporal persistence of the self—has never been an a priori given.[6] These works—thanks to the logical indeterminacy aesthetic production—are able to produce a critical understanding of French Caribbean history and culture and to imagine a social order and a human subject beyond the instrumentalization of society and the self at work in that region.

ON THE FOOTHILLS of Mount Matouba on the small island of Guadeloupe in the French West Indies, the former Fort Richepance, recently rebaptized Fort Delgrès, stands abandoned beneath the dazzling sun, where it gazes emptily toward the horizon in mute testimony to the revolt against Napoleonic troops that occurred there two centuries ago. A small sign at the entrance commemorates Louis Delgrès's 1802 revolt against Bonaparte's emissary bearing news of the reimposition of slavery, Richepance. On any day, a few locals and curious tourists will walk through the ruins, now a historic monument, peering through a portal toward the dense jungle on the hills above. In May 1802, Delgrès and his remaining troops escaped through this opening when surrounded by the French and made their way under cover of night and tropical forest to the Habitation Danglemont. There, they patiently mined the ground, and as French troops rushed in upon them, the wounded Delgrès lit the tail of powder on the ground below him in a final suicidal explosion, a tropical Masada whose echo was quickly absorbed by the luxuriant, paradisiacal forest around him, unheard and largely forgotten for a century and a half.

Below Fort Delgrès in the former capital of Basse-Terre, the French citizens of Guadeloupe, since 1946 a Départment d'Outre-Mer (DOM), or overseas department, theoretically no different than the Hauts-de-Seine or Yvonne, go about their business. Were you to question them, young or old, chances are they would know the basic story of Delgrès's heroism, often repeated since 1946. When I was living in St. Anne and traveling each day across the island to the Departmental Archives to research historical representations of Delgrès, I discovered that this story of Guadeloupe's flash of independence was familiar to many of the people to whom I described my project. These included my friend Emmanuel Laurent, a fellow musician and a wind-surfing instructor whose livelihood depends upon the French and Canadian tourists flocking to the exotic beaches of St. Anne and St. François, and Christian Frolleau, a young French bureaucrat at the archives possessing a European Community passport and secure employment by the state, whose ancestors had been brought by force to the island from West Africa centuries before.

Such turns of history inform contemporary Antillean experience: no longer absent, this once-repressed past has instead become a commodity, offered up in newspapers; on local television; in annual commemorations and historical speeches; and on plaques, steles, and fortresses. The monumental, death-like rigidity of these structures, like the compulsive, ritualized repetition each year of fetishized names and dates (May 27, 1802), often seems merely to re-entomb the search for human autonomy encapsulated in Delgrès's actions.[7] In tandem with the consumerization of Antillean society, memory itself has become a commodity, circulating throughout society as mnemonic spectacle. When my friends and acquaintants spoke of Delgrès's sacrifice for human autonomy from within a world rendered utterly dependent upon the support of the French state, this was no mere question of bad faith. Instead, the ritualized invocation of a mummified past occurring throughout Guadeloupean society obliquely and compulsively points to the soft, postmodern transformation of the ever-present trauma of enslavement, penetrating to the core of a people's daily lived experience: dependency.

ON MARCH 19, 1946, the French National Assembly unanimously voted into law the departmentalization of the French colonies of Guadeloupe, Martinique, Guyane, and Réunion, at a stroke turning these regions into the juridical *sosies* of their metropolitan sisters.[8] For all its retrospective incongruence with the contemporaneous beginnings of African decolonization, such a transformation followed a definite historical tendency and was widely sought both in the colonies concerned and the metropolis. Local councils in Guadeloupe and Martinique had repeatedly argued for such a development from the end of the nineteenth century onward. During the second world war, both the Comité Martiniquais de Libération Nationale and the colonial conseil général had demanded Martinique's "complete assimilation" into France, with Martinique's communist representative, Aimé Césaire, asserting publicly that "[juridical] assimilation should [henceforth] be the rule" (qtd. in Aldrich and Connell 74).

If Antilleans sought this transformation to strengthen and consolidate social rights and protections (health care, employment, education), for the French government, departmentalization logically culminated a centuries-old colonization. Departmentalization brought to fruition the ideology of centralization and assimilation, a French tradition Jean-Pierre Sainton traces back beyond Napoleon and Louis XIV to the reign of Hugues Capet (Emeri et al. 31). Only in hindsight has departmentalization become a twentieth-century anomaly. In 1946, French decolonization was still years ahead, while events such as the Colonial Exposition of 1931 remained potent in the French imagination (Miller 90–117). Concerning only French

Guyana and four small islands, each bearing populations of well under half a million, departmentalization assured at minimal cost the global imprint of French geopolitical interests for a country preoccupied with rebuilding a shattered postwar economy. Amid the second scramble for "colonies" that initiated the Cold War, departmentalization assured France a lever of intervention against United States hegemony in the Americas.[9] Nonetheless, by 1961 Aimé Césaire openly recognized the failure of departmentalization: "In a world in the midst of decolonization, the French Antilles remain in the Caribbean, indeed in the entire world, *one of the rare lands of colonization*.... The great misfortune from which the Antilles suffer is to remain *colonies,* the last and only French colonies" (qtd. in Oruno D. Lara 232). In 1981, Edouard Glissant, in *Le discours antillais*, could conclude that departmentalization was in fact "one of the rare 'successful' colonizations of modern history."

The predominant structural trait of the Antillean DOMs is an unparalleled degree of dependency upon the métropole. The DOM economies receive regular injections of federal funds primarily directed toward tertiary economic structures and away from the development of local means of production. This practice was no novelty suddenly thought up in Paris in 1946 but was a perfection of the mercantilism that had been determining French colonial practice since Colbert. The *Exclusif,* promulgated in 1727, assured not only that France would monopolize trade with its colonies but that their trade would be thoroughly and insidiously complementary: no products might be produced in the colonies that would compete with metropolitan production. Thus only rarefied, exotic goods impossible to produce in France (sugar, bananas, fur) were cultivated, while the colonies imported all other goods from France, ensuring a global market for metropolitan producers. From the institution of French colonialism in the seventeenth century, the Antilles have thus been marked by a monocultural mode of production that determines social life at every level, from patterns of employment (and unemployment, which has regularly surpassed 30 percent since the 1980s) to the structures of Antillean subjective experience expressing this dependency.

In the Antilles, economic exports were almost entirely limited to sugar and its derivatives into the early twentieth century. A slight diversification in Guadeloupe prior to World War II reflected only the planting of a second tropical product, the banana, in the face of growing competition to sugarcane farmers from the sugar beet. This tendency only increased with departmentalization. In Guadeloupe and Martinique, imports more than doubled between 1973 and 1977, and if the gross domestic product rose

71 percent in Guadeloupe and 97 percent in Martinique during the same period, this was mainly as a result of payment transfers from France.[10] Richard Price remarks that in a local market near his house in Martinique, 84 percent of the goods were imported in 1983, "from 31 countries and from every continent except Australia" (155). What little production does exist is directed predominantly at local markets, and production costs are such that it is generally cheaper to import goods from Europe than to produce them locally.

While productive capacity in Guadeloupe and Martinique has declined steadily throughout the twentieth century, the tertiary sector (commerce, transportation, and administration) grew dramatically in the postwar period, passing from 62 percent in 1966 to 75 percent in 1975, while agricultural and industrial production continued to decline.[11] This systematic underdevelopment results in "elevated salaries in unproductive sectors; habituating the population to a high level of free social expenses (education, health); [and] considering the State as the unique employer of the region. In short, this is an economy of consumption without real production" (*DA* 65). Public service has become the largest employer; ironically, as productive capacity waned, a panoply of new bureaucracies such as the Fonds d'investissement pour les Départements d'Outre-Mer (FIDOM) appeared, reinforcing the very transformation they sought to combat. The French government's budget for the DOMs *quintupled* in a decade, passing from 2 to 10 billion francs in 1970–80.[12] The transfer of the French Welfare State to the DOMs, while markedly improving inhabitants' quality of life in such areas as infant mortality, actually reinforced this decline of production, thus ensuring continued dependency upon the métropole. Undeniably, the physical conditions of existence are strikingly superior in the DOMs to those of neighboring islands. And yet, in accepting such poisoned gifts, commentators such as Glissant and Patrick Chamoiseau have maintained that Antilleans are driven into a sort of permanent social immaturity, selling off the promise of autonomy for a momentary historical stability.[13]

Aside from enlarging bureaucracies and increasing social welfare payments, the only area of economic growth in the Antilles has been in tourism. Though superficially giving the appearance of dynamic development, tourism has largely served to increase the imbalances of Antillean society. As a whole, tourism has tended to increase dependency on the vagaries of the French public's discretionary income, while tourist-sector investment and thus profits flow largely in a closed loop from the métropole and back, locking out Antilleans from even this form of economic development.[14] And yet, even the gleaming commodities of the tourist industry

9   *Introduction*

can reflect the region's historical past, and these "products" may at times take on an afterlife of their own, condemning the same commodification and dependency that produced them as the kitschy objects of touristic consumption.

I FOUND just such an image of the commodification of Antillean historical experience in one of the souvenir shops that line the waterfront in St. Anne, Guadeloupe. Home since 1966 of a Club Med resort, St. Anne is itself a symbol of the passage of French Antillean society through a century-long decline of agricultural production to a contemporary dependency upon a French-controlled tourist infrastructure. A poster-sized blowup of a colonial bank note presents a complex representation of the erasure of Antillean communal memory and its replacement by the commodified memory-image. This fantasy projection of colonial existence was inscribed on banknotes by the Institut d'émission des Départements d'Outre Mer between 1954 and 1965. It shows a woman holding a container of fruit as if offering it to an unseen presence. Behind her lies a forest of palm trees, while signs of the bill's value, "cinq mille francs" and "contre-valeur de 50 nouveaux francs," and the names of the overseas departments float around her. The bill's image was painted by Eugène Poughéon, who painted not only the other images adorning the DOMs' paper money of the period but those found on the majority of French paper money of the postwar period. Until 1951, each overseas department issued separate bank notes. From 1959 to 1974, the same notes were issued for all three American departments, while, beginning January 1, 1975, the Institute of Emission circulated the same notes as in metropolitan France, replacing this remnant of the colonial period.[15] Ironically, given the importance of finance to the colonial project, the Antillean banking system was one of the last sectors to resist full assimilation into the metropolis. Buffon explains this as an atavistic historical epiphenomenon, given the near total lack of real autonomy of Antillean financial institutions (*Le systeme bancaire* 81). Indeed, Poughéon's image itself derisively testifies to the structural inconsequence of this "autonomy," as I will argue in what follows.

Poughéon's painting flattens a five-hundred-year history of conquest, genocide, enslavement, colonization, economic exploitation, abolition, and modernization into a timeless visual mythology. The image testifies to the reduction of historical, qualitative time to mere spatial quantity that Henri Bergson first depicted in his *Essai sur les données immédiates de la conscience* (1888). There, Bergson described the reduction of the lived experience of "real duration" to the spatial world of "homogenous time"

10   *Introduction*

Figure 1. French Antillean five-thousand-franc note, circa 1957

(81) exemplified by the identical abstract movement of a clock hand (80).[16] Walter Benjamin subsequently developed Bergson's insight into a model of critical thought, the goal of which was to explode the frozen mythology of timeless nature, whether of a noncommodified original nature, or "golden age," or the "second nature" that mystifies actual social relations as absolute, eternal givens.[17]

The "epistemo-critical prologue" that introduces Benjamin's *Origin of German Tragic Drama* calls for the critique of the related phenomena of nature, of mythology and its partner fate—understood as the absence of historical and ethical consciousness—and of the artwork's semblance *(Schein)* of static eternity. The work of critique, in this view, is not to celebrate the putative eternal profundity of an artwork, but rather to "erode" and decompose its illusion of eternity, to reveal the artwork as a historical, fabricated object amid its "consciously constructed ruins" (qtd. in Hanssen 70).[18] The paradoxical nature of this allegorical critique is to historicize and thus bring to life the artwork, breaking its frozen illusion of eternity in a process that destroys in order to reconstruct dynamically the artwork as an object of knowledge: "Criticism means the mortification of works. . . . And if it is questionable whether the beauty which endures does still deserve the name, it is nevertheless certain that there is nothing of beauty which does not contain something that is worthy of knowledge" (qtd. in Hanssen 71).

As an object of our critical attention, stripped of its mystified status as the bearer of a universal exchange value, Poughéon's fascinating image comes alive, operating across a wide range of symbolic levels. Most explicitly, it objectifies an eroticized female Other, equating her with the eternal, unchanging Nature that surrounds her. The woman is in the dress of the *doudou*, the metonymical, sexualized representation of the folkloric exoticism that perpetuates an ahistorical, mythical ideology of Antillean natural beauty, the Caribbean "paradise."[19] Patrick Chamoiseau and Raphael Confiant, in their 1991 study *Creole Letters,* describe the literary field of *doudouisme* that grew up at the turn of the century around this French Antillean cultural archetype:

> This literature uses Creole reality, thus returning to some extent to the [Antillean] world of one's existence, but one returns to it as a tourist, that is to say with a European vision, an exotic and therefore superficial vision. And this superficial gaze upon oneself and one's own world only retains the paradisiacal, the blues of the sky, the white of the sand, the flowers and little birds, and above all what the traveler appreciates more than anything: the *doudou,* a bewitching creature who searches out the means of improving her bad luck by charming passersby. (89)

The doudou engages the colonizer with her offer of fruit. She looks away, however, rather than straight ahead: the viewer is not immediately conflated with this colonizer. This gesture allows the viewer to forget his—the metropolitan female is excluded from this libidinal/economic circulation of power—historical participation in the erotic and monetary economy inscribed in the bill he is holding. A simulacrum has replaced the real individual who posed for this image (Who was she? Why did she pose? What were Poughéon's instructions to her?), and her image has become a mere marker of value exchanged between men.

On another level, the image represents the historical interpellation of the colonized within the process of assimilation, which integrates the French Caribbean subject into French civilization. In this more dynamic dimension of the image, the woman appears to have turned her back on the jungle that evokes the uncivilized Africa of a racialist colonial mythology. The warm colors of the background—yellow, red—are muted, decipherable as an attenuated reference to the African's "uncivilized" drives and behaviors. Furthermore, the sloping red line of the mountain charts the decay of this primal energy, from its hidden origin above the forest at the volcano's summit to its tepid descent into the ocean. The clothes of the doudou, once made from the scraps and leftovers of the slave mistress's gowns, evoke the creativity of a syncretic plantation culture, where African and European traditions once met. In the image, the African origins of this clothing are softened, and what might have once been a *boubou* now appears as a white lace shawl adorned by a string of pearls, hoop earrings, and folds of rich fabric that say Dior, not Dakar. The doudou's hands are those of a woman behind the perfume counter at Galleries Lafayette, not one returning from chopping sugar cane. Her hair appears relatively straight, and her features correspond to the French ideal of *les traits fins* (i.e., the "delicate features" of the European). Her skin color is light, nearly that of the *chabine*—or light-skinned, almost red-skinned—*mulâtresse*. The image magically erases the animosity and hatred of the slave. Only her look of apparent kindness harbors a last trace of resistance in a certain rigidity of her gaze and dynamic tension, as if Poughéon's model were thinking, "I'll pose for you because I have to in order to survive, but I won't give you the pleasure of seeing me smile."

The bill's image forcefully dramatizes the dilemma of commodification at the heart of the French Caribbean experience of history. The doudou's gesture, holding out the "fruits" of her people's labor to the colonizer, eternalizes into a frozen spatial representation both the exotic mythology of an Edenic land of plenty and the colonial project to exploit those "raw materials" to serve the needs of the "civilized" mother country. The image represents a dualist division of nature and culture, and the doudou's movement from one to the other is inscribed by the signs of reification—literally, "thingification," that rigidification and rationalization that the Marxian critic Georg Lukács saw at work in the passage of capitalism beyond mere economic processes and into the constitution of human subjectivity.[20] The varied writing characters in the image invoke a division between an eternal nature and the historical incursion of France's "civilizing colonial mission": the flowing script naming the three French overseas departments ripples and glides like rain over the leaves on the palm trees behind her, while the block capital letters ("L'INSTITUT D'EMISSION") impose a rigid form on top of the background. Furthermore, a primary nature, the forest of trees behind her, has itself been stamped with a value ("cinq mille francs"), and the fruit she holds, once a symbol of fertility and the productive union with nature, has been stripped of its ties to the land and made to fit into a rigid Cartesian container.

Poughéon's doudou appears frozen and objectified like the fruit she holds, caught in the dilemma that structures and determines experience within the French overseas departments: while in the midst of nature, subjectively at home in an autonomous space in which Antilleans are numerically far superior to the metropolitan French, a series of highly developed structures, structures suggested here by the universal exchange mechanism of money, work to objectify and pacify her. These processes—a centralized schooling system that creates French citizens on a distant Caribbean island; employment in the local French bureaucracy; an economy based on tourism, bureaucracy, and service that is largely dependent on the importation of French staple items—have created a situation of material and psychological dependency that negates the geographic independence of these small islands. This web of dependency enlists the Antillean subject in its constitution and perpetuation. The doudou is the metonymical representation of this reification, where psychological and political autonomy are abandoned for a unit of exchange that today equates Mercedes-Benzes and BMWs instead of sugar cane and rum.[21]

The image of the Antillean doudou offers a striking visual representation of neocolonial alienation and dependency.[22] Its overt legibility testifies to the "success" of Antillean colonization, blatantly calling attention to the reification and exploitation at work in commodity exchange. In its self-referentiality, Poughéon's five-thousand-franc note triumphantly mocks those caught up in the encroaching objectification of subjectivity it represents to them. While the bill (as money) takes on power only through its effects upon other objects, negating their specific use-value in the universality of exchange, so Poughéon's image began life representing colonial mythology, interpellating its subjects into a dreamlike world of dependency. And yet, as a mass-produced object circulating throughout colonial space, this image outlived its original functions to become a spur to critical reflection. Blown up to ten times its original size, its objective effects became uncontrollable, and this seductive call to a world of dependency became equally decipherable as a mocking indictment of the exploitation in which Antillean culture finds itself embroiled in a global postmodern age.

Poughéon's image announces, decades before its analysis by Jean-François Lyotard and Jean Baudrillard, the amnesia characteristic of the postmodern sublime in which a fragmented human experience finds itself unable to comprehend the formal and temporal totality of the world in which it takes part. The image's overt coupling of the reified simulacra of Antillean experience with the processes of (monetary) commodification points to an obliteration of subjective identity in Antillean society, while its circulation through neocolonial networks of tourism and exchange paradoxically allowed it to recover a critical dimension. To read Poughéon's image today as an indictment of neocolonial reification is to refuse emphatically the enthrallment to a putative world of total simulation—in which all ideological critique is deflated as a mere effect of simulacra themselves—that terminates in the questionable glorification of desubjectification characteristic of Baudrillard's work.

14 Introduction

In 1997, President Jacques Chirac signed a law granting to the French overseas departments full equality of social benefits relative to the metropolis. Fully fifty-one years after Aimé Césaire instituted departmentalization as a sort of colonial equal rights amendment, the French government at last grudgingly lived up to the agreement it had signed in a moment of postwar euphoria. The ambiguities of departmentalization remain unabated, however. The French Antillean remains, in Glissant's words, an "impossible yet satisfied European" (*DA* 289). With the institution of the Euro on January 1, 2002, the regional specificity of the French franc, like that of Poughéon's colonial five-thousand-franc note, was itself erased by the juggernaut of globalization. The tiny islands of Guadeloupe and Martinique were thus symbolically assimilated into the exchange mechanisms of Europe, enlarging the scope of their dependency to an entire continent.

Reification and Alienation in Antillean Experience

The result of Antillean neocolonial dependency, Edouard Glissant has argued, is an experience of "history as neurosis," a history to which one passively submits (*DA* 133, 137).[23] The absence of history, what Glissant calls a *raturage*, or erasure, is an effect of the process of reification visibly at work in the image of the doudou. To understand Antillean historical experience, René Ménil argued in his essay "Psychoanalysis of History," we must focus not on the factual minutia of that history but on the social and existential contradictions that inform Antillean subjects' perceptions of that past: "The mystery of our impossible history lies not in the absurdity of the past but in the incoherence and inconsistency of our present social consciousness. The prerequisite to any history of Martinique is the study of our consciousness as it exists today" (47). Glissant's analysis pursues this project begun by René Ménil to describe the mechanisms and manifestations of Antillean amnesia as products of cultural, historical, economic, and political alienation and reification. In the process, both Ménil and Glissant explicitly place Antillean culture within the larger contradictions of capitalism, modernity, and historical experience that have informed much of modern and now postmodern experience in the West. In this view, the Antillean subjects of French colonialism are neither the mere "victims" of modernity nor its absolute Others. Rather, while the constitution of Antillean society was a liminal project of modernity, the subjects it produced—slaves and the colonized—reconstructed the project of enlightenment in their drive for emancipation.

The Caribbean and postmodern critiques of the unavailability of history as an effect of social commodification build upon the ontological critique of transcendental, teleological Historicism elaborated by Martin Heidegger in *Being and Time*. There, Heidegger attacked the practice of *Historie,* the historiographic, analytical conceptualization of the past as a series of occurrences that are gradually totalized within a narrative of presence. In this recuperative process, each event is made present to a transcendental "Cartesian" subject through its re-presentation in a historical narrative. Time itself is divorced from subjective experience, quantified into "an objectively present multiplicity of nows" that stretch forward and back to infinity (383). All events are lived only within their relevance to the present, a series of moments in which the Hedeggerian subject *(Dasein)* loses itself.

In contrast to this historicist *Historie,* Heidegger's seductive narrative proposes the notion of *Geschichtlichkeit,* or "historicity."[24] In this view, historicity overcomes the tradition-bound closing-down of existence by History, the reduction of historical understanding to the merely conservative memorializing of the past. Instead, Heidegger's historicity recognizes the opening of human experience onto its futurity, the transformative dynamic of a human subject projected into "the ecstatic and horizonal constitution of temporality" (387). The being of Heidegger's Da-sein is based not on identity but on its constant nonidentity with itself, its "throwness" beyond the limits of self-same identity. Instead of closing down and limiting human experience within a transcendent narrative (whether of the subject as self-identical foundation of experience or of History as an infinite series of reified "nows"), Heideggerian historicity describes a subject never fully present to itself as conscious representation, a subject that recovers history not as the closing down of being through the repetition of what has already been but as an open future of possibility implied necessarily by Da-sein's ontological appearance in the world. In the most recent English translation of the work, Heidegger's tortuous prose describes how "Already-being in-a-world as being-together-with-innerworldly-things-at-hand means, however, equiprimordially being-ahead-of-oneself" (296).

Heidegger's description of the lived experience of historicity places the subject within a single triangulated temporal realm in a process he terms "anticipatory resoluteness": "only because Da-sein in general *is* as I *am-*having been [i.e. in the process of living my relation to the past], can it come futurally toward itself in a way that it comes-back [i.e. comes back to its authentic self in projecting itself into its future]. Authentically futural, Da-sein is authentically *having-been*" (299). Heidegger's discussion of historicity and temporality is not only an insightful critique of academic

German historicism but, via the French recuperation of Heidegger, serves as one foundation for Edouard Glissant's notion of a "prophetic vision of the past" that I will discuss in chapter 6.[25]

Heidegger's 1927 critique is a fundamental moment in the questioning of a teleological understanding of history that extends back at least as far as Nietzsche's early text, *On the Advantage and Disadvantage of History for Life,* and the prolongation of that critique in the writings of Wilhelm Dilthey (Bambach). While *Being and Time* pursues the critique of *Historie* in great depth, its argument suffers from the voluntarism of Heidegger's existential ontology. On the one hand, Heidegger offers a compelling critique of the Cartesian division between subject and object in favor of the differentiated totality he terms Da-sein's being-in-the-world. At the same time, like the earlier critique of Bergson, the transition from history to historicity Heidegger argues for is mystified as a simple change in perspective. Heidegger retains the Kierkegaardian category of free will (the existential subject's "decision" to pursue its authenticity) while dressing up this process in a language of subjectless, mystified ontology: "History . . . takes place on the occurrence-basis of the coming."

Heidegger's discussion of "handiness" ("Handiness is the ontological categorical definition of beings as they are 'in themselves'" [67]) buries the empirical critique of use-value familiar from Marxian thought beneath the rural mystique of the "workshop." There, the reduction of objects to their sheer instrumental use value is presented as "taking care" of things: "The forest is a forest of timber, the mountain a quarry of rock, the river is water power. . . . In taking care of things, nature is discovered as having some definite direction on paths, streets, bridges, and buildings" (66). Even the authenticity of Da-sein, however, is merely an apotheosis of this instrumentalization, in which use-value is displaced onto the subject itself, who is called upon to sacrifice itself to its futurity in an endless deferral of self-realization, in which Da-sein exists not for itself, but for its futuricity, its "being-unto-death."

Heidegger's critique neglects to investigate the sociohistorical determinants that render access to historicity by actually existing subjects impossible. It is not that the category of the social is simply absent from *Being and Time.* Heidegger's famous discussion the "worldliness of the world," of objects such as hammers and pens, describes these objects in their handiness; that is to say, their use-value to human subjects, while his conception of the "they" thoroughly condemns the rampant alienation of individuals in modern industrial society.[26] The pursuit of the authenticity of Da-sein in its "wholeness," however, abandons the Marxian category of totality as a critical tool that might show how society, as a contradictory totality, blocks access to an experience of historicity by actually existing individuals.

It may well be true, as Heidegger argues, that historicity as the opening of Da-sein onto its futurity and possibility is ontologically prior to the experience of *Historie*, and even that historicity itself is not a transcendental category of being but is necessarily entwined in its historical unfolding (Ziareck 89). Yet, without a critical understanding of a subject in search of historicity, one who is fundamentally blocked from it at every level of experience by society, Heidegger's Da-sein is reduced to the interiority of the experience of the self in its putative ontological priority, a subject whose "throwness" remains mythological wish fulfillment, devoid of concretion and empirical content.[27] If the construction of an Antillean aesthetic this book charts is precisely a counterpoint to such a mythology of Being, the Marxian critique of social reification taken up by Glissant and Césaire predetermines this Antillean aesthetic, offering in the process a critical corrective to the Heideggerian mysticism of Being and historicity.

GEORG LUKÁCS's original use of the term "reification" describes not only, in Martin Jay's words, the "petrification of living processes into dead things, which [appear] as an alien 'second nature'" (*Marxism and Totality* 109) but underlines as well an externally determined, preformed subjectivity that is merely reactive and lacking agency. Stripped of autonomy, the subject becomes, according to Lukács, "a mechanical part incorporated into a mechanical system . . . in which . . . activity becomes less and less active and more and more contemplative" (*History and Class Consciousness* 89). The generalized reduction of use-value to the mere exchange of equivalent commodities extends throughout society to encompass subjectivity itself, destroying all traces of organic community and experience. In Marx's formulation, "a definite social relation between men . . . assumes, in their eyes, the fantastic form of a relation between things," and consciousness itself becomes a commodity (qtd. in Lukács, *History and Class Consciousness* 86).

"All reification is a forgetting," Theodor Adorno observed in a letter to Walter Benjamin. "Objects become purely thing-like the moment they are retained for us without the continued presence of their other aspects: when something of them has been forgotten" (321). Reification—the reduction of an entity's uniqueness to a state of abstract identity, capable of exchange and exploitation—breaks the chain of memory that unites the past to present, dividing objects into isolated, quantifiable units that, as Marx described the commodity, "confront [the individual] as invisible forces that generate their own power" (qtd. in Lukács, *History and Class Consciousness* 87).

Benjamin argued that the shock of modern society, in which individuals are increasingly exposed to forces that threaten their psychological and even physical existence, leads individuals to shunt experiences to unconscious forgetfulness; mere fragments, prefabricated signifiers and sound bites, stand in our consciousness for unique events, and the experience of unique events becomes available only to the representational capacities of memory. In Antillean culture, the power of the reified object within postcolonial consumer society gives colonized objects the hollow aura of the fetish, an object standing in for something absent and forgotten; from the fetishized imported auto redolent of an island's economic and psychological dependency to the exoticized bottle of tropical rum that might metonymically recall centuries of enslavement and exploitation along with the pleasure of a midafternoon *'ti punch,* the objects of consumer society stand in for something forgotten.[28]

This auratic reification hides not only these objects' modes of production but also their temporal situation within larger developmental processes of historical mutation. Memory is no ontological constant but is a variable human potential, to be developed or stifled with each generation, as the historian Maurice Hwalbachs argued (Yerushalmi 13).[29] With the gradual transformation of Antillean society into an almost pure consumerism since 1848, the experience of time as the substantive perception of difference and nonidentity in their temporal dimension has grown weaker, erased under a hegemonic law of exchange of abstract equivalency. At the same time, paradoxically, the past itself has become an increasingly accessible commodity (as plaque, newspaper article, or web page). Following the reduction of both the French Antilles and the slaves who worked that land to objects of exploitation and exchange-value, this active dispossession instituted a commodified Antillean subjectivity through the generalized symbolic self-representation of the Antillean as overseas French citizen.

The Martinican poet Aimé Césaire was the first to describe these processes of reification at work in colonialism. In the opening pages of his seminal 1939 poem, "Cahier d'un retour au pays natal" (Notebook of a return to my native land), Césaire's striking description of a prostrate, impotent Martinique, wrought by dependency and unfreedom, condemned colonialism in its reduction of humans and the geographical space they inhabit to passive objects of exploitation: "spread-flat, stumbling over its good common-sense, inert, gasping beneath the geometric burden of its eternally returning cross, resisting its destiny, mute, frustrated at every turn, unable to grow with the riches of this earth, hampered, whittled away, reduced, split-off from fauna and flora" (*Poésie* 10).

Césaire addressed the issue of reification more explicitly in postwar texts such as the 1955 *Discourse on Colonialism*. Here he develops the insight that slavery itself can be seen as the prototypical reduction of human relations to the form of commodity exchange. In this influential polemic, Césaire adopts the term *chosification* or "thingification" to describe the processes at work in colonization. The *Discourse* draws the consequences of enlightenment as it denounces a "universal regression" (11) that instrumentalizes human relationships. Césaire appropriates the mathematical logic of this process, holding up to the colonizers the objectified image of their barbarity: "Colonization=thingification" (19). The affirmative stance of Césaire's text is itself performative, a negation of the deadened passivity of the colonial subject. The *Discourse* constructs a rhetorical montage of heterogeneous objects in which the waste products of colonialism are reappropriated to weigh in against a barbarity masquerading as civilization.[30]

Césaire's colleague, the Martinican critic René Ménil, explicitly linked the process of colonization with the dysfunctional status of Antillean historical experience. The "degradation of temporal and spatial experience," Ménil wrote in "Psychoanalysis of History," "is a result of the colonial relations of a society split off from its vital interests–its geography, its past, its economic materiality" (49).

Edouard Glissant, the Martinican poet, theorist, and former student of Césaire, went on to delineate the parameters of Antillean dependency in his influential 1981 study *Antillean Discourse*. Here, Glissant articulates the material foundations of the erasure of memory in French Antillean society, describing the unfreedom of French Caribbean economic, cultural, and historical experience. Glissant locates the passivity of Antillean subjects in the objective economic and political structures that encourage dependency and what he terms a "mimetic impulse" toward a dominant metropolitan culture (42).

Such a misbalanced social structure—in which every dimension of daily existence is predicated upon the continued largesse of France—determines as well the patterns of behavior and experience of the Antillean populace. The result of this dependency, in Glissant's provocative terms, is to render any form of creation—economic, artistic, or political—a "scandal." To the scandalous status of creativity corresponds an erased, discontinuous history, "history as neurosis" (133), a past experienced passively as the persistent trauma of slavery, and the impossibility of a subjective "projection into the future" (88).

The Antillean subject's mimetic impulse leads to the absorption or assimilation of his or her culture in that of the metropolis. Glissant's provocative argument shows how symbolic expression itself, in the form of Creole, is itself rapidly adopting a French-derived syntax and vocabulary, serving only as local color in a context in which it has little remaining systemic function. Antillean subjects become both alienated and reified, experiencing their subjectivity not only—as Fanon described it in *Black Skin, White Mask*—as their objectification within white society, but within Antillean society real social relations are mystified and experienced passively as "morbidity." In Glissant's words: "We go away. Physically or mentally. Exiled or sick. Sick from the absence whose sign can be established inexhaustibly: a record of derision" (*DA* 119).

In Simone and André Schwarz-Bart's 1967 text, *Un plat de porc aux bananes vertes*, an old Antillean woman, abandoned in a Parisian old-persons' home, describes with enlightened lucidity this incapacity to delve into the memories that are her only possession:

> In fact, I know I'm not crazy, and that in my skull I too hold the threads of my life wound into a ball. But something prevents me from unraveling the past: fear. These women [her French neighbors in the asylum] are able to choose only those threads that they wish to, while I'm an awkward worker whose fingers are caught up in my memory, and each time a memory returns to me that destroys me. That's why I prefer to remain in the present, where I live as though I were born in this asylum. (18–19)

The isolated Mariotte stands as a cipher for the degree to which members of Antillean society are driven both to resist unwinding the filaments of memory and to reflect upon this resistance in aesthetic and theoretical writing. Her self-characterization as an "awkward worker" points to the contradiction at the heart of this refusal. Like other Antilleans, she is a "worker" from a land without work; the irony in her insistence in defining her own identity so inappropriately only underlines the radical disjuncture between her subjective desire for agency and those external structures and forces that render that agency practically impossible and virtually unthinkable. Mariotte, like the Antillean community for which she stands, is trapped in a French environment in which citizens are dependent upon a corps of functionaries and bureaucrats for handouts and a network of support systems in which "nothing exists beyond the chamber pots of sister Marie des Anges" (18).

If the white French inhabitants of the asylum can roam freely amid their memories ("they ramble freely upon the heights of their childhood"), where the subjective freedom of rêverie softens the blows of objective constraint, the traumatic character of Mariotte's buried memories makes even a present filled with chamber pots and bedsores preferable to delving into the past. Schwarz-Bart's despondent allegory of the objective economic dependency and preformed, commodified subjectivity presented by Césaire, Fanon, and Glissant represents only one half of the story of Antillean historical experience, however. The assimilation and the destruction of memory they describe have consistently met corresponding forces of resistance to the colonialist interpellation of Antillean subjects, and nowhere have the antinomies of contemporary French colonialism been more forcefully underlined than in the work of Aimé Césaire.

Negritude, Externalization, and Production-based Subjectivity

Aimé Césaire's response to the situation of Antillean dependency he first described in texts such as the *Cahier d'un retour au pays natal* has not been to postulate an imaginary resolution to the unfreedom of colonialism. Rather, he has consistently striven to demonstrate the inadequacy of existing social relations in the French Antilles to the concept of freedom. To do so, he has proceeded via an immersion of his aesthetic and critical sensibility within the material of Caribbean historical experience.

In 1939, Césaire's epochal poem *Cahier d'un retour au pays natal* first presented to the world the neologism "negritude." The poem traces both the passage of a colonized subject from prostration and heteronomy to freedom, while continuing to acknowledge the full force of social and psychological forces that undercut any notion of freedom that would bypass ongoing alienation. Though chapter 2 will examine in detail the doubled, antinomical structure of Antillean subjectivity Césaire presents in that poem, it is important here to describe the effect of his neologism as a determinate response to the alienation he observed in Caribbean experience.

Negritude refers to a collective self-understanding of the African diaspora emerging from a common experience of subjugation and enslavement. Césaire writes in the *Cahier:* "Negritude, no longer a cephalic index, or plasma, or soma, but measured by the compass of suffering" (77). Both Césaire's term and the subsequent cultural movement that took this name emphasized the possible negation of that subjugation through racial struggle and affirmation, of which the Haitian Revolution is emblematic ("Haïti where negritude rose for the first time" [47]).

Negritude as a concept encompassed and distilled a wide range of previous historical moments and generated a diverse field of debate that has, in its use of the term, extended, and at times even contradicted, Césaire's original intervention (cf. Nesbitt, "Negritude").

The implications of negritude as a poetic and historical intervention remain, I want to argue, productive beyond the historical stasis of the negritude debate of the 1950s and 1960s. Césaire's negritude of 1939 is a critical, protean concept, one that possesses a divided, objective status. By this, I mean that the poem presents something more than the unambiguous affirmation of a self-identical black subject many have seen in it. Césaire's concept of negritude externalizes the self-alienation of colonized subjects through an act of creation: the neologism. In Césaire's usage, an alienated subject is forced to confront itself as a reified object, a subjectivity in fact already constituted by society itself:

> my negritude is not a stone, its deafness hurled against the clamor of the day
> my negritude is not leukoma of dead liquid over the earth's dead eye
> my negritude is neither tower nor cathedral
> it plunges into the red flesh of the soil
> it plunges into the ardent flesh of the sky
> it pierces opaque prostration with its upright patience
> (*Collected Poetry* 69, translation modified)

Césaire's poem uses the freedom of aesthetic creation to orchestrate a complex critical apparatus. It postulates negritude as self-estrangement, standing before individuals as an externalized object. Césaire's poem, via what James Arnold has called a "phenomenological . . . dialectic of negritude," constructs a self-consciousness subject that overcomes its enslavement by confronting its self-alienation (*Modernism and Negritude* 155–57)[31] "To become aware of one's self as belonging to a subject people," Edward Said has noted, "is the founding insight" of the literature of decolonization. "We must not minimize the shattering importance of that initial insight—peoples being conscious of themselves as prisoners in their own land—for it returns again and again in the literature of the imperialized world" (214). Césaire's revolution in perception turns the process of objectification he perceives at work in Antillean society on its head, reappropriating it to the needs of the colonized. In marked contrast to those post-Hegelian critiques of objectification, most notably Sartre's, that find in it a sheerly negative alienation, Césaire's work recovered for the realm of colonial subjectivity the affirmative moment lodged in the Hegelian concept of objectification.

In Césaire's poetic activity, as Sartre observed in *Orphée noire,* "the poem objectifies" (260) an existential crisis (slavery, colonialism) through the work it performs upon an astonishing array of preexisting historical and aesthetic material. As such, however, Césaire's poetic work stands in contrast to the conflation of objectification—the fabrication of objects—and alienation—a specific modality of objectification in which individuals are made into unfree objects of exploitation—typical of much Marxian thought.[32] Césaire's neologism and its subsequent historical trajectory demonstrate that "alienation" harbors a transformational moment in which the individual's putatively "natural" existence—in this case the ideological subjugation of the colonized within a schema of racism and exploitation—is determinately negated for an artificial, self-created one. Césaire's neologism, in this view, is the performative instantiation of the very process it describes, tracing the liberation of an unfree, colonized subject through a confrontation with racism and colonialism.

Césaire's poem can thus be understood as the aesthetic analogue of the "heroic subject" Alexandre Kojève describes abstractly in his contemporaneous (1933–39) Parisian lectures on Hegel. In its productivity, Judith Butler observes in her analysis of Kojève, "work that exemplifies [for Kojève] human being as transcending the natural and which occasions the recognition of Others is termed *historical action*. As the efficacious transformation of biological or natural givens, historical action is the mode through which the world of substance is recast as the world of the subject. Confronting the natural world, the historical agent takes it up, marks it with the signature of consciousness and sets it forth in the social world to be seen" (68). Thus Kojève's heroic subject, like its poetic contemporary, Césaire's subject of negritude, initiates its historical existence through the application of a transformative instrumental rationality, confronting an inert, ahistorical nature to form it via the application of its autonomous agency. "The ultimate project of desire," Butler writes of Kojève's subject, "is less a dialectical assimilation of subjectivity to the world, and the world to subjectivity, than a unilateral action upon the world in which consciousness instates itself as the generator of historical reality"(69).[33] Césaire's neologism affirmed the radical creativity of constituent subjectivity, redeploying the force of the productive imagination against colonialist racism.

At the very historical moment when the idealist subject of Kant, Hegel, and the young Marx appears historically invalidated, when the theories of Nietzsche, Saussure, Freud, and Heidegger seem to dissolve the solidity of that subject's identity in a range of objective determinations, Césaire's poetic tour de force portrays the historical process of de-subjectification as simultaneously true and untrue: true insofar as it designates the actual dehumanization of enslaved and colonized subjects, yet untrue insofar as negritude constitutes a refusal to accept such dehumanization as history's final word. In this view, the celebrated "death of the subject" is no prognosis of an impending disappearance but rather the apprehension that, if colonized subjectivity has heretofore remained a zombified living-death, human subjectivity, as the full actualization of human potential in a given historical moment, has yet to be instantiated.

Externalization

Césaire's act of creation follows the logic of *Entäusserung,* or "externalization," developed in G. W. F. Hegel's 1807 *Phenomenology of Spirit*.[34] Césaire's neologism appears at a crucial historical moment within the development of what I wish to call a "production-based" model of subjectivity. This model originates in Giambatista Vico's equation of truth with that which humans have rationally produced *(verum et factum conventuntur)* and reappears in idealist form in Kant's analysis of reason as the creator of the objective world of human understanding via the spontaneous capacity of the mind's "productive imagination" (*Critique of Pure Reason* 256–57).[35] Hegel's description of productive labor's emancipatory implications for the enslaved subject, however, offers the key elaboration of this concept fundamental to postcolonial theory. One might argue such a reference to European theory—the notoriously racist Hegel in particular —reproduces the justifiably criticized gesture of using colonial texts as the raw material for high Western Theory (P. Hountonji).[36] While the very real racism of figures such as Kant and Hegel that Paul Gilroy describes in *Against Race* is relevant to that author's critique of racial experience, the focus of this study lies elsewhere. French Caribbean thought is obviously no mere rewriting of Hegel; my intention is rather to dig beneath an "exotic" surface to explore less visible layers of thought informing it as a refractive participant in Western Modernity. This book is thus an attempt to construct critically a constellation of heterogeneous materials spread throughout space and time, from Haiti to Hegel, that takes its cues as much from Glissant's *Discours antillais* and Richard Price's *The Convict and the Colonel* as from Benjamin's notion of the constellation.

It would take us too far afield to describe in detail the origins and development of Hegelian "externalization" and its transformations and vicissitudes in the work of Marx and subsequent Marxian thought on the problem of production.[37] In reference to negritude and given the centrality of Hegel's dialectic of the master and slave to all of postcolonial theory, however, it is important to determine the key elements in this materialist prefiguration of Marx's critique of labor. The analysis of labor is one of the fundamental elements in Hegel's systematic philosophy. This analysis has often remained underappreciated, however, since its most explicit elaborations occur in Hegel's early, lesser-known writings (the so-called "First" or "Jena System" and the "System of Ethical Life" of 1802–6). Herbert Marcuse's *Reason and Revolution* argues compellingly for this materialist dimension fundamental to Hegel's early thought both in Hegel's critical analysis of alienated labor and, in its negative impact, in Hegel's already conservative idealist conclusions. Marcuse traces, on the one hand, the origins of German idealism to the Lutheran primacy placed upon spiritual interiority (14) and a conciliatory, conformist tendency that sublimated the impulse for social transformation Hegel inherited from the French Revolution to the call for "sacrifice," "submission," and "disciplining" (55, 59) of the individual to and by the state. This tendency would culminate in the *Philosophy of Right*'s defense of the authoritarian Prussian monarchy.

At the same time, Marcuse examines Hegel's early philosophical writings (1800–1809) to show that Hegel's ever-increasing conservatism is in fact a betrayal of the philosophical principles that structure his entire system of thought: while empiricist and later positivist philosophy "confined men within the limits of 'the given,' within the existing order of things and events" (20), Hegel's early writings explicitly announce Marx's critique of capitalism (77–79). Hegel denounces the alienation of individual laborers within the fictional universality of private property (53) and describes prophetically the same material and psychological reification Lukács would analyze in greater detail over a century later: "The utmost abstractness of labor reaches into the most individual types of work and continues to widen its sphere. This inequality of wealth and poverty, this need and necessity turn into the utmost dismemberment of will, inner rebellion, and hatred" (qtd. in *Reason and Revolution* 81).[38]

Hegel's early idealism critiques a society (late German feudalism before the Napoleonic invasions) in which an "irrational" society thwarts the human potential to come to correspond with its own idea or concept of an enlightened "humanity" (60, 89). Hegel thus redefines the "real" as a utopian futurity in which phenomenal objects (above all, humans, able self-consciously to conceive and temporally project themselves) will attain the full possibility contained in their concept (65).

The majority of these early writings were not published until the twentieth century. In their place, Hegel's *Phenomenology of Spirit* (1807) submerges this critical dimension, bowing in its conclusions to the reality of a blocked, monolithically conservative society it leaves behind unchanged for the realm of Absolute Spirit. In its idealist apotheosis, the *Phenomenology* affirms Hegel's abandonment of the call for the dialectical negation of the false, merely existing world via that world's encounter with its own true concept, in deference to the hollow affirmation of its mere sublimated likeness, the Absolute Spirit (Marcuse 91–92). And yet, attention to the text's description of the encounter between master and slave, now relegated by the mature Hegel to a mere moment in the advance of Spirit, reveals the subterranean persistence of the materialist dimension of Hegel's idealism.

The *Phenomenology of Spirit* describes the complex relations inhering between a predominant, unfree society and the capacity of human imagination to construct freedom from within this very enslavement and predetermination. Hegel's argument locates the origins of self-consciousness within the interaction between an enslaved subject and the objective, phenomenal world that has determined it; more specifically, within the transformative work the slave operates upon specific objects of his or her labor. "Through work . . . the bondsman becomes conscious of what he truly is." Hence the clear relevance of Hegel's argument to the experience of the colonized—an argument that Fanon would later adapt to compelling effect in *Peau noire, masques blancs*—as containing the seeds of its own negation and transcendence. "The negative relation to the object [i.e. its transformation via work] becomes its form and something permanent, because it is precisely for the worker that the object has independence." Prefiguring Marx's analysis of the commodity, Hegel's worked-upon object takes on a life of its own. It confronts the worker with an image—constituted via the application of rational formal categories of construction—of both his bondage and obligation and his capacity to transform that world of unfreedom through his own acts. "It is in this way, therefore, that consciousness, *qua* worker, comes to see in the independent being [of the object] its *own* independence" (*Phenomenology* 118).

Crucially, Hegel argues that self-consciousness arises from the specific experience of lived contradiction.[39] In Hegel's analysis, it is specifically *enforced, unfree* work that he finds productive of transformative insight, since unavoidable contradiction throws before the slave the true nature of his or her experience, *at once* enslaved and autonomous. Marx and Lukács would go on to emphasize the unfreedom of work as "alienation" *(Entfremdung)* and reification, in which capitalist control of the conditions, means, and products of labor, over and against the worker, determines the thing-like reign of commodity fetishism. Their analysis lies at the root of Césaire, Fanon, and Glissant's critique of Antillean alienation described above.[40]

Hegel, however, unlike Marx and Lukács after him, stresses that an act of creation, even and especially within conditions of dependency, carries a transformative, utopian charge. For Hegel, the article of the slave's creation, though externalized, is not simply an abstraction. Instead, it is a representation of his or her subjective experience, given phenomenal form and existence, and is thus understandable, a representation that produces what Hegel's 1802–3 writings called a "practical consciousness," "the real rationality of work" in which "concepts . . . are wrenched from nature" (Hegel, *Le premier système* 81; *Système de la vie éthique* 124, 123).[41] "The shape does not become something other than himself through being made external to him; for it is precisely this shape that is his pure being-for-self, which in this externality is seen by him to be the truth. Through this rediscovery of himself by himself the bondsman realizes that it is precisely in his work wherein he seemed to have only an alienated existence that he acquires a mind of his own" (*Phenomenology* 118–19).

The created object produces insight because it serves to mediate subject and object; as such, labor constructs a subjectivity that expands beyond the abstract interiority of alienation and suffering to encompass subject and object as a differentiated, contradictory totality. Work reveals the "disparity between Notion and reality . . . [a disparity] learnt by consciousness from experience in its work"(244). Subjectivity, in this sense, arises from this dialectical interdetermination of subject and object, in the forms (from houses to language, all "buildings" or human constructions in the widest sense of that which is rationally built) humans create. Thus the notion of "externalization" initiates dialectical *experience* as a specific concept of subject-object relations that finds self-conscious subjectivity to arise from the productive externalizations of labor.

Hegel's notion of externalization implies the fabrication of a specifically *historical* experience, insofar as the enslaved subject is transformed, or negated, in the experience of work; in other words, the experience of labor not only transforms the object (a tree into a wheel) but the subject him or herself is transformed via self-understanding. From an unthinking, merely reactive slave, he or she *becomes an other,* in this case a simultaneously enslaved worker and a free creator of the objective world, through this insight into the contradictory nature of both the self and the phenomenal world.[42] In becoming aware of both his or her determination within a context of social unfreedom and the capacity to transform that world, the slave is himself transformed into an objectively new being. The slave becomes conscious of both this negative unfreedom and its contradiction with the immanent possibility (the idea) his teleological activity proves: that he may and must become truly human, and this by transforming the world. This critical root of Hegel's idealism shows self-understanding to exist in dialectical relation with objective determinations and in the transformation of those determinations through insight and the subsequent capacity to act rationally upon them.

This dialectical movement of self-externalization and ensuing insight into the self and its place in the world transforms the slaves Hegel describes —and thus they enter into a properly *historical* existence. As such, they become alienated from their former selves in a process constitutive of the modern self, destroying what came before and passing forward into a transformed, novel existence. Hegel's analysis is no mere historical curiosity; the importance of constructed concepts such as "negritude" for the self-understanding of the colonized points to the relevance of his insight for the process of decolonization. Furthermore, Hegel's understanding of labor's capacity to constitute consciousness grows increasingly important amid the globalization and de-materialization of labor. Hegel's notion of a "practical consciousness" first theorized labor as implicated in the construction of subjectivity and of the human itself; and his vision of a transformative, emancipatory labor is only now becoming a real possibility with the potential reorientation of production toward a life-based bioethic, a possibility I will return to in chapter 6 (Hardt and Negri 432, 441; see also Bidima 20 and Lefebvre, *La fin de l'histoire* 24).[43]

THE APPEARANCE of Césaire's *Cahier* in 1939 is thus historically incisive on at least three levels. It proceeds through an immersion in the content of African diasporic history, invoking the historical figure of Toussaint Louverture at the very moment Césaire forms his most powerful neologism. "Haïti, where negritude rose for the first time and stated that it believed in its humanity ... (TOUSSAINT, TOUSSAINT LOUVERTURE)" (47). Secondly, both the *Cahier* and the concept of negritude in turn engendered a vast range of material effects during the decolonization movement, where they served as a primary point of reference and inspiration to the generation that brought an end to juridical colonization. Finally, the concept and word *negritude* is the model of an autonomously created object that negates the objectivity of enslaved existence itself—where humans are putatively reduced to pure objects—in a becoming-human. Humans, in Marx's words, "distinguish themselves from animals as soon as they begin to *produce*" (150). Furthermore, as language, Césaire's neologism represents a specific type of "labor." The poet is, in Hegel's words, "the artificer," and in his or her poetic labor "Spirit has raised the shape in which it is present to its own consciousness into the form of consciousness itself and it produces such a shape for itself.... [The poet] has become a spiritual worker" (424). As labor upon *language,* the poet's work transcends the limited interiority of the isolated worker to begin the construction of an intersubjective linguistic community, an immanent "universal consciousness" (242).

As an act of negation and externalization, Césaire's aesthetic production is quite literally an example of the negativity of what Nietzsche termed the "slave morality [that] from the outset says No to what is 'outside,' what is 'different,' what is not itself" (qtd. in Butler 208). This act of negation, which Nietzsche condemned as nihilistic, is in a sense to Césaire's credit. Césaire refuses Zarathustra's *amor fati;* instead, the experience of slavery engenders a reaffirmation and reformulation of the Hegelian practices of critique and negation. Rather than internalizing the demand of society to affirm immediately its sacrificial logic, then mystifying that internalization as an abstract "affirmation," Césaire subjects his world to unceasing critique in an attempt to "negate" it. In this view, the true slave morality would be the Nietzschean one that calls itself free while affirming a world in which its freedom is predicated upon the unfree labor of others. Though the postwar ideology of negritude betrayed its own ideals as it became a mere catchphrase of public debate, Césaire's original use of the term remains suggestive. No essentialized category, Césaire's negritude describes the very contradictions that open the colonized subject to the possibility of self-transformation and enlightenment beyond the circularity of identity politics.[44]

THE IDEA of a French Caribbean historical experience that this study seeks to elaborate develops the notion of *Erfahrung,* or "experience," first described in Hegel's *Phenomenology of Spirit* and subsequently transformed in the critical thought of Walter Benjamin and Theodor Adorno.[45] Hegel's *Phenomenology* determined not only the contours of postwar French thought in general but more specifically that of French Antillean thinkers such as Aimé Césaire, Frantz Fanon, and Edouard Glissant. The dialectical historicism of thinkers such as Hegel, Marx, Lukács, Hyppolite, and Kojève offered compelling tools with which African diasporic writers attacked French colonialism. Primary among these was a notion of experience marked by a complex understanding of the relation between subject and object as one of mediation and negation in the face of the violent, abstract objectification and dehumanization of the colonized.

As we have seen, Hegel's notion of "Externalization" implied a specific reworking and reanimation of the static, frozen relation between subject and object at work in capitalist (and slave-holding) culture. In this act of conscious creation, the slave externalizes aspects of his or her subjective experience. In so doing, the slave gains a measure of insight into both his determination by the forces that work to objectify him as slave and his capacity to act upon the world as an autonomous subject. The relation between the slave and the created object is not one of absolute separation and difference. Instead, the object is in this view an objectification of the slave's subjectivity. The movement from the abstract inwardness of immediate experience, the uncomprehending pain of enslavement, to insight into both the nature of that determination and the possibilities of its transformation form Hegel's idea of a dialectical truth-content.

In the preface to the *Phenomenology* he describes this transformation as a movement of consciousness: "The immediate existence of Spirit, *consciousness,* contains the two moments of knowing and the objectivity negative to knowing.... Consciousness knows and comprehends only what falls within its experience; for what is contained in this is nothing but spiritual substance, and this too, as *object* of the self" (21). Here, the idealism that Marx would critique in the *1844 Manuscripts* is striking (I will return to it below) and would seem to render such a formulation useless for the concrete historical processes of slavery and colonialism. What the previous discussion of "externalization" has hopefully made apparent, however, is that Hegel's *Phenomenology,* for all its dubious conclusions, engages a powerfully historicized method of critique that contests the very sufficiency of immediate experience, showing how the most concrete occurrences impinging upon and molding human bodies in terrifying ways actually call forth reflection, understanding, and their own transformation and overcoming in what Hegel calls "the tremendous power of the negative"(19).

Prior to Hegel, the German word *Erfahrung* (experience) had implied an active, domineering process of subjective inquiry into a passive world of objects.[46] With Kant, the notion undergoes a logical schematization; he understands experience as the a priori logical categories of reason processing the material of sensible intuitions ("appearances") in the act of synthetic judgment.[47] As such, the Kantian notion of experience is one of sheer interiority; it occurs entirely within the faculty of reason, "only in me.... We have no insight into the possibility of [things in themselves], and the domain outside of the sphere of appearances is empty (for us)" (*Critique of Pure Reason* 429, 362).

Hegel's dialectical reformulation of *Erfahrung* attempted to reintroduce the mediation of subject and object into human experience that this Kantian "block" on experience of the noumenal "things in themselves" refused. Hegel argued that the Kantian noumenal was merely an empty "abstraction" and "figments of subjective thought" and, as such, not an endpoint and blockage of thought but the point at which consciousness must begin if it is to actualize the truth contained in its notion (*Logic* 489, 36). The essence of Hegel's argument was precisely to demonstrate the formal interaction of subject and object, then to trace that process through all of human historical experience as he knew it. The preface to the *Phenomenology* describes abstractly the movement at work in the slave's act of production: "But Spirit becomes object because it is just this movement of becoming an *other to itself,* i.e. becoming an *object to itself,* and of suspending this otherness. And experience is the name we give to just this movement, in which the immediate, the unexperienced, i.e. the abstract ... becomes alienated from itself and then returns to itself from this alienation, and is only then revealed for the first time in its actuality and truth, just as it then has become a property of consciousness also" (21). The model of truth Hegel proposes here is not based upon a reified objectivity separating the scientific observer from the observed facts. This Hegel critiques as the merely formal, external understanding *(Verstand)* of Kant that is no more than an empty "table of contents." Instead, he argues that truth can only arise from the subject's immersion within the immanent object itself, its "surrender to the life of the object" (*Phenomenology* 32).

HEGEL'S MODEL of experience has not gone uncriticized in Francophone postcolonial theory. Frantz Fanon's work in particular interrogates the seductive explanatory force of this notion of productive experience in which the subject's encounter with the object and his return to self-same experience glides along the well-oiled rails of dialectical automatism: "the abstract ... becomes alienated from itself and then returns to itself from this alienation, and is only then revealed for the first time in its actuality and truth" (*Phenomenology* 21). Fanon's critique of Hegel reworks that of Marx, first elaborated in the *1844 Manuscripts.* There, Marx had erased Hegel's explicit focus on the slave to develop a more general critique of alienated labor. Though Marx praised Hegel for having grasped "*labor* as the *essence* of man," he concludes that Hegel "sees only the positive, not the negative side of labor" (112). Marx, of course, proceeds to reverse

Hegel's assessment 180 degrees and describes "objectification as *loss of the object* and *object-bondage*" in which "the worker becomes a slave of his object" (72–73, emphasis in original). Hegel's idealism, Marx concludes, falsely hypostatized a self-conscious subject and, in so doing, left behind concrete, suffering individuals in a flight of philosophical fancy: "Within the sphere of abstraction, Hegel conceives labor as man's act of *self-genesis*. . . . Real man and real nature become mere predicates . . . a *mystical subject-object* or a *subjectivity reaching beyond* the *object*" (121, emphasis in original).

Fanon's critique recovers the Hegelian focus on the slave, now, however, in light of Marx's analysis of alienated labor. Fanon's investigation reveals the ideological nature of Hegel's reconciled, de-alienated model of the subject. Hegel's return to the self from its moment of alienation is possible, Fanon argues, only in a society in which identity and agency are transparent and unproblematic. Colonial society, however, places itself, as it were, between the subject and any unproblematic constitution of self-understanding. As both colonized subject and psychoanalyst, Fanon revealed the problematic nature of experience at the point of an extorted reconciliation ("dis-alienation") in Hegel. In a context of systematic dehumanization in which "the Negro is not a man" (*Peau noire, masques blancs* 6), Hegel's "surrender to the life of the object" becomes a pathological desubjectification enforced upon colonized subjects by society. Hegel's notion of "experience," in this view, is ideological due to its sheer inwardness; it can maintain an image of a freely moving subjective experience only if the agency of that movement is understood to be uncoerced. In the unfree world of colonialism, however, the subject is compelled to systematic alienation at every level of experience: language, culture, economics, geography, politics.

Peau noire, masques blancs reveals to its readers, via ideological critique, the extent of this unfree alienation in which they are entangled, working through the blockage, at once psychological and material, that colonial society visits upon its subjects. For Fanon, "all critique of material being implies a solution" (50). Despite its thematic condemnation of Hegel, Fanon's utopian gesture can be seen to reappropriate Hegel's "labor of the negative" to generate what Fanon calls "the ideal conditions for the existence of a human world" (188). Fanon's critique of colonial alienation is not so much opposed to Hegel's notion of experience as it is an attempt to work through the limitations of the latter's failure to problematize sufficiently the contradictory, conflictual relations inhering between colonized individuals and society. As such, the Hegelian model of experience is not abandoned and rendered outdated by writers such as Césaire, Fanon, and Glissant but rather emerges transformed by their critique, informed by the determinate specificity of colonial alienation that Hegel's hypostatization of a transparent unity between individual and society elides.

A DIALECTICAL model of experience, I would maintain, underpins Antillean literature's encounter with history. For if the abstract objectivity of a scientific historiography has its place within the constellation of Antillean letters, in the vexing context of exploitation, dependency, and alienation at work in colonialism, this discursive model undervalues the need of the colonized for insight into the concrete relations between the phenomenal world and the individual's search for freedom. In such a context, neither an abstract, value-free description of that world nor the sheer inwardness of poetic reverie is sufficient. Faced with the need for human autonomy, Antillean authors have constructed the means to confront their objective, historical determination via the representation of subjective experience.

This construction of an autonomous Antillean subjectivity, mediated through the production of aesthetic objects, occurs in response to the material context of the "successful" colonization and heteronomy of Martinique and Guadeloupe registered by authors such as Césaire, Fanon, and Glissant. In the French overseas departments, the creation of this literature serves a critical function in a culture that has become dependent on the arrival of cargo planes and ships from France at regular daily intervals. Indeed, Maryse Condé has argued for just such a social function of literature in these islands, remarking that "writing [in the Antilles] is a refuge and site of power." In a situation in which nearly all business and political decisions depend upon the whims of metropolitans, "writing bestows a power," Condé argues, a power markedly lacking in daily life (Maryse Condé, personal communication, Feb. 23, 1995). Following Césaire's initial displacement of Hegelian and Marxian externalization from the actual slave's work to the imaginative, aesthetic work of the poet in *Cahier d'un retour au pays natal*, later Antillean literature sustains this sartrian relegation of effective intentional consciousness to the imaginary in the face of overarching economic dependency.[48]

In this context, the World War II blockade and occupation of the islands by the Vichy government has come to represent for writers such as Daniel Maximin, Edouard Glissant, and Raphaël Confiant a paradoxically Edenic period in which forced isolation obligated inhabitants to develop a self-sufficiency that had been stamped out since the 1848 induction of all citizens into the island's system of limited commodity consumption. Employment in the French bureaucracy provides a security that compensates for the inherent insecurity of being a small island faced with the threat of imminent devastation every August to October (hurricane season) in a community whose numerical inconsequentiality leaves it open to the changing whims of each new metropolitan government. The patent instability resulting from such exposure to the elements and remoteness from the metropolitan center helps explain the manic character of French-Caribbean experience that Glissant has so fruitfully explored (*DA* 361).

The French Caribbean writing described in this volume, when viewed as a compensatory mechanism capable of imagining novel social relations, is fundamentally dual: it arises from and is determined by historical, material conditions, and yet it refuses to accept the present state of things as inevitable, generating a utopian vision informed by the historical past. Max Horkheimer, in a passage from his essay "Critical Theory," described this radical promise encapsulated in history: "What has happened to those humans who have fallen, no future can redeem.... Amid this immense indifference only human consciousness can become the higher instance where injustice can be abolished/overcome.... Historiography *(Historie)* is the only court of appeals that present humanity, itself fleeting, can offer to the protests coming from the past" (qtd. in Löwy 37). This anticipatory dimension of history determines the attraction of a historical poetics in the postcolonial Caribbean context. There, history recuperates the buried suffering of history's conquered, refusing to subordinate subjective experience to the demands of an "objective" history that Benjamin famously described as "the triumphal procession in which the present rulers walk upon the bodies of those who are lying vanquished today."[49] This historical poetics is not the abstract freedom to write anything, a "history" of pure creation utterly undetermined by historical, objective facticity, but the construction of historical texts that dialectically mediate documentary evidence and the critical experience of colonized Antillean subjects. What I am calling Antillean historical experience is neither a theory of historiography nor of memory but rather a description of the objectification of a historically determined subjective experience within aesthetic objects.

Antillean writers have been forced to approach the past fitfully and surreptitiously in order to recapture its lost dimensions. In so doing, they enter into dialogue not only with the poets and novelists who serve as their models but also with a wide-ranging tradition of French academic and positivist historiography, to which they offer a more or less explicit counter-model.[50] To speak of an "academic' and "positivist" historiography is to indicate differing aspects of what can be taken as a single, differentiated field of production. The former points to the self-positioning of a given historiographic discourse within a discursive structure of socioprofessional norms, a discourse functioning through a logic of accumulated social capital in an academic and/or literary field. The latter, in turn, refers not only to the putative epistemological transparency of Third-Republic historians such as Ernest Lavisse, Charles-Victor Langlois, and Charles Seignobos[51] but also, for example, to the orthodox Marxist "scientific" discourse of Pierre Vilar, who, in "History after Marx," speaks of "model[s] . . . concepts, hypotheses, and theories,"—as opposed to a historiography of "stylistics"—the proper manipulation of which confirms for the author Marx's insight that "the entire realm of the human, in space and time, can be brought within the compass of scientific analysis" (qtd. in Revel and Hunt 76.) Even more recent historians and philosophers of history such as Jacques Le Goff and Paul Ricoeur maintain a surprisingly uncritical understanding of historical objectivity (Le Goff 10, Ricoeur, *La Mémoire* 182).

French Antillean literature strives to engage history and its modes of narration to recover for subjective experience the material of history: "Only poetic knowledge," write Confiant, Bernabé, and Chamoiseau in their *Eloge de la Créolité*, "can reveal us, perceive us, bring us back, evanescent, to a reborn consciousness" (qtd. in Price 170). Postcolonial Antillean writers have cultivated the representational means of voicing history and memory while attending to its negative, utopian exploration of possibility.[52] "The first obligation of our generation is to prepare for future generations the arms in the fight against forgetfulness," Vincent Placoly writes in *Frères volcans*. "There will be no peace for those who have died as long as the cancer of forgetfulness eats the flesh of their children. . . . Of course we owe it to ourselves to reconstitute the exceptional events of the past. But not as if this past no longer belonged to us, or as though we were rid of it. . . . The historian of the Antilles must be an architect of tomorrow" (119, 11, 10). The danger confronting such an enterprise, in contradistinction to a rigorous academicism, is an insufficient immersion in the objectivity of historical material. The ensuing chapters will follow French Caribbean authors in their negotiation of this problematic. Their various constructions of a historical poetics seek to ensure that the past, while rigorously attended to, will always signify beyond its immanent meaning as a "prophetic vision of the past" (*DA* 132), to break down and reanimate the reified materials they feed off.

Aesthetic Construction

The aesthetic, since Alexander Baumgarten invented the concept from the Greek "aisthetikos" in his *Reflections on Poetry* of 1735, has been tied to matters of the human body in ways that underscore its relevance to the Antillean experiences of enslavement, torture, and suffering. Baumgarten demarcates two spheres of experience: rational scientific cognition and—subordinate to it in Baumgarten's view—a secondary process addressed to the objects of bodily, sensuous perception that is the aesthetic (78).[53] Baumgarten first theorized the impoverishment of experience by scientific-technological reason this chapter describes. From its inception, the aesthetic implied a mode of cognition that proceeds differently from that of scientific, classificatory rationality, an alternative form of experience to the instrumental reason inextricable from the historical projects of European colonization and slavery.

Kant sustains this distinction between two forms of understanding in the opening passage of his Third Critique: "The judgment of taste is . . . not a cognitive judgment, hence not a logical one, but is rather aesthetic, by which is understood one whose determining ground *cannot* be *other than subjective* [i.e. sensuous rather than a priori]" (*Critique of the Power of Judgement* 89, emphasis in original). Kant describes "an entirely special faculty for discriminating and judging" (90) whose principal characteristic is that "the taste for the beautiful is a disinterested and *free* satisfaction" (91, emphasis in original). Kant's aesthetic cognition thus avoids the instrumental, means-oriented teleology of rational calculation and represents instead a model of that which has value in and for itself and not in its mere use for another; fundamentally, a full human subject and not the slave-object useful only as a quotient of labor.

Aesthetic cognition takes objects in their specificity (using what Kant terms "singular judgments" [100]), avoiding the categorical, abstracting logic of reason *(Verstand)* that mediates aesthetic perception via the application of preformed universal concepts (101). Aesthetic cognition, through a process Kant terms the "free play of the faculties of cognition" (103), allows for the generation of new concepts after the fact, so to speak, from an attention to the aesthetic object itself in which "only the particular is given and the universal has to be found for it" (qtd. in Bernstein 306).[54] Aesthetic cognition is the mode of an autonomous thought, irreducible to absolute logical and social determination (the beautiful cannot be decreed). Robert Kaufman argues that Kant's notion of aesthetic judgment, insofar as that judgment strives toward a universality that must necessarily be free of coercion (to force another to agree on an object's beauty is to invalidate that judgment), provides "the grounds and springboard for a rational, noninstrumentalized, noncoercive constructionism" ("Red Kant" 713).[55] In this view, aesthetic critique is more than the act of dissolution at work in Benjamin's concept of the allegory; it is simultaneously a construction of critical understanding in which the objects of cognition achieve a qualified priority over any (eventual) universal concept.

Unlike Kant, who maintained the ultimate irreducibility of the object world (the "noumenal") to a totalizing human subjectivity, Hegel systematically reduced the aesthetic to an inferior way station on the march to Absolute Spirit, prior to the moments of religion and philosophy. Indeed, the very relation to sensuous experience that I am arguing underpins the validity of aesthetic quasi-cognition for Antillean experience is what invalidates the aesthetic for Hegel, for whom its relation to intuition limits it to an inferior position within the totality of Spirit (Eagleton 144).

For Marx, however, the aesthetic consideration of subjugated bodies implies the representation of a human society in which individuals become ends in and for themselves. Marx, it will be recalled, articulates a materialist critique of the Hegelian model of productive experience whose implementation is obstructed by the impediments to autonomous experience inherent in capitalist society. In consonance with his rejection of Hegel, Marx reaffirms the aesthetic as a model of the production of nonalienated, self-sufficient use-value: "A writer does *not* regard his work as a means to an end. They are an end in themselves; so little are they 'means,' for himself and others, that he will, if necessary, sacrifice his own existence to their existence" (qtd. in Eagleton 204, emphasis in original). Here again, Marx does not discard the analysis of production Hegel presents in the *Phenomenology* but retains it as a model whose instantiation is made impossible by actually existing society.

Thus Marx does in fact pose, but as an ideal, the nonalienated production Hegel seems to presuppose: "It is only when objective reality universally becomes for man the reality of man's essential powers and thus the reality of his *own* essential powers, that all *objects* become for him the *objectification of himself*, objects that confirm and realize his individuality, *his* objects, i.e. *he himself* becomes the object" (qtd. in Eagleton 205). Marx's debt to the model of production-based subjectivity Hegel offers in the *Phenomenology* could hardly be more blatant. Despite this Marxian reaffirmation of production, and for all its clear relevance to the colonial experience of alienated labor and subjectivity, Terry Eagleton rightly points to the masculinist, ethnocentrist bias of the production model of experience

(221). As such, the Marxist-Hegelian model of production must be rearticulated if it can hope to inform the dilemmas of Antillean experience.

SUCH A REARTICULATION can perhaps begin with the distinction between an instrumental, goal-oriented *production* and a noncoercive model of *construction*.[56] A model of aesthetic construction would emphasize an uncoerced creativity in which human imagination generates new formal constellations that, as in collage, allow objects to persist in their specificity rather than serving as mere raw material to be transformed into commodities, commodities that only have value in their equivalency with other commodities. Such a model of construction is in fact developed in Theodor Adorno's reworking of Kantian aesthetics in his posthumous *Aesthetic Theory*.[57] The change "from a focus on a goal (or on productionism's goal, the product)," Robert Kaufman observes, "allows for concentration on the problem of construction (of imagining and making the form) itself" (721).

Adorno warns against any absolute, nondialectical affirmation of construction following Benjamin's celebration of surrealist collage (56). He instead investigates construction as a contradictory aesthetic process, one in which the antinomies of an unfree society, and of the dominated subjects in it, may be represented and worked through in a process that is itself a form of reification: "Construction is the extension of subjective domination, which conceals itself all the more profoundly the further it is driven. Construction tears the elements of reality out of their primary context and transforms them to the point where they are once again capable of forming a unity, one that is no less imposed on them internally than was the heteronomous unity to which they were subjected externally" (57). In this process of aesthetic reification, Adorno argues, the artwork simultaneously reproduces and distances itself from the reification of a society determined by alienated labor. In its distance from physical labor, the laborious construction of the artwork—reaffirmed in every act of conscious, laborious reception as well—offers the possibility of coming to understand social reification. "This *work* of the artist," Proust observed in a premonition of Adorno's insight, "alone expresses for others and makes us see our own life, that life that cannot 'observe' itself, [a life] whose appearances as observed by [the artist] must be translated and often read backwards and deciphered with enormous effort" (*Temps retrouvé* 300, emphasis added). Proust's timeless artwork is not life but rather, Frankenstein-like, it "recreates true life" to reveal the falsity of what merely passes for life (our "mundane," *mondain* existence).

Fredric Jameson argues in his book *Late Marxism* that Adorno's treatment of reification effects a complex reworking of the traditional Marxian dualism, described above, of objectification and alienation. The ethical and political foundation of Adorno's attention to the persistence of objects in their nonidentical specificity "historicizes the problem [of reification] and includes reification as such (as an intensified effect of commodity production) within even nonalienated objectification today" (21). Jameson argues that the foundation of Adorno's highly abstract analysis of the dialectics of identity and nonidentity is in fact the emphatically material Marxian investigation of use and exchange values (23).

As a form of reification, the *work* involved in the construction of every "artwork" signifies its participation in an untrue, coercive society, yet the artwork simultaneously abstracts itself from this society and turns away from it as purposeless *art pour l'art*. Through its autonomy, art affirms an external, utopian critique of the reified society of which it is a product: art "becomes social by virtue of its oppositional position to society itself, a position it can occupy only by defining itself as autonomous" (qtd. in Jameson, *Late Marxism* 179).[58] In its autonomy, the artwork offers a model of a subjectivity that would operate through something other than the endless reduction of difference to identity: "The reconciled condition would not be the philosophical imperialism of annexing the alien. Instead, its happiness would lie in the fact that the alien, in the proximity it is granted, remains what is distant and different, beyond the heterogeneous and beyond that which is one's own" (Adorno, *Negative Dialectics* 191).[59]

Within the overarching historical dilemma of reification, *aesthetic* reification, Adorno's "construction" of artistic images, offers an alternative to both Kantian reason *(Verstand)* and Hegel's dialectical reason *(Vernunft)*. For all its suppleness, even the latter must depend upon the conceptual universals of language, which, Jameson observes, "in trying desperately to designate what is other than the universal, continues to use an abstract terminology and the very form of logical opposition or dualism to convey its protest against the operations of that language and that logical form. To say 'particular' is to reinforce the 'universal,' no matter what you go on to do with these words" (*Late Marxism* 29). Instead, as Kant first argued, aesthetic construction is an only *quasi*-rational process. On the one hand, "although artworks are neither conceptual nor judgmental, they are logical" (Adorno, *Aesthetic Theory* 136.) Despite this inherent logicality, artworks, Adorno argues, neither turn away from rationality to mystical intuition nor are they fully given over to discursive logic. Instead, "art corrects conceptual knowledge because, in complete isolation, it carries out what conceptual knowledge in vain awaits from the nonpictorial subject-object relation [i.e., from abstract reason]: that through a subjective act what is objective would be unveiled. Art does not postpone this act ad infinitum but demands of it its own finitude at the price of its illusoriness" (113).

Artworks thus take up homeopathically, in Adorno's felicitous image, the process of reification that, as Hegel first pointed out, holds the historical promise of self-consciousness and freedom. In so doing, the artwork turns reification against its dereliction in an existing society given over to the totality of exchange. Aesthetic constructionism, in contrast to positivist historicism, responds to the vitiation of a historical experience reduced to the mythological, seemingly eternal spatial relations of reified society: "Universal history has no theoretical armature. Its method is additive; it musters a mass of data to fill the homogenous, empty time. Materialist historiography, on the other hand, is based on a constructive principle" (Benjamin, *Illuminations* 262). As an example of the construction Walter Benjamin called "rememoration" *(Eingedenken),* the artwork, informed by the suffering of past generations, points toward a recovery of qualitative historical experience through its own ossified form.

As an *aesthetic* process, this rememorative construction undoes reification not in its own self as artwork, but, if it is successful, in those who contemplate it. If the artwork conveys in its expression the memory of suffering, if it gazes back at us but does so blindly (as Benjamin once put it), this is because it has itself already imbibed the deathly poison of reification in the process of its construction. Every successful aesthetic construction takes reification into its innermost being not for the sake of its own freedom, but awaits us so that we may look upon its deathly ossification as our own reflection and become free in understanding our own immersion in unfreedom. Every successful artwork is a martyr for freedom.

CARIBBEAN LITERATURE and art transform the reificatory logic of the society from which they arise. They construct aesthetic objects from scraps and leftovers, stolen from the master's house, to improvise historical awareness and self-understanding in the blind gaze these objects cast back upon humans. The neologisms, fortresses, paintings, and sculptures of the Caribbean offer representations of subjectivity that describe not the triumph of a transcendent subject but its unfree determination, its thorough preconstruction by society. Caribbean art retains the category of the subject, but in order to pass through it and to confront the observer's identity with the artwork's opaque inscrutability. A Haitian *bòkò* (expert in the supernatural), named St. Jean, made one such construction, called a *wanga*.

41 Introduction

Designed to bring good luck to the American anthropologist for whom it was made, a Barbancourt rum bottle is filled with sediment, perfume, and shavings from a human skull recovered from the graveyard next to the bòkò's house. Inside the bottle, three pins are held in place by the force of the magnets stacked around its neck, each there to hold things in place

Figure 2. Haitian *wanga*. (Courtesy Elizabeth McAlister and Fowler Museum of Art)

through visible and invisible forces. Three strips of cloth, once the colors of the Haitian flag and each linked to Vodou gods or Lwa such as Ogun and Bawon Samdi, hide the bottle's contents. Open scissors symbolize the four limbs of the human body, menacingly guarding the bottle's contents. String is wrapped tightly around the bottle, containing the forces St. Jean placed within it. Finally, four mirrors around its circumference gaze back powerfully, yet blindly (McAlister).

St. Jean's *wanga,* while manifestly a product of aesthetic construction, refuses in its inscrutability to be reduced to the outcome of a teleological human project. Instead, its undecidable objective status (at once an object of human labor that nonetheless transcends the mere sum of its elements) materializes the contradictions of Caribbean experience distilled in Edouard Glissant's competing notions of "relation" and "opacity." Glissant's notion of "relation" expresses the differentiated totality in which objects such as St. Jean's *wanga* take their place, becoming comprehensible, the *"tout-monde,"* where objects develop their determination in relation one to another. "The universe, . . . multiple and extended to every element of the Real and all the countrysides that constitute the One" (*IP* 51). Glissant's repeated defense of the right of the colonized to their "opacity," however, simultaneously places a limit on relation in order to prevent the relapse of this infinite process of differentiation into an absolute Hegelian identity of subject and object within an idealist totality of spirit.[60]

In this sense, the contradiction between "opacity" and "relation" and, indeed, St. Jean's *wanga* itself, confront one of the fundamental philosophical problems of postcolonial theory: the epistemological status or "knowability" of the Other. Glissant's theoretical contradiction between the interrelated totality of the world and those zones of opacity that refuse reduction to that totality reworks a conflict that received its archetypal form in the dispute between Kant and Hegel. Kant, it will be recalled, placed a block on the pretensions of human reason to encompass the absolute, a block he termed the "thing-in-itself." In so doing, he theorized one of the principal dimensions of Enlightenment thought: the systematic refusal to ponder the essence of things-in-themselves that Voltaire and D'Alembert adapted from Newton's scientific methodology (Cassirer 84–85).

Kant differentiated between objects, the constructions of human reason achieved through the synthetic application of the logical categories to the intuitions received from sensuous experience, and the unknowable "things-in-themselves," devoid of all determination, since the mind is unable to "reach beyond the boundaries of the objects of experience [i.e., the realm of appearance]" (*Critique of Pure Reason* 361). The effect of this block was to erect a novel dualism in place of the Cartesian separation of subject and object Kant's system overcomes. The Kantian subject is on the one hand the autonomous creator of its "empirically real" world,[61] synthesizing objects via the productive imagination following the laws of synthetic a priori judgments, expanding its scientific mastery of the world subject to the laws of causality. At the same time, Kant absolutizes the world of unknown things, pushing it beyond the realm of human experience. The effect of this radical separation is that every advance in human understanding of the world of experience remains in a sense false, the knowledge of mere appearances, while knowledge of the true world-in-itself is banned for human cognition.

Hegel's dialectical logic refuses this absolute Kantian limitation of experience, arguing that spirit can come to encompass the totality of being. Though Hegel's rejection of the Kantian thing-in-itself operates through a blatant misreading of Kant,[62] Hegel's hypostatization of the noumenal as a thing "devoid of all determination" nevertheless points to the inherent fragility of Kant's attempt to limit the thing-in-itself to a negative constraint on reason: any conceivable attempt to think such a boundary is nonetheless a positive act of representation.[63] Hegel's critique of the noumenal, however, itself ends in a new blockage of reason caught in a logical contradiction: on the one hand, the noumenal must exist because, Hegel has argued, any posited, differentiated entity exists only through its negation of its other (so that like salt, which exists only as the "negation" of pepper, the world of absolute reason is conceivable only in its opposition to another (noumenal) realm it does not encompass).[64] On the other hand, the noumenal as a realm beyond representation cannot exist, because even to state that it *is* not, that it *is* only a limit, is always already to posit it as a representation, as a determined entity.

Yet to accept this contradiction as itself the final word on the existence of things unreduceable to our reason would be to absolutize the validity of the law of noncontradiction. To accept that reason can invalidate the existence of things-in-themselves because their existence and nonexistence are equally impossible to conceive is to presuppose the validity of the absolute idealism that critical thought sets out to investigate; that is to say, to presuppose that the world of things obeys the same laws of noncontradiction as logic. Instead, the persistence of this contradiction underscores the critical thrust of Glissant's reworking of this two-hundred-year-old dispute in his development of the concepts of "relation" and "opacity."[65] For opacity, the irreducibility of otherness to the identity Glissant terms "l'Un" provides the critical passage beyond the circularity of the Hegelian dialectic. Hegel's dialectic, to the extent that it strove critically to *construct* universals from an immersion in the experience of determinate objects—rather than the hypostatized imposition of prefabricated absolutes that it became in his later teaching—remains compelling beyond the allergies and anxieties of influence of French poststructuralist criticism. Hegel's early thought in particular refuses the complacency and conservatism of the abstract and undetermined, and of the reification of the world into the rigid, absolutely separate entities of the understanding *(Verstand)*; Hegelian critique undertakes the dissolution of that reification into the historical movement of dialectical negation.

The fundamental difficulty with Hegel's thought is rather its systematization of circularity; in both the Kantian realm of experience and its transformation in Hegel's dialectic, the objective world that the mind produces is tautological. That is to say, if the mind understands the world to be the result of its own acts of objectification, then it really knows and produces only further determinations of itself. While Hegel mythologized this tautology as the actual instantiation of subject-object unity in the Absolute Spirit, the Kantian noumenal, like Glissant's opacity, critically refuses to transcend the persistent separation of thought and world via a retreat to the realm of spirit. Glissantian opacity, as a barrier and limit to an all-encompassing reason, implies that the reified world of productive human subjects, in which the objects we produce and claim to understand confront us as alien entities, is historical, not an absolute. The more knowledge expands to construct the world in its image, the more alienated it grows amid this world of products. As such, Glissant refuses to absolutize either relation or opacity; instead, the relation of relation and opacity is dialectical: "Identity for the colonized is at first an 'opposed to,' that is to say a principle of limitation. The true work of decolonization will be to pass beyond this limit" *(PR* 29).

Glissant's critical investigation of Antillean culture shows the historical dynamics of slavery and (neo-)colonialism to lead to both reification and alienation; the conflict between relation and opacity inherent in his work reproduces at the level of concepts the contradictions of French neocolonial culture. Glissant's poetics of relation thus undertakes the impossible task of describing the nonidentical object that refuses relation, an object whose construction has not yet reduced it to the identity logic of the commodity. This poetic description cannot be a transparent communication of data between identical, abstract subjects but is rather the attempt to carry an indescribable and fragile difference within a language that constantly threatens to reduce that difference to the universality of language itself: "What is necessary . . . is in fact not a language of communication (abstract, disincarnated, 'universal' in the manner we're familiar with) but on the contrary the possibility of a communication . . . between mutually independent opacities, differences, languages" (*IP* 50). If the expanding logical functionalism of human productivity inevitably furthers the alienating reification of the world, then only the quasi-logic of aesthetic constructionism—embodied in objects such as the statues, sculptures, and architecture of artists like St. Jean or Médard Aribot—can hope to peer over the wall reason has constructed around itself and describe what it has seen without regressing into irrationalism (on Médard, see Price 110).

The actual existence of opacity as a given of human experience is not an ontological absolute but an effect of the increasing commodification of that experience. The subject cannot overcome this opacity by dissolving regressively into undifferentiated unity with society or nature; instead, subjective experience must be transformed by maximizing the process of differentiation—the knowledge of the other and the self as determinate specificities—to arrive at a situation in which individuals exist in their difference in a state free of domination; that is to say, as true individuals (*PR* 23). "For the individual, this simple obligation: to open and to ravish the body of knowledges" (*IP* 51). The aesthetic constructionism Glissant calls the poetics of relation is thus an effort to reach this autonomy of objects by passing through subjective experience, maximizing its determinations in a poetic quasi-logic rather than eliminating subjectivity in deference to an engulfing scientific positivism.

CARIBBEAN LITERATURE and art as a whole demonstrate that this autonomy of the object is extensive not only in space but in time as well. Their immediacy is in fact itself thoroughly mediated, reconstructed from found historical materials ranging from Baudelaire, Rimbaud, Leautréamont, and the Haitian vodou pantheon in the poetry and theater of Césaire to the bones, empty bottles, and scraps of cloth found in Haitian garbage heaps and cemeteries. In an unfree world of violence and exploitation, themselves objects of exploitation in the global flow of so-called "naïve" art and "postcolonial literature," these works strive to sustain the otherness of the past in their recourse to objectification. The construction of a complex individual experience of interdependency is the overarching project of Antillean literature. Antillean literature is less than a solution but perhaps something more than a mere reaction formation to the block society has placed on the institution of noncoercive, universal interrelation. The process of representation, writing often opaque and difficult literature and poetry, foregrounds its guilt and uselessness (as the mere aesthetic image of reconciliation amid unfreedom and dependency) and yet it nonetheless points beyond its guilt, silently, by image and example, to freedom.[66]

The history of modern Antillean literature is in many respects an attempt to articulate the interaction between the objectivity of historical fact and the fleeting experience of colonized subjects, registering the turmoil and affirming the resistance of the subject in the face of ongoing colonization and globalization. The imaginative creations of Aimé Césaire, Maryse Condé, Daniel Maximin, Edouard Glissant, Edwidge Danticat, as well as a series of other novels including Vincent Placoly's *Frères volcans*, Patrick Chamoiseau's *Texaco*, Raphaël Confiant's *L'archet du colonel*, and Tony Delsham's *Négropolitains et euro-blacks*, each engage a complex interrogation of the Antillean past.[67] History here serves as the material, the concrete difference and nonidentity, that shatters the veneer of the neocolonial world.

While an attention to the materiality and documentary status of historical fact allows these works to articulate an immanent, situated truth content, their lyrical creativity reinvests historical events with the productive force of subjective memory. Their exploration of history, memory, and freedom recognizes and underscores the impossibility of subjective freedom amid material conditions of exploitation, dependency, and violence. The alienation their aesthetic construction attacks is not indebted to a universal essence (Frenchness, Humanity, or Negritude) but instead confronts the violent alienation of human potentiality, the loss of possibility of lives cut off before their time. Their work confronts the colonial and postcolonial violence that Jean-Godefroy Bidima calls the "obturation of the possible" (173).

Their work articulates an ethical imperative to care for the living of the past, present, and future.[68] While their critique of alienation shows that already we who are supposedly alive do not yet truly live, that we are walking dead colonized by a global consumer society, for us there is still hope we will awake. A pressing ethical imperative arises as well, however, from the claims of those who lived and died without realizing their promise. To recognize and begin to work through those claims, to carry and transmit something of those past lives forward not as lifeless history but as living memory, the deathly still of language must struggle to become both testimony to the past and the poetic semblance of the lives lost to the march of history.

These texts underscore the antinomical status of Antillean existence itself: insofar as this subjective experience is always-already constituted by the objective social forces determining its dependency, it can never attain its own ideal of freedom perpetuated as a negative image in the memory of slavery. And yet, the critique these authors elaborate uses the semblance of rationality that is aesthetic construction to pursue such a freedom as an interminable project. In pointing to an actual absence of Liberty, Equality, and Community, French Antillean literature calls for a transformation of the subjective and objective dependency it portrays. In a disenchanted, reified world, Antillean literature articulates the need for an expanded concept of human reason, one both critical yet able to describe and carry the fragile experience of individuals caught up in anonymous processes that transcend them. These texts mobilize a vast range of materials to construct a self-conscious individual, a subject whose awareness in turn necessarily passes through this individualism to pursue and construct a noncoercive, global dependency and relationship. Antillean literature addresses a global community of readers in order to cultivate critical insight and self-understanding. As such, French Caribbean literature steadfastly posits a freedom of noncoercive relations as a regulatory ideal, its critical poetics sustaining a transformative dynamic of enlightenment.

1   The Vicissitudes of Memory
Representations of Louis Delgrès

> Au bout du petit matin ces pays sans stèle, ces chemins sans mémoire, ces vents sans tablette
>
> —Aimé Césaire

ON MAY 5, 1802, a fleet of ships under the command of Napoleon's commissary General Richepance arrived in Guadeloupe. They, like the troops of General Leclerc who at the same moment were engaged in an unsuccessful struggle to retain the island of Haiti for France, sought to reaffirm the colonial power of an increasingly reactionary Napoleonic France. In the eyes of many in this period, French dominance had been weakened and dispersed during the Revolutionary period. Following the abolition of slavery in 1793, a large number of black as well as *mulâtre* (mixed race) troops had been incorporated into the French army in Guadeloupe. The revolt of May 1802 was precipitated when one of the highest-ranking of those *mulâtre* officers was denied promotion by General Lacrosse. Though he had been a much-liked commissioner in Guadeloupe under the Convention in 1793, when Lacrosse returned to power in 1801, a rapid series of events signaled the return of the old order and turned public opinion against him: arrests, unpopular taxes and graft, the return of exiles whose lands had been confiscated, and, perhaps most important, a return of forced labor and accompanying brutality that foreshadowed the reimposition of slavery.[1] When he denied promotion to Colonel Pélage on account of race—and instead took the promotion for himself—the local troops rose up against him. Lacrosse promptly fled to neighboring St. Lucie to await help from the French authorities. Pélage himself remained faithful to French authority through the entire rebellion. For this, he was subsequently rewarded by Napoleon with the prison cell in France from which he wrote the memoirs he hoped would clear his name for posterity.

The actual revolt itself occurred only after it became clear to the black troops and their mixed-race leaders that Richepance intended to restore to power the now-hated Lacrosse. When Richepance failed to show the signs of respect demanded by protocol to the black troops who welcomed him and when he then proceeded to attempt to disarm them, the leaders of those troops—Colonel Delgrès, a *mulâtre* officer from Martinique, and Ignace, who has been variously described as a black pro-independence revolutionary and a *mulâtre* artisan—fled with as many of their troops as they could gather. A series of battles ensued in which the badly outnumbered Guadeloupean army attempted to stave off defeat and assert their refusal to reenter the bonds of slavery. Delgrès issued a proclamation—though it was written by an aide—defending their cause, attacking Lacrosse, and stating their preference of death to the reimposition of servitude.[2] Finally, Ignace and Delgrès split their troops. The former soon found himself irremediably cornered just outside the capital, Pointe-à-Pitre. There, he and his soldiers met a gruesome end, slaughtered by French troops, their leader's head displayed on a pike as an example to any who might consider similar resistance to French domination.

Delgrès himself escaped along with his troops from the vulnerable Fort-St. Charles into the surrounding foothills of the volcano La Soufrière and the plantation known as Habitation Danglemont. When, on May 28, 1802, it became apparent that no further resistance was possible, Delgrès's troops mined the plantation with explosives and, upon the entry of the French, sent hundreds of soldiers from both sides, as well as women and children, to their death. Their rebellion thus ended, all remaining participants were executed, exiled, or returned to slavery. A brutal repression and period of reaction followed in which it was made illegal even to discuss the events of May 1802, and the island of Guadeloupe returned for the next forty years to pre-Revolutionary social relations, including the immediate reimposition of the ownership of one human by another—though the word "slavery" remained taboo.[3]

Tracing the Event: L'histoire éffacée

An examination of the historiography of these events of May 1802 and the figure of Louis Delgrès can reveal the complex development of historical experience in Guadeloupe since 1802. Instead of attempting to discover what *really* happened in 1802, I will instead ask, "What has the 1802 revolt represented for Guadeloupeans over the last two centuries?" Looked at in this light, a variety of texts, from the well-known *Histoire de la Guadeloupe*, published by August Lacour in 1855, to long-forgotten newspaper articles and the *Etat Civil* registries of 1848, all hold ciphers of a people's memory of this revolt.[4]

51   *The Vicissitudes of Memory*

At the inception of this history lies the silence surrounding Louis Delgrès from his defeat in 1802 until well after the second world war. In *Le discours antillais,* Edouard Glissant states:

> When colonel Delgrès blew himself up with three hundred men on the powder magazine of Fort Matouba in Guadeloupe (1802) . . . , the sound of this explosion did not immediately resound in the consciousness of Martinicans and Guadeloupeans. Delgrès was in fact vanquished a second time by the muffled ruses of the dominant ideology, which managed for a time to disfigure the meaning of his heroic act and to efface it from popular memory. . . . Today, however, we hear the roar of Matouba. To rediscover the moments of its history, the Antilles needed to break through the gangue that the colonial web had woven around their shores. (131)

Similarly, Oruno D. Lara describes how "a complex machinery was put into place by 1848 to guarantee a production of forgetfulness" (151). Such statements categorically assert the near-total repression of discourse and awareness of Delgrès's revolt since 1802. Their pronouncements are a spur to the investigation that follows: to what extent did this repression actually occur? This chapter draws the contours of the representational field that has arisen around the events of May 28, 1802. Newspapers, novels, political tracts, typed essays deposited at the archives, history books, and the registry of newly freed slaves in 1848 constitute the various objects strewn about this discursive field. Was the suppression of which Glissant spoke total, or were there in fact traces of the explosion on Matouba that remained in the Guadeloupean vernacular culture after 1802?

Mnemonic Resistance in Guadeloupe: 1802–1848

The first problem confronting the reconstruction of the general knowledge of Delgrès in the nineteenth century is the fact that after Matouba and Ignace's defeat at Baimbridge and until the abolition of slavery in 1848, a near-total silence in the archives envelops Delgrès and his companions. As violent as the repression of the years following 1802 had been, it seems highly improbable that the people of Guadeloupe would have suddenly stopped discussing this momentous confrontation. Delgrès and his followers had the entire island in a state of war and in open rebellion against France for nearly a year; and many of the surviving soldiers, in large part former slaves from all corners of the island, returned to their families and friends following their violent defeat and the barbarous reimposition of slavery. Both the violence of these events and Delgrès's striking sacrifice at Matouba make it likely that the survivors continued to discuss the revolt covertly. The triumph of the French colonialist regime, however, and the repression that it installed after 1803 forced all discourse on these events to go underground.

This centralized repression failed to eliminate the resistance of Guadeloupean slaves to the colonial land-owning powers, as Josette Fallope has convincingly shown in her documentation of the life of Guadeloupean slaves during the nineteenth century. Beyond the multiple acts of open resistance that Fallope describes in the period leading up to Abolition (revolts, poisonings, fires), there occurred an immense variety of infinitesimal daily acts of resistance. Such acts were hidden from the dominating gaze of the slave-owner, each of them designed to enlarge the psychological or material perception of freedom that the slave defended in the daily fight for a more human existence. It is in this atmosphere of repression, Fallope maintains, where "the truth cost the slave dearly, and [where] he had learned by experience that it was necessary to lie to protect oneself, . . . [that] simulation [became] a necessity in a community dominated by oppression and a reality in day-to-day resistance" (192).

There were, however, other forms of resistance at the level of daily existence that were less striking than poisonings and arson but that nonetheless played a fundamental role in the slave's psychological survival. At the level of symbolic production the slave maintained a margin of action that material existence often denied him or her. Dance, the African-derived music of the *gwo-ka,* songs, and perhaps most obviously the *conte antillais* have all transmitted to posterity traces of this daily micro-resistance arising from within a largely oral culture. At the level of symbolic creation, certain traces of Delgrès's revolt may have persisted, to preserve an event that "represents in the collective memory of Guadeloupean slaves in the Nineteenth century, the nostalgic image of a lost freedom whose restoration is keenly desired" (201).

There remains at least one source of documentation that has transmitted testimony to us from the slaves of the period: at the moment of Abolition (1848), all slaves were required to have their name, age, and place of birth inscribed upon the lists of the authorities' *Etat Civil* to ensure their recognition as voting citizens of the Republic.[5] Much has been written on the importance of names in West-African societies,[6] and the evidence from the various slave-holding societies of the Americas indicates that the slave's autonomous attribution of names remained fundamental in the face of impositions on the part of the master into daily life. From the pleasure taken in devising names in the various black American cultures (Brazil, Antilles, USA, etc.) to the existential affirmation of Malcolm X's auto-baptism, the attribution of a proper name is a fundamental gesture across the black Atlantic world.

Were there, then, slaves who chose to inscribe the memory they carried within them of their revolution and of their refusal to submit to slavery upon a highly reliable medium—that is, in the name that a human carries from birth and is transmitted to his or her descendants? Among those born in the years following Delgrès's revolt, did slaves, for whom all other means of commemorating this event were strictly forbidden, choose to give their children names made famous in the days of May 1802? Among the five thousand names appearing in the lists of newly freed slaves in Guadeloupe (Capesterre and Petit-Bourg) in 1848, not a single Delgrès is to be found. This is hardly surprising, for two reasons. First, quite simply, the ascribing of a family name was normally not left up to the free choice of the slave; and even though from time to time that did occur, in the climate of repression and violence of the period, the name Delgrès would have attracted the master's violence toward a child and his parents.[7]

This atmosphere required a different strategy on the part of the slave. Henry Louis Gates Jr.'s theory of "signifyin'" suggests another possibility. In the context of the plantation, where rare moments of open contestation are rapidly and violently suppressed, hidden revolt becomes the daily medium of resistance, and often this takes the form of a play of ambiguity in which a subaltern person hides his or her revolt behind a split signifier. In this manner, through parody and irony, the slave appropriates a signifier that has been imposed through the master's discourse, colonizing it and evacuating it of its traditional meaning, then reinvesting it with a new, contestatory sense. The interest and indeed pleasure of this technique lies in the creation of a margin of ambiguity more or less unreadable by the master, one that nonetheless remains entirely evident to the slave, who, through this ambiguity, avoids the reprisals of the master while satisfying his or her own existential needs. This practice occurs in certain *contes antillais* and in various contemporary African American practices, including jazz, rap, and the "dozens" (Gates 1988).

In the situation in question here, beyond a certain number named "Solitude" and "Ignace," a name—one that normally would pass unnoticed —frequently recurs. This was Delgrès's common first name, "Louis," a name that might well have hidden, in its very banality, the consecration of a historic event that disappeared before the master's gaze at the same moment as it mocked him. What more ambiguous signifier, in fact, than "Louis," hiding behind so many representatives of French royalty traces of an overt revolt against that same tradition. In fact, the first name "Louis" achieved a sudden popularity among slaves born in the years following 1802. In the communes of Capesterre and Petit-Bourg, there occurred double the proportion of slaves named "Louis" born in the period 1803–4, and a dramatic septupling, on average, in the years 1805 to 1809, relative to the years 1801–2. In later years and until 1848, the number of slaves named "Louis" varied one and one-half to six times compared with the number recorded in 1801–2.[8] Though not a complete survey of records of the period, these figures imply a substantial rise in the popularity of the name "Louis" in the years following 1802, qualifying Glissant's assertion of a total erasure of historical memory in Guadeloupe.

Nineteenth- and Early-Twentieth-Century Historians of Delgrès

The only other testimony surviving from before 1848 are the memoirs of a number of French officers concerned more or less directly with these events, including those of General Richepance, the head of the French force; Lacrosse, the despised local officer; and the Guadeloupean Pélage, all of whom were writing for a French reading public unquestioning of the justice of Napoleon's decision. These officers saw in the actions of Delgrès and his followers only a revolt against the lawful rule of French colonial power. The first text that addresses, at least in part, a Guadeloupean reading public is also a product of this same colonio-centrist viewpoint. This is the history of Guadeloupe written by Colonel Boyer-Peyreleau in 1825, a book that also happens to be the first history of the island written since the seventeenth century. This text is important, although it considers Guadeloupe only as an object of military-colonial knowledge, because its narrative inaugurates a series of discursive processes regarding Delgrès and the 1802 revolt that will be reproduced by numerous commentators in the ensuing century.

From the opening of his preface, the author makes clear the ideological choices that have structured his historical narrative. He assures us that, as a good historian, his text has been written with total objectivity and that "men and events are treated therein dispassionately; all matters touched upon are based upon authentic documents" (Boyer-Peyreleau v.) Despite the author's claims to objectivity, many contemporary readers would be immediately struck by how deeply Boyer-Peyreleau's narrative is marked by the essentialist racial discourse of the time, a discourse that surrounded the entire colonialist project in the nineteenth century.[9] Although Boyer-Peyreleau never enters into the subtle considerations of racial typology or of the roles of physiology and culture in the formation of races typical of

Gobineau, he shares his conclusions on the innate inferiority of blacks. These prejudices insinuate themselves into the structure of his narrative, and from there, they are reproduced in the analyses of those authors who build upon his work into the twentieth century.

The most distinctive characteristic of Boyer-Peyreleau's discourse is the author's uniform incapacity to imagine the events in question from the point of view of the Guadeloupean; instead, he adopts what I would call a "colonialist focalization." Each battle, each military strategy is considered only in relation to its utility relative to the eventual triumph of the French army. For the author, Guadeloupe is an object whose future must be decided by France without consulting those who will be most affected by these decisions, the island's blacks who will ultimately be returned to slavery for two generations. "On every side people [*on*: the French? Guadeloupeans?] demanded the reestablishment of the former code, which had for so long made its possessions proper, as being the only legislation that might suppress the spirit of revolt and restore calm" (70).

The Guadeloupeans are implicated by the author in a narrative structure where the attribution of pronouns freezes them in an objectifying, manichean structure, oscillating between the "nous" of the French soldiers and greater French political and economic interests and the Other always represented in the third person: "As long as *they* had in *their* possession Fort St. Charles, which looks over the city, *we* [*on*] could take little account of the advantages *we* had recently won. It was thus necessary to resolve ourselves [*se résoudre*] to lay siege to the fort following normal practices" (130–31, emphasis added). This strategy of focalization robs the reader not only of any knowledge of the military strategies of both sides, but also—and more important—it informs the author's basic interpretation and explanation of these events. For Boyer-Peyreleau and for all those since who judge the events of 1802 from the viewpoint of the necessary, teleological triumph of French colonialism, Delgrès and his companions are seen as rebels who revolted against an administration thoroughly justified in its violent actions.

The author attributes this rebellion, moreover, not to a refusal to submit to a reimposition of slavery and its emissary Lacrosse—which the text of Delgrès's proclamation makes clear that it was—but rather to the fear that Delgrès was supposed to have had of Lacrosse. Boyer-Peyreleau tells us that "this fear led him to raise the flag of rebellion" (127). The "rebels" themselves are described as cowards [*fuyards*] (136). Later, they are described as a band of "nègres" (142), but never is it admitted that they might be "soldiers," humans in search of freedom, nor, to risk a historical anachronism, "Guadeloupeans" possessed of a nationalistic impulse. Although he attributes a certain blind nobility to Delgrès's final gesture, Boyer-Peyreleau vilifies his companion Ignace, whom he describes as "the ferocious Ignace, who burned and massacred all he encountered" (136). This distinction will be reproduced well into this century, between the "black" Ignace, incapable of rational reflection, who kills and massacres in an orgy of violence, and the "noble" mulatto Delgrès.

At the end of his history of Guadeloupe, in a narrative profoundly implicated in a Francocentric interpretation of these events, Boyer-Peyreleau gives an interesting clue to the possible awareness Guadeloupeans of the period preceding abolition had regarding the events of the 1802 revolt. Concerning the freeing of French prisoners held at Matouba just before the explosion, Boyer-Peyreleau, writing in 1825, tells us that "various rumors have circulated regarding a spirit of generosity out of character for the spirit of destruction that animated these rebels; it is said that before blowing themselves up they sent back eighty white soldiers whom they had taken prisoner" (143). For all its racial prejudice, Boyer-Peyreleau's comment offers us a precious clue: his remark clearly indicates that, despite the government's interdiction, an oral discourse regarding the 1802 rebellion had indeed continued to circulate among the Guadeloupean population.

Guadeloupean Historiography: Auguste Lacour

After Boyer-Peyreleau's text, it is not until the publication in 1855 of Auguste Lacour's *Histoire de la Guadeloupe* that we find another reference to Delgrès in the archives. The newspapers of the period involved in the fight for the abolition of slavery never mention Delgrès's name as a precursor to their struggle; one of the only references to the events of 1802 from the period doesn't mention the participants.[10] It is the testimony of a metropolitan senator, M. de Castellane, who, during a debate on abolition, refers to Napoleon and to "St. Domingue" (Haiti), mentioning that "you well know, it was necessary to shed rivers of blood for the reestablishment of slavery in Guadeloupe."[11] The incongruity between Boyer-Peyreleau's fairly extensive commentary and the near total silence in contemporary metropolitan and colonial newspapers, even in contexts in which such a reference seems logical, appears to indicate that, despite a lively interest on the part of Guadeloupeans in this subject, Delgrès's name was not a part of either official or counter-discourse of the period, and that, while his memory had perhaps maintained a continuous presence in certain social classes (among slaves and the historically minded bourgeoisie), it would take a century for his name to replace that of Victor Schoelcher in the discourse of the Guadeloupean Left.

Delgrès's name reappears in 1855, however, in Lacour's monumental text. This historian's work, the most significant history of the island written until the twentieth century, has been criticized for taking sides with the elite white bourgeoisie in its analysis of events. Although this influential magistrate unavoidably reproduced many of the prejudices of his class (as, for example, when he defends slavery, or, more subtly, when he defends Delgrès for his romantic greatness of soul and generosity in a manner not far removed from that of Boyer-Peyreleau), his study reveals a level of research and firsthand knowledge of the object of his investigation that goes far beyond those of many who have written on Guadeloupe before or since.[12] As a native Guadeloupean, Lacour is divided between a double allegiance: he is at once a representative of colonial power (as judge) and a distinguished member of the bourgeoisie and participant in the island's power relations; the result is a conflicted, quasi-nationalist desire to commemorate his island's history.

This double optic leads Lacour to become the first historian to speak positively of Delgrès's actions. For Lacour, the Martinican is the only participant on either side to have judged the situation with clarity. He tells us that "Delgrès alone appears to have appreciated these events in their full measure. Emotion never blinded him. He sustained no illusion as to the consequences of [his] audacious enterprise" (250). With Lacour, one perceives for the first time the events from the Guadeloupean point of view, and he goes so far as to analyze the complex series of mental judgments that led to Delgrès's decision to rebel against Richepance. Lacour is the first to explain this decision as the blacks' refusal to reenter slavery. The limits of his sympathy for the revolutionaries are nonetheless evident in Lacour's description of Ignace. He condemns what he calls Ignace's "insane undertaking" (317). According to Lacour, Ignace was fighting for the island's independence, and he further blames him for the bloody reprisals that followed his defeat at Baimbridge. In the end, this representative of the established social order refuses to give his accord as Guadeloupean historian to the overthrowing of the world he defended each day as judge.

Lacour left more than secondary accounts of Delgrès based upon testimony from historical witnesses to the period. A brief comment regarding his historiographic method gives us another indication of the continuing presence of Delgrès in the minds and discourse of Guadeloupeans in the mid-nineteenth century. Lacour spent decades in search of every documentary source regarding his subject. Beyond the various archival sources he exploited with rare tenacity, Lacour also sounded the oral memory of the island's population. He conducted many interviews with those still alive who had lived through the Revolutionary period, and in one of the rare descriptions he gives of his technique, he tells us, "I wished to obtain a few details regarding the life and psychological habits of Delgrès. In Basse-Terre there was a man who *supposedly [qui passait]* had been present with this rebel leader till his final moments. This man had a mutilated hand and *everyone was convinced* that this was the result of a wound received in the battles against Richepance's soldiers. . . . Well! I questioned him in every manner conceivable: he assured me that he had no knowledge of the facts I brought to his attention" (tome 1: 3, emphasis added.) For all its inconclusiveness, Lacour's commentary reveals indirectly that there were still ongoing discussions that continued to evoke enough general interest, curiosity, or pride that they turned into gossip, rumors, and tales regarding Delgrès. Guadeloupeans' interest in 1802 thus continued to be both lively and generalized throughout the first half of the last century, despite its total absence in the documentation of the epoch. Though we can no longer obtain direct proof of it, it seems reasonable to assume that memory of this rebellion survived much as Richard Price found memories of the 1925 massacre in Diamant surviving into the 1970s in Martinique. His encounters with local inhabitants led Price to conclude that "Martiniquan peasants and fishermen did preserve a heroic, anticolonial vision of the past and that collective amnesia was more an invention of bourgeois intellectuals than a rural reality" (171). Although the archive's silence makes us believe that Delgrès's exploits were buried beneath a mantle of forgetfulness for over a century, Lacour's comments indicate that their memory likewise continued to exist within an oral culture that left almost no traces of its convoluted path.

The Colonizer's Gaze: Pardon and Gustave Aimard

Toward the end of the nineteenth century, two works appear that are interesting for their heterogeneous discursive strategies as much as for a certain deeper ideological resemblance. These are an 1881 *Histoire de la Guadeloupe* written by Jean-Marie Pardon and a historical novel, *Le chasseur de rats: Le colonel Delgrès,* written in 1876 by Gustave Aimard, a French author of exotic fiction best known for his writings on the American West. Pardon's text seems at first of little interest; he reproduces the racial prejudice of Boyer-Peyreleau along with the same narrative perspective that privileges events as seen by the French. For Pardon as much as Boyer-Peyreleau, all events are perceived from a coloniocentric optic. Furthermore, the events of 1802 appear to so little merit Pardon's interest that he passes rapidly over the entire revolt in the space of eight pages. And yet, an important modulation in historical perception of Delgrès occurs in this text.

In the case of Gustave Aimard, the events of 1802 are described in great detail over the course of an entire novel. Formally, the novel resembles the Hugolian historical novel of the period. It describes in minute historical detail the Revolution of 1802, and, next to the novel's fictional characters, one finds Delgrès, Ignace, Pelage, and other historical persons. The confrontation between Delgrès and Ignace on one side and Pelage and Richepance on the other is reenacted by Aimard, along with a midnight rendezvous in the sordid alleys of the colonial capital and scenes of bravery and romance, all in the by-then-well-worn tradition of Hugo and Eugène Sue.

At first these two books seem quite opposed to one another; one presenting itself as a work of history, preoccupied with a transparent narration of historical facts, the other a novel concerned with the libidinal thrill and verisimilitude of its narrative. Pardon, moreover, is careful to distance himself from novelists like Aimard when he says in his preface: "This is no work of the imagination or fantasy in which creativity *[l'esprit]* plays a greater role than reason: it is simply the narration of the events that occurred in this singular country from its discovery to the current era" (6).

This act of ideological distantiation, however, is undermined at two levels; first, that of enunciation, where each author utilizes what could be called a historicizing discourse that attempts to convince the reader of the objective truth of the facts being recounted. Second, the two authors agree in the utilitarian function they attribute to their work. The differentiation Pardon makes between an objective historical discourse and that of fiction does not resist close examination of these two texts. For all his presumed objectivity, Pardon tells us very little in the eight pages hastily recounting the events of 1802, while Aimard's narrative is filled with details of all sorts regarding the island of Guadeloupe. Not only is there a detailed exposition of the events of the revolution, but there are geographic descriptions of the island, racial typologies of its inhabitants, and even *contes créoles* transcribed directly by the author. In his sheer quantity of largely credible documentary information, Aimard the novelist far surpasses the historian Pardon.

Even from the point of view of historical accuracy, nothing permits one to claim that Pardon's academic discourse renders a more transparent vision of the past than literary historical narratives of the period. Although

Aimard created imaginary dramatizations for his novel, and dialogues and interior monologues for his historical characters, Auguste Lacour had no hesitation in doing the same for those he was studying. The learned familiarity that the nineteenth-century historian had gained with the object of his inquiry justified this imaginative creation in the discursive norms of the period. The creative analysis that both Lacour and Pardon produced is in fact entirely typical of the imaginative method of historiography championed by Augustin Thierry in the 1820s. This historiography was diametrically opposed to the academic historicism typified by Leopold Von Ranke, which one finds in less rigorous form in the work of Boyer-Peyreleau.

This imaginative discourse met the needs of Republican historians of the 1820s who were attempting to save the memory of the Revolutionary period, a memory that the Restoration had tried to overwhelm in both forgetfulness and reactionary legislation. In such a context, the narrative style of Thierry—which applied to the writing of history the technique of the historical novel as developed by Walter Scott—served to revivify a hidden past of which readers were unaware (White 637). In a similar manner, for both Lacour and Aimard, writing somewhat later in the century, the imaginary aspect of their narrative serves to ensure Delgrès against the threat of oblivion that decades of official silence had threatened to impose. That said, it is essential to note that Aimard mixes the process of imaginary creation without distinction with a more scientific spirit of observation based on personal experience and documentary sources. Numerous historians of Delgrès until the end of the 1960s will in fact cite Aimard's necessarily imaginary descriptions of Delgrès's thoughts and moral character without indicating that these observations were taken from a novel.

Both Pardon and Aimard explicitly situate their discourse within the French colonialist project of the late nineteenth century. For Pardon, the Antilles remain badly known by the French, despite their being, as colonies, parts of France. "It is therefore a duty for he who has seen and studied them to make known to the public their history in every detail, so that one may appreciate them in light of the moral and material interests that unite them to the motherland" (5). His text is therefore hardly disinterested; the author recognizes that the success of colonialism depends upon both a certain will to domination on the part of the French that he dresses up as the "moral interests" of the French in Guadeloupe, as well as upon a knowledge of the colony's functioning—"material interests"—that can assure an uninterrupted extraction of profits. Aimard as well wishes to instruct the French regarding life in one of their colonies, in order, he tells the reader, to show by "what fierce struggles [Guadeloupeans] fought for [their rights] . . . in order to remain French" (2).

Each author explicitly ties his project to the knowledge of the Other that is necessary for the functioning of the colonial system. Far from being objective investigators devoid of ideological interests, each is a metropolitan French citizen whose discourse is profoundly implicated in his country's colonial project. This implication is apparent in the multiple structures and mechanisms that led them to focus their research upon a given object (the colony of Guadeloupe) and the related structures that allowed them to complete their research on site, to gain familiarity with previous colonial research, and to present their work to a public of French readers (unlike Lacour's study, for example). Unavoidably, each narrative is formed and determined by these multiple contexts. The exploratory gaze of Aimard, in a libidinal fervor, traverses an island-become-fetishized-object, revealing its flora and fauna while simultaneously scanning the bodies of its inhabitants, submitting them to the fixity of a pseudoscientific racial typology.[13] From our distant perspective, it may seem odd for a convinced colonialist to glorify a man who rebelled against the imposition of that very authority, but for the reader with Republican sympathies in the 1870s, Delgrès's actions would most likely have seemed quite admirable. In Aimard's novel the Martinican colonel is called upon symbolically to play the role of the noble Republican who rebels against the unjust tyranny of a Napoleon.

Pardon as well pursued a colonialist project, his elitist and pitiless discourse working to justify in its every phrase the subjugation of the island by the French in the face of an inferior race. Matouba was for Pardon a dirty trick, an act of "horrible vengeance" (133) on the part of the blacks, for which he regrets only the loss of life of the French. Delgrès's troops are for him mere rebels who do not even merit the name of "men"; they are more like wild animals devoid of reason, which the French were obliged to subjugate. He observes: "It is distressing that so much blind courage was put at the service of such a detestable cause as that of revolt; but it was impossible to do otherwise, the Negroes [les noirs] had entered into such a furious rage that they were utterly unmanageable, they were wild beasts, mortally wounded, who sought to avenge themselves upon their enemy!" (133–34). Pardon's vilification of the revolutionaries, far from the neutral study it purports to be, devolves into an organ of racist, antirevolutionary ideology that serves to further the ends of colonialism at least as much as those of historical knowledge.

Schoelcher and Delgrès in the Guadeloupean Press

In the Guadeloupean newspapers of the turn of the twentieth century, there exist no discernible references to Delgrès. This absence is as eloquent as any positive evidence could be regarding historical memory of Delgrès at the time; in numerous contexts, a reference to Delgrès should logically have occurred and yet does not. At the moment of the centenary of his revolt, for example, neither the papers of the political right such as *L'Indépendant de la Guadeloupe*, which nevertheless did not forget to remind its readers of the centenary of Victor Hugo two months before in March 1902, nor the socialist papers mention this event. One of the latter, *Le Réveil social*, exhorts its readers week after week to revolt against the injustice of capitalism and to "strike with redoubled blows the worm-eaten edifice that will quickly fall beneath the weight of our combined efforts"[14] without ever referring to Guadeloupean history in any form. The primary historical point of reference in the socialist rhetoric of the period, even in Guadeloupe, remains that of the metropolis and 1789.

Le Socialiste, a paper of the period that openly attacked the formerly radical black politician Légitimus and his party,[15] never speaks of Delgrès but rather evokes with incessant regularity and overwrought rhetoric Victor Schoelcher, liberator of the black slaves. "Who is the descendant of slaves," one commentator asks us, "who in his moments of reflection does not think of the venerable Schoelcher?"[16] This focalization upon Schoelcher rather than the subjects of Guadeloupean history is typical of the period and will remain so until the 1950s, when Delgrès's name will replace that of Schoelcher in the official public discourse of the Guadeloupean Left.

Even in Légitimus's paper *Le Peuple*, Delgrès seems totally forgotten, and Schoelcher remains the obligatory reference. In an article on "Le Socialisme aux Antilles," the only name that is mentioned regarding the events of 1802 is that of Napoleon. "Five years after the abolition of slavery in the Metropolis, abolition of slavery in the Antilles. The Napoleonic reaction confiscates public liberties in France, and reinstates slavery in the colonies."[17] In a ritual in which the name of Delgrès will later replace that of the liberator of 1848, *Le Peuple* signals to its readers on July 4, 1900, not the anniversary of Matouba but rather that "in the evening of June 20, a fraternal banquet brought together at the office of the Central Committee a certain number of members of the French Workers' Party, come to celebrate the memory of the illustrious philanthropist Victor Schoelcher, liberator of the black race."[18]

This situation continues in a similar manner in the left-wing Guadeloupean press through the second world war. In 1926, the workers' paper *Le Cri du peuple* piously commemorates the memory of Schoelcher in an article entitled "Modern slaves": "Schoelcher, the great Schoelcher, to whom all politicians hearken back, found [slavery] to be bad and inhuman. He struggled to bring it to an end and succeeded. It was beautiful. It was sublime, everyone exulted joyously. Alas! Today, the word boss has replaced that of master."[19]

WHEN THE same paper announces on July 21, 1926, that M. Hanna-Charley will deliver "a speech in memory of Schoelcher before the bust of the great philanthropist," the author (ironically) underlines the moral good that this gesture will perform for "a collectivity ignorant of its own history." A series of articles from the month of August 1926 inform readers of a debate between two leading political figures of the period, M. Valentino (who was also director of the *Cri du Peuple*) and M. Boisneuf, with the title, "Did slaves contribute to the abolition of slavery?" Each of the debaters reveals an extremely vague knowledge of the events of 1802 and never identify Delgrès or his companions in relation to the revolt against the reimposition of slavery. Valentino, who is defending the role of the slaves, seems incapable of naming the Guadeloupean resistors, though he is quite familiar with the opposing French forces: "In 1802, Lacrosse and Richepance, in the name of Napoléon, will reestablish slavery, despite a bitter and desperate fight on the part of the former slaves. Many of them will refuse to submit and will become maroons."[20] Without mentioning Delgrès, their debate quickly degenerates to focus on the outrage Valentino is presumed to have caused to the memory of Victor Schoelcher by defending the thesis of the slaves' free will.

During the 1930s and until the end of the war, this scenario hardly changed, even in left-wing papers just before the Vichy government invaded the island. An article on blacks in France in *La voix du peuple de la Guadeloupe: Organe Officiel du Parti de l'Union Socialiste, Républicain, et Schoelcheriste* from March 2, 1940, for example, once again describes the reimposition of slavery by Napoleon without mentioning Delgrès's name.

Intimations of Negritude

The silence in the archives on the subject of Matouba during this period is not total. A lone voice reminds Guadeloupeans of this far-off event. In

1921, Oruno Lara published his *Histoire de la Guadeloupe*. The study's preface is interesting because, well before Leon Damas, Aimé Césaire, and the other participants in the negritude movement, Lara proclaims his pride to be a "writer of the black race" and states that his book forms "the image of the painful and formidable creation of the American continent steeped in African blood and tears" (1).[21] The author wants his book to serve "our advancement"; that is to say, that of the black race, and he continues: "It is truly up to one of us to write our history; and when, born yesterday, we seem to possess neither past nor civil rights, it is up to one of us to edify a more beautiful past, by drawing from the source of our very days a more beautiful human expression, in sacrifice and probity" (1).

Reminiscent of the early work of W. E. B. Dubois, these lines open the interwar discourse on the social advancement of blacks; they predate the Harlem Renaissance as well as negritude. Unfortunately, Lara's text fails to rise to the challenge the author has set for himself. Instead of the historical critique of the island's history the preface leads us to hope for, revisiting and rewriting the work of the often-racist white historians who preceded him, Lara's *History* is a pastiche of citations from his sources, with the author's voice scattered among the quotations. Frequently, one finds three or four paragraphs of citations per page, taken principally from Boyer-Peyreleau, Auguste Lacour, and Gustave Aimard. The author makes no distinction between these, drawing upon them at random, citing Aimard's minute description of Delgrès's office, for example, as if it had originated in documentary sources instead of the imagination of a novelist. When Lara speaks, it is almost never to attack the conclusions of his sources, which constitute the body of his text, but rather to move the reader on to the next stage of his linear narrative before withdrawing behind another citation.

That said, the portion of his book dedicated to Delgrès and Ignace shows a truly innovating spirit. This is especially true in the case of Ignace, for Lara is the first commentator to champion the cause of Delgrès's companion. He speaks of the "noble heart" of this "family man" (148). "Ignace is ours," he goes on to say, "a child of the people, he rose up through his own effort, he is of our soil, he is of our race, he is of our sufferings of yesterday and our hopes for tomorrow. Our grandchildren must know him and love him, in his heroism and his sacrifice!" (149). This defense of Ignace will be echoed in coming decades, when Guadeloupeans informed by the revolutionary spirit of the 1960s will proclaim Ignace the avatar of Guadeloupean independence.

The Rise and Fall of Delgrès: *L'Etincelle*

After the second world war, Delgrès becomes the focus of a veritable explosion of interest, first in newspapers and then, from the 1960s, more and more frequently in history books. Attention to the various transformations in the perception of this event, as registered in archival documents of the period, draws a compelling image of the gradual replacement of a (largely subterranean) lived historical experience with a preponderance of mnemonic image-commodities accompanying Guadeloupe's transformation into a consumer society utterly dependent upon the central French state an ocean away.

In 1948, Guadeloupeans erected a marble plaque in Delgrès's memory near the site of the Habitation Danglemont at Matouba. Suddenly, after over a century of neglect and historical amnesia, this stone monument eternalized Delgrès's instantaneous explosion of the unquestioned homogenous historical continuum of French colonization. The plaque freezes the historical dynamic of a complex, conflicted revolutionary act into a unidimensional, timeless spatial representation, effectively entombing within the realm of natural myth the "memory" of "Delgrès and his companions" and along with it the "spark of hope," to redirect Walter Benjamin's phrase, their act contained.

In a series of remarkable articles from the organ of the Guadeloupean Communist Party, *L'Etincelle* (The spark), we can follow the emergence

Figure 3. Memorial plaque to Louis Delgrès (Nick Nesbitt)

of discourse on Delgrès over a period of twenty-five years as the paper makes itself into the defender of this now-celebrated hero of Guadeloupe's past. During this time, this discourse makes its timid beginnings after the war, then gradually achieves a certain sacralization—verging on banalization—of its theme by the 1970s. In the edition of *L'Etincelle* from July 15, 1950, there appears the first evocation of Delgrès in the archives in decades. The article in question is entitled, "The Battle of Delgrès, Ignace, and Their Companions for Liberty, against Slavery." The article is unsigned, but already since early 1950, the paper had been receiving dispatches from the Quartier Latin from a certain "young compatriot Henri Bangou" (for the last thirty years the Communist mayor of Pointe-à-Pitre and a respected historian of Guadeloupe) who was perhaps researching his own *Histoire de la Guadeloupe,* soon to appear in installments in the pages of *L'Etincelle.* Whatever the case, this 1950 article describes in detail the events of 1802, events that were little known at this point to Guadeloupean readers, without offering any commentary on their significance.

Two years later, at the moment of the one-hundred-fiftieth anniversary of Matouba, the *Etincelle* of May 17, 1952, reminds "all Guadeloupeans in love with liberty" that May 28 is "a date of historical importance." The paper continues: "An hommage must be rendered unto him. Let us be ready, camarades." This commentary is perhaps the first indication that Delgrès's name is beginning to move beyond the level of a simple event to become reified within the official left-wing discourse of Guadeloupe. In the same edition of the paper, we learn that the politician Rosan Girard had requested the modification of the name of Fort Richepance, where the most important battles of the revolt occurred, to that of Fort Delgrès, a request that would be repeated over the next three decades until it finally was granted in 1989. "The hour has now arrived," the *Etincelle* tells us, "to wash the spit from the face of Louis Delgrès and his companions from so-called historians who present them as rebels against French authority. . . . The honor of elevating Delgrès and his companions to the pantheon of heroes in the fight for freedom from tyranny and slavery falls to today's combatants."[22]

The *Etincelle* thus began in 1952 a veritable revaluation of values in which the Guadeloupean communists attempted to rewrite a history they judged to be unfairly Francocentric and tied to exploitative capitalist interests. In this view, Delgrès, whom they describe as a "martyr," represents the world's exploited masses, a freedom-fighter transcending issues of race and ethnicity. This construction makes of Delgrès a universal symbol in which the uniquely Caribbean aspects of his exploit are minimized. This totalizing ideology of Delgrès is in fact entirely typical of the period. It both reproduces the reigning Cold War master narrative and testifies to the universalist mentality that Aimé Césaire would reject four years later, in 1956, in his celebrated "Letter to Maurice Thorez." There, Césaire resigned from a P.C.F. accused of dissolving the cultural and historical specificity of the Antillean situation within the global communist project.

Two weeks later, in June 1952, Girard, communist deputy and the paper's "political director," invites readers to "commemorate" the memory of Delgrès and his companions by means of a "pious and fervent reflection," expressing his desire that "the streets of our cities bear their names." For Girard, the visible and durable traces of the names of these heroes will serve to save them from forgetfulness, integrating their memory into the daily existence of the city.

In 1956 there appears for the first time an article that cites Delgrès in passing without being consecrated to his rememorization.[23] This allusion to Delgrès during a quite general discussion of legitimate resistance to colonialism indicates that it is from this period that his name begins to replace that of Schoelcher as a point of primary reference in general discourse surrounding the antislavery movement in Guadeloupe in the nineteenth century.

On May 28, 1956, the paper publishes another article summarizing the events of 1802, this time accompanied by the text of Delgrès's proclamation, in order to remind readers of the historical facts of this event. The following year, however, in June 1957, it is no longer a question of reminding readers of historical details that are becoming widely known but rather to discuss the formal construction of this memory and how the revolt is to be commemorated. The Communist Federation, which signs the article, wants to move beyond traditional acts of commemoration fit only to "stir the masses into unbridled enthusiasm," and the authors tie this Guadeloupean event for the first time to the calls for colonial independence that had begun to be heard in the late 1950s: "Time passes, and we find ourselves at a turning point in our evolution. Nearly one hundred fifty years after the tragedy of Matouba, we are becoming foreigners on our own soil, the detritus of colonization."[24]

On May 31, 1958, an article exhorts readers to be "nombreux au Matouba" for the annual ceremony, then offers a new interpretation of 1802: "For the bourgeoisie the enemy is no longer the English . . . but the Negroes of Guadeloupe who must be returned to the irons of slavery. Louis Delgrès, Jean Ignace at the head of the fighters for liberty symbolize this heroic resistance. . . . Brilliant armed struggles on the part of this improvised army, a genius for military prowess, such as Ignace's break-out from Dolé, mark this campaign." This last phrase points to a change in this discursive field: throughout the nineteenth century, it will be recalled, Delgrès was admired for the nobility of his actions, and their idealization as a paragon of "sacrifice" accorded with already anachronistic romantic values of a noble caste. From 1958 onward, however, the celebration of the brilliant military strategist overtakes the idea of Delgrès as a generous, gallant soul who sacrifices his life rather than going back on his word of honor.

IN MARCH 1959, Henri Bangou, who had been publishing in the newspaper extracts from his *Histoire de la Guadeloupe* each week over the past year, reaches the period of 1802 in his discussion. In a comparison between the 1802 revolution and the 1848 abolition, Bangou makes explicit the change already noted over the previous years in the paper, namely that, in Bangou's estimation, Delgrès's actions were more determinant in the island's history than those of Schoelcher insofar as they show a will to self-determination not implied in the undertakings of the "liberator of the slaves."[25] Already, in this same series of articles in 1958, the author had presented a militaristic, phallocratic Delgrès whose memory put to shame the island's current dependency and lack of resolve: "In this period the man of color possessed ten times more political and material power than today. [Guadeloupeans] had no fear of Bonaparte, while today, we do not wager upon our strength, but rather upon our weakness. France muscles us with a C.R.S. uniform attached to a club on the Place de la Victoire [in Pointe-à-Pitre], and America strikes us frozen in terror before the letters that compose this word. Guadeloupe in 1958 is a cadaver beside the living Guadeloupe of 1802. And it is this cadaver that French colonization invites us to admire."[26]

The "Hommage à Delgrès" the paper presents in its issue of June 6, 1959, implies a certain commodification of the Martinican revolutionary; Delgrès has moved beyond the status of a contestatory radical whose actions only a few Communists commemorated each year and has instead become integrated within the Guadeloupean social habitus. The article describes a now annual ritual of the Guadeloupean bourgeoisie:

> Thursday, May 28 at 6 PM, a group composed of the personnel of the Association of the Friends of Delgrès came together before the Monument to the Dead, and its President Dr. Chartrol deposited there a magnificent spray of flowers.... There, before a good-sized audience, the floor was taken in turn in order to retrace the heroic epic of Delgrès and his companions, by the young

Néraulius, our camarade Plumasseau, Jean Antoine, and the good Dr. Chartol. We left one another each with our hearts filled with a bit of local history. . . . An imposing crowd of men and women of every age and political affiliation, come from every corner of the island, renewed the great pilgrimage from the City Hall of Sainte Claude to the crossroads of Liberty at Matouba, on the Danglemont property, where the flame of remembrance was renewed.

The events of 1802 ("a bit of local history") dissolve into the background of the article, and a long list of the Guadeloupean *gauche caviar* of the period who attended the event (including mayors, professors, and the director of the official printing press) takes their place. Still, the article manages to proclaim in closing, as a sort of afterthought: "Workers, you will come next year to draw energy and hope."

By 1963, the paper can presume its recovery of Guadeloupean history to have been successfully accomplished: "They may well have systematically maintained multiple generations of our people in ignorance of the real meaning of the events of May, 1802, the ten-volume Larousse may well never have mentioned the name of Delgrès, Radio Guadeloupe may well refuse fearfully to pronounce the date 28 May; History has all the same been reestablished. Delgrès has passed down to posterity."[27]

The tone of these articles grows more radical throughout the 1960s, adopting an orthodox communist analysis to describe an event whose regional and historical specificity is frequently erased. In its edition of May 30, 1964, while commemorating 1802, the paper tells its readers that "faced with the machinations of a moribund colonialism and its hired valets, the contestatory organizations of Guadeloupe judge that it is not inappropriate to remind the people engaged in the fight for liberation of the memory of its heroes Ignace, Delgrès, and their companions."[28] By now, Ignace's name is appearing before that of Delgrès in the enumeration of the heroes of 1802, reflecting his growing significance for independence-minded commentators.

January 1966 marks the entry of Delgrès into the circuits of capitalist commodification, which had grown increasingly pronounced on the island since the 1946 departmentalization. At this time, the *Etincelle* announces the sale of the book, *L'Epopée Delgrès,* by the historian Germain St. Ruf, at the bookstore *La Renaissance.* The communist paper sings the praises of this historical study: "What a beautiful story M. St. Ruf has to tell us! How we read it easily and with what joy! . . . We cannot recommend highly enough to all democrats the reading of this book . . . which contains, what is more, precious lessons for all Antilleans."[29]

As if to underline this commodification of Delgrès, the same article/advertisement reappears word for word the two following weeks. On March 5, 1966, Delgrès's revolt is reduced to the object of a banal farce, when the paper announces that the police have confiscated a window display carrying the inscription, "Ask for *l'Epopée Delgrès* by G. St. Ruf," despite the protests of the store's employees. We soon learn, however, that the display was returned by the *préfecture,* "who had taken it from afar to be an organ of subversion."

In May 1967, the annual evocation of Delgrès adopts the stilted language and conservative attitude of Soviet bureaucracy: "Today, with progress in the art of guerilla warfare, an infinite number of us would allow themselves to rectify the political strategic errors of the "rebels" of 1802. . . . Today, with progress in revolutionary science, our sacrifice is above all that of patient and extenuating work for the organization of the working class and revolutionary elements, in view of the multiple daily battles against the modern enslavers, to institute a socialist society and to reinforce this society throughout the 1/3 of the globe where it already exists."[30]

From 1968 on the commemoration of Delgrès seems to become, at least for the *Etincelle,* a sort of civic duty to be performed as quickly and painlessly as possible, and whose significance no longer seems as vital as it had appeared twenty years before. An article from May 18, 1968, is perfunctory in the extreme: "Sunday, May 26 . . . Commemorative demonstration before the stele of Delgrès. . . Meeting at 9 AM before the City Hall of St. Claude—March to Matouba—Deposition of sprays—Speeches—All Guadeloupeans are invited to this important demonstration." The following year, the paper lets May 28 go by unnoticed, shirking its now apparently cumbersome duty. Finally, in the issue of May 20, 1972, there is no commemoration of Delgrès's revolt but instead a brief reference to the "great party organized by l'Etincelle. Win a Volkswagen 1200 for two francs." Delgrès himself has been disposed of, replaced by consumable commodities of more recent vintage.

Monumentalism and the Annihilation of Culture

What explains this outburst of interest in Delgrès following the second world war, after a hundred and fifty years of relative silence in the archives? It is remarkable that the reappearance of Delgrès in postwar Guadeloupean society coincides so thoroughly with the "departmentalization" begun in 1946. The incorporation of the French Départements d'Outre Mer (DOM) into West European consumer society occurred in this period, while the metropolis consistently demonstrated its indifference or active hostility to any indigenous initiative that might undermine a quasi-total dependence upon the importation of all categories of goods (foodstuffs, consumer appliances, employment opportunities largely limited to the French bureaucracy, and cultural products).

In fact, renewed interest in Delgrès during this period has often served to assure not the irruption of history into the experience of his descendants but rather the disappearance and erasure of that experience behind monuments and commemorative speeches that merely freeze the experiential core of his gesture. Walter Benjamin described this commodification of memory in the context of European modernity as the encroachment of a homogenized, empty time. In the overarching consumer culture of the DOMs, historical experience is itself quite literally *consumed;* memory becomes mere representation and comes to serve the paradoxical function of reaffirming a static, ahistorical status quo (the neocolonialist consumer order).

The erasure of Guadeloupean collective memory is analogous to that of postwar European Jewish culture, whose liquidation in the Holocaust bears direct implications for Guadeloupe, despite obvious differences in the magnitude of each tragedy.[31] It is only at the moment of the disappearance of a culture (the prewar Yiddish or pre-departmental Guadeloupean plantocracy) that monuments to memory tend to be erected, monuments that testify to a transformed experience of the past. The Delgrès of before and after 1946 are not the same, just as Guadeloupe itself had been transformed. We have seen how Delgrès did not at all cease to exist for Guadeloupeans after 1802, that he continued to be present in people's daily life, that his first name became popular among slaves in the first half of the last century, that he was the subject of stories and gossip—all this despite his absence from official discourse. His memory remained a presence in Guadeloupe, living on in daily life and speech. There still existed at this time a generalized experience of both oral history and the *conte* and thus a lived relation with the past, which has been greatly attenuated—if not, as Maryse Condé has insisted, completely obliterated—by a consumption-based neocolonial *société du spectacle*.[32]

THIS HISTORICAL modification of French Caribbean experience of the past is an African diasporic variant of the changes Walter Benjamin saw at work in Western European subjectivity in the 1930s. Benjamin described the conflict between a living, dialectical interaction with the past he, adopting the Hegelian teminology described in the introduction, called *Erfahrung* [dialectical experience], and the deathlike, abstract objectification of the past that he named *Erlebnis* [immediate, lived experience].[33] Benjamin uses the latter term to indicate the mere reified lived moment in which the modern historical subject first described by Baudelaire loses the capacity to integrate phenomenal events within his or her understanding. Typified by the newspaper, the novel, and academic historiography, these events remain pure information, abstract and distant from the subject as they float, ghostlike, upon the page. Memory itself becomes the mere recollection of facts and dates *[Erinnerung]*, isolated and with no purchase on the present, and this hollow memory keeps at bay the pain of experience *[Erfahrung]*. Benjamin implies—somewhat schematically—that the encroachment of capitalism and, presumably, the reign of commodity fetishism as analyzed by Marx and Lukács, is responsible for this "increasing atrophy of experience."[34]

After the war, Guadeloupean intellectuals experienced a radical transformation of the island as it became ever more integrated with Europe and the structures of global capitalism. As was argued in the introduction, this increasing immersion within globalization worked to alienate Antillean subjects from historical experience as a lived totality. Delgrès was a symbol of the resistance to Guadeloupean assimilation, and the Guadeloupean students in Paris in the 1950s such as Henri Bangou, Jacques Adelaïde-Merlande, and Germain Saint-Ruf were among the first to reclaim the legacy of his revolt. They began to study Delgrès, to celebrate him, to erect plaques and street signs for him, to search through the archives to discover what really happened in 1802, at the very moment he disappeared from Guadeloupean historical experience. And yet, in a Caribbean inflection of Hegel's ruse of reason, the efforts of these postwar intellectuals to recover Delgrès as an object of Antillean consciousness appear ironically as a mere moment in Guadeloupe's further immersion within globalized consumerism via the commodification of symbolic production.

Indeed, one might argue that Delgrès was put to death twice over, first by Napoleonic nationalism and racism and more recently by this commodification of experience. Delgrès, in this view, is one more frozen, cryonized, sterilized, decontextualized victim of the entombment of the past within the world of simulacra described by Jean Baudrillard (1983). The commodification of memory, Baudrillard argues, increasingly degenerates into the pathological drive to conserve, command, and govern the real in the face of its liquidation beneath a totalizing logic of simulation. A "nostalgia for the 'ancestral' way of life," Richard Price has observed, "is omnipresent in 1990s Martinique. Celebration of the *patrimoine* permeates the press, radio, and TV, animated by artists, musicians, dancers, taletellers, writers, theater groups, and cultural associations—with considerable financial support from the state (for example, the Conseil Régional). Commercialized folklore is available at every village fête and large hotel, and it floods the airwaves" (180). Public commemoration of Delgrès today manifests a Guadeloupean variant of this process. As Mireille Rosello has argued, the Martinican rebel serves as a phallocentric historical representation of the Antillean capitulation to a logic of sacrifice and death; Delgrès's exploit has become a highly overdetermined Antillean allegory for the deathly interment of contemporary experience within the mausoleum of the commodity in globalized neocolonial culture.

Figure 4. Delgrès memorial commemoration, 2001

This radically static vision of a Guadeloupe frozen into a world of commodification—like the objectified doudou described in the introduction as the cipher of this commodification—has its counterpoint in the various critical and imaginative responses to Antillean alienation that have appeared in Antillean culture, responses whose richest and most complex and articulate manifestation is perhaps found in the work of Edouard Glissant. Indeed, this logic of commodification—which first arose in the Antilles not with the coming of departmentalization but with that primary commodification that was slavery itself—has been challenged at every step in the region's history. Within the context of plantation society, the tendency to develop alternative modes of historiography arising from the oral traditions maintained in the diaspora was encouraged by force of circumstance. This is for two reasons: in a context where literacy and the techniques of memory developed in the West since Herodotus were often unavailable to slaves, they instead relied on vernacular techniques freely available to them, stretching back to the centuries-old practices of the griots.[35] Thus understood, this vernacular historiography existed alongside European techniques of memory, adopted in varying degrees according to the individual circumstances of biography (access to education), personality (drive to assimilate Western learning), and psychology (identification with the European). At the same time, a second, less circumstantial tendency reinforced this recourse to vernacular techniques of historiography. For history in slave-holding or racially divided society is a depository of power and is thus protected by the custodians of mnemonic capital. The capacity to perceive the world as mutable, to see that present social relationships have no absolute, eternal validity, is an insight that has at times exploded into societies with great power and is thus subject to multiple forms of control. In light of these controls, the historical memory of those who could not afford to forget was forced to take on forms that allowed for the reproduction of memory without incurring the suppression of its material incarnation by the slave-holding elite. Memory thus was forced underground, making up its various disguises from the materials that lay at hand, in this case those of the vernacular (including the *contes,* music, *signifying,* and even the naming of one's children).

In the less overtly repressive context of twentieth-century Antillean existence, the suppression of the memory of revolutionary figures such as Louis Delgrès and Ignace has not disappeared, but rather techniques and strategies have changed. There has been no simple, one-sided "disappearance of a sense of history," as Fredric Jameson has argued of postmodernity in general, but a series of multi-dimensional, often contradictory shifts and mutations in historical consciousness that manifest both consumerist, alienating dimensions alongside the utopian, critical spirit of enlightenment (qtd. in Huyssen 88).[36] Antillean writers have been at the center of these changes, constructing aesthetic, critical representations of these historical transformations. Their "departmentalized" world of increasing dependency required new techniques of critique that might revive suppressed memories of the Caribbean past within a social totality where immediate material interests encouraged either utter historical oblivion or the romanticization of Delgrès's sacrificial logic. Aimé Césaire invented such techniques of a critical historical poetics in his *Cahier d'un retour au pays natal;* the poem's paradoxical destiny was to begin the unraveling of the French colonial world at the very moment its author negotiated the legal assimilation of the Caribbean departments into the French mainland.

2 Antinomies of Double Consciousness in Aimé Césaire's *Cahier d'un retour au pays natal*

> "Ethics" means the negativizing of narcissism within a practice. . . . Given this insight, one cannot ask that "art"—the text—emit a message which would be considered "positive": the univocal enunciation of such a message would itself represent a suppression of the ethical function.
>
> —Julia Kristeva

CRITICAL THOUGHT, awkwardly yet necessarily divorced from practice and in debt to the experience that sustains it, brashly names the objects of its desire because the moment for their realization that would annul that debt may already have vanished. "Freedom," "autonomy," "liberation," these ideals constituted the dream-life of the twentieth century's drive toward decolonization. To affirm such dreams, to commit them to paper, might already be to disincarnate what is left of them in a shell of positivity, to betray their historical reality in a mere linguistic semblance, a lifeless effigy. "The people who struggle, the people who, thanks to their struggle, set forth and know this new reality, advance, freed from colonialism." Withdrawn from praxis into psychological inwardness, critique constructs these ideals as the sublime residue of its own powerlessness, then, transferring the guilt of society onto itself, silently falls into line at the call to arms of the already compromised revolution (*Les damnés de la terre* 186).[1]

And yet we cannot escape a commitment to naming such dreams, for not to do so is to give free rein to repression and to forget that this dream might once have been, and might once again be more than mere hope. If the poets of French decolonization—Aimé Césaire, Léopold Sédar Senghor, Léon Gontran Damas, David Diop, and many others—dared to assert a counterreality to colonialist ideology, they did so in the hope that their words would take on something of the violent charge that animated their existential refusal of the world that had formed them. That they were at all successful, that their poetry did in fact impel concrete historical effects, however, is no excuse for confusing those aesthetic objects with the ideals they name.

Such is the dilemma confronting any interpretation of "committed" literature. For if the latter is at all successful, more than mere ideology, it has found an approach to the insoluble task of being at once historical and literary, both action and reflection. And yet to read the critics of the movement's greatest poet, Aimé Césaire, one might be excused for thinking that his poems had miraculously instantiated the world he dreamed of. In the sixty years since its publication, Aimé Césaire's 1939 poem *Le Cahier d'un retour au pays natal* has come to stand as a fundamental intervention and reference in anti- and postcolonial literature. The poem did in fact serve as a call to arms for a generation of young African intellectuals in the 1960s and became the centerpiece of many pedagogical programs in postcolonial Africa. In the 1994–95 school year, the French government put the *Cahier*, along with Césaire's *Discours sur le colonialisme*, on the reading list for the *terminale* year of studies preceding the *Baccalauréat*, along with Sophocles, Shakespeare, and Montaigne. The poem has been the object of countless articles, and at least a dozen longer studies undertake its explication.

The many readings and interpretations it has sustained over this period have rarely failed to invoke the stunning lyrical force with which the poem both condemns a racist colonial order and effects a revaluation of values in its poetic institution of the subject of negritude. Given the *Cahier*'s preeminent role in the awakening of black diasporic consciousness of this century—a process Césaire famously designated "negritude"—criticism of his immensely rich and complex poem has understandably stressed its affirmative character. The many critical encomiums to Césaire and negritude arose in a specific historical period of African independences and the struggle for civil rights throughout the black Atlantic world, and black intellectuals and revolutionaries seized upon Césaire's compelling vision of freedom for its efficacy within this process. Even close textual readings of the work, for all their attention to detail, have tended to discern in the *Cahier* a unilinear developmental process, a movement from the submission and quasi-enslavement of colonialism to the freedom of the poem's ascending vision in its final lines.

I will argue in what follows for the *Cahier d'un retour au pays natal*'s inherent ambiguity or double character. In this view, the affirmative stance of the *Cahier* is haunted by a specter: that of its historical failure to enact the liberation it describes in a world that will remain unjust after the *Cahier*'s appearance.² This foreboding works its way into the poem's core, persisting through its final transcendent images. Césaire's poem presents the ascendancy of negritude as a complex historical process where the forces of violence and exploitation weigh in against the author's utopian project even in its triumph. It is this elaborate portrayal, in which the diverse resources of Césaire's poetic, philosophical, and anthropological inheritance are masterfully combined and redirected against social injustice, that marks the poem's great accomplishment: Césaire refuses to bypass the contradictions that will complicate negritude's historical instantiation, and instead dramatizes the antinomical character of a freedom postulated amid ongoing social inequity. In this manner, I take Césaire's *Cahier* to be a first, most-imposing working-through of the traumas of slavery and racism in Francophone culture, one that steadfastly refuses to represent existence as the mere teleological unfolding of subjective wish fulfillment.

I will begin by situating Césaire's poetic portrayal of a contradictory French Caribbean historical experience as a development of W. E. B. Dubois's influential notion of "double consciousness." I will then initiate my analysis by means of a passage that seems to me particularly productive in its ambiguity, calling as it does for the poetic subject's "strangulation" at the moment of his seeming liberation. This thematic contradiction is further considered in light of an overall formal movement in the poem: from a complex scoring of a free rhythmic multiplicity during what seems the moment of greatest prostration in the poem's opening sections, Césaire goes on to orchestrate his poetic subject's final ascent to freedom via the pounding regularity and terrifying monorhythmic pulsation of the closing passages. In closing, I underscore the double character of Césaire's lyric construction by confronting the poem with an incontestably aporetic artwork whose strikingly homologous historical situation, thematic and formal procedures, and ethical concerns throw light upon the *Cahier*'s hidden ambiguities.

CÉSAIRE COMPOSED the *Cahier* while a student in Paris from 1931 to 1939. As a brilliant colonial *miraculé* (socially subaltern student able to advance through the French educational system), Césaire pursued his studies amid the historical and intellectual ferment of the period, surrounded by the rise of fascism and the fall of the Popular Front, the rediscovery of Hegel in Kojève's lectures at the Ecole des Hautes Etudes, the debates over surrealism and communism, and the growing condemnation of colonialism evident in journals such as *La Voix des nègres* (1924), *La*

Race nègre (1927), *Le Cri des nègres* (1931), *Légitime défense* (1932), and *L'étudiant noir* (1934), to which Césaire contributed his first published work.³ Though many of these events would register in his discourse only after 1945 when he returned to Paris as a communist deputy in the National Assembly, Césaire devoured the many cultural and aesthetic references he encountered over the years he prepared his *agrégation* in a defiant act of cultural cannibalism that formed his protean intellectual perspective.⁴

If, as I will argue below, an ambiguous doubling that objectifies an unresolved existential duality lies at the heart of the *Cahier*, Césaire was hardly the first to have registered the incursion of an antinomical social existence within the expressive structures of black consciousness itself.⁵ René Ménil, in his contribution to the single issue of *Légitime Défense*, described the profound assimilation of Antillean subjects within French culture as an "objective, unconscious hypocrisy" (7), while Jean Price Mars's *Ainsi parla l'oncle* (1928) attacked the alienation of what he termed a Haitian "bovarysme collectif." Césaire's poem is, in this view, a response to W. E. B. Dubois's celebrated diagnosis of a black "double consciousness" in *The Souls of Black Folk* (1903): "The Negro is a sort of seventh son, born with a veil, and gifted with a second sight in this American world,—a world which yields to him no true self-consciousness, but only lets him see himself through the revelation of the other world. It is a peculiar sensation, this double consciousness, this sense of always looking at one's self through the eyes of others, of measuring one's soul by the tape of a world that looks on in amused contempt and pity" (3). If Dubois in this famous passage confronts "double consciousness" with the Hegelian ideal of "self-consciousness," the *Cahier* is in similar fashion Césaire's first gesture in his lifelong pursuit of an inter-subjective self-understanding that he, like Dubois himself, would undertake through his multiple poetic, historical, and political interventions. Writers and critics such as Frantz Fanon, Richard Wright, James Baldwin, Edouard Glissant, and, most recently, Paul Gilroy have in turn developed the insights into "double consciousness" first expressed in the work of writers such as Césaire and Dubois (see Gilroy, *Against Race* 77).

The striking originality of the *Cahier d'un retour au pays natal* lies in its violent critique of colonial Antillean society. Its effect of shock arises in part from its uncompromising representation of exploitation, misery, and alientation. Cutting through the stultifying decay of an exotic, reified *doudouisme* and colonialist hypocrisy, it takes up and affirms (black) existence in a liberating moment of *amor fati*. At the core of this triumph, however, Césaire stages a conflict that will both poetically and historically complicate the instantiation of negritude: the affirmation of black freedom evinced in the poem occurs in the guise of a much-remarked rejection of Western rationality. In its ascendancy, the black subject appears to hand over a newfound autonomy to a transcendent totality that would dissolve the individual subject in the universal sublime.

This surprising gesture occurs as the poetic subject announces his desire to be "tied" and "bound" in the poem's final lines. The poem thematically abandons the mediating force of reason in favor of what Césaire termed "flaming madness" (*Poetry* 49), while the poetic subject's final moment of freedom is ambiguous, producing negritude's promise of sovereignty via the seeming dissolution of that subject's autonomy. This dissolution is represented affirmatively in a "progression from the individual to the collective consciousness" (Irele, *Cahier* 148) in the final lines of stanza 173: "embrace me unto furious us / embrace, embrace US."[6] And yet, the constant reversion, through the poem's closing line to the first-person singular ("I will now fish the malevolent tongue"), underscores the fragility of this sentiment, as the poet risks abandoning his community to an insubstantial, merely textual freedom. The contradictory nature of the "freedom" at the core of Césaire's discourse thus provides, through its unresolved status, the impetus to the Martinican poet-statesman's future exploration of the relation between theory and practice and between historical knowledge and the objective impact of the latter in the political, poetic, cultural, and theatrical work that would follow the *Cahier*.[7]

Herein lies the ethical thrust of the poem. While this is clearly "a poem in which the sense of individual destiny is not only located within the framework of a necessary implication in the collective but is also associated with the operative values of human responsibility and moral obligation which flow from that essential relation" (Irele, *Cahier* xliii), it nonetheless would betray its own vision of a free black subject were it to overlook that subject's still insubstantial, utopian nature. This ambiguity is in fact the true measure of the poem's remarkable achievement. Césaire's *Cahier* simultaneously articulates both the aesthetic semblance of an autonomous black subjectivity and its immanent critique. The poem announces with prophetic insight the tragedy that would soon come to dominate Césaire's aesthetic and political reflection in works such as the *Discours sur le colonialisme*, the historical study *Toussaint Louverture*, and his theatrical masterpiece *La tragédie du roi Christophe*: the degeneration of the promise of negritude into tyranny and violence amid the utopian aspirations of the newly independent African and diasporic states.

Despite the many analyses of the *Cahier*, it has never received a sustained examination of the contradiction inherent between the desubjectifying forces of the irrational and Césaire's positive affirmation of the subject of negritude.[8] Césaire's poem is, I maintain, far too complex to be reduced to a single, celebratory interpretation based on its manifest theme of black liberation. The poem's embrace of the irrational is, to be sure, both therapeutic and liberatory when Césaire proclaims:

> "Reason, I crown you evening wind. . . .
> Because we hate you
> and your reason, we claim kinship
> with dementia praecox with the flaming madness
> of persistent cannibalism." (49)[9]

Julia Kristeva has described this revolutionary capacity of a certain poetic language both to confront and dismantle the ideological practices that constrain and disengage human agency:

> Recovering the subjects' vehemence required a descent into the most archaic stage of his positing, one contemporaneous with the positing of the social order; it required a descent into the structural positing of the thetic in language so that violence, surging up through the phonetic, syntactic, and logical orders, could reach the symbolic order and the technocratic ideologies that had been built over this violence to ignore or repress it. To penetrate the era, poetry had to disturb the logic that dominated the social order and do so through that logic itself, by assuming and unraveling its position, its syntheses, and hence the ideologies it controls. (*Revolution*, 83)

And yet, the *Cahier* is no simple celebration of the irrational. The poem refuses the path of least resistance as it consistently places its own stated intentions in contact with the forces that would eliminate human freedom. The text of the *Cahier*, like the poetic discourses of Rimbaud and Lautréamont that inform it, initiates a "process that exceeds the subject and his communicative structures" (Kristeva 16), while surpassing those influences in its refusal of the real, material destruction of colonized subjects. In its excess, "beyond good and evil," the destructive potential of the irrational can and has set upon any object, regardless of a putative racial solidarity forged "at the compass of suffering." This terrifying fluidity of human violence in fact goes to the heart of Césaire's exploration of the vicissitudes of colonized subjectivity.

THE POEM'S most obvious aporia lies in its final lines, where the triumphant ascendance of the poet and the dove occurs only when the former has uttered this surprising request:

"devour wind . . .
and bind, bind me without remorse
bind me with your vast arms to the luminous clay
bind my black vibration to the very navel of the world
bind, bind me, bitter brotherhood
then, strangling me with your lasso of stars
rise,
Dove
rise
rise
rise
rise" (84)[10]

The verb *lier* here alternates between two distinct meanings. The coexistence of its sense of "mettre ensemble, rapprocher, unir [to bring together, to unite]"—manifest in the passage "au nombril même du monde"—with that of restriction, "attacher, enchaîner [to attach, to bind, to enchain]"— as where Césaire writes "lie-moi de tes vastes bras . . . m'étranglant de ton lasso d'étoiles"—underscores the ambiguity of the poet's entreaty. He is clearly asking not simply to be "linked" to the world but also to be "bound" by it. While overtly an expression of unity with the forces of nature, the passage unavoidably recalls the images that have marked the black subject's loss of freedom: enchained slaves and the frenzy of the lynch mob. Coming at the poem's moment of greatest freedom, this voluntary imposition of a new form of bondage has generated surprisingly little commentary.[11]

When A. James Arnold cites these lines, his brief explication describes the poetic subject's unambiguous need to remain tied to his people: "The heroic figure who emerges in the final movement of the poem calls upon the wind, his Lord, to assure his bond with the black world for which he claims to speak" (*Modernism and Negritude* 166). Arnold's important 1981 study of Césaire's poetry is worth considering more fully, however, since it offers a detailed analysis of Césaire's theme of irrationalism. His incisive commentary draws out the equivocal nature of this theme in the historical context of the 1940s and fascism, though he applies his critique only to René Ménil.

Arnold places Césaire's entire poetic output from 1939 to 1945 under the sign of irrationalism (68). In bringing together the texts from this period, including the *Cahier*, the wartime journal *Tropiques,* and the poems of *Les armes miraculeuses,* he underscores two influences in Césaire's use of the irrational: surrealism and the thought of Leo Frobenius. While Frobenius is commonly mentioned in genealogies of negritude, Arnold's analysis alludes to some of the more troubling aspects of this parenthood. Arnold points out how Césaire, following Frobenius, argues in the article "Poetry and Cognition" (1945) for a primitive, pre-rational immediacy to be rediscovered through poetry. To quote Césaire: "It is an error to believe that knowledge, to be born, had to await the methodical exercise of thought or the scruples of experimentation. I even believe that man has never been closer to certain truths than in the first days of the species. At the time when man discovered with emotion the first sun, the first rain, the first breath, the first moon" (qtd. in *Modernism and Negritude* 58).

Three years earlier, when introducing Frobenius's writings in *Tropiques,* Césaire allied himself with the biological conception of negritude that he has since taken great pains to disavow: "There flows in our veins a blood that requires of us a unique attitude toward life . . . we must respond . . . to the special dynamics of our complex biological reality" (qtd. in *Modernism and Negritude* 38). The theme of blood appears in many guises throughout the *Cahier,* at times implying an essentialist evocation of racial unity ("Blood! Blood! all our blood aroused by the male heart of the sun" [69]).[12] It was only in 1950, in the *Discours sur le colonialisme,* that Césaire would explicitly evoke and condemn the fascist ideology of a sanguinary nationalism. No less troubling are Césaire's "ambiguous" feelings toward Gobineau. Gobineau's racialism allowed Senghor to affirm that "Art is black," an affirmation that Césaire implies was attractive to himself as well in the 1930s, when he composed the *Cahier* (*Modernism and Negritude* 41).

While manifestly antithetical to social oppression, in hindsight Césaire's references to pre-rational immediacy and "Negro blood" in 1942 and 1945 merely invert and hence participate in the ideological categories of Hitlerian fascism. Thematically, Césaire's work describes from beginning to end an unambiguously antitotalitarian project. *Tropiques,* the review in which these phrases appeared, was itself a call to resistance against the Vichy regime of Admiral Robert in Martinique, the opening pages of its first issue in April 1941 stating, "We are among those who say no to darkness" (Toumson and Henry-Valmore 75). However, while the poem explicitly allies itself with the downtrodden of the world ("I would be a / jew-man / a Kaffir-man / a Hindu-man-from-Calcutta / a harlem-man-who-doesn't-vote" [43]),[13] in its defense it uncritically deploys the ideological tools of fascist and racist oppression. The risk of this discursive contamination seems not to have troubled Césaire's wife, Suzanne, who, in her 1941 article on Frobenius in *Tropiques,* explicitly concludes that "a world brought to its present catastrophe by the Hamitic characteristics of Euro-American civilization can only be redirected through the renewal of the Ethiopian strain: whence the special mission of negritude" (qtd. in *Modernism and Negritude* 38–39).

To the Nazi's theories of racial purity, Suzanne Césaire postulates negritude as a counterdoctrine of racial rejuvenation. Indeed, as late as 1973, Senghor was to point out with pride how, in the midst of Hitler's rise to power and the ensuing genocide,

> We had to wait for Leo Frobenius before the affinities between the "Ethiopian", that is the Negro African, and the German soul could be made manifest and before certain stubborn preconceptions of the 17th and 18th centuries could be removed. . . . Frobenius tells us that, like individuals, ethnic groups are diverse, even opposed, like the Hamites and the Ethiopians, in their feelings and ideas . . . that each ethnic group, having its own *paideuma*—once again its *soul*—reacts in its own peculiar way to the environment and develops autonomously. . . . And [Frobenius] concludes: "The West created English realism and French rationalism. The East created German mysticism . . . the agreement with the corresponding civilizations in Africa is complete" (qtd. in *Modernism and Negritude* 40).

Senghor, even at this late stage, preferred not to explore the connection this mystical German racism (where the term "soul" has replaced any references to "blood") might have held with its dialectical negation in the hyper-rationalism of Auschwitz. These surreptitious correspondences between the antithetical discourses of fascism and negritude form the negative image of Césaire's articulation of black autonomy.

The closing lines of Césaire's 1939 poem thus participate in and displace a discursive practice common to French intellectuals of the period such as Roger Caillois and Georges Bataille: a questionable espousal of authoritarianism to *counter* the forces of an encroaching fascism (Hollier 179–97). The pre-critical incorporation of these images within the discursive structures of the *Cahier* and *Tropiques* participates obliquely in what J. Michael Dash, speaking of the Haitian indigenist movement contemporary to the publication of the *Cahier,* terms a "totalitarian temptation" in which "fascist politics are a hidden dimension to indigenist poetics" (*Other America* 75). Césaire's "demi-urgic poet" functions in this view as a sublimated transformation of the authoritarian leader: "One of the ironies of this phase of Caribbean modernism is the way in which a rejection of the tyranny of reason leads to the poetics of closure and authority" (80). That said, the *Cahier* nonetheless sets the stage for both Césaire's reasoned critique of postcolonial violence in later works such as *La tragédie du roi Christophe* and his subsequent rejection of biological essentialism.

James Arnold leaves implicit the links between Césaire's irrationalism, his and Senghor's early biological racialism, and the global context of fascism in which these theories were developed and expounded.[14] Arnold's analysis describes the literary dimensions of a psychological "regression," both in terms of the poetic subject's relationship to society and within Césaire's actual poetic material (260). He depicts an ahistorical psychological subject of negritude actively divorced from the world. By the same token, Arnold does project a historically engaged critique of the glorification of the irrational onto another figure involved in Tropiques: René Ménil. Describing Ménil's contention in 1941 that discoveries in psychoanalysis and ethnography would render propaganda obsolete, Arnold observes that "there is something frighteningly naïve about these predictions when one considers that they are contemporaneous with Hitler's crowd-swaying speeches and Leni Riefenstahl's film making in Nazi Germany, both of which appealed to the 'vitally engrossing energies' [Ménil's phrase] in a culture" (*Modernism and Negritude* 89).

In the *Cahier d'un retour au pays natal,* this totalitarian resonance of imagery reappears up through the moment of submission occurring in the *Cahier*'s final lines. The *Cahier*'s triumphant ascension, "[the] image of a spiral that unites the one and the multiple, in the explosion of a single movement" remains compelling and should be sustained as an element in its structure of truth (Dash, "Le bateau ivre césairien" 160). In accord with the poem's own effort to instantiate negritude as an unassimilated moment of difference and nonidentity, however, Césaire's poetic constellation proceeds dialectically, containing images of both a utopian autonomy and the conditions preventing its establishment.[15] The ambiguity of the grammatical subjects of the poem's final passage, from the syntactical "vent" [wind] ("coil, wind, around my new growth" [83]), and the "fraternité âpre" [bitter fraternity] ("bind, bind me, bitter brotherhood" [85]), to the more general referent "mon pays," [my country] should be acknowledged. While they each manifestly appeal to a liberated, intersubjective community of the black diaspora, notions of "country" and racial "brotherhood" have nonetheless repeatedly motivated a century of genocide and terror. Retrospective historical experience must inform the ethics of our reading of the poem, calling forth images ranging from the Rwandan catastrophe to the pre-individual collective of pogroms and Kristallnacht to interrogate not Césaire's program, but his methodology. It takes only the slightest change in perspective for one famous passage to resonate disturbingly with fascist iconology, à la Leni Reifenstahl, evoking both the propaganda poster and the coming Hitlerian "apocalypse": "And we are standing now, my country and I, hair in the wind, my hand puny in its enormous fist and now the strength is not in us but above us, in a voice that drills the night and the hearing like the penetrance of an apocalyptic wasp (77).[16]

Like many involved in the fight against fascism in the period, if Césaire's poem uncritically adopts images of blood, community, and racial solidarity, it does so to undertake their determinate negation. Césaire refuses simply to turn away from injustice and subjugation. Instead the poem confronts and takes into its very poetic material the elements of a racist and fascist discourse that would obliterate black and indeed human subjectivity, and forces us to face the degree to which irrational negativity is not foreign to, but rather inherent in, the categories of our own action, perception, and subjectivity. The poem's final lines place us before the antinomical status of freedom itself, in which the notion of an emergent black subject threatens to become ideological, a locus of submission and mere "support" to the domination of society, and where subjectivity may only find its "freedom" in submission to absolute imperatives.

The *Cahier* must thus be understood as no mere exotic undertaking, alien to the larger concerns of its time. Written in Europe by a Paris-educated black subject of French colonialism, it thrust onto the world stage at the moment of Kristallnacht and the Stalinist show-trials the drama of colonial alienation and racism. What is perhaps the best-known example of Stalinist art from the 1930s stands not only as the ideal image of the fascist ideology Césaire's poem reappropriates but was in fact on public display in Paris during the period Césaire was composing the *Cahier*. At the 1937 Exposition Internationale, atop the Soviet Pavilion stood a monumental testimony to the dialectical reversal of the drive for freedom into the cult of personality and its consequent obliteration of stubbornly individualized subjects. Césaire, as a student at the Ecole Normale Supérieure from 1933 to 1939, undoubtedly visited the site at the Trocadéro, and most likely followed the contemporary debate surrounding the Stalinist show-trials that intellectuals such as Breton and Gide famously denounced at the exposition's inception. The statue stands in rigid, mute testimony to the obscure terror inherent in the passage in the *Cahier* cited above.

The very disproportion between Vera Mukhina's immense sculpture entitled *Worker and Collective Farm Girl* and the tiny, buglike observers that swarm around it is striking. The statue speaks of the paralysis of enlightenment and hands over its implementation to the police state. Césaire's poem protests and works through this process, not by turning away from it toward an insubstantial racial utopia but by tarrying with the contents of racial and ideological heteronomy. The *Cahier*'s manifest content and program remain the conquest of autonomy by the black subject. And yet, the dialectical reversals that process would necessarily undergo in the period of decolonization are here reflected in their contemporary historical form as Césaire's images imbricate the phenomenological progression of black subjectivity within the contemporary threats of colonialism and Stalinist and Nazi fascism.

Figure 5. Vera Mukhina's *Worker and Collective Farm Girl* at the 1937 Paris Exposition Internationale

THE FINAL image of Césaire's *Cahier* is itself a provocative, unresolved contradiction, a compelling moment and starting point in the phenomenology of black consciousness Césaire's entire literary and political career will effect. The central paradox of the *Cahier* is that, for each step the subject of negritude makes toward conquering freedom, each movement away from slavery, human commodification, and dependency into self-consciousness and autonomy, there results an ever greater estrangement from nature within the isolation of an individual subjectivity. As Césaire presents the antinomical logic of this pursuit, in its affirmation of autonomy, an increasingly isolated poetic subject must turn *toward* a "reconciliation with nature" and the irrational as a means of recovering this lost subject-object unity (Irele, *Cahier* 85).[17] And yet such a gesture abandons a sought-after individual autonomy and self-preservation, strips the subject of its free will, and turns it into an instrument of blind nature. The poem circles again and again from an immersion in the prostrate suffering and heteronomy of the Martinican and black peoples, to an affirmation of upright triumph, and back again (Irele, *Cahier* 85–86). In tracing the movement of the subject of negritude toward a moment of de-subjectification, capitulation, and self-abandonment in the moment of its greatest triumph, Césaire follows relentlessly the dictates his aesthetic material presents to him.

The poetic subject in the *Cahier* clearly invokes a becoming-animal, a becoming-vegetal as an escape from Reason:

> From staring too long at trees I have
> become a tree . . .
> from brooding too long on the Congo
> I have become a Congo resounding with
> forests and rivers." (51)[18]

And yet it is easy to overlook the note of impossibility and pathos in this gesture encapsulated in Suzanne Césaire's 1941 article on Frobénius: "No, Man did not create civilization, no, civilization is not the work of Man. Man is on the contrary the instrument of civilization, the simple means of expression of an organic force that infinitely exceeds him. Man does not act, he is acted upon ["il est agi"], moved by a force anterior to humanity, a force comparable to the vital-force itself, the fundamental 'Païduma' [Frobénius's term]" (qtd. in Combe 31).

Man as the "instrument of civilization" and of an "organic force": this is what awaits the subject of negritude in its imagined flight from the rational. In this view, one could read the *Cahier* as a tracing of dystopia: the greatest moment of autonomy in the poem lies not in its final embrace of/submission to a natural "organic power" but rather in the mimesis of its objectification of the Martinican landscape. *"Au bout du petit matin"* ("At the end of the wee hours"): the *Cahier*, by invoking Céline's *Voyage au bout de la nuit* at its moment of inception, places the subject of negritude squarely before the horrors from which Céline's Bardamu flees, as though, dreaming, the poet awakens to confront the true nightmare (see Arnold, *Modernism and Negritude* 142). The black subject witnesses the objectification of "this inert town and its beyond of lepers, of consumption, of famines, of fears squatting in the ravines, fears perched in the trees, fears dug in the ground, fears adrift in the sky, piles of fears and their fumaroles of anguish" (37)[19] and in this very confrontation with heteronomy delineates the parameters of a dialectical autonomy. This description allows the poetic subject to measure its own experience against its material surroundings. If the former is found wanting, guilty of a pathos of distance the poetic subject gradually overcomes ("j'accepte, j'accepte tout cela" ["I accept, I accept it all"] [77]), in the face of ongoing, objective social contradiction, s/he can only achieve an imaginary resolution of antinomy and fusion of subject and object.

That Césaire at once searches for and dramatizes the impossibility of any "return to nature" is the measure of his revolutionary insight. His poetic subject never in fact becomes-animal, becomes-tree, but must continue to speak of doing so.[20] The *Cahier* maps not the actual process of abandonment to the irrational but rather the mastery of the irrational through the gradual imposition of a gridlike rhythmic structure upon the flows of an uncontrolled reality. The unrelenting opacity of Césaire's poetry—its refusal of a norm of transparent communication—dashes any hope for a recovered subject-object unity. In this Césaire has moved far beyond a simple "return to nature" and instead confronts us with its very impossibility in the moment of its invocation. It is this highly articulated contradiction that gives Césaire's poetic language its full critical, transformational force, in contradistinction to the often unidimensional poetry of black liberation generated during the subsequent colonial independence movements.

The *Cahier d'un retour au pays natal* explores the dialectic of freedom and enslavement in more than its thematic material, however. The poem brings a newly liberated black subject into contact with a repressive totality that would annihilate all traces of resistant subjectivity through the element of its form that holds out the greatest promise of freedom: rhythm.

ANAPHORA—repetition—and parataxis—the juxtaposition of clauses without connectives—stand out as the *Cahier*'s organizing rhythmic devices. These create a nonmetrical, "pre-reflective" rhythm, according to the critic Dominique Combe. For Combe, Césaire's irrationalism is not simply a thematic element in the poem but, rather, finds its immanent tracing in rhythmic processes, which, as "mere" repetition, Combe links to the supposedly frenzied beat of the tribal drum and dance.[21] Combe describes the poem's structural flow as lacking sequential linkages, consisting rather of a series of "illuminations."

Combe's analysis throws a new light upon the problem of the irrational in the *Cahier* as an element emanating from its rhythmic structuration. At a general structural level, the poem effects a movement from "prose" to "verse".[22] This differentiation between the poem's "prose" and "verse" passages is in fact the measure of its overall temporal structure, as opposed to the minutiae of its innumerable and highly complex metrical variations. Although it is not always possible to differentiate clearly between the poem's prose and verse sections, in the poem's first section ("At the end of the wee hours . . . that other dawn in Europe" [35–43]), approximately thirty-three sections or paragraphs of prose encounter only two distinct sections of verse along with four short verse sections. In the final section ("I say that this is right . . . in its motionless veerition!" [65–85]) this pattern is largely reversed, and seventeen generally shorter prose sections are mixed in with approximately fifty-eight sections of verse.

Two largely distinct rhythmic practices thus characterize the poem, while an overall rhythmic structure prevails in which the latter gradually replaces the former. Anaphora is the fundamental rhythmic process only of the poem's later stages, while its earlier prose passages obtain their rhythmic force from what Combe suggestively terms "the rhythmic cell." These cells form around a number of recurring phrases that introduce nominal expressions: "At the end of the wee hours," "What is mine," "Eia for," "I accept." The explanation, I want to argue, for the poem's rhythmic development, its movement from highly complex, dense rhythmic "cells" to the repetitive anaphora of its final section, lies in the relentless working-through of the implications of its own material and its articulation of the poetic subject's problematic relation to both nature and society.

Césaire's poem moves from a freely characterized natural world in its opening descriptions of the *pays natal* to the terror still visited upon black subjects enciphered in the rhythms and images of the poem's closing moment of transcendence. In the *Cahier,* the anaphora of its closing section marks the progression from the flowing, undifferentiated "prose" of its introduction to the reactive "acceptance" in the poet's moment of triumphant autonomy:

> I accept . . . I accept . . .
> the yaws
> the mastiff
> the suicide
> the promiscuity
> the bootkin
> the shackles
> the rack
> the cippus
> the head screw. (75)[23]

The pounding regularity of this list of the terrors of slavery evokes a reified world of mechanized, prosthetic torture, one that appropriates instrumental rationality to drive the black subject to submission. Aesthetic mimesis momentarily dissolves the poet's critical subjectivity in a pattern of compulsive repetition, abandoning dialectical reflection for an immediate confrontation with the horrors of slavery. As the poem attempts anamnestically to recall and move beyond a prior enslavement, the final section of the *Cahier* compulsively transfers an identitarian rhythmic logic into its formal structures. The *Cahier* is most compelling in precisely such aporetic moments, as it masterfully works through a traumatic past while formally calling attention to the totalizing procedures it would condemn.[24] And yet, Césaire even here posits nonidentity within a field of signifiers ("bootkin / shackles / rack / cippus / head screw"), each of which carries its own specific dimension of suffering, never interchangeable with another.

The received reading of this "acceptance" sees it as the necessary precursor to the stance of negritude, the negation of the denial of blackness and African roots traditional to the mulatto world view. We need not abandon this reading in pointing out the impossibility of Césaire's undertaking. Césaire describes a subject torn between a striving for autonomy and its negation in the means adopted—the flight from Western rationality into nature. His genius, in turn, was to push this antinomy to its furthest limits in his poetic material. Césaire's poetry autonomously develops an equivalent to the surrealist montage technique, "[the] innumerable 'ands' [that] link nothing" (Combe 77), abandoning developmental processes to the force of shock, juxtaposition, and accumulation. With flourishes of technical virtuosity, Césaire renders unattainable the natural immediacy his poem so longs for.

THE *Cahier d'un retour au pays natal* is at once the triumphant call to negritude it has always been seen as and a measure of the enormous difficulties facing its immanent realization. If Césaire, after the transformational process of the *retour au pays natal,* can affirm

> Et elle est debout la négraille . . .
> debout
> et
> libre[25]
>
> (*Poésie 55*)

this very claim remains threatened by the specter of its incompletion. The accomplishment of Césaire's project lies in its taking in the negativity of reality, confronting it, and presenting its implications without forcing a resolution of its contradictions that would bypass social untruth. In this, the poem transcends the mere celebration of victorious negritude. Dominick LaCapra's description of writing that effectively works through traumatic memories pertains to Césaire as well: the *Cahier* "elaborate[s] a hybridized narrative that does not avoid analysis or ideologically deny trauma by projectively representing empirical reality as the simple realization or teleological unfolding of wishes and values" (199).

Césaire's achievement is to follow his material through to its consequential moment of regression and confront us with the need to go beyond it. The objective impact of Césaire's negritude was decisive for a colonial world calling into question the doxa of colonialism. The *Cahier*'s aestheticized phenomenology of black consciousness remained, however, to be instantiated, and Césaire would soon drive beyond the inwardness of the poetic "zone of incandescence . . . of the 'I'" that marks his early work (qtd. in Delas 115). Its antinomical structure enjoined a fuller confrontation between theory and practice, between historical forces and the self-understanding of the colonized, as the project of negritude entered the stage of world history. To underscore this doubled, ambiguous nature of the literature of decolonization via critique is not to be unfaithful to its invocation of a liberated subject but rather to pursue the only means available to recall its dream of the transformed society that history goes on betraying, endlessly.

Coda

No isolated event in twentieth-century history, Césaire's *Cahier* stands within a constellation of creative works that struggled with the contradic-

93 *Double Consciousness in* Cahier d'un retour

tions of fascism in the period leading up to the second world war. To speak of the rhythmic processes at work in the *Cahier* is to invoke the foundation of lyrical creation: music. While one might presumably find processes analogous to those in the *Cahier* at work in any music that concerns itself with human freedom, an over-determined confluence of formal and historical homologies occurs between the *Cahier* and one musical composition in particular. Written within months of one another, each a response to the terrorization of the individual growing ever more pronounced in the years leading up to 1939, Césaire's *Cahier* and Dmitri Shostakovich's Fourth Symphony developed formal aesthetic responses to this terror that are strikingly similar. To bring them into contact is to underscore their central position within a more general historical gathering of objects created in response to fascism, announcing the link between fascism and colonialism that Césaire would only explicitly develop after the war in his *Discours sur le colonialisme*. No mere abstraction, such a comparison serves as well to drive the *Cahier* beyond the interiority of its status as mere poem, even as *anticolonial* poem, underscoring its participation in a broader historical context of the search for human autonomy without erasing its specificity as a critique of the colonial world.

The closing notes of Shostakovich's stunning Fourth Symphony (1936) mirror the *Cahier*'s final image ("strangling me with your lasso of stars / rise, / Dove, / rise / rise / rise" [85]) in their formal representation of double consciousness and an antinomical social totality. Shostakovich withdrew the piece from rehearsal in 1936 in the midst of his sudden condemnation for putative "left deformation" in the pages of *Pravda* (Taruskin 22, Wilson 115–25). Though nonprogrammatic, the symphony's free- form rejection of classical models and its violent, thundering gestures mimetically condemn the processes of violence and totalization. Like the insistent alternation in the *Cahier*'s final stanzas between an idealized autonomy and the starkness of real suffering and degradation (Irele, *Cahier* 138), the unadorned polyrhythm[26] of Shostakovich's final figure leaves unresolved the conflict between a bureaucratic terror and the promise of a utopian resolution of antinomy. As the tympani and contrabasses obsessively intone a pianissimo triplet pattern on the tonic fundamental C, the ethereal notes of the celesta drift upward to the farthest harmonic extensions of the final C-minor chord, their duple rhythm seemingly oblivious—yet ultimately bound—to the ominous, quite literally deranged, pulse.[27] Like Césaire's white dove that "strangles" the poetic subject as it rises in a death-like moment of transcendence, Shostakovich's Fourth clutches at the promise of freedom even as its final notes fade into silence, *morendo*.

94 *Double Consciousness in* Cahier d'un retour

Figure 6. Closing passage from Shostakovich's Fourth Symphony, 1936 (rehearsal nos. 255–259)

Despite their similar concerns with the liquidation of the subject (from the enslavement of Africans amid colonization to Soviet collectivization and Stalin's Terror of 1936–39), the *Cahier* and Shostakovich's Fourth Symphony are not simple mirrors of each other's resistance. In fact, their encounter is truly productive insofar as they mediate one another through their points of *dis*-similarity. For if the *Cahier* has long been seen as a quintessentially and unambiguously engaged artwork,[28] Shostakovich was traditionally viewed, at least in the West, as hopelessly compromised by his ties to the Soviet state and Communist Party. Today, however, Shostakovich is more subtly recognized as the quintessential example of artistic double consciousness, the Russian *yurodivy*, or fool, who successfully hides his evocations of a free human subject within the inherent ambiguity of the musical signifier. That these two artists, unknown to one another and working in quite different mediums, find such similar solutions to a single problem transforms our understanding of them both: While the *Cahier*'s radical historical engagement underscores that more hidden aspect of Shostakovich, the Soviet composer's complex and undeniable ambiguity makes that same dimension of the *Cahier* more readily apparent, a tarrying with the negative that is perhaps the most effective response to a world marked by murder in the name of higher ideals (communism, the humanization of "savage" Africans). In both artworks, the aesthetic representation of freedom by its very nature bears witness to the capacity of thought to posit a space beyond the destruction and terror Césaire and Shostakovich witnessed and condemned. Produced and determined by this devastation, the evocation of freedom in their work transforms that negation to become a liminal experience of the not-yet-real.

3 Aimé Césaire, *Présence africaine,* and Black Atlantic Historical Experience

TODAY, HAVING gone through and emerged at the other end of the so-called "death of the subject" announced from Nietzsche to Foucault and Baudrillard and beyond, it is apparent that the radicality of an ever-renewed gesture that starts as an ideological critique is itself inherently ideological. If such critique of the subject fails to confront this dilemma and remains unambiguously and blindly affirmative of the subject's dissolution, it ends up lamely echoing the course of the world. As such, historical example shows that the notion of an autonomous subject cannot be affirmed emphatically, and yet it remains a project beyond the limits of postmodern immanence in a time of transnational and consumerist capitalism.

The *Cahier d'un retour au pays natal,* the previous chapter argued, pursues such dialectical work when it describes the basic structure of Caribbean subjectivity as an antinomical doubling of experience. If the surface logic of negritude is indeed a high modernist hypostatization of a transcendental, autonomous subject, that gesture cannot be simply forgotten and discarded but instead must be worked through as a simultaneously productive and mystificatory effort. Césaire's project to create a subject of negritude in a historical context in which subjectivity was historically denied amid the violence of slavery and colonialism was a Promethean effort to engage critically the breadth of western modernity and African tradition to forge a New World self-consciousness.

Understood in this light, the category of Antillean subjectivity as it appears in Césaire's work must itself be understood historically, as Fredric Jameson has argued in a different context: our "view of the 'great' modernist creators [among whom I am emphatically counting Césaire] ought not to argue away the social and historical specificity of those now doubtful 'centered subjects,' but rather provide new ways of understanding their conditions of possibility" (*Postmodernism* 306). Though arising from the basic contradictions of Antillean experience, an examination of Césaire's work that would do justice to its diverse and still-productive historical implications must indeed take into account the specific context–the "conditions of possibility" from which it arose. This investigation must in turn build upon the self-understanding of these texts to discover the homologies and effects of their aesthetic interventions upon the multiple fields in which they came into play. Only in this manner can Césaire's poetry be perceived as more than the (illusory) subjective freedom of the poet amid the objective compulsion of Antillean and postcolonial society.

Through the amassing and deft manipulation of intellectual discourses, Césaire not only created a new aesthetic; he simultaneously accumulated a mass of intellectual capital that had material implications for both the author himself and for the constitution of Francophone letters within a preexisting intellectual field.[1] Césaire was not the first black student to attend the Ecole Normale Supérieure. He was, however, with Senghor, perhaps the most *successful* of that group. More precisely, Césaire was successful as few Francophone black intellectuals had ever before been in learning to deftly rearticulate a vast range of discourses. These discourses, as they existed within the social space of the French intellectual world, each possessed a quantum of value that Césaire the student appropriated: surrealist, proto-Afrocentric (Frobénius), Judeo-Christian, Marxist, philosophical, and classical Greek and Latin discourses, to name only the most obvious of Césaire's sources.

Rather than the teleological appearance of a mystical Sartrian *projet originel*[2] arising from the author's originary consciousness, Césaire made a series of choices (aesthetic and political) in a context in which the *Cahier* and negritude existed only as structural potentialities. In a context in which the historical, formal development of an art form must be expressed in each new artwork (even and especially the most avant-garde) in order for it to achieve recognition as innovative, the greater an artist's familiarity with and mastery of his or her inherited material, the greater will be the persuasive power of his or her art. The accumulation and masterful manipulation of various discourses thus serve to facilitate the entry of an unknown artist into a preexisting field of producers.

The aesthetic choices and operations of Césaire the poet had material effects not simply upon the trajectory of Césaire himself but upon the constitution of a new cultural field. From this perspective, the appropriation of discourses and their effective incorporation within a body of work are not simply aesthetic processes. Each of these discourses preexisted Césaire, and he encountered them with their attendant values within a historically developing intellectual field. Césaire, however, not only took on certain social roles he encountered in French society (surrealist poet, politically engaged intellectual, politician); he simultaneously created a previously nonexistent position for himself within the French intellectual field of the second half of this century. In a manner structurally akin to that of Sartre—and in the field of music, Pierre Boulez[3]—Césaire became the prototypical black poet statesman. Though others occupied (or attempted to occupy) similar positions (Senghor, René Ménil, Sékou Touré, Camara Laye), none so successfully combined poetic gift with a capacity for progressive political leadership.

Prefigurations of Césaire's Trajectory: Disposition and Entitlement

Césaire's sensitivity to his own and others' blackness and status as colonized subjects necessarily coexisted with an equally strong sense of his own entitlement, a fundamental belief in the rightfulness of his own equality. This sense of entitlement made it impossible for him to accept the stigmatization of his blackness as simply the way of the world. The experience of a fundamental cultural conflict brought to an unbearable pitch is a characteristic Césaire shared with many other artistic innovators (Flaubert and Sartre are obvious examples).[4] In Césaire, this conflict provided not only the psychological impetus to his creativity; it formed, as the previous chapter showed, the immanent problematic he worked through in his artistic material. Césaire's family occupied a dominant position (the black intellectual and economic elite) within a dominated group (black colonial bourgeoisie). Césaire's biographers agree that his family's status in Martinican society made it part of both an economic and, especially, intellectual (through the influence of his father and grandfather) elite (Ngal, *Césaire* 26–29; Toumson 24). Martinican blacks were barely two generations removed from slavery at the time of Césaire's birth, and, although Césaire's family was economically better off than the majority of Martinican blacks, intellectual achievements were particularly valorized in Césaire's family as the path to social success.

Césaire's subsequent fame has obscured the fact that he very nearly became an anonymous *instituteur colonial* in Martinique before going on instead to achieve global literary renown and political power. After failing his *agrégation* in 1939, he returned to Martinique and began teaching Latin and Greek at the Lycée Schoelcher: "When I entered the ENS, I continued to prepare my *licence* [B.A.]. Very early on, I underwent a crisis, a physical and moral crisis: all these classical studies that I was doing seemed so far from life, so far from what I wished to do.... I prepared the *agrégation* exam with extreme negligence. Then I started writing poetry. The result was that my tutor for the agreg' told me that a composition I had written was a poem. I was disadapting myself [for the exam]" (qtd. in Toumson and Henry-Valmore 40, 68). Pierre Bourdieu describes in detail the astounding absence of reflection and investigation involved in the preparatory education Césaire underwent. One particularly cynical *khagne* English professor states to Bourdieu: "I never give out a bibliography—there would be no point. They have to be able to speak on any topic without really knowing anything. I bring them predigested knowledge." Bourdieu describes the narcissistic products of this education in their utter conformism:

> Given that this enterprise of hothouse cultivation is carried out on adolescents who have selected themselves according to their attitude toward the school, in other words, according to their *docility*, at least as much as their academic ability, and who, shut up for three or four years in a protected universe with no material cares, know very little about the world other than what they have learned from books, it is bound to produce *forced* and somewhat immature minds that, more or less as Sartre writes about some of his reading at age 20, understand everything luminously and yet understand absolutely nothing." (*State Nobility* 95, 91)

Perhaps, in fact, Césaire's refusal to adapt himself to the intellectually stultifying demands of the *agrégation,* an examination he was presumably capable of passing, was in fact a form of self-elimination from certain socially designated roles. In this case, however, it was a denial become creative, forcing a *retour au pays natal* instead of the provincial teaching position that he would have had to accept had he passed the exam. On the other hand, Césaire's encyclopedic incorporation of a body of knowledge in preparing the *agregation* provided the basic form, rigor, and intellectual material that make his subsequent revolt so rhetorically compelling in comparison with other anticolonial thinkers unable convincingly to give the impression of bringing the entirety of the Western intellectual tradition into the scope of their accusation. Césaire's success was not unique; it was in fact a structural possibility inherent in the French colonial system that other French Antilleans and Africans ("les miraculés") have successfully occupied before and since. Césaire, however, was able to modify this space, creating a new, dominant position for himself within it, his poetic creation attracting powerful forms of symbolic capital to the author as it appeared within an intellectual field to which it was at once perfectly adapted and a radically new intervention.

A GRADUAL mutation occurs in Aimé Césaire's aesthetic production from the publication of *Cahier d'un retour au pays natal* in 1939 to the publication of *La Tragédie du Roi Christophe* in 1963. The wartime articles published in the Martinican journal *Tropiques* and Cesaire's writings on Victor Schoelcher from 1948 demonstrate a nascent concern for the problem of historical praxis. Nonetheless, rather than arguing for the intellectual's attempt to influence historical events directly, Césaire at this time (1939–48) continues to call for the elaboration of a separate, poetic realm: "To defend oneself from the social by creating an incandescent zone, within which there may flourish in a frightful security the unknown flower of the 'Self.'"[5]

This desire to create a space independent from political and social determination undoubtedly owes much to the wartime Martinican conditions of intense censorship and cultural regression. At the same time, Césaire here indirectly articulates a description of the primary antinomy structuring intellectual practice as a whole, the contradiction between critical thought and systemic marginalization. Intellectuals from Flaubert and Baudelaire on have understood themselves to be actors independent from society as a whole. This relative independence allows a margin of intervention in historical practice through the development of critical reflection and the objectivation of sociohistorical processes. This isolation is both real (intellectuals and artists function within a field only indirectly tied to the dynamics of politics and economics) and idealized (this field nonetheless is concretely determined by, and not without effect upon, social totality). In the *Tropiques* articles Césaire the poet directly implicates himself as demiurgic creator: "But one man saves humanity, one man returns it to the universal concert, one man marries a human flourishing to the universal flourishing; that man is the poet."[6]

Although statements such as this give the impression of a hopelessly idealist aestheticism (as well as perhaps confirming Confiant's prognosis of a "hypertrophy of the ego"), Césaire's work from the *Cahier* on maintained a concrete engagement with the historical process of decolonization. During the period of *Tropiques,* this engagement was counterbalanced by an emphatic, vanguardist modernism perhaps reinforced by the monolithic character of fascist Europe. Texts such as Césaire's preface to Victor Schoelcher's *Esclavage et colonization* (1948) and the *Discours sur le colonialisme* (1955) announce Césaire's turn to history and a new, more radical grappling with historical facts as augurs of material revolution. Seen in isolation, Césaire's writings appear the quixotic intuition of an incipient decolonization. In fact, Césaire's contribution can more accurately be understood when seen within a larger context of black Atlantic and, indeed, postwar French intellectual history. Within these fields Césaire was a foundational figure of a larger historical process involving many actors. One of the primary vectors for the articulation of the philosophy of decolonization was a group project in which Césaire participated during the postwar period, a project that came to redefine the parameters of the African diasporic world: the journal *Présence africaine*.

ALIOUNE DIOP'S *Présence africaine*, launched in Paris in 1947 by a team of researchers including Aimé Césaire, instigated one of the signal interventions of African diasporic thought of this century.[7] Its appearance marked a shift from the typical intellectual review of the 1930s.[8] The reputation of the most influential literary journal of the prewar period, André Gide's *Nouvelle Revue Française*, had been tainted by wartime collaboration. Taking its place as the bellwether of Parisian intellectual fashion, Jean Paul Sartre's *Les Temps modernes*, launched in 1945 immediately following the war, dominated a field in which its rivals constantly defined themselves in relation to this overpowering competitor.

Journals such as *Les Temps modernes* had come to represent a tactical necessity in the postwar literary-intellectual field. With the ever-increasing extension of education throughout the French populace and the concurrent expansion of the reading public from the Third Republic into the postwar period, a new audience that comprised students and professors had appeared, an audience to which *Les Temps modernes* catered. This public thronged to Sartre in 1945, giving him a previously-unheard-of status as a mass-market intellectual. Within this context, *Les Temps modernes* allowed for the concentration of various knowledges (philosophical, literary, political) within a space that provided Sartre with a forum for his interventions.

Following the appearance of *Les Temps modernes*, a number of influential journals, including *Critique, La Table Ronde,* and *La Nouvelle Critique,* appeared in the period 1946–48. Each of them exhibited a distinct affiliation with Sartre's journal through critical or positive reactions to both existentialism and its editorial *prises de position*.[9] For these new journals it was impossible to ignore *Les Temps modernes;* their own survival required them to define a space either in opposition, offering an alternative ideology, or in support of *Les Temps modernes*. George Bataille's journal

Critique, for example, had a constructive relationship with *Les Temps modernes*. Its eclectic, hermetic, largely apolitical editorial policies formed a complement to *Les Temps modernes* that posed no threat to the latter's hegemonic position as the voice of prophetic engagement.[10] Others, including the conservative *La Table ronde* and the French Communist Party mouthpiece, *La Nouvelle critique*, had distinctly antagonistic relationships with *Les Temps modernes*, the latter in particular constantly taking Sartre and his team to task over their sociopolitical pronouncements. Possessing limited cultural capital—social origins, scholastic degrees, and intellectual renown—when compared with Sartre, Beauvoir, and Merleau-Ponty, the writers of *La Nouvelle critique* compensated for this lack by allying themselves with a socially dominant structure, the French Communist Party.

This same recourse to patronage holds true for the black intellectuals of Césaire's generation, who nonetheless tended to avoid the *Nouvelle critique* with its Stalinist orthodoxy and authoritarianism. These colonized intellectuals' political alliance with communism certainly owed something to expediency, given the immediate conflict Césaire felt as a member of the party hierarchy: "Early on, I had the impression that the Communists were assimilators. Within the P.C., I found myself in precisely the situation of a colonized subject" (qtd. in Delas 78). Césaire's problematic relationship with the P.C.F. was conditioned at a primary level by the independence imputed by his status as a black intellectual. The specific force with which Césaire experienced this conflict stemmed from his status as a black colonial subject forced into a pragmatic alliance: the P.C.F. was the only party that was at all sympathetic to the concerns of the French colonized. It was only in 1956, after eleven years of relative submission to party doctrine, that Césaire was able successfully to start his own political formation, the Parti Progressiste Martiniquais.

THE APPEARANCE of *Présence africaine* in 1947 occurred as part of this general tendency within a French intellectual field moving toward the concentration of cultural capital within the literary forum of the intellectual journal. Significantly, its founders refused to ally themselves with preexisting vehicles such as Sartre's *Les Temps modernes*. Their need for intellectual autonomy is already noticeable in the prewar journals of Paris-based black intellectuals and students such as the *Revue du monde noir, Légitime défense*, and *L'Etudiant noir*. The difference between these earlier, short-lived and (at the time) unnoticed journals and *Présence africaine*, however, is the concerted mobilization within the latter of resources that, occurring within a context of nascent decolonization, allowed for its worldwide impact. This strategy of accumulation was fundamental to the successful reception of the postwar French intellectual journal:

> The logic of the market leads to concentration and accumulation. Recourse to the journal as a means of achieving these ends conforms to the logic of a particular form of capital, intellectual capital, which necessitates, in order to convert itself from individual property to a collective patrimony, a symbolic operation capable of producing and imposing the image of a collective reality. In bringing together individuals within a single forum, the journal constitutes these individuals as a distinct and visible group, a structured and structuring ensemble, wielding the right to include and exclude membership, a site that marks and consecrates. (Boschetti 179)

Présence africaine was no exception to the "logic" of this market. The title of the journal itself translates this desire to impose a "collective reality" and opposes the self-limiting orientation of the earlier *L'Étudiant noir* to envisage an incursion within a wider field.[11] From the journal's first issue, this dual orientation is apparent: on the one hand plotting a space within a general, preexisting field dominated by *Les Temps modernes*, while at the same time pursuing a new, Afro-Atlantic orientation made possible through the accumulation of cultural capital acquired in this first field via the support of established intellectuals such as Gide and Sartre. The effectiveness of *Présence africaine* depended upon the successful exploitation of both these tactics.

THE TITLE page of the journal's first issue is revealing: rather than posing as a direct competitor to *Les Temps modernes*, *Présence africaine* appears as a creation of the most influential names of the intellectual field in which it is appearing. The first name to appear under the rubric "comité de patronage" is that of André Gide. Gide's support gives the newborn journal the stamp of authority from the dominant literary figure of the interwar period. Thanks to Gide's turn to the Left in the 1930s and his denunciation of colonialism in *Voyage au Congo,* his patronage conferred unmistakable weight to such an enterprise. Gide's name, isolated at the top of the page, is followed by those of four negrophile French intellectuals (P. Rivet, Th. Monod, P. Maydieu, E. Mounier), in turn followed by those of three black intellectuals (C. S. Senghor, P. Hazoume, Richard Wright). Next come three leading voices of the preexisting intellectual field in which *Présence africaine* is appearing: J. P. Sartre, M. Leiris (then writing for *Les Temps modernes*), and A. Camus. Aimé Césaire's name appears with the title "direction revue internationale," followed by the twelve members of the "comité de direction" and, at the bottom of the page, the name of the journal's director, Alioune Diop. This typographical disposition is eloquent, favoring those voices that will confer upon the journal the authority to pronounce upon the events of the African diaspora.

The introductory articles that lay out the journal's editorial orientation make explicit a divided allegiance between an intended readership of French intellectuals and a nascent African intellectual community. Both

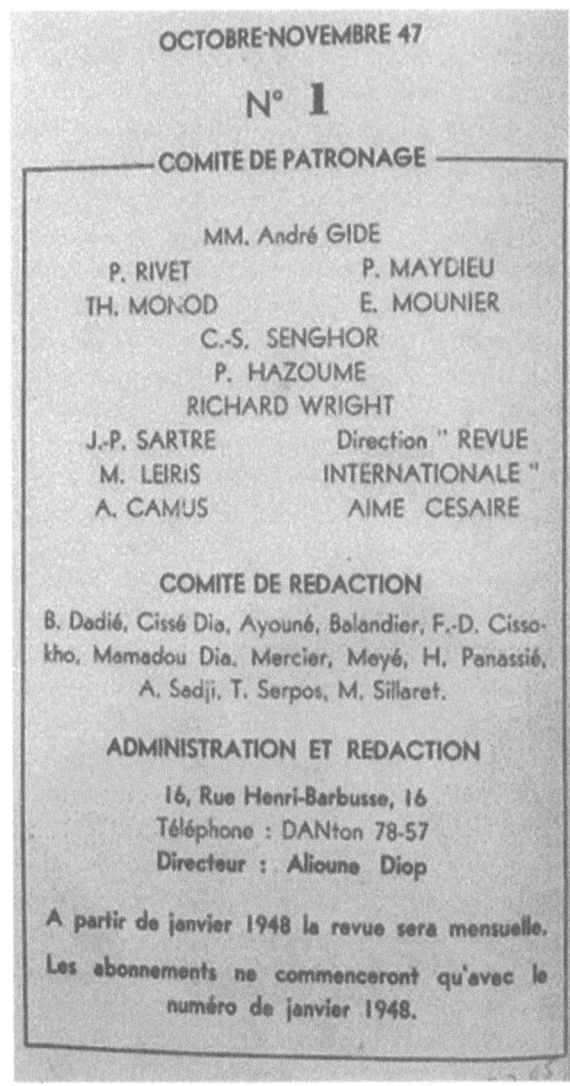

Figure 7. *Présence africaine* title page, 1947

Gide and Sartre provide articles with the former group in mind. Gide's "avant-propos" invokes a *nous* who have only begun to understand the black world through its art and music (3–5). It is only at the end of his piece that Gide, in deference to Alioune Diop, makes a halfhearted, paternalistic gesture to a hypothetical black intellectual community: "The present journal hopes to reach a black audience with what we have to say to them; but moreover and above all, it hopes to offer them the means to speak to us" (5).

Sartre's article "Présence Noire" is also directed at a European readership, with Sartre posing as the bad conscience of a racist culture, a culture both condescendingly tolerant of the few blacks present in the French metropolis and entirely alienated from the injustice occurring within the countries from which those few students and bureaucrats have come. Like Gide, Sartre invokes a white, European *nous,* yet his invocation takes on an interesting ambiguity, since, as the dominant intellectual of his field, he is also the director of *Les Temps modernes*. Addressing a new player in the field of intellectual journals, Africa, he states, has been an "absence" in the area of "our concerns." "Yesterday Germany, today the U.S.S.R. and the United States" (28). While these may be the major geopolitical concerns of the majority of Europeans in 1947, more to the point, these are exactly the topics that *Les Temps modernes* ("nous") was routinely addressing during that period. *Présence africaine,* in other words, is to be understood not as a competitor for Sartre's hegemonic position but rather as a complementary participant, occupying a structural opening that *Les Temps modernes* has left unaddressed.

Taking its place between the articles by Gide and Sartre, Alioune Diop's article, "*Niam n'goura* or the Reasons for the Existence of *Présence africaine,*" explicitly states—in opposition to his French patrons—that "we address ourselves principally to African youth" (8). While this might seem to argue for an ideological opposition between Diop and Sartre, the former's rhetoric clearly marks his location within the field of existentialism: "We have no choice. We are henceforth engaged in a heroic phase of history. Either one accepts death (when one obstinately hangs on to individual happiness), or else one conquers salvation and the chances for greatness" (14). The combination of Diop's personal, evangelical fervor with a Sartrean existentialist discourse of *engagement* is patent. While such statements appear to have only limited relevance to the editorial purposes of Diop's article, they in fact perform a crucial function in asserting the journal's *présence* within a cultural field from which it has been heretofore absent, appropriating, through the mastery of a socially dominant discourse (Sartrean existentialism), a form of cultural capital crucial to the success of the journal.

Further evidence of this discursive appropriation occurs in J. Howlett's "Absence et Présence." A philosophical reflection on the terms of its title, the article appears an extreme abstraction relative to the journal's concerns, instead pursuing an existentialist interrogation of Being: "There is nothing for [Man] which is not the experience of a lack of Being, in any case his plenitude can only be imagined as that of a pure in-itself" (51).[12] The inclusion of this article, however, serves to confirm the philosophical seriousness of *Présence africaine,* bestowing essential credentials for any journal that hoped to compete in a field dominated by *Les Temps modernes.* Each issue of the young journal engages Sartre. In issue number three, M. M. Davy's review of *Situations I* appears; no explanation is offered for the review's presence in a journal of the African world, nor is any attempt made to describe the book's relevance to the concerns of the journal. This constant reference to Sartre's thought and literary production has a performative—rather than strictly intellectual—function, consistently serving to place *Présence africaine* beside its more famous rival and to solicit Sartre's continued support by paying homage to him.

Aimé Césaire's participation in the first issues of *Présence africaine* did not occur in the form of his own contributions. Rather, Césaire's name appears in each of the early issues of the journal, along with frequent, laudatory reviews of his work. Issue number two includes a short review of the *Cahier,* number three an evocation of "Two black poets of the French language: Aimé Césaire et Léopold Senghor," while the journal's fourth issue features the longer article, "Aimé Césaire, Poet of Freedom" by Hubert Juin. Following this early support of the young poet,[13] only two references to Césaire appear until the journal's restructuring in 1955: brief comments on Césaire in George Balandier's "Black Literature in French,"[14] a brief review of *Discours sur le colonialisme* in issue 10–11, and "Negritude: Reality or Mystification?" which in fact consists almost entirely of "reflections on [Sartre's] 'orphée noire'" by Albert Franklin, in issue fourteen from 1952. Césaire's authorial absence is perhaps explained by its coincidence with his most intense period of political engagement; this tendency reaches its extreme as Césaire quietly disappears from the list of the editorial board in the last two issues (8–9, 10–11) of the first series.

THE APPEARANCE of *Présence africaine* in a "New Series" in 1955 marks far more than a moment in its publishing history. This little-noticed occurrence was in fact the first in a series of events that quietly initiated a fully mature phase of the decolonization movement within the sphere of cultural production.[15] It left its only traces in the pages of the first issue of the journal's new series, whose editorial board had changed radically from the older edition. The previous domination of the French intellectuals whose names gave symbolic weight to the journal, consecrating it within a competitive intellectual field, has been overthrown. In fact, there is now only a single communal "comité *Présence africaine*." Césaire's name here reappears within this group purged of French intellectuals. The makeup of the journal's new committee, as well as the typographic layout in which it is presented, serves as a faint, precocious historical prefiguration of the more familiar aesthetic interventions that announce the imminent political upheavals of decolonization; "Here too," as Edward Said has observed of the literature of decolonization in general, "culture is in advance of politics, military history, or economic process" and the production of a new, postcolonial subjectivity initiated in Césaire's 1939 *Cahier* would soon force the abandonment of a highly conservative French colonialism (200). As such, Césaire's aesthetic production stands among the most dramatic confirmation of Hardt and Negri's assertion of the profound "power of cultural movements" (275) to force the adaptation of fundamentally conservative processes such as colonialism: "resistance is actually prior to power, . . . When imperial government intervenes, it selects the libratory impulses of the multitude in order to destroy them, and in return it is driven forward by resistance" (360).

Présence africaine's discreet 1955 transformation heralds the debate that was to explode onto its pages (and indeed into all of the French intellectual field of 1955–56) regarding "national" poetry. No longer relying on the borrowed symbolic capital of Gide, Sartre, & Co., by 1955 *Présence africaine* had apparently acquired sufficient resources to strike out on its own. This gesture of independence would soon be repeated over and over again, in the most diverse realms: the aesthetic (Césaire's refusal to accept the normative authority of Aragon's "national" sonnet), cultural (*Présence africaine*'s 1956 Paris conference and its proclamation of black cultural independence), political (Césaire's 1956 letter to Maurice Thorez announcing his resignation from the P.C.F.), and finally world-historical (the actual African independences, led by Kwame Nkrumah and Sékou Touré). This multidimensional maturity received its clearest articulation in Césaire's letter to Maurice Thorez: "We, men *[hommes]* of color, in this precise moment of historical development, have become conscious, taken possession of the entire field of our singularity and we are ready to assume, on every level and in every domain, the responsibilities that

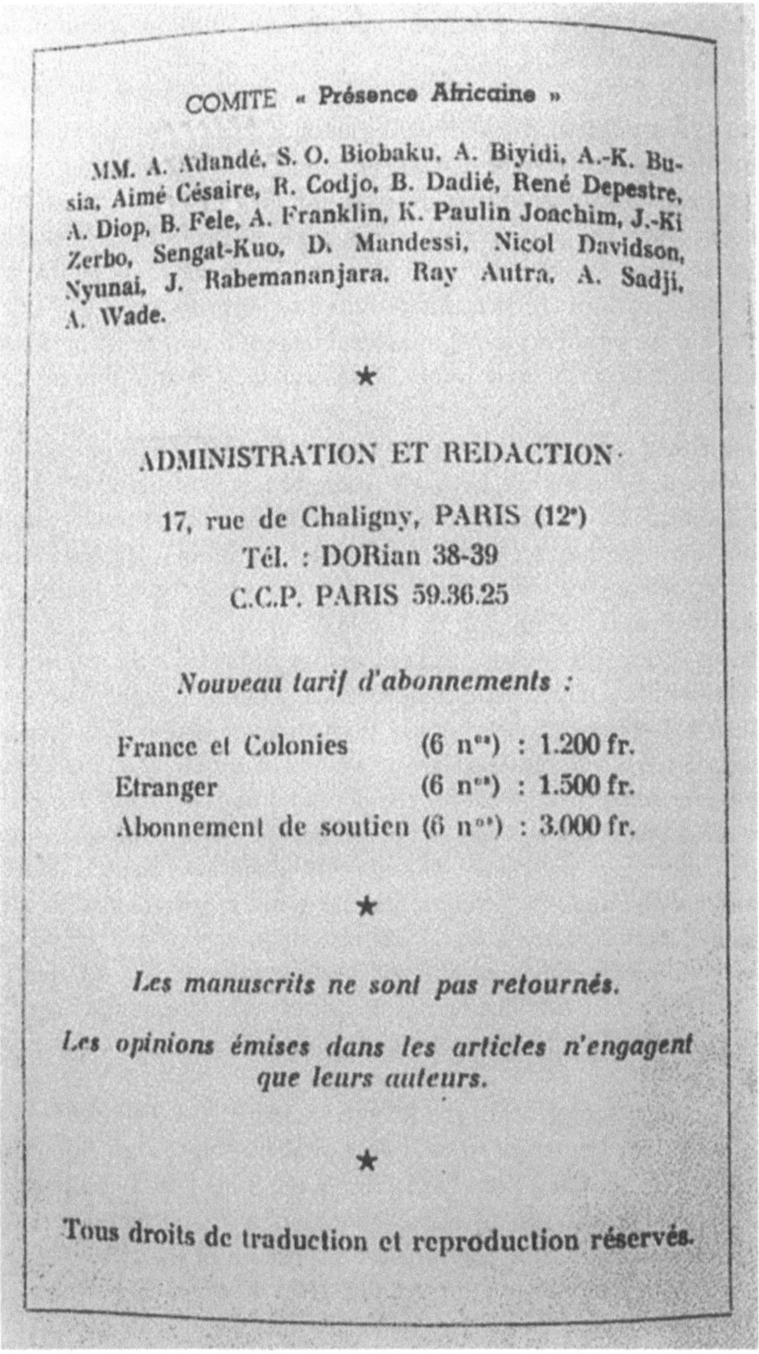

COMITE « Présence Africaine »

MM. A. Adandé, S. O. Biobaku, A. Biyidi, A.-K. Busia, Aimé Césaire, R. Codjo, B. Dadié, René Depestre, A. Diop, B. Fele, A. Franklin, K. Paulin Joachim, J.-Ki Zerbo, Sengat-Kuo, D. Mandessi, Nicol Davidson, Nyunai, J. Rabemananjara, Ray Autra, A. Sadji, A. Wade.

ADMINISTRATION ET REDACTION

17, rue de Chaligny, PARIS (12ᵉ)
Tél. : DORian 38-39
C.C.P. PARIS 59.36.25

Nouveau tarif d'abonnements :

France et Colonies   (6 nᵒˢ) : 1.200 fr.
Etranger   (6 nᵒˢ) : 1.500 fr.
Abonnement de soutien (6 nᵒˢ) : 3.000 fr.

Les manuscrits ne sont pas retournés.

Les opinions émises dans les articles n'engagent que leurs auteurs.

Tous droits de traduction et reproduction réservés.

Figure 8. *Présence africaine* title page, 1955

proceed from this awakening of consciousness" (qtd. in Toumson and Henry-Valmore 161).

FURTHER EVIDENCE of this increasing autonomy can be found in Césaire's celebrated poem "Le verbe marronner," which first appeared in *Présence africaine* in 1955, the same year as the journal's mutation into an independent "New Series." The poem castigates René Depestre for his capitulation to Louis Aragon's demands for a "national poetry" along the lines of socialist realism (Arnold, *Modernism and Negritude*) 180–84). It is written in the intimate tone of one friend to another, every attempt being made to minimize the appearance of a hierarchical relationship between the two poets. Depestre is the "valiant cavalier of the tom-tom," Césaire evoking their camaraderie through the use of the first-person plural ("will we maroon ourselves?"). Césaire's recurrent image of blood ("I accuse the bad manners of our blood"), the depository of a millennial culture, here evokes the ties that unite the two black Antilleans. The poem itself is structured around the opposition of two worlds, that of France and its intellectual traditions and the world of Brazil and the greater black Atlantic. The poet's voice is a call to freedom arising from the *mornes*, the Antillean hills to which marooning slaves historically escaped, urging the enslaved (Depestre) to break away from their subjection. The series of images that make up the poem create a mood of nostalgia (or, more pertinently, *saudades brasileiros*) for the poet's home and nature. Images of two areas predominate: those of the Antilles *(Boukman, tam-tam, rhum, vodou, mornes, canne à sucre, Dessalines)* and those of Brazil *(macumba, Brésil, Bahia, Botafogo, Batuque, favelas)*. Césaire, perhaps already planning his departure from the P.C.F., contrasts this evocation of a shared existential and geographic homeland with the alienating effects of Depestre's prostration before the bureaucrats of culture, who are more concerned with "the relation between poetry and the Revolution ... and the dialectical detour."

The poet, however, is not speaking to Depestre from their native land, urging the latter to return from a place of alienation to their homeland. He is himself speaking from Paris ("From the Seine I send you in Brazil my greetings"), the seat of Francophone political and cultural power. Through this contingent geographical disposition of the two poets, the subtle disproportion between them that gives the poem its performative force is reintroduced. The warm, gently prodding and nostalgic tone of the poem sugarcoats the fact that Césaire, in 1955, now felt himself authorized to tell Depestre how the latter should be writing poetry. Césaire had by this time effectively attained a position remarkably similar to that of the Breton who twenty years before had strategically reaffirmed his (Breton's) dominance of the French avant-garde when he designated Césaire's *Cahier* as "the greatest lyrical monument of the age." Similarly, Césaire in 1955 felt himself empowered to define the parameters of valid poetic discourse within the Francophone black diaspora. That Césaire was acting as his objective placement in the intellectual field called upon him to do, and not vainly striving for an effect he was not qualified to produce, is suggested by the poem's friendly tone and simultaneous forceful assuredness. Moreover, the poem, perfectly adapted to its field, produced exactly the effect desired. In the interchange regarding "national poetry" that appeared in the pages of the subsequent issue of *Présence africaine,* Depestre abandoned his defense of Aragon and, instead, submitting to a poetic alpha male, yielded to a new figure of cultural authority: "On the grounds of lyricism, and its black [nègre] possibilities, nothing, absolutely nothing, in principle, can now separate me from the aesthetic position that Aimé Césaire defined last year" (qtd. in Mouralis, *Litérature et dévéloppement* 445).[16]

The reactions to Césaire's *prise de position* in this debate in his article "Sur la poésie nationale" confirm his domination of the now-independent cultural-intellectual field created by *Présence africaine.* Following Césaire's introductory poetic explication, a series of commentators (Senghor, David Diop, Amadou Moustapha Wade, Georges Desportes, along with Depestre himself) proceed to align themselves behind their leader, Césaire, with each marking off a slight interpretive personalization. None, however, offers a critique of Césaire's fundamental position.[17]

ALONGSIDE THE increasing autonomy of *Présence africaine* during the 1950s, Césaire's poetry came to articulate the historical call for decolonization as it grew more concrete and historically rooted. Although even the *Cahier* had shown a concern for the depiction and critique of social injustice, its attack had remained generalized, anonymously evoking the miserable conditions in Fort-de-France; the poet's revolutionary proclamation of negritude was a cry for rebellion against the status quo of racism, poverty, and black self-hatred. The wartime poems collected in *Les Armes miraculeuses* continued to reveal a surrealist concern for a revolutionary symbolic practice. By the time of the publication of *Ferrements* in 1960, however, Césaire was writing about slain Martinican dockworkers, the newly independent African states, and other topical subjects. Perhaps most typical of his turn to a historically referential poetry is his 1957 poem in memory of the revolutionary hero Louis Delgrès, whose refusal to submit to Napoleon's reinstatement of slavery and subsequent martyrhood had been largely forgotten by the Guadeloupeans for whom he had sacrificed himself.[18]

The theory of artistic practice that Césaire developed in this period adheres to an existentialist concept of the engaged intellectual able to enlighten his readers and lead them to revolutionary consciousness through a production-based model of autonomous, creative subjectivity. Césaire's 1959 speech before the Second Congress of Black Writers and Artists in Rome illustrates this stance: "Cultural creation, precisely because it is creation, disturbs. It overthrows, firstly the colonial hierarchy, where of the colonized *consumer* it makes a *creator*. . . . And this is why we must create. . . . It is up to poets, to writers, to men of culture, stirring up in the daily sufferings and denials of justice, memories and hopes, to constitute these great reserves of faith, these great silos of forces from which the people draw in critical moments the courage to assert themselves and to force the future. Some have said that the writer is an engineer of souls" (qtd. in Delas 132–33).

This move away from the aestheticism of the *Tropiques* articles did not imply any reduction in the self-aggrandizement of the poet Césaire had proclaimed during the war. He now calls upon the "man of culture," however, to play a prophetic, godlike role as the "engineer of souls."[19] Césaire here makes explicit both the transformative potential of the production-based subjectivity first harnessed in the *Cahier* as well as its grandiloquent, elitist glorification of a narcissistic subjectivity. The gradual evolution of Césaire's creative production toward a more politically engaged practice in this period is directly traceable, if not abstractly reducible, to the biographical changes he himself had undergone since the writing of his first mature work. On one level, this change can be explained as a result of Césaire's own increasing militancy as he grappled with the historical dilemmas of the postwar colonial world. The specific form this evolution took, however, was a direct result of the conjunctural possibilities Césaire encountered as his own renown increased. The most obvious of these preexisting structural possibilities was his gradual abandonment of the stance of the isolated poet in favor of the Sartrean model of the engaged, prophetic intellectual.

As he achieved fame within the limited circle of those designated as intellectually competent to judge his poetry on purely aesthetic grounds (Breton, Gide, Sartre), Césaire was able to use this acquired capital to address a wider audience, one less able to judge his poetry against the larger field of its influences (Baudelaire, Rimbaud, Lautréamont, Appolinaire). Césaire himself has explained that this process was motivated by "the desire for a simpler language to converse not only with my students, but with peasants and workers" (qtd. in Toumson and Henry-Valmore 187). Once again, the parallel with Sartre's postwar mutation from academic philosopher to social critic and playwright is striking; it is to be explained not by any conscious mimicry but rather through Sartre and Césaire's occupation of homologous positions within intellectual fields, French and black Atlantic.[20]

Césaire's adoption of the prophetic model of intellectual engagement also corresponded with a crisis in international power relations occurring at the moment of the drive for independence and the subsequent formation of newly independent African states. As with other periods of political upheaval in a French society in which intellectuals had historically played important roles (the consolidation of the Third Republic and the Dreyfus Affair, the appearance of the Front Populaire in the 1930s, and Sartre's role as a public intellectual at the end of the second world war), the end of French colonialism created a number of new political entities in need of social legitimization. Césaire's move to an engaged aesthetic practice is thus part of a historically recurring pattern, here taking novel form amid the historically unique process of decolonization.

This mutation occurred as Césaire occupied a previously existing structural opening within the intellectual field marked by the failure of journals such as *Les Temps modernes* to address black Atlantic culture and history. One of the effects of Césaire's increasing intellectual prestige was the attendant obligation that he speak for the voiceless masses. Here his engagement largely replicated the inherited practice of powerful intellectuals stretching from Hugo's "L'histoire d'un crime" to Zola's "J'accuse" and Malraux's "La Tentation de l'Occident." This transformation was one of the primary markers of Césaire's gradual accumulation of symbolic capital. Not only was he a consecrated poet; he had been the political leader of Martinique since 1945. This historical process had the effect of giving weight to his pronouncements, making him someone whose opinion on matters of decolonization would be listened to and taken seriously.

Césaire's appropriation of the role of *intellectuel engagé* was thus both active and reactive. For although he was taking up a position that functioned in largely prefashioned ways, with the intellectual's capacity to pass judgment sanctified by the battery of analytical tools he had mastered, the actual immanent form Césaire's incursion took moved in directions not immediately predictable from the examples of metropolitan intellectuals such as Zola or Sartre.

Following his interventions within the pages of *Présence africaine* in 1955, Césaire once again disappeared from its pages until the 1959 publication of the poem "Hommage à Louis Delgrès" and his article "The Political Thought of Sékou Touré." The latter marks a defining moment in Césaire's intellectual project, while the issue in which it appeared presents a synchronic *aperçu* of the Francophone black Atlantic field circa 1959. The article served to consolidate Césaire's clearly dominant position within the intellectual field the journal had come to define, as well as to articulate a uniquely and problematically affirmative moment in Césaire's lifelong struggle to actualize the goal of autonomy within African diasporic experience.

AIMÉ CÉSAIRE's article "The Political Thought of Sékou Touré" appeared in the December 1959 issue of the journal *Présence africaine* entitled "Guinée indépendante!" On September 28, 1958, the citizens of the French West African colony of Guinea-Conakry voted by the margin of 95 percent to reject Charles de Gaulle's call to participate in a West African community of states in continued association with France. Guinea thus became the only French colony to choose democratically the path of immediate independence in the history of French colonialism. While colonies such as Sénégal and Côte d'Ivoire remained within the mantle of colonialism and chose to wait for France to grant their independence largely on its own terms, Guinea asserted its autonomy in a gesture that echoed across the remnants of the crumbling French empire.

De Gaulle made good on his word, conceding Guinea full and immediate autonomy; the former colonizers quickly withdrew, destroying archives and infrastructure—as one Guinean alive at the time said to me, taking even the light bulbs, then coming back for the sockets. Guinea found itself an isolated, underdeveloped country confronted with the huge task of forming a nation with little more than its human resources. The early years of Guinean independence appeared to make good on these promises, seeing schooling rates more than triple from 9 percent in 1957 to 33 percent in 1962. The later years of President Sékou Touré's rule until his death in 1984, however, saw this once-proud trade unionist resort increasingly to human rights abuses against his real and imagined foes in a cycle of ever-increasing paranoia.

The utopian aspirations of African independence contained in the country's historic "no" vote of September 1958 echo throughout this issue of *Présence africaine*, taking us beyond an abstract condemnation of Sékou Touré's plunge into totalitarianism. Guinea—like so many of the objects of Aimé Césaire's reflection—offers an irresolvable contradiction, where a spirit of determinate, utopian freedom calls forth its simultaneous realization and negation in the birth of a new, autonomous nation and future dictatorship.[21] This ambiguity is crystallized in Césaire's contribution to "Guinée indépendante!" Like the articles of Alioune Diop, the French Marxist historian Jean Suret-Canale, Jacques Rabemananjara, David Diop, and Léonard Sainville, among which it appears, Césaire's text points to the enormous promise of independence and freedom, at once political, economic, moral, and existential, encapsulated in this historic moment. At the same time, our hindsight allows us to watch with dismay as an insightful, brilliant poet and politician unwittingly betrays that hope in the act of actually affirming the reality of a free Guinean state, the positive image of a putative utopia that could never coincide with the violent world that was newly independent Guinea.

Alioune Diop inaugurates this issue with his "Impressions of a Voyage." Diop underscores the importance of Guinea's gesture: not merely a "political independence," the country's vote implies an accession to autonomy that he terms "political sovereignty" (4). Diop then immediately breaks off his argument, and the fatal flaw that will undermine in various degrees each of the articles in this issue of *Présence africaine* appears. For in speaking of Guinea's "political sovereignty," Diop has opened a chasm between a putative empirical, real, and existing sovereignty and his representation of it within his discourse. In actually naming Guinean "independence," the word is stripped of its promise. When Diop calls upon it to coincide with a phenomenal world to which it does not yet correspond, the promise of a noncoercive society encapsulated in the notice "Guinée indépendante!" stands revealed as hollow ideology.

Diop must struggle to span this chasm between the referent and the real, and he works to cover the insufficiency of his own assertion through a regressive gesture of invocation: "That [e.g., the primacy of political sovereignty] is, at least, the feeling of the Guinean leaders: the primacy of the political, the primacy of a political sense of the actual circumstances, via the autonomy of each type of activity or human knowledge.... Political comportment appears to them the privileged domain of reflection for developing countries. It offers the only appropriate language by which a people can immediately confront, appreciate, and know itself, recognizing its functional unity and personality" (4). Not only is he, Diop, merely *speaking* of independence, but he is now speaking of others speaking of independence. The editor of *Présence africaine* can only formulate the wishful assertion of the existence of Guinean autonomy, when in fact such a freedom can have validity only in its phenomenal realization. Faced with this antinomy, Diop is forced to fall back on external authority, as he echoes the assertions of the Guinean leaders.

Here, the celebration of autonomy betrays its own terms, and *Présence africaine*, the organ of the intellectual maturity of the African diaspora, hands over its independence to the ideological program of the nascent state bureaucracy that would soon imprison and liquidate its opponents, real and imagined: "Dedicated to loyally serving their people, to whom they [the political leaders of Guinea] have vowed their undivided faith and a jealous love, they judge that culture is less an object of politics than a constitutive element of politics" (4). Wavering in its intellectual independence, Diop's text continually threatens to become political propaganda. The specter of bureaucratic totalitarianism appears even in his ringing defense of the country's enthusiasm: "In the smallest villages, weekly conferences bring together the inhabitants to discuss, one by one, international issues, African affairs, and Guinean affairs. The government takes care that none of these great decisions remains unnoticed or misunderstood by the people" (5).

The fundamental weakness of Diop's text is its lack of experiential content: despite the assurance of his title that he is relating firsthand impressions of a voyage, his short text is little more than a series of empty declarations. And yet, Diop's hollow phrases nonetheless allow for an echo of the uniqueness of this historical moment to persist and reach across time to us: "The fundamental conviction that [Guinea] has drawn from its cruel colonial experience is that it can only depend upon itself and its own resources. This is doubtless the most revolutionary and original aspect of the Guinean Event. . . . This Guinea for whom some in the West still express scorn, this Guinea at her birth, abandoned to isolation and nudity, this Guinea wounded and fragile, is ready to be transfigured by her faith, her courage, and her initiatives into a privileged site of African dignity" (5, 7).

The article following Diop's, written by the historian of colonialism Jean Suret-Canale, could hardly be more different. Entitled "Guinea Within the Colonial System," it remedies the lack of content that weakened Diop's article, tracing the history of the French colonial occupation of Guinea through the end of the second world war and the political awakening of the country. The article is richly researched, synthesizing portions of the research presented in Suret-Canale's massive three-volume, fifteen-hundred-page study of the social and economic history of West Africa through 1960. The author observes that the country's inhabitants themselves were almost entirely absent from earlier studies by the governors and military men of the colonization of Guinea. Suret-Canale's article, in contrast, focuses for perhaps the first time upon the impact colonial processes had, in his words, upon "Guineans themselves, who worked the earth in the brush, suffering beneath their burden along the paths of the interior" (9).

The author compresses nearly a century of French exploitation, duplicity, massacres, and both passive and active support of ongoing slavery into some thirty-five pages. In Suret-Canale's words, "Forced cultivation, military duty and recruitment, and taxes, these were the benefits that the 'French Peace' bestowed on the people, especially the most humble, the former captives, crushed more than ever, despite all the 'humanitarian declarations' written for the edification of European public opinion" (34). In 1935, after a half-century of French colonization, Suret-Canale reports that there existed 6,558 primary school students from a population of 2 million and no secondary schooling, whereas Mungo Park at the turn of the nineteenth century had found Coranic schools in the smallest villages of the Fouta Djallon (42). "At the onset of the Second World War," the historian concludes, "for the mass of the Guinean population—that is to say the peasantry—the results of colonization appear absolutely negative. The meager colonial infrastructure of railroads, post offices, telegraphs, trails and a port only served to hand over the peasants to the usurers of international commerce and to intensify his or her exploitation. Schools and hospitals were accessible to only a privileged few. The peasant continued to live and work as did his ancestors, except that he worked more and ate less" (44). Malnutrition regularly recurred as the French eradicated local farming in favor of monocultures for exportation.[22]

Aimé Césaire's article "The Political Thought of Sékou Touré" was written amid a series of better-known works exploring the vicissitudes of independence in the African diaspora. It appeared in *Présence africaine* four years after Césaire's 1955 polemic *Discourse on Colonialism* and immediately preceded the poet's two meditations upon Haitian history, *Toussaint Louverture* (1960) and *La Tragédie du roi Christophe* (1963) (discussed in the following chapter).

Knowing as we do today Touré and Guinea's historical development since independence, Césaire's homage sits uneasily amid the *Discourse*'s equation of colonialism and Naziism and the analyses of the descent of a free nation into tyranny and dictatorship in his two later works. Despite its lapses into blind affirmation, Césaire's article gains rhetorical force through its constant dialogue with quotations from Sékou Touré himself, beginning with Sékou's most famous pronouncement in the days leading up to Guinea's historic "no" vote: "We ourselves have a primary, indispensable need, that of our dignity. And there is no dignity without liberty. We prefer poverty amid freedom to riches amid enslavement" (66). Césaire here briefly participates in the cult of personality that he would soon critique in Haiti's Christophe, referring to Sékou as "the decisive African Man."

As he would in those later works, Césaire posits Guinean independence in terms of a Hegelian coming to self-consciousness after the two moments of a precolonial immediacy and subsequent self-alienation in colonialism. In Césaire's view, the passage into physical independence engenders a corresponding "psychological transformation" from the alienation of the colonized into "liberated man" (68). Both Césaire, who had yet to walk upon the continent, and Sékou Touré himself repeatedly invoke a hypostatized "African personality" that will supposedly furnish the content of Guinean self-consciousness.

Despite Césaire's assurances that this personality is only a process or a project, the specter of those who disappeared into Sékou's death camps after refusing to recognize themselves in his "African personality" constantly reappears with the virtue of our twenty-twenty hindsight. Witness the impossible balancing act of Césaire's description of Sékou Touré's political project: the Guinean state will result from "the active cooperation of all, in which the individual will disappear and at the same time fully recognize himself, for the first time" (68). Here, the logic of a sublime erasure of the individual within the absolute state overtakes—as it would again in *La tragédie du roi Christophe*–the pursuit of freedom. As he had in *Discours sur le colonialisme,* Césaire condemns the process of Western "abstraction" that, in its reduction of human subjects to mere fungible objects, has resulted in much of the genocidal violence and tyranny of this century. At the same time, he ignores the degree to which his and Sékou Touré's discourse is complicitous in this very abstraction. Césaire supports Sékou Touré as the latter condemns free thought to the domination of an unmediated "reality of the people." In Sékou Touré's words, "Society is not made for principles, for a philosophy, for a doctrine, for a science, but on the contrary, science, philosophy, and principles of action must be determined for the people and as a function of the realities of the people" (70). Sékou Touré's pronouncements announce the condemnation of free thought and its utopian capacity to move beyond the tyranny of the merely existing world at the very inception of a Guinean independence and transformation he was responsible in bringing about.

Césaire would henceforth avoid such positive affirmations of concretized social utopia, instead returning to its negative representation in his works of the 1960s, culminating in the 1966 condemnation of Mobutu's coup d'état in the play *A Season in the Congo*. And yet, beyond the horror of Sékou's infernal *Camp Boiro*, intimations of autonomy and enlightenment offer themselves to us in the traces of that independence found in the music and dance of Guinea's *Ballets africains;* the writings of Camara Laye, Alioum Fantouré, and Williams Sassine; and even in the ambiguous words of Sékou Touré himself, with which Césaire's essay concludes: "The African, . . . kept apart from a world that had made him inferior through the practice of domination, this man stripped of everything, a foreigner in his own country, naked and diminished amid his own riches, . . . suddenly reemerged into the world to reclaim the entirety of his human rights and full participation in universal life. . . . Africa, yesterday a plaything and object of unbridled desires, is today fully engaged in the march toward freedom" (72–73).

The unique circumstances of an incipient Guinean independence—actively claimed rather than bestowed by a benevolent colonizer—implied a radical development of self-consciousness and autonomous historical development to the black intelligentsia writing in *Présence africaine,* a promise that was soon betrayed by the tyranny of the African independences. At the moment of its realization, Guinean independence represented for these intellectuals the unification of theory and practice and the active instantiation of the utopian ideals intimated in Césaire's concept of negritude. The subsequent isolation of Guinea, rarely perceived as anything more than economic tragedy, did in fact preserve a measure of those utopian ideals of 1958, not as Sékou Touré's affirmative, pseudocommunist ideology, but rather through the historically ambiguous act of self-abstraction. Guinean isolation, at once disastrous and utopian, captures even today the promise of autonomy as a refusal of assimilation in the juggernaut of economic globalization. The richness of contemporary Guinean culture that was preserved amid this isolation condemns the pretensions of a putative New World Order through the only means available to an economically underdeveloped country: self-sufficiency.

4 Cannibalizing Hegel
Decolonization and European Theory in *La tragédie du roi Christophe*

> Human history, the history of the progressing mastery of nature, continues the unconscious history of nature, of devouring and being devoured.
> —Theodor W. Adorno

IN HIS AESTHETIC works of the late 1950s and early 1960s, Aimé Césaire increasingly objectified both the historical process of decolonization and the complex role to be played by the prophetic intellectual, the "griot of his people." To do so, he drew upon a vast range of intellectual materials at his disposal, the most striking of which was the Hegelian model of dialectical historicism. Césaire's dialectical thought can be understood as a black Atlantic variant of the mode of understanding that forms the deep structure of postwar French thought in Hegelian Marxian thinkers such as Sartre. Sartre, like Alexandre Kojève before him, combined a utopian outlook with a prophetic stance in which he spoke to the unenlightened as the voice of truth. Both intellectual fashion and the antinomies of the postwar period themselves drove such thinkers to embrace dialectical thought as that most appropriate for an understanding of and working through of the dilemmas of history.

Aimé Césaire's appropriation of this dialectical historicism, while of the greatest consequence for his own original aesthetic creations, was hardly the inspired act of an isolated autodidact coming upon a long-forgotten author. The rediscovery of Hegel and the articulation of a new understanding of the implications of his 1807 *Phenomenology of Spirit* was one of the defining features of the Parisian intellectual world of the 1930s (its heroic phase, limited to a small group of the initiated in Kojève's seminar), the 1940s (which saw the gradual infiltration and consecration of this text within the Parisian intellectual milieu), and the 1950s (marked by the dominance and eventual contestation and toppling of what had become an intellectual idol). This rediscovery of Hegel occurred as a generational rejection of the institutionalized philosophies of Henri Bergson (at the

Collège de France) and Léon Brunschvig (at the Sorbonne) on the part of intellectuals of Sartre's generation in favor of German philosophy (Hegel and Kierkegaard as well as Heidegger, Husserl, and Scheler).[1]

This movement was inaugurated by a 1929 study by the French philosopher Jean Wahl on Hegel's *Phenomenology*, and it was spurred on by the influx of a group of East European intellectuals to Paris, including André Koyré and Alexandre Kojève. Césaire, as a brilliant, intellectually inquisitive *normalien*, and, later, poet, intellectual, and communist politician, was ideally placed to appropriate this intellectual fascination with Hegel and the symbolic capital gradually accumulating to his thought. While the Afrocentric use he was to make of this acquisition differed radically from that of the famous European members of the Parisian intelligentsia, Césaire's Hegelianism nonetheless placed him within a field in which a certain Hegel came to be the stamp of intellectual sophistication and a powerful mark of a thinker's participation within an intellectual elite.

In the aftermath of French poststructuralism in the 1970s and 1980s, attempts to salvage productive aspects of Hegel's multidimensional philosophy all but disappeared from French and Francophone studies. And yet, Vincent Descombes argues that French thought from the 1930s on itself grew out of the encounter of an entire generation of intellectuals with Alexandre Kojève and Jean Hyppolite's commentaries and translations of Hegel's *Phenomenology of Spirit*. Michel Foucault himself described the persistence of Hegel within the context of his generation's attempt to escape from Hegel's specter as he took over Jean Hyppolite's chair at the Collège de France on December 2, 1970: "But truly to escape Hegel involves an exact appreciation of the price we have to pay to detach ourselves from him. It assumes that we are aware of the extent to which Hegel, insidiously perhaps, is close to us; it implies a knowledge, in that which permits us to think against Hegel, of that which remains Hegelian. We have to determine the extent to which our anti-Hegelianism is possibly one of his tricks directed against us, at the end of which he stands, motionless, waiting for us" (235). True to Foucault's warning, Hegel's thought has not been surpassed. A crippled, merely instrumental reason, a parody of Hegel's notion of Absolute Spirit, has infiltrated our world to make it "reasonable" in only the most impoverished sense. The opportunity to make the world "rational," for it to attain its inherent potentiality, was missed; instead, this potentiality lives on as a feeble trace amid "rationalized" bureaucratic disempowerment, global hunger, and genocide, and we inherit only the painful memory of a *rendez-vous manqué* that persists as a dimly perceived imperative to realize reason's potentiality.

RECENTLY, IN fact, attention has begun to be paid to the legacy of Hegel in French thought.[2] For an entire generation of writers born in France's overseas colonies, a Paris-based education meant an immersion in an intellectual milieu in which Hegel's *Phenomenology* was the signal philosophical reference. For nearly three decades—from Kojève's 1933–39 lectures on the text[3] to the appearance of structuralism in the 1960s—the *Phenomenology*, seen through the lens of Hyppolite and Kojève, served within the Francophone world as the gold standard of one's assimilation of the highest realms of Western thought. The writings of Aimé Césaire, Alioune Diop, Léopold Sédar Senghor, Frantz Fanon, and Edouard Glissant were concretely affected by their education within this milieu, and their work bears the marks of the reigning existentialist and Marxist Hegelianism of the period within both its thematic content and extending into its deepest formal structures. Ato Sekyi-Otu has, for instance, recently shown how Frantz Fanon's *Les Damnés de la terre* incorporates Hegel's *Phenomenology* in its themes, structure, and theoretical methodology, and that a failure to recognize this intellectual heritage has led to widespread misunderstanding of Fanon's famous text.

Two decades before the appearance of *Les Damnés de la terre,* however, Césaire read the *Phenomenology* following its 1941 publication in Hyppolite's translation. He has recently recalled the youthful excitement he felt at discovering Hegel's philosophical elaboration of his own existential concerns: "When the French translation of the *Phenomenology* first came out, I showed it to Senghor, and said to him 'Listen to what Hegel says, Léopold: to arrive at the Universal, one must immerse oneself in the Particular!'"[4] Césaire's self-recognition in this putatively "alien" European object stands as a striking historical confirmation of the very process of alienation and self- recognition Hegel's text describes. Furthermore, an analysis of the dialectical, Hegelian tenor of Aimé Césaire's work is essential to fathom the Promethean undertaking he termed negritude. Such an examination can hope to underscore not only Césaire's crucial role in postwar French thought but also the astonishing intellectual virtuosity he brought to bear in moral outrage at the injustices of racism, colonialism, and human exploitation.

Although the socio-intellectual field constituted by the existentialist "Hegelians," led by Sartre, long ago achieved mythical dimensions, one important element in this constellation has been largely neglected. While Césaire is now acknowledged as one of the greatest poets of the twentieth century, his status within this second intellectual field is rarely mentioned. And yet, recognition of his appropriation of Hegel, possessing both constructive and limiting dimensions, is essential to an overall understanding of Césaire's work. This recognition broadens our conception of the postwar Parisian intellectual field, underscoring the presence of Afrocentric voices within this otherwise culturally homogenous sphere of production, voices that redirected the theoretical legacy of the West to critical ends. What Edward Said claims of Fanon applies equally to his teacher Césaire: "Both Fanon and Foucault, have Hegel, Marx, Freud, Nietzsche, Canguihelm, and Sartre in their heritage," Said comments, "yet only Fanon presses that formidable arsenal into antiauthoritarian service" (278).[5]

Césaire was inextricably bound to the culture he critiqued. Césaire was a student, like Sartre and Nizan before him, at the prestigious Lycée Henri IV and later at the even more celebrated (and selective) Ecole Normale Supérieure de la rue d'Ulm from 1934 to 1939; in addition, he was a deputy in the French Assembly, representing the overseas department of Martinique from 1946 to 1983. Following the postwar publication of his *Cahier d'un retour au pays natal* by Bordas, he became both a guiding voice of French Caribbean culture and an active, innovative, and ideologically autonomous presence on the Parisian intellectual scene.

Césaire's work was not only a crucial element in that constellation, but, as the previous chapter showed, he forged for himself a role structurally homologous to that of the Sartrean total intellectual in which Césaire accumulated intellectual and political capital by positioning himself as the archetypal black poet-statesman. His proximity to and familiarity with the existentialist movement and the functioning of that intellectual milieu (former *normalien,* consecration by Breton, growing fame in Francophone literary circles, Parisian presence as both an intellectual published in *Les Temps modernes* and *Présence africaine* and a deputy) allowed him successfully to fulfill this role.

Of these factors, his status as a former *normalien* most powerfully determined his participation in this field of intellectuals. For within the highly centralized French university system, that elite preparatory school for university professors formed in each generation an intellectual aristocracy that would dominate the Parisian intellectual world of its time.[6] While Césaire's success despite all odds within this system served to prove the (minimal) functioning of what was ideologically presented as a meritocracy, his temperament and irreducible difference (as a black colonial subject) made it impossible for him to assimilate entirely within the network of working and personal relationships in a field soon dominated by Sartre.

In this context, a web of influences and relationships determined Césaire's aesthetic and biographical trajectory as well as the preexisting structural openings and possibilities that he both discovered and created. The reigning dialectical historicism of the period was crucial for Césaire in both these respects; it formed the substance of his philosophy of history, and it offered him the culturally valorized ideological and structural foundation for his meditations on the dual historical problems of Caribbean history and the incipient African independences in the 1950s and 1960s.

Postcolonial Dialectical Historicism

A dominant tendency of Césaire criticism has been to examine the author's role in the historical decolonization movement. And yet, the relative lack of interest on the part of critics in the models and cultural materials Césaire appropriated in this area of his pursuits perhaps arises from the fact that an emphasis upon Césaire's intellectual *métissage,* drawing attention to his European "roots," would contradict an ideology that sees in negritude an Afrocentric black liberation theology. Césaire never varied in his opposition to the cultural "assimilation" of blacks within Franco-European society, from the *Cahier* and *Tropiques* through thirty years at the head of his Parti Progressiste Martiniquais. Though Césaire's many Franco-European influences are readily apparent, his politically engaged speeches and interviews often downplayed those influences in favor of the African and African American cultures celebrated by negritude.[7]

A second tendency in Césaire studies, however, has been concerned primarily with questions of artistic and theoretical influence in the area of aesthetic creation. Césaire applied his extensive intellectual faculties to the vast range of primary materials appearing both explicitly and in transformation throughout his poetry. Graziano Benelli, attempting to enumerate the range of these references, offers a useful and impressive summary of these fields of knowledge within Césaire's grasp: the mythological, including Greek antiquity, Christianity, Egyptian mythology, and most importantly the African and Antillean pantheons (primarily Yoruba, Bambara, and Vodou); geographical (references to rivers, mountains, deserts of Africa, the Third World, and the Americas predominate, with Europe and France in particular being almost entirely absent); references to historical characters (mainly African and Caribbean world historical figures such as Toussaint, Delgrès, and Lumumba); a vast range of rare fauna (mainly African) and flora (mainly Caribbean); and linguistic erudition, including extremely rare French terms of Greek, Latin, Provençal, Italian, English, Arabic, Portuguese, Dutch, Hebrew, and Russian origins, as well as other terms borrowed from various African languages. Within the scholarly literature on Césaire's influences, references to philosophers are extremely rare and almost never go beyond a cursory mention of Marx and Hegel.[8] Contrary to this perceived limitation of the range of Césaire's influences to the strictly aesthetic, his appropriation of a vast range of critical social thought, much of it European in origin, influenced in decisive fashion the entirety of his productions in poetry, prose, and theater.

SARTRE'S FOUNDATIONAL essay "Orphée Noire," written as the preface to Léopold Senghor's 1948 collection, *L'Anthologie de la poésie nègre et malgache,* is remembered mainly for its inflammatory description of negritude as an "antiracist racism," the negative moment in a dialectical movement toward "a race-less society" (280). The essay was also, however, the first to apply a Kojèvian reading of Hegel's *Phenomenology* to the black world. Sartre links the suffering and violence of slavery and racism to the entry of blacks into historical existence ("Suffering... becomes historical insofar as the intuition of suffering confers a collective past and assigns a goal in the future" [276]). Sartre's theorization of this process develops Kojève's excursus on the historicization of human experience through the violence of slavery understood by the latter as the destructive negation of cyclical, natural time, replaced by historical becoming and linear transformation: "Race is transmuted into historicity, the black Present explodes and becomes temporal, Negritude inserts itself with its past and its future into Universal History, it is no longer a state nor even an existential attitude, it is a becoming; the contribution of blacks in the evolution of humanity is no longer a flavor, a taste, a rhythm, an authenticity, a bouquet of primitive instincts: it is a dated enterprise, a patient construction, a future" (277).[9] Although "Orphée Noire" may have been one of the instigators of Césaire's articulation of the historical problematic that would result in *La tragédie du roi Christophe,* Césaire'a reflection went beyond such brief comments found in Sartre's essay, instead finding its formal logic in the Hegelian philosophy that underlies Sartre's comments.

CÉSAIRE'S POETIC production preceding the publication of *La tragédie du roi Christophe* often outlined a Kojèvian dialectical historicism. In a passage of the *Cahier d'un retour au pays natal* that directly prefigures the problematic to be explored in *La tragédie du roi Christophe,* the poet calls upon his people to move forth out of the repetition of Nature ("au pas du monde") and to accede to a historical, fully human existence through a construction ("faire") that will not necessarily preclude violence ("conquérir")

> because it is not true that the work of man is finished
> that we have nothing to do in the world

that we parasite this world
that it is enough for us to fall into step with the world
but
the work of man has only just begun
and it remains for man to conquer all
interdictions immobilized in the corners of his fervor (51).[10]

The prophetic tone of the *Cahier* appears again in the poem "Corps perdu," first published in the collection of that name in 1949. The poet here recovers the memory of his people ("I hiss yes I hiss very ancient things" (243). Césaire's violent, demiurgic *prise de parole* attempts to shatter the preexisting world, bringing a new one into being, thus inaugurating a historical process of development:

[I] shall raise a scream so violent
that I shall splatter the whole sky
and with my branches torn to shreds
and with the insolent jet of my wounded and solemn bole
I shall command the islands to be (245, translation modified)[11]

Although written a decade after the *Cahier*, the tone has not noticeably changed.

By the publication of *Ferrements* in 1960, however, Césaire's rhetoric has moved much closer to the historically referential form it would acquire in *Christophe*. The poem "The Time of Freedom" takes its inspiration from an actual historical event: the death of twelve protesters during the French repression of anticolonial riots in the Côte-d'Ivoire on January 30, 1950 (Toumson and Henry-Valmore 110). Césaire articulates the poem around the distinction between the traditional, colonialist prejudice of an ahistorical, natural Africa ("Africa is asleep") and a series of precise, dated events that by their very articulation imply the continent's participation in historical processes ("the Governor's wireless had peddled his lies . . . it was 1950 in the month of February" [321]). Beyond the precise nature of the events the poem recounts, the poem's alliance of Africa's entrance into a universalist history ("History I tell of Africa as it awakes") with a thematic of violence ("when under the composite memory of chicotes / they piled up the knotted black fire") evokes Kojève's insistence that the accession of humans to historical existence can be achieved only through the violent, revolutionary negation of a previous state of existence ("when in the breathing of the best men the colonialist tsetse will have disappeared" [321]).

125 Cannibalizing Hegel

FURTHER EVIDENCE of the vast range of Césaire's theoretical influences appears in one of his most celebrated speeches, "Culture et colonization," given at the Sorbonne in 1956 on the occasion of the Premier Congrès des Ecrivains et Artistes Noirs (Arnold, *Modernism and Negritude* 184–87). Although the speech itself is a fascinating document in the history of the decolonization movement, it is particularly eloquent in displaying Césaire's wide-ranging erudition. In Césaire's poetic production, this erudition generally appears in the guise of a fabulous lexical virtuosity, one that rarely evokes actual source material. In this 1956 speech, on the other hand, Césaire mounts a veritable tour de force of historical references in the span of a dozen pages. This spectacle was hardly gratuitous; it in fact functioned as the unacknowledged illustration of the speech's thesis: that the task of "black men of culture" in 1956 was to integrate freely their multiple heritages, European and African, into a new culture, a culture free from the distortions inherent in a colonial context.[12]

Césaire's self-understanding as the enlightened voice of the downtrodden, as the intellectual vanguard of the colonized, here produced a contradictory, compromised utopianism. Though he ends by deferring the act of cultural creation to "the people, our people, liberated from their chains, our peoples and their creative genius finally rid of what hinders and sterilizes them,"[13] the modesty of this formulaic gesture is belied by Césaire's entire speech, which parades a panoply of names before his audience, assembled at the Sorbonne from every corner of the globe. Césaire includes long quotes from Hegel's *Introduction to the Philosophy of History* and *Logic*; Marx (*Capital* vol. 3); Marcel Mauss; Spengler's *Decline of the West*; the *Courrier de l'UNESCO* of 1956; Margaret Mead; Malinowski (*Introductory Essay on the Anthropology of Changing African Cultures* and *The Dynamics of Culture*); Toynbee *(The World and the West);* the American anthropologist Kroeber; Captain Cook's description of his voyages to the Hawaiian islands; two long citations from Nietzsche's *Birth of Tragedy* as well as references in passing to the ethnologists Frobénius, Schubart, Roger Callois, Béguin, and Panniker; Lenin; the politicians Deschamps and Doumer; the historian Berr; and the Hawaiian prince Kamehamela II. This gallery is crowned by Césaire's untranslated citation of an obscure Roman prefect from the fifth century AD named Rutilius Namatianus, whom Césaire draws upon as an illustration of the fact that the mentality of colonization goes back at least as far as Rome's occupation of Gaul.

This virtuosic assemblage of discourses was neither gratuitous nor unprecedented. It occurred within a context (the 1956 Premier Congrès des Ecrivains et Artistes Noirs sponsored by *Présence africaine*) in which, implicitly, the capabilities of black intellectuals were to be demonstrated to the world. The manner in which Césaire proceeded replicated the tactic that had served Sartre: the assertion of mastery through the accumulation of discourses. This tactic marks Césaire's poetic production in general. Within this speech, however, the context and the unambiguous use of source material visibly demonstrate this mastery to his assembled peers.[14]

Though the heterogeneous nature of black culture is recognized by Césaire, his argument here is against a theory of *métissage culturel,* judging this *métissage* to have generally occurred within a distorted social structure in which appropriation by the colonial subject occurred only insofar as it was sanctioned by the structures of a colonial system. Instead, Césaire evokes a necessary act of assimilation of multiple exterior elements within a single totalizing and unified subject, in an act of cultural and intellectual cannibalization: "The borrowing [of cultural materials] is only valid when it is balanced by an interior state that *calls for it* and that definitively integrates it to the subject assimilating it, . . . that makes what is exterior interior" (117).[15] In this passage, Césaire clearly articulates for colonial experience the general model of historical experience inherited from Hegel's *Phenomenology* described in the introduction: "Experience is . . . this movement, in which the immediate, the unexperienced, i.e. the abstract . . . becomes alienated from itself and then returns to itself from this alienation" (21).

In his speech, Césaire postulates a unified postcolonial subject not as an actuality but as a project or process marked by a dialectical relation between subject and object. His speech itself, as with his neologism "negritude," is thus performative in nature and follows the Hegelian logic of an expressive subjectivity able to recognize itself in the creations (or "expressions") of its production that defines Western critical thought of the period, from Lukács to early Habermas.[16] Césaire's performance can be seen as an objectification of the newly autonomous subject of negritude, embodied by Césaire himself, at the heart of the objective world that both enslaved it and gave it the materials to construct its freedom (Paris, and the Sorbonne specifically). Césaire's speech, demonstrating at once the subject's alienation within the objective materials of Western Civilization and its "[return] to itself from this alienation" is a display of precisely that process the speech takes as its thematic object of investigation.

Césaire's drive to totalize the vast range of intellectual material at his disposal, beyond any narcissistic "hypertrophy of the ego" (Confiant, *Traversée paradoxale* 99), resulted from the particular form of education administered by the French system of the Grandes Ecoles.[17] This primary disposition was reinforced, as in the case of Sartre, by a biographical trajectory in which Césaire was both creating and to a large extent dominating a new intellectual field, a situation in which the totalization of knowledge—"the form that the ambition for absolute power takes in the intellectual field" (Bourdieu, *Regles de l'art* 295)—within the consciousness of the "man of culture" appeared as a disinterested, intellectual credo, while also (unconsciously) offering a perfect tactic for Césaire's dominance of a nascent field.

La Tragédie du roi Christophe

In writing *La Tragédie du roi Christophe* in 1963, as commentators from Lilyan Kesteloot and Barthélémy Kotchy on have remarked, Aimé Césaire drew upon Caribbean history as a means of addressing the process of decolonization and the creation of African states occurring all around him. The play, as René Ménil remarked in an article from 1964, expresses the historical consciousness fundamental to Césaire's aesthetic perception: "The historical vision of the play comes not from the fact that its material is historical–the death of Christophe that occurred in Haiti around 1810. It is rather the opposite that is true: the choice of a historical subject is made necessary by the historical conception of the world that is proper to the author himself. Césaire has of the world, of society, of men and of things an original vision in which things, men and institutions spontaneously appear as processes, as transitions, as passages rather than solidifying into eternal realities" (180). In this view, Césaire's work serves as the aesthetic critique of the mythological eternity of colonial ideology in which colonizers naturally dominate the colonized, to undertake instead a prophetic reading of the past. "Paradoxically," Ménil comments, "it is not the past that [Césaire] invites us to witness in the historical reconstruction he undertakes, but rather our future. A future that takes on meaning and consistency in its contradictory confrontation with a distant past and a present [the African, Asian, and Caribbean independences of the 1960s] undergoing a difficult gestation" (181).

Generally regarded as Césaire's finest theatrical achievement, *La Tragédie du roi Christophe* tells the story of the first king of an independent Haiti, who reigned from 1811 to 1820, as he attempts to actualize the freedom implicit in his country's victory against France in 1804. In so doing, Christophe ends up re-enslaving his subjects in the name of freedom and ensures their eventual rebellion when his force of will abandons him and he falls, paralyzed, before the specter of his crimes against his people. *La Tragédie du roi Christophe* describes an Antillean counterpart to the

French Revolutionary Terror, tracing Christophe's descent from idealistic terror to suicidal dementia.

Césaire's choice of subject is instructive: rather than turning to the revolutionary hero Toussaint, as he had a few years before, a hero whose image as a martyr remained largely untarnished by the ordeals of practical politics, he here looks to Henri Christophe, an ambiguous historical figure who took it upon himself idealistically to bring his people out of the tutelage of slavery by forging a modern, independent Haitian polis. Christophe, at once former slave and brilliant and ruthless military tactician, combined an abstract utopian idealism with an instrumental recourse to violence in his visionary pursuit of moral ends by the most violent of means.

Césaire articulated an incisive reflection upon the dialectical nature of history in this, his second play. With its virtuosic mixing of diverse historical and intellectual materials, from Hegelian dialectical thought to the gods of the Yoruba and Vodou pantheon, Césaire constructed a unique form of Caribbean historiography. While forgoing traditional positivist models of historical writing, Césaire's work in turn achieved concrete historical effects extending far beyond those of the Antillean academic tomes devoted to Louis Delgrès considered in chapter 1. Césaire here created a historical knowledge that decisively altered fields as diverse as the Parisian postwar intellectual scene and West-African and Caribbean colonial and postcolonial politics.

The play's central contradiction is that of the conflict between the drive to instantiate the immanent freedom of historical individuals and their recurrent political and ideological subjugation in the name of a transcendent, utopian autonomy. Five years after his ringing defense of Sékou Touré's Guinea in the pages of *Présence africaine,* Césaire here identified at an early stage of the decolonization movement the dialectic of autonomy and violence that has structured debate on African postcolonial politics from Sékou Touré to Mobutu and beyond. The instantiation of an ethical, postcolonial community implicit in the process of the Haitian Revolution vanishes as the play commences. The last trace of this hope disintegrates as Christophe orders the killing of Metellus, who had rebelled against his rule in the name of that ethical community that he recalls before being put to death: "We were going to found a country / with each individual persisting in the whole! *[tous entre soi!]*" (43). The movement toward a Haitian community is blocked in Christophe's self-aggrandizement as "king," and in this Haitian Terror "The lord of the World becomes really conscious of what he is . . . in the destructive power he exercises against his subjects" (*Phenomenology* 293). Césaire articulates this conflict between freedom and re-enslavement around the pivotal image of the citadel that Henri Christophe builds upon a mountain using the labor of tens of thousands of Haitians. Césaire's focus upon the citadel is crucial to his analysis of the antinomies of emancipation. The term "citadel" is itself inherently double, implying both a haven from outside invasion and a fortress that ensures the subjugation of the populace. Its original meaning, coming from the Italian for "little city," renders it symbolic of the new Haiti Christophe dreams of creating. Its modern meaning encompasses that of a "fortress commanding a city, which it serves both to protect and to keep in subjection." Not only was the actual Haitian citadel able to protect some fifteen thousand citizens at a time, it was also a jail for those who displeased him.

In a hallucinatory vision at the end of the play's first act, Christophe sees "a citadel! Not a palace. Not castle to protect my personage. I say the citadel, the liberty of a people. Built *by* the people as a whole, *for* the entire people!" (*Christophe* 63, emphasis added). Despite his idealism, the slippage in the king's language between a palace built both *for* and *by* the people reveals that the ambiguity of enslavement in the name of liberty is present in Christophe's very conception of the citadel. Although Christophe envisions the citadel as ensuring his citizens' freedom (newly independent Haiti faced the constant threat of invasion, particularly following the fall of Napoleon), its construction required sixteen years of forced labor. As such, the citadel becomes a menacing presence dominating the city of Cap Haitian, a sign of Christophe's terror and oppression against his own citizens. His subjects soon come to see him not as a benevolent leader but as a black version of the enslavers they had fought so hard to drive out. As one peasant states, "I tell myself that if we've driven out the whites, it was to have it for ourselves, this land, not to toil on the land of others, even black, to have it for ourselves" (74). Césaire's evocation of Haiti's attempt to construct a new nation thus served as a politically engaged meditation upon the difficult relation between freedom and idealism that would confront each postcolonial African leader as former colonies achieved independent statehood.

The citadel, however, is more than a simple emblem of the ambiguity of violence and utopianism. As a product of human construction, an objectification of the labor of the Haitian populace, it is intimately tied to the productive model of subjectivity that underlies Césaire's entire oeuvre, drawing upon a dialectical model of history to explore the Caribbean past. The citadel's enormous, immobile stone mass towers menacingly above the Haitian populace it surveys from a strategic mountain peak, while its shiplike prow seems to slice through the sky three thousand feet in the air, breaking away from the historical determination that has limited the Haitian accession to freedom from 1804 to the present. This combination of stasis and movement, solidity and molecularization, oppression and liberty, make it an ideal crystallization of the dualistic conception of history at the root of Césaire's play.

Césaire's appropriation of the dialectical model of historical understanding decisively oriented his exploration of the problem of historical experience in *Christophe*. Whether or not Césaire was conscious of doing so, from its thematic emphasis to its innermost structure, the play freely reworks the material of the *Phenomenology of Spirit* that so impressed Césaire upon his first encountering it on his return to Paris in 1945. Césaire's play shows a further similarity with Alexandre Kojève's influential commentary upon the *Phenomenology*. What Kojève refers to as his "Dualist Ontology" differentiates between two spheres: on the one hand, that of nature, characterized by a cyclical, repeating process of reproduction based upon identity; nature is devoid of history in Kojève's reading of Hegel, because this reproduction of identity, the cyclical reappearance of the same, allows for no unique historical event. Opposed to nature is man, who enters into history through negativity insofar as he negates the present in order to create a new future. This linkage of history with negation underscores Kojève's Nietzschean notion of the violence of historical becoming.

Christophe and the *Phenomenology* share a common historical background; the latter is often considered Hegel's commentary on both the French Revolution and the ensuing Napoleonic wars. The world order brought into being by Napoleon, upon which Kojève places so much emphasis, was, from the perspective of the black Atlantic world, creative less in its successes (Guadeloupe, Martinique) than in its most grandiose failure. For the field of conflict of the Napoleonic wars extended far beyond Europe, Russia, and North Africa; it was Napoleon who sent his generals Leclerc and Richepance to Haiti and Guadeloupe respectively in 1802 in order to maintain control of those highly profitable French colonies in the face of local revolution. The Haitian Revolution led by Toussaint Louverture and his lieutenants Dessaline and Henri Christophe has become an international symbol of anticolonial contestation, well known as the world's only successful overthrow of a slave-holding society by the enslaved themselves.

More concretely, Susan Buck-Morss has argued that Hegel's famous description of the master-slave dialectic was very precisely engendered by his reflection upon the Haitian Revolution. Buck-Morss answers a question that has long troubled scholars of Hegel: "Where did Hegel's idea of the relation between lordship and bondage originate?" (842). Buck-Morss marshals convincing archival evidence to show that Hegel, a notoriously avid reader of newspapers and journals, "knew about real slaves revolting successfully against real masters, and he elaborated his dialectic of lordship and bondage deliberately within this contemporary context [of the debate surrounding the Haitian Revolution of 1804]. . . . In perhaps the most political expression of his career, he used the sensational events of Haiti as the linchpin in his argument in *The Phenomenology of Spirit*" (844, 852). If Buck-Morss is correct, the central theoretical role played by Hegel's *Phenomenology* in the process of decolonization in the twentieth century should be understood not merely in light of the metaphorical relevance of its argument to this project. Instead, the *Phenomenology* concretely inaugurated the philosophical reflection at the heart of this process: "The actual and successful revolution of Caribbean slaves against their masters is the moment when the dialectical logic of recognition becomes visible as the thematics of world history, the story of the universal realization of freedom" (852).

Seen against this background of violent social upheaval, both the *Phenomenology* and *Christophe* can be interpreted as studies of the aftermath of slavery, barbarity, and war, addressing the problematic process by which humans overcome a state of terror and violence.[18] This point implies a second, deeper similarity: the primary concern of both works is to articulate the historical, temporal development of mankind away from an existence of unconscious, brutal repetition toward a fully historical human existence. This distinction between the cyclical and the linear locates Césaire's play within a larger field of discourse derived from Kojève's "Dualist Ontology."[19] The parallel between Césaire's play and Kojève's dualism of nature and history is thorough: in this view, Henri Christophe attempts to bring his country out of an ontological, eternally recurrent past of servitude, dependency, and abjection into a process of historical becoming and overcoming of the self. This transformation, however, is fundamentally linked with violence, as Christophe's abstract negation of the past is acted out upon real individuals whose ideals fail to correspond with the king's own. The play's tragedy thus unfolds as Christophe realizes the impossibility of making the world, in its torpor, inertia, and sheer nonidentity correspond to his monological revolutionary ideal.

In order to begin this dialectical development, Christophe first confronts an Other from which he is estranged, the Haitian people. The entire first act explores the conflict between multiplicity and unity, identity and nonidentity, as Christophe rejects his assimilation within his opponent

Pétion's parliament, affirming his autonomy, his "right to be *non-identical*" (*Phenomenology* 343). After the civil war in which he accedes to power in the north of Haiti (Act I, Scenes 1–6), Christophe drives the Haitian people toward a nascent self-transformation. Christophe's monologue in scene 7 crystallizes this gesture as he describes how, through the alchemy of the word, the bestowing of names upon his subjects, they will achieve "a new birth" (37). From this focus upon an animalistic mass ("thousands of half-naked blacks that the waves vomited up one evening" [38], they will be born into subjective self-awareness by Christophe himself, the midwife of a "shattering power of word and action, of construction, of building, of being, of naming, of linking, of rebuilding" (38). Christophe's alienation from his subjects is total; they represent for him either an unconscious organic totality that he despises ("What was there in this country before the arrival of King Christophe? . . . Shit, nothing but shit!" [97]) or absolute abstractions, citizens whose freedom is purely formal and who serve as the mere legal recipients of his decrees (76). Christophe's ethical orders are visited upon passive citizens without consultation, for whom "the ethical order exists merely as something *given*" (*Phenomenology* 214).

Christophe's the vocabulary of "constructing," "building," and "redoing" serves to locate the play within the Hegelian production-based logic of an expressive communal subjectivity. This community, however, remains blocked by Christophe's Terror, and he abandons his brief vision of a collective Haitian *nous,* announcing Christophe's final narcissistic glorification of his own demiurgic subjectivity: "so I will take them / I know their weight / and I will carry them!" (38).

Christophe's development in the play, complexly rendered by Césaire, progresses from the Terror of abstract idealism to the hopeless interiority of moral impotence. However, Christophe's idealism remains compelling, in its very uncompromising abstraction. Unlike the worldly cynicism of his secretary, Vastey (80), Christophe is guided by an unswerving fidelity to his ethical ideal. The Haitian king rejects for his subjects a freedom by decree handed down from above, proffering instead "something which, if need be by force, forces [the people] to be born unto itself and to overcome itself" (23). *La tragédie du roi Christophe* offers an extended meditation upon the nature of historical freedom, clearly placing his protagonist within the discourse of enlightenment so powerfully appropriated in the Haitian drive for independence. In consonance with the Kantian moral philosophy contemporary to the Haitian revolution, freedom for Christophe's subjects cannot be conferred (by a government or a leader) but must be autonomously legislated by each individual's faculty of reason such that its compelling force demonstrates its universality. Otherwise those individuals are not truly free, for their freedom has been bestowed heteronomously upon them by an outside, empirical source, making them subject to the natural world. In their idealism, Christophe's ambiguous statements shuttle between a utopian freedom lying somewhere in the future and the material violence of an external obligation that, like Rousseau's prescription for a free society in the *Social Contract,* would force those subjects to be free regardless of their own volition. The Haitian people are finally the mere means to realize Christophe's project, sacrificed to the future and "smashed to pieces" (*Phenomenology* 221) exactly as Hegel's mature philosophy of history sacrificed consciousness of the real suffering of individuals in the present—what Hegel dismissed as "sentimental reflection"—to the "true result of universal history": the World Spirit (qtd. in Löwy 76).

Christophe attempts to prime a dialectic of self-overcoming in the Haitian people. He conceives of this development as a veritable re-invention of humanity: "The human material itself must be refounded. How? I do not know. We will undertake this process in our corner of the world! In our own small workshop!" (62). Christophe's effort to reinvent the Haitian people in a negation of their former selves mirrors Kojève's description of the enslaved subject's productive self-alienation: "Its sustained existence thus signifies for this Self: 'not to be that which it is (as a static and given being, a natural being, as an "innate character") and to be (that is to say to become) that which it is not'" (12). The concept of humanity thus stands in negative relation to the historical individuals over whom Christophe rules; *La tragédie du roi Christophe* posits humanity as an ideal yet to be achieved, an ideal to be constructed. Christophe's absolute idealism, however, sacrifices his actual subjects to this vision, ensuring that his steadfast pursuit of a "humanitarian" goal determined only by his pure faculty of reason will drive his real living subjects into utterly animalistic suffering and unfreedom.

Christophe's domination over his people has two consequences. First, his dissatisfaction with the status quo: despite his recourse to violence, he is not content to be a tyrant over a quiescent, obedient populace (84, 92). To achieve satisfaction, Christophe the master must invoke the self-consciousness of those who would recognize him as their king by means of "something thanks to which this transplanted people takes root, flourishes, throws in the face of the world the perfumes and fruits of its flowering" (23). The manner in which Christophe acts to bring about self-consciousness in the Other similarly corresponds to two steps of the Hegelian Spirit's movement toward Absolute Knowledge. On the part of the Haitian people, this movement occurs through productive work, specifically the construction of Christophe's palace by slave labor. For those Haitians surrounding Christophe in his court, on the other hand, this process is enacted in the realm of culture.

Following the logic of a production-based subjectivity, Césaire shows the Haitian people's progression toward self-understanding to arise through work. Through their forced labor, the Haitian peasants of the play enter into history. The citadel they build under the threat of death appears before them as the objectification of their own enslavement to a brutal dictator, a monument to unfreedom. And yet, their capacity to transform the world is simultaneously hewn in this gigantic stone construction, announcing the violent uprisings that will end Christophe's tyranny at the play's close.

If, through work, the peasants leave behind the cyclical world of nature of the Haitian countryside, Christophe remains utterly alienated from their experience, ruining any movement toward the Haitian ethical community his ideal implies. Césaire's play stages a rigid binary opposition between the peasants' putatively timeless world, a dehistoricized, rural Haiti ("amid the highlands, . . . the high plateaus and the savanna, the violence and the tenderness of the people, the Artibonite river . . . casts out and divulges everything from the high mountains of Dominicanie to . . . the Great Savanna" [65]) and the historical, linear world of the revolutionary leader and king, the ex-slave who has entered into history through a violent confrontation with death (the Haitian Revolution). Christophe is in this Kojévian reading the formerly enslaved, unconscious being who, through a violent negation of his former natural self, an act of self-alienation, became an autonomous, law-giving subject. Moreover, through their unfree labor, the Haitian people themselves become increasingly conscious both of their own creative power and of the identity of given historical moments. "The country [Nature], is good, but this time we live in sure isn't" (73), observes one of the peasants.

The Haitian peasants in the play reveal a resolute sense of self-consciousness that belies their putative relegation to an absolute "nature," what Christophe can only perceive as mere "shit." They comment perspicaciously upon their own misfortune and the events in their country. However, in *Christophe,* Césaire's glorification of "the masses" remains as formulaic as it had been in his earlier 1956 speech. The intimations of their entry into historicity never fully develop into a true moral contestation in the play, and the Haitians' revolt against Christophe's domination at the play's end remains a distant abstraction beside Christophe's final suicidal display of agency. It is, rather, the nobles of his court and the military who concretely abandon Christophe when he grows too weak to impose his will. Césaire's Haitian peasants remain indissolubly tied to their land in a historical stasis: "To tell you the truth, *compère* Patience, my love is with the land. I believe in the land I work with my own arms and that the fat king wants to keep from us" (110).

Césaire's affirmation of Antillean nature and natural, cyclical time nonetheless marks a refusal of the violent abstraction of instrumental reason implicit in both Christophe's terror and colonialism itself. In the play, the postrevolutionary Haitians have already destroyed the "second nature" of the plantation, negating their former world of slaves and masters through a violent confrontation in which "the Slave has risked his life in a Fight for recognition, ceasing in this manner to be a Slave" (Kojève 113). This Haitian Enlightenment remains blocked, stuck at the unmediated extremes of Christophe's idealism and the peasants' passive suffering.

For Césaire, as for Hegel, culture is a realm of self-creation superior to the brute interiority of hard labor. My introduction examined how, in the process that Hegel refers to as "alienation," the individual's natural existence is negated for an artificial one in which "[the self's] actuality consists solely in the setting-aside of its natural self. . . . The self knows itself as actual only as a transcended self" (*Phenomenology* 298–99). For Césaire, as again for Hegel, this process of intersubjective acculturation is accomplished through the medium of language. If, in labor, the isolated individual becomes aware of his or her capacity to transform the world, the constructive work of language as communicative self-understanding builds toward an intersubjective ethical community (*Phenomenology* 308). In language, Hegel comments, self-awareness is objectified and becomes intersubjective: "Language is the *real existence* of the pure self as self; in speech, self-consciousness, *qua independent separate individuality*, comes as such into existence, so that it exists *for others*" (309, emphasis in original). Césaire as well views the poet's creativity as lying essentially in the demiurgic force of his or her enunciation to instantiate a novel intersubjective reality. As such, the poet is an autonomous producer of the subjectivity embodied in the concept of negritude.

In *La tragédie du roi Christophe,* this process of subjective production is dramatized by Césaire through that ritual so common throughout former slave-owning societies in the Americas: the reappropriation of one's own name, replacing the name given by the slave owner with one autonomously chosen. The process of objectification (the slave as object being attributed a name rather than choosing it him or herself) is thus reversed, as Régis Antoine has observed, by Christophe, who refers to the European masters with a condescending "on" (48). "These new names, these titles of nobility, this crowning! Formerly our names were stolen from us! Our pride! . . . Pierre, Paul, Jacques, Toussaint! These are the humiliating stamps with which they obliterated our true names. . . . Do you feel the pain of a man who doesn't know his own name? . . . Alas, only Mother Africa knows that name!" (37).

Here again, however, the impulse for this transformative act has come from Christophe himself rather than from the subjects who will bear these names. As in the final passages of the *Cahier* twenty years earlier, Christophe's speech again veers between the singular and plural, first and second person: "with names of glory I wish to cover your slave names, / with names of pride or names of infamy, / with names of redemption our names of orphans!" (37). Thus the antinomy recurs between Christophe's desire to develop his subjects' autonomy and his own compulsive reproduction of the systems of objectification from which all Haitians were attempting to escape.

Though Christophe strives to bring about the transformation of those in his court, the negation of a former self symbolized in the slave names of his subjects falls victim to the same shortcomings Hegel describes. As in the court of Louis XIV in Hegel's analysis, the values to which these individuals adhere are not autonomously generated but are accepted from the all-powerful ruler. Although they were required to make a conscious effort to adhere to these values, thus implying a certain increasing "spiritualization," this activity quickly degenerates into conformity and sycophancy (Hegel 300; Césaire II 2). Henri Christophe's actions can be understood as Césaire's self-critique. The former acts out the role Césaire had only a few years before—at the 1959 *Présence africaine* conference in Rome—prescribed for the "man of culture," whose job it is to "bring order to the cultural chaos" (qtd. in Delas 134). *Christophe* reproduces the antinomy at the heart of Césaire's aesthetic theory, in mediated form. Césaire's assertion at the Rome conference that it must be the "people" who effect a cultural renewal runs directly counter to his belief—expressed everywhere from the article "Poésie et connaissance" in 1945 ("But one man saves humanity . . . that man is the poet") through the two *Présence africaine* "culture" speeches (1956 and 1959)—that it is the poet or the "man of culture" who must work that change upon a largely passive, receptive, and subordinated "people." In like manner, Christophe is ineluctably entrapped by the sterility of his prescriptive gesture. His invocations of "this people" only underline his total alienation from them, whether they are the nobles of his court or the peasants who will build his citadel. Césaire thus objectifies in the character of Henri Christophe the dilemma that underlies his work from the *Cahier* onward in the form of a contradiction between the promised autonomy of negritude and the appropriation of that autonomy by the vanguard intellectual whose freedom substitutes for that of the colonized masses. Moreover, *La tragédie du roi Christophe* undertakes a critique of the ideological degeneration of the concept of negritude plainly visible by 1963 in the tyranny of Guinea's Sékou Touré, "Papa Doc" Duvalier's Haitian "Noirisme," and even Senghor's manipulation of the concept in newly independent Senegal. The tyranny of Henri Christophe announces these twentieth-century betrayals of the concept of negritude, and Césaire overtly thematizes this degeneration and his own foundering hopes in Christophe's act of naming his subjects: "You are 'black' [nègre]. . . . I baptize you, name you, consecrate you 'black'" (146). If, in 1939, Césaire's neologism ("negritude") held out the promise of an intersubjective ethical community of the Black diaspora, by 1963 he ironizes the pretensions of the poet, ("the kingfisher . . . inventing himself a daybreak of drunken sunlight *[un petit matin de soleil ivre]*" 144), recasting the hopes of the *Cahier* ("au bout du petit matin") as mere "drunken" fancy and mythical invocation.

La tragédie du roi Christophe describes not the teleological development of a postcolonial "absolute knowledge" but the static confrontation of unyielding absolutes, a dialectic whose only movement is the putrescent degeneration of Christophe himself. Christophe's recourse to violence in his pursuit of a Haitian utopia dooms his effort to failure. He gradually withdraws into the interiority of Sans Souci, an objectification of his own bunkered subjectivity, immersing himself in the mythical realm of the Haitian Vodou gods. The play's invocation of the spirits of Haitian Vodou in Christophe's dying moments reworks the Hegelian critique of "revealed religion" (i.e., Christianity). In a striking parallel, Christophe blocks the Haitian people's access to a postcolonial ethical community precisely as the Christian Christ stood, in Hegel's analysis, as the "mediator" blocking access to a non-transcendental Christian community (*Phenomenology* 476).

La tragédie du roi Christophe constructs its complex model of historical consciousness dialectically, using elements of both Hegel's *Phenomenology* and the historicism expressed in the religion of the West African Yoruba, from which so many Afro-American religious traditions, including Vodou, derive. Throughout the play, Yoruba and Vodou ceremonies are represented both onstage and in various comments by different characters (I, 4; II, 8; etc.).[20] A principal aspect of the play's striking originality lies in this mixture of such heretofore-distinct discourses: that of European historical and philosophical discourses of the revolutionary period with the mythical figures of the black Atlantic (former slaves, Vodou, and the Yoruba gods). This mixture is far from gratuitous; the deities, or *orixas* of the Yoruba pantheon, Ogun in particular, are fundamental to the play's evocation of the movement of humans out of a state of nature and into history through a process of violent negation.²¹ Kojève and Hegel, of course, are never mentioned in the play. On the other hand, Ogun Badagri, the Haitian transformation of the West African deity Ogun, appears onstage, the literal black Atlantic incarnation of a dialectical historicism uncannily similar to Kojève's reading of Hegel.

Césaire's description of Ogun's personality, like that of Shango and Baron Samedi, is meticulous, based largely upon Alfred Métraux's 1959 study of Haitian Vodou (Pestre de Almeida). The Vodou Lwa are intimately linked with the play's meditation on historical experience. Ogun in particular, the god of iron, is linked with all that is warlike and violent, "a violent warrior, fully armed and laden with frightening charms to kill his foes" (Barnes 2). Ogun symbolizes the forces of violence and destruction. Ogun, however, is a highly complex deity, for his violent nature is intimately tied with its negative image, creativity. "Ogun kills and he creates" (Barnes 16). It is for this reason that Ogun, the destroyer of the old and creator of the new, is so closely linked with a historical, event-based, noncyclical existence. Ogun Badagri/Baron Samedi's speech is filled with markers of temporal existence: "Excuse my *lateness,* Mesdames and Messieurs. You know, I'm *always* the one who arrives *late.* . . . In the *end,* we arrive *on time* and that's what counts for the *minute* of silence . . . the master dancer who incarnates an outraged civilization, proclaims far and wide to *History* that there's nothing to be done with Negroes, although . . ." (148, emphasis added).

This final phrase, explicitly recalling Christophe's desire to instantiate his subjects' entry into historical existence, evokes a characteristic of Ogun's personality even more essential to the play's philosophy of history. Ogun, despite his destructive nature, is simultaneously "the metaphoric representation of [the] transformation brought about by human effort" (Barnes 17). Ogun is tied with many of the fundamental inventions that mark off human existence from that of other animals:

> Ogun was responsible for society's most important innovations. His praises were sung by many Yoruba-speaking groups as "Master of the World," the innovative deity who "showed the way" for others; the deity who brought fire; the first hunter; the opener of roads; the clearer of the first fields; the first warrior; the introducer of iron; the founder of dynasties, towns, and kingdoms.

> Each of these acts was in some way revolutionary. Each was in some way a "first".... Ogun brought a new political order through civil war or conquest, a new economy through clearing the fields, a new technology through the introduction of iron, and a new way of life through the founding of towns and cities. (Barnes and Ben-Amos 57)

Ogun is the god who initiates this humanization of animalistic man through invention and production. The evocation of Ogun by Baron Samedi at the play's end underscores an intermingling of the historical creation of man and the death of a transcended self. While Ogun symbolizes the historical creativity of humanity, he also signifies its link with destruction and death (149).

Hegel's conception of absolute spirit claims the possibility of an actual overcoming of subject/object alienation in which the subject recognizes itself in the phenomenal universe.[22] Hegel, Kojève, and Césaire's Christophe each attempt to overcome the subject-object antinomy that structures modern experience. Each articulates a possible synthesis that would, they maintain, render this moment of identity immanent, universal, and absolute. In the wisdom of our hindsight, in turn, each can be seen to have failed to instantiate the ideal they described. If history has shown that the immanent noncoercive community Hegel identified in his description of "Absolute Knowledge" was, as Merold Westphal has argued, both historically naïve and an extorted *deus ex machina* given the logic of the *Phenomenology* itself (200, 227), Christophe's suicide merely extends the compass of his absolutism to embrace death itself.

Césaire dramatizes this absolute abstraction of death in the final scene of *La tragédie du roi Christophe* where it takes the form of the flight from civilization into nature, repeatedly thematized in his work from the *Cahier* on. As two porters carry the king's coffin to its burial site, it grows heavier and heavier, as it is drawn down toward the earth. Rather than burying him in the ground, Christophe's coffin is set vertically into the ground, in an intermediary position between earth and sky, becoming an arborescent link between the physical and the spiritual, becoming himself "SHANGO ... Force of the night, tide of the day" (152). Christophe thus momentarily appears as the realization of Kojève's "anthropodeism." Christophe has become Absolute Spirit.

WERE IT to stand as Césaire's final gesture in *La tragédie du roi Christophe*, this narcissistic resolution to the antinomies of freedom structuring the play would merely reproduce the antagonisms of history and nature and of reason and the unconscious that underlie the *Cahier*. Chapter 2 shows how that poem's rejection of reason and flight into nature threaten to abandon the self-conscious subject the poem constructs to the unfreedom of nature. The poem's representation of this antinomy, while immanent within its structure, remains largely unthematized in deference to a transcendent teleological conquest of freedom ("Et elle est debout la négraille / debout / et / libre"). In *La tragédie du roi Christophe,* however, Césaire overtly stages the material confrontation between the autonomously imputed freedom of a self-same individual (Christophe/Shango) and that individual's confrontation with the unfree world and suffering subjects in it. Christophe's own physical degeneration demonstrates that there is no true freedom possible for an isolated subject in a world that remains unfree. For all its pious invocations of Absolute Spirit, this nonidentity of the world and our understanding of its perfectibility is also what dominates the final pages of the *Phenomenology,* a world in which "what enters consciousness as the in-itself [i.e., the idea of the world's perfectability] . . . is a reconciliation that lies in the beyond, . . . is the world which has still to await its transfiguration" (478).

Césaire refuses to close *La tragédie du roi Christophe* with a gesture of transcendence that would bypass the antinomies of Caribbean existence. For the force of the final lines of *La tragédie du roi Christophe* arises from their inscription of the contradictions of the Haitian history they describe: Christophe's unbridled pursuit of autonomy ultimately brings not objective freedom but the liquidation of subjectivity. His pursuit of autonomy has neglected any concrete immersion within the experience of the Haitian people to become the obstruction Hegel terms "Absolute Freedom." As in the latter's analysis of the French Revolutionary Terror, Christophe has enforced an abstract, absolute freedom upon his subjects that is in fact death itself. The roar of Christophe's cannon, turned against his own people, signals the terrifying fulfillment of his dialectic of enlightenment. These individuals become abstract for Christophe when they refuse to conform to his equally abstract ideal. Devoid of material individuality for him, they can only truly conform to his utopian ideal through their absolute negation in death: "The sole work and deed of universal freedom is therefore *death,* a death too which has no inner significance or filling, for what is negated is the empty point of the absolutely free self. It is thus the coldest and meanest of all deaths, with no more significance then cutting off a head of a cabbage or swallowing a mouthful of water" (*Phenomenology* 360). Christophe's unmediated pursuit of the humanization and historicization of his people leads instead to their animal-like slaughter and their absolute de-historicization in death. Likewise, Christophe himself abandons all engagement with the phenomenal world in the play's final scenes, losing all control of his body, withdrawing into his castle; his freedom—culminating in suicide—is absolute negation, utterly devoid of content and reality.[23]

The emptiness of Christophe's final free act of suicide engenders the erasure of his specificity as a human subject.[24] As such, Christophe attains a universal, total freedom "which effaces all distinction and all continuance of distinction within it" as Hegel says, but at the cost of his human subjectivity in a death "with no more significance than cutting off a head of a cabbage." In so doing, as he had already done for his people, he now sacrifices his own human experience to the sublime universal, achieving an abstract unity with the divine Lwa and the forces of nature evoked by his African page: "Force of the night, tide of the day / SHANGO / I salute you" (152).

While Christophe has passed into the world of absolute spirit, the unfreedom he sought to overcome persists in the world he deserts. He has left behind a nation of Haitian subjects freed only of his attempts to liberate them. Césaire's final words in *La tragédie du roi Christophe* evoke this sublime impasse structuring *Christophe,* pointing to the falsity of Christophe's absolute, ultimately insubstantial freedom that echoed at the time of the play's appearance in the unfreedom of Haitian president Duvalier's "*Noirisme*" and the Tonton Macoutes. Denying the possible resolution of an extorted return to nature in a world riven by antinomy, the play's final lines draw the measure of a contradictory existence and chart the Antillean drama of historical immobility and dependency "upright, / suspend[ed] over the abyss."

BY ARTICULATING a black Atlantic variant of the dialectal historicism dominant in postwar French letters, Aimé Césaire's *La tragédie du roi Christophe* accomplishes more than the mere adaptation of his generation's philosophical master text to the demands of his poetic sensitivity. Thematizing the development of nature into history also allowed Césaire to address the primary problematic that confronted him as an Afro-Caribbean, French intellectual in the 1950s and 1960s. At stake were the unfolding drama of the accession of the various African colonies into independence and their attempt to move from servitude and dependence toward autonomy and substantial freedom.

Césaire's redeployment of Hegel's famous text in his articulation of a philosophy of history implies more than a simple thematic relevance. This adaptation should be understood to arise from the context of a series of aesthetic choices Césaire made as he evolved from an unknown Martinican student and poet to his position as the dominant intellectual of his field. The dilemmas Césaire faced as black poet-statesmen were implicitly explored in *Christophe*, as they were more directly examined in Césaire's articles and speeches of the period. If the political excesses and absolutism of Christophe are at odds with the author's benevolent, long-lived political practice, the problematic exploration of the subject's distantiation from an objectified mass that proved to be the king's downfall recur throughout Césaire's aesthetic practice.

This was not a matter of bad faith, with Césaire professing sympathy for the masses while acting out of professional self-interest. Césaire's constant exploration of the problematic relation between the individual artist and his audience bears witness to his refusal to remain content with the modernist elitism of his early texts and the alienation from the Antillean masses that is a feature of his poetic work even today, when more "accessible" authors such as Maryse Condé or Tony Delsham are better known in the Antilles than Césaire the poet.[25] Rather, he repeatedly searched for ways to mediate the antinomy between his bond with the "people" and the movement away from them implied by his creation and occupation of an isolated space for the intellectual/poet.

Dialectical historicism, in its Kojèvian variant, carried a strongly positive value within the French and nascent pan-African intellectual fields in 1963. Césaire's subtle, unacknowledged use of Hegel's *Phenomenology of Spirit* both to structure and to provide thematic philosophical depth to the play placed it within a concrete European philosophical tradition. By analogy it invoked the lineage of Sartre's philosophical theater and implicitly placed it within the postwar vogue of Hegelianism. Césaire's appropriation of dialectical historicism provided subtle intellectual rigor to a nascent African theater. Simultaneously, his manipulation of a Yoruba/Vodou cosmology and philosophy of history allied *Christophe* with a millennial tradition of compelling spiritual force.

The symbolism of *Christophe* thus has a direct relationship with the historical context in which the play appeared. Not simply a warning to the new leaders of Africa, as so many commentators have suggested; rather, the play itself is historically performative. The fact of its appearance in 1963 within an intellectual and social space the author had negotiated and created over the previous thirty years, produced in turn effects within the field of black Francophone letters. The central symbol of the construction of the citadel thus takes on an additional sense: the play itself is an attempt to concretize through language the African diasporic ethical community that Christophe himself failed to achieve, its verbal architecture existing both on paper as objective artifact and on stage via the actors (including the brilliant Douta Seck) who would bring it into existence before an African public at the 1966 Dakar festival of Black Arts (Lemoine).

The play enacts this construction on both an individual and collective plane. Individually, Césaire explores a key moment in the history of the African diaspora, using a series of historically inherited discursive strategies (the Yoruba/Vodou and Hegelian philosophies of history) to produce an artwork that occupied a preexisting field (postwar French *théâtre engagé*) due both to the cultural capital Césaire had previously accumulated and the mastery of historical material (philosophical, poetic, anthropological, and rhetorical discourses) that the play itself displays. This successful insertion within a European intellectual field—the play became, for example, the first by a black playwright to be performed at the *Comédie Française* in 1991, and in 1996 it became the first to be performed in the Court d'Honneur at the Avignon festival in fifty years of summer festivals—was complemented by the play's domination alongside the *Cahier* of the nascent field of black Francophone letters. If Césaire's earlier incursions into this field were essential in the definition and constitution of its parameters, the performance of *Christophe* at the Dakar Black Arts Festival in 1966 can be seen as a critical moment in the field's canonization.

In addition to the masterful incorporation of a series of European intellectual discourses within the play, Césaire was one of the first Caribbean writers to use what has become a common trope of literature in the postcolonial Americas: the juxtaposition of a narration of suppressed historical material with the cosmology of the Orishas and Lwa of the Yoruba-derived syncretic religions. The presence of these gods in Césaire's play must be understood as accomplishing more than adding "local color"; instead, they are essential to both the organic functioning of the play's symbolic logic and its conquering of a novel intellectual field through the masterful accumulation of discourses. The presence of Ogun—"the metaphoric representation of a transformation brought about by human efforts" (Barnes 17),—brings together what might seem to be two heterogeneous discourses, Old World and New, into a new synthesis.

Césaire's invention of negritude had already proven essential to his reception by the French intelligentsia. Had he been only another surrealist-inspired poet, a former student at rue d'Ulm, it is unlikely that Breton, Sartre, and their followers would have taken interest in him. It was the combination of an accumulation of cultural capital that they themselves recognized (diplomas, mastery of historical and poetic material) with the manipulation of a topical theme they were incapable of evoking authentically (colonialism, racism, negritude) that explain Césaire's success. If Sartre, in particular, attempted to place the philosophical stamp of the total intellectual upon these problems in "Orphée noire," it was essential that he do so within the context of a collective publication of black poets *(Anthologie de la nouvelle poésie nègre et malgache)*. His analysis was unavoidably weakened by his "situation," in which he spoke in the place of others who were claiming their right to self-expression. Sartre's self-positioning as spokesperson for the anticolonial movement could never achieve the total dominance he had achieved in other cultural fields. Césaire thus responded to a structural opening in the postwar French intellectual field, becoming, along with Fanon, one of the most influential theorists of the decolonization movement through the recognition he received in both worlds, French and black Atlantic.

Césaire's historical incursion within the black Atlantic intellectual field thus has more than a simply subjective importance within the dynamic constitution of his own position within that field. The performative nature of *La tragédie du roi Christophe* remains ambiguous, an act of objective (self-)construction by a black Francophone intellectual. In this manner, the play encodes within its formal and symbolic processes and structures a historical dynamic that transcends Césaire's own biographical trajectory. Henri Christophe's construction of the citadel, itself a towering monument to negritude by the world's first black emperor, is the symbolic objectification of the play's own sociohistorical activity.

The appearance of *La tragédie du roi Christophe* marks the inauguration of a monument in the history of the black Atlantic world. It substantially transformed African diasporic culture via its representation of the production of a self-conscious black subjectivity, confronting that culture with a critical image of its own unfreedom. The impact of Césaire's play was truly monumental, in the many contradictory senses of the term, completing the process begun by his lectures in Port-au-Prince in 1944 that had produced such an explosive, revolutionary effect upon his audience, "destroying in their passage the grasses of every baseness of spirit, devouring taboos, slicing with great knife-strokes every habitual association" (Depestre) in Césaire's struggle to decolonize Antillean subjectivity.

5 Dreaming of the Masters
Jazz and Memory in Daniel Maximin's *L'Isolé soleil* and *L'Ile et une nuit*

THE PUBLICATION of Daniel Maximin's novel *L'Isolé soleil* by *Editions du Seuil* in 1981 signals an Antillean crisis of representation. At precisely the moment Euro-American theorists posited postmodernism as a conceptual reality, the novel presents a panorama of Caribbean history that refuses to articulate a grounded centerpoint of either narrative consciousness or historical perspective, moving from the plantation to Delgrès's 1802 revolt against Bonaparte's troops, to the island's occupation by the Vichy government in World War II, and on to the present. Multiple narrators in the novel constantly search for the modes of expression that might adequately represent this act of anamnesis in a self-referential *mise en abyme*. In so doing, they undertake an autocritique of historiography in the French Caribbean while offering the reader an evocation of the past no less rigorous than many a historical monograph.[1] The novel offers a rich mosaic, moving from historiographic pastiche to the interrogation of these same acts of mnemonic (re-)construction by the various French Caribbean intellectuals who serve as the novel's narrators. The latter are confronted by a confiscated history that fitfully unveils itself within a society still bearing structural characteristics inherited from the colonial dependency upon the French metropolis. In so doing, *L'Isolé soleil* offers a model of Antillean subjectivity that addresses the dispersion and multiplicity of postmodern Caribbean experience via an immersion in the objectivity of critical historical experience.

If *L'Isolé soleil* attempts to work through such a crisis in historical and epistemological representation, it is not so much as a refusal of the notion of totality, as a caricatural postmodernism would have it, as through a reinscription of totality as a historical dilemma within a pervasive Antillean fragmentation. As such, the problem of representation in *L'Isolé soleil* serves to denote, more than the stigmata of aesthetic inwardness, the elitist narcissism of "the poet" who continues to create lyric images amid political and historical alienation—though the novel certainly does thematize such issues, the protagonist, Louis-Gabriel, understandable as a Caribbean Nero, fiddling while Pointe-a-Pitre burns at the behest of its Napoleonic invaders.

The fragmented narrative of *L'Isolé soleil* posits totality as its negative image and itself struggles to represent the incapacity of Antillean subjects to conceptualize historical alienation as an overarching global movement whose origins stretch back to slavery and the plantation and whose fulcrum point is the island's 1946 departmentalization. The crisis in representation the novel addresses is thus a predicament of understanding in which subjects struggle to grasp these processes of alienation, dependency, marginalization, and dispersion as localized instantiations of global historical processes. Aesthetic representation serves as a marginalized remnant amid the historical vitiation of production and political autonomy. Here, poetry becomes the sole sphere of autonomous production still available in an era of globalization and dependency. At the same time, the aesthetic forms a refuge for nonidentity in which play, in the form of poetic creativity and language games, persists as a zone of noninstrumentalized use-value in a context of increasingly total instrumentalization and commodification (of language, of history, of political representation, of production).

With inspired economy, the title *L'Isolé soleil* itself articulates the drama of Antillean subjectivity described in the introduction to this volume: the dissolution of the subject via the reification ("isolation") inherent in the historical course of departmentalization. The title *L'Isolé soleil* invokes Aimé Césaire, the architect of departmentalization, via the signal image of his poetic voice: the "sacré soleil vénérien," the "dernier des derniers soleils," the "soleil serpent," the "sang de soleil brisé," the "soleil cou coupé." In this manner *L'Isolé soleil* announces the novel's engagement of historical material, both on the level of aesthetic influence and of history itself.

Maximin, however, rejects the disalienated reconciliation with nature postulated by Césaire's *Cahier*.[2] He instead produces a representation of the "nonmaîtrise du quotidien" (Glissant, *DA* 113) and of the continuing alienation and isolation of a land administered from and dependent upon a metropolis four thousand miles away. The metonymical signifier of nature *(soleil)* is typographically dominated in the title by its rearticulated, manipulated objectification: the anagram *L'isolé*. This anagram—in which the organic totality of the word is broken down into its reified components (letters) only to be reconstructed in its various logical permutations—is itself the poetic inscription of Antillean reification and historical alienation. The anagram as such traces "the petrification of living processes into dead things, which [appear] as an alien 'second nature'" (Jay, *Marxism and Totality* 109). Maximin's entire text—in its disarticulation of the Antillean subject into a series of discursive fields—redirects the force of this trope to refuse the complicitous semblance of a utopian harmony, to confront instead Antillean society with its own shattered image.

Maximin's anagram, however, accuses Antillean society of the untruth of alienation without reducing the text to a mere documentary reproduction of the social totality it condemns. It produces instead an image of objective dependency via the freedom of aesthetic creativity. Verbal play traverses the novel in the form of word games, neologisms, and poetic invention: "I wanted to be *SOLEIL* [sun] writes the narrator, Adrien. "I played with words / I found *L'ISOLÉ* [lone]" (*IS* 105) *L'Isolé soleil* thus participates in the "overdetermined *coexistence* of play as *mise en abyme,* as implicit organizing principle, and as metaphor for writing and living ... specific to modern texts" that Susan Rubin Suleiman identifies in the work of authors such as Beckett, Perec, and Robbe-Grillet (*Subversive Intent* 4). The gratuitous character of Maximin's wordplay is in itself a critical gesture; its creativity refuses the reduction of Antillean existence to its mere exchange value within global politics and capitalism at the same time that its form retraces this very process.

Aesthetic semblance in *L'Isolé soleil* forms a relationship of simultaneous identity and nonidentity with the society it describes. It perpetuates in complicity with transnational capitalism the marginalization of critique within Antillean society to an ineffectual zone—Caribbean literature as the sandbox of postmodern geopolitics—while cultivating an articulate refusal to accept the commodification of every realm of Antillean experience. Within this contradictory, perhaps quixotic undertaking, the struggle to represent a fractured, unavailable history becomes paramount. The successful representation of this fractured history promises that an Antillean subject who grasps the complex articulations of his or her social predetermination, unfreedom, alienation, and increasing dissolution within the global community might thereby attain a furtive purchase upon a never-complete self-understanding and autonomy.

Jazz and History

Critics such as Clarisse Zimra have evoked Maximin's project, inherited from Césaire and Edouard Glissant, to recover a forgotten Antillean past. *L'Isolé soleil* continues the historico-poetic recovery of the Antillean heroes of the Revolutionary period enacted in Césaire's *La Tragédie du roi Christophe* and Glissant's 1961 play, *Monsieur Toussaint*. This historical aspect of the novel is among its most essential. The formal innovation of *L'Isolé soleil* is to have raised reflection on the problem of history in the French Caribbean to a new level through a self-referential narrative structure that puts in question our ability to know the past. *L'Isolé soleil* is a prototypically postmodern novel, as Chris Bongie has observed, one that "grounds itself in words already said (notably those of Césaire and the surrealists) and events already lived (various episodes from a pointedly revisionist history of Guadeloupe)" (*Islands and Exiles* 355). Rather than rehearsing this explicit thematization of historical reflection in *L'Isolé soleil* that a number of critics have previously studied with great insight,[3] in what follows I wish to explore one of the novel's themes and underline its at once profound and hidden ties with the recovery of Caribbean memory.

Jazz is thoroughly linked to *L'Isolé soleil*'s production of meaning, a driving force in its historiographic machine that formulates and generates constructions and critiques in ever-new combinations of once-buried memories. Jazz and Maximin's historiography are united more profoundly than their mere thematic juxtaposition might suggest. The exterior dissimilarity between musical and linguistic signifiers hides what the Anglophone Caribbean writer and critic Kamau Brathwaite calls a "subterranean unity." Maximin the poet-historian is thus able to draw upon the oral cultural practices of the African diaspora to give form to a suppressed, often ambiguously valorized past. Both jazz and Caribbean literature address critically the dilemmas of historical representation to work through an alienated subjectivity with hidden similarities belied by their surface heterogeneity.

Blues Analysis in a Caribbean Mode

The music of the cultural and geographic area that Paul Gilroy has called the "black Atlantic world" is omnipresent in *L'Isolé soleil*. The novel returns again and again to the presence of music in the daily existence of African America. The music and instruments of European origin appropriated and personalized by Antilleans, including the waltzes the fictional character Louis-Gabriel plays on his violin during the invasion of Napoleon's troops in Guadeloupe, properly Caribbean creations—such as the *Gwo-ka* and the beguine—and the musics of the greater African American world—including steel bands, Afro-Cuban music, and jazz—are all described extensively. The latter two musics receive particular attention in Maximin's novel. The Afro-Cuban music the character Siméa hears in Paris during the 1940s perfectly translates the emotional turmoil she is experiencing, allowing her better to understand the Antillean poets she admires. American jazz is even more fundamental to the novel's narrative. Siméa's partner, Ariel, is a saxophonist who introduces her to this musical world before leaving for New York, Forty-second Street, and the bebop of Charlie Parker and Dizzy Gillespie. Maximin evokes the great moments of jazz in the twentieth century, and two periods in particular are preeminent in the novel: bebop and its precursors, including the music of Coleman Hawkins in particular, and the free jazz of the 1960s and 1970s. Given this fundamental narrative focus on jazz in *L'Isolé soleil*, I wish to consider further its function within the novel's overall structure.

Judging solely by the descriptions of this music made by the narrators, Maximin's use of African-derived musics reproduces French stereotypes from the 1920s and 1930s, when "le Jazz Hot" and the blues of Louis Armstrong seemed—to unfamiliar ears—to escape from a morass of musico-theoretical strictures, and the black bodies of performers such as Josephine Baker were celebrated as vehicles of sexual desublimation. Although African American music is mentioned in numerous passages in the book, its description rarely seems to rise above typical clichés of black exoticism and gender-based stereotypes.[4] In this vein, *L'Isolé soleil* rewrites the famous culminating passage of *La Nausée* in which the saxophone melody Roquentin hears and the voice of a black singer ("Some of these days"), transported across time, are "saved"; and their art redeems, for the narrator, the hope lost in the moment of each individual's disappearance. Maximin redirects this Sartrean experience of jazz, to be filtered now through the subjectivity of a black Antillean woman, one who fully participates in the world she describes. Maximin's rewriting rejects Sartre's intellectualized and phallocentric vision of this moment of enlightenment to evoke a poetic, expressive fusion of listener and player.

The cultural references that allow Siméa to understand this music come from the black Atlantic itself, and, for all its reliance on clichés, her sympathetic rapport with the Caribbean music and the musicians she finds in Paris is less shocking than the gaze, at once ethnographic and voyeuristic, typical of the Parisian intellectual of the twenties and thirties: "But all your words hurt me this evening, you, Cuban singers and Antillean poets, your male bodies are enclosed within words and amorous stratagems, that can only be broken by the rhythm of improvised jazz and sweet or furious madness of words" (134–35). Siméa goes on to compare Coleman Hawkins's saxophone to "a great, deep phallus [un grand sexe grave] [that] improvises in solitude its shameless call with the deep and exalted vehemence of repressed desires" (144).

Looked at thematically, the clichéd tone of the passage presents jazz as part of the historical milieu of 1940s Paris in which "Black Exotica" (Lock 70) functioned as cultural commodities and signifiers of sublimated sexual desire. The novel's explicit thematization of jazz artists focuses on the libidinal investments of its fictional listener at the expense of an appreciation of that artist's practice, whether understood in musical, sociocritical, or spiritual terms. Jazz, for Siméa as for the Parisian intellectuals of the 1920s, functions as a vehicle for the liberation of repressed sensuality and desires.

And yet, to sustain this reading of jazz in *L'Isolé soleil* would be to judge a cultural phenomenon solely in terms of the desire and pleasure created between performer and listener. Although this relatively immediate level of appreciation is an important aspect of musical performance, to dwell there is to disregard the levels of insight and awareness that the greatest masters have achieved in their practice. In a similar manner, one could simply enjoy Marie-Gabriel's text as a merely affective, expressive creation ("I aspire through writing to create desire" [106]), ignoring the complex aesthetic manipulations she operates upon her historical and poetic materials. In conjunction with the formal complexity of *L'Isolé soleil* itself, it is essential to understand the more profound function of this theme (jazz) by clearly elucidating the relation between jazz and Afro-Caribbean culture, as Maximin practices it.

What then is the relation between jazz and literature, two highly dissimilar signifying practices? This question can be addressed on many levels. The nonreferential nature of musical signifiers makes any attempt to articulate their content highly problematic, and René Ménil is perhaps the sole Antillean critic to have explored the difficulties this poses for any rigorous appreciation of African diasporic music as a cultural phenomenon:

> It is not easy to penetrate to the essence of musical compositions in order to grasp significations that are not given unambiguously *[toutes faites]* in the impression they make upon us. Music, like all the arts, does not reveal immediately to logical reason the secret of its messages since it addresses itself to our sensibility "without a concept" (Kant). What's more, the musical message will be naturally enigmatic and mysterious since music is not figurative as a painting might be: its material, consisting of sounds and rhythms, is invisible and the space in which it operates—duration in time—is itself invisible. Given these difficulties, in failing to grasp musical action itself, [cultural criticism] naturally offers discourses on music rather than restituting the truth of music itself. (252)

Unquestionably, however, African-derived musics are a privileged form of expression and communication throughout the Americas. It is thus essential to reflect upon their means of signification if we are to understand the interaction of these two registers of expression (musical and poetic) in *L'Isolé soleil;* we must take seriously the possibility that highly developed reflection and commentary might reside in the cultural practices traditional to a fundamentally oral society rather than solely in European-derived criticism or theory (Gates, "Editor's Introduction" 15). It is thus a question not of making pedantic lists of intertextual and intercultural influences in Caribbean literature, whether these be European, African, or other, but rather of grasping the productivity of an aesthetic act of *bricolage* (vernacular construction), objects that resulted from and yet transcend their mere influences. The attempt to release the cognitive force of such vernacular material is fundamental: if black Atlantic critical theory is to amount to more than the wielding of prefabricated, preestablished norms and categories ("Identity Politics," "Créolité," and "Afrocentrism" being the most notable examples), if this theory is to satisfy its own demands for insight, it must immerse itself in a vernacular productivity that appears opaque to our understanding in its primary form as unmediated aesthetic expression.

Such is the challenge Paul Gilroy has laid before theorists of the black Atlantic world. "Taking the music seriously," as Gilroy puts it, does not simply mean apprehending its status as aesthetic object but demonstrating the capacity of black Atlantic aesthetic objects to serve as "the expression of a class of organic intellectuals whose immanent critique of society arises from within their art, rather than any discourse or overtly political activity exterior to that practice" (*Black Atlantic* 76). No simple equivalence can pertain in such a matter; art is not theory. And yet, insofar as the latter is to retain a measure of creativity and, indeed, insight, it must turn toward the objects most antinomical to its own nature, risking methodological fragility for the flashes of insight that can arise from its self-estrangement.

Clearly, a surface resemblance exists between jazz and black Atlantic fiction and poetry as processes of critical reflection and creation. Despite a long-standing perception of jazz musicians as "natural" artists possessing an essentialized, inherited talent, the music's high level of complexity has required an intense analytical and critical sophistication on the part of its creative figures. Whether this awareness was built upon oral or graphic modes of learning and whether it was acknowledged by media often bent upon portraying musicians as marginal exotics, the standards of jazz as a practice have required that even those musicians concerned only with stylistic imitation acquire a thorough knowledge of past genres. Furthermore, creative artists have used that knowledge of the past to create new, highly sophisticated languages. As with any evolving language, communication was possible only through the incorporation of recognizable elements brought together in new formations according to the dictates of personality and temperament, historical milieu, and imagination. From bebop to free jazz to the neoconservatism of the 1980s and 1990s, jazz musicians have depended upon this dialectical reforging of tradition in their acts of expression and communication.

Likewise, if we take Maximin as an example, the creative writer moves to develop an awareness of his culture's history attained through a long period of stylistic and archival research and reflection upon the problems with which an idealized, imagined future text confronts him. Indeed, *L'Isolé Soleil* can itself be understood as the critical representation of this process, as it follows its narrators' investigations of their inherited cultural materials and their attempts to give those materials an innovative and appropriate aesthetic structure. This process of apprenticeship to the past remains the same for any creative artist. Whether their style is primarily monolingual (as with a writer who might use a single style or voice, or a jazz musician who might play only in a hard-bop or free style) or heterogeneous and multiple, as with a writer building up symphonic structures around multiple narrations and voices (Maryse Condé's *Traversée de la Mangrove*—to be considered in chapter 7—typifies this process), or a musician whose eclectic constructions move from one mood or voice to another (Charles Mingus, for example), both musician and writer build upon the foundation laid down by their predecessors.

Given the enormous importance of music in the black diaspora, both in culture and in literature, numerous attempts have been made to theorize a "jazz aesthetic" of literature. A staple of African-American studies in the work of writers such as Amiri Baraka and, more recently, Albert Murrey, reflection on jazz and other New World musics of African origin has also enjoyed the attention of Caribbean critics.[5] In the field of Antillean letters, René Ménil in particular has shown an ongoing affinity for jazz as early as his 1944 *Tropiques* article, "The Situation of Poetry in the Antilles." There, Ménil clearly announces, in schematic form, the relation of jazz to Antillean historical experience that Maximin will pursue: "It is notably the crucial phenomenon of jazz that, more certainly than any critical reflection, has allowed us to grasp the *historical* character of the artwork, in its content and form" (121, emphasis in original). Edward Kamau

Brathwaite's study *Jazz and the West Indian Novel* offers in turn a suggestive, yet frustratingly limited, analysis of anglophone Caribbean literature. Brathwaite uses the categories of improvisation, riffs, and call and response as a series of metaphors for understanding Caribbean literature. As a whole, this school of criticism describes the jazz/literature relationship in terms of surface similarities, limiting itself to comments on the relations in jazz between soloist and group, improvisation and composition, call and response, and similar categories typically seen to function as metaphors for a utopian intersubjectivity.

Following this approach, it is possible to find in passages of *L'Isolé soleil* a "jazz aesthetic" in the novel's moments of linguistic play. In this view, the narrators manipulate words and letters to engage a textual improvisation that sustains and renews the Schillerian defense of aesthetic play as the moment in which autonomous human subjectivity appears.[6] Starting with a linguistic fragment, *L'Isolé soleil*'s narrators modify this motif through all its possible permutations, using processes of augmentation, diminution, modulation, and tension and release (178). Such a formalist understanding of the "jazz aesthetic"—though not without interest—is ultimately limited by its erasure of the novel's dynamic relationship with historical processes of both mnemonic recovery and imaginative transformation.

While it has seemed obvious to many commentators that jazz has played a radical and revolutionary role in American culture, few have attempted to theorize just what form the structural functioning of jazz as a social practice might take. Edouard Glissant and Edward Kamau Brathwaite have described a "subterranean unity" (Brathwaite) of the black Atlantic. This unity ties together Brazil and Cuba, Trinidad and New Orleans, Haiti and New York, despite surface differences of language and cultural heritages from the colonial period. A passage in *L'Isolé soleil* traces the historical recovery of this unity: "They tried to make us reject our nature as African Blacks and the pride in our bodies and the memory of our ancestors and we fought for the respect of this originary dimension. As to America, you'll agree that it's only since the [Second World] War and the blockade of the Antilles that we've discovered ourselves at the center of this continent, and perhaps one day we'll learn that Cuba and Haiti, Bahia and New York are closer to us than Paris. After all that, do you think it's healthy for us to choose history over geography?" (225). As theorists from Melville Herskovitz to Antonio Benítez-Rojo have argued, these geographically dispersed communities have a common social structure with its roots in the plantation system and an African-derived culture that remained in some measure intact, though "subterranean," after its passage to the New World.

Common to these various theories of African American unity is an emphasis on the cultural value of music in societies where other forms of communication, creation, and resistance were often unavailable. Maximin himself has emphasized this role of music; for him, music is "a means of circulating; music circulates faster than ideas, and [to speak of music] is thus a way of showing a solidarity between diverse regions."[7] Thus, Maximin focuses upon music as a way out of the impasse of the sublime terror of absolute freedom that I argue encloses Césaire's *Christophe* and the process of decolonization it mirrors (chapter 4). Christophe's pursuit of absolute freedom leads to the negation of subjective experience in the abstract terror of death. Henri Christophe ends his life, I argue, with the dissolution of any particular and immediate experience within absolute abstraction, visiting upon his people a Caribbean Terror of death and destruction in the name of freedom.

As Mireille Rosello has argued, *L'Isolé soleil* undertakes a critique of the death-based sacrificial logic of texts such as Césaire's *Et les chiens se taisaient* and the various examples of phallocentric hero-worship that have marked the growing historical attention paid to Louis Delgrès since 1946:[8] "Suicide is the only heroism of our islands crushed beneath the squadrons of the continents: entire Carib villages threw themselves from cliffs, slaves poisoned themselves and their families, smothering their new-born. There lies so much blood in our memories.... Sometimes I ask myself if it wouldn't be better to do away with all these fathers who have only left us death as a dazzling memory" (86; see Rosello 41–70).

Breaking free of this "dazzling memory of death," Maximin turns to music as a counter-model of subjective experience forged in the black vernacular. For Maximin, language (when musical or poetic) strives to circumvent the annihilation of the particular in universal abstraction, where, as Hegel observed, "the sensuous This that is meant *cannot be reached* by language, which belongs to consciousness" (*Phenomenology* 66). Maximin's musical language attempts to maintain the fleeting particularity of aesthetic, living expression while operating as a vehicle of a noncoercive communal experience. Maximin's writing constructs, as Chris Bongie observes, "a space that is between the oral and the written, and that puts into question the (inescapable) binary thinking that would cordon them off from one another" (*Islands and Exiles* 400). His focus on music transports the fleeting lived experience of musical performance within the frozen rigidity of language. Music has traditionally functioned as the privileged vector of intersubjectivity within black Atlantic culture. Blues describes the determinate experience of the suffering, unfree individual in society within the construct of an equally real and actual creative freedom. In musical, as in poetic practice, a preexisting language carries one into relation with a community that has created certain norms of expression. In turn, the poet/musician brings to bear the particularity of her subjective experience to saturate linguistic expression with torment and joy. Maximin's literary voice uses music to mediate the expressive and structural dimensions of language. As such, a critical understanding of jazz implies its engagement as far more than a mere theme in Maximin's novel. For jazz to inform our understanding of *L'Isolé soleil*, we must pursue the former's concretion, refusing to let the constellation of jazz, Antillean literature, and historical experience remain the mere abstraction of cultural jargon. Only then can we hope to describe the link between this political, creative music and a novel preoccupied with the past and future transformation of the French Caribbean world.

JAZZ, FAR from being an occasional theme in *L'Isolé soleil*, is profoundly engaged in the novel's principal project of articulating a Caribbean historical experience that can avoid a stifling academicism, one that would respond to the narrators' desire to "make poetry and history cohabit" (272). The novel's thematization of jazz adopts a revolutionary ideology; it evokes music as one of the primary vectors of historical transformation in the black Atlantic. The music Siméa hears in Parisian jazz clubs carries "messages of revolution" (135), while her friend and correspondent Ariel later asks her, "Isn't music the only freedom that we've truly conquered to this day in the three centuries of our oppression?" (172). Near the end of the novel, the revolutionary implications of jazz reappear, this time during a discussion between Adrien and Antoine, when the former describes his love of the free jazz of Sonny Murrey and Chicago's AACM and its Art Ensemble of Chicago (266–67). Adrien, however, is more skeptical than Antoine regarding any simple equation between jazz and revolution such as that offered by Stokely Carmichael: "The only revolutionaries [Carmichael] had met were jazz musicians playing in a club. . . . I think he was wrong: music can never effect a revolution. The two can only dance together from time to time, like two bodies in love improvising their movements in tune with the rhythm, when the revolution has a moment of liberty" (90). Toward the end of the novel, the same debate over jazz as libratory practice reappears, this time in the context of Antoine's desire to unite *gros-ka* and free jazz with radical theater (266). These examples of Maximin's use of jazz in *L'Isolé soleil*, while maintaining a certain critical distance, testify to a faith in jazz as a practice at once pan-American and concretely implicated in the larger historical development of these societies. What might constitute this social content of a music that must use nonverbal means to communicate subjective—and objective—insight?[9]

Musicians like Charlie Parker in the 1940s and John Coltrane and Archie Shepp during the 1960s played a significant role in the Civil Rights and Black Power movements; less clear is how one might actually conceptualize the linkage between a nonverbal musical practice and more general cultural phenomena and historical tendencies. While a poem, for example, might make specific reference to injustice, outrage, revolution, etc., jazz commentators have in general been limited to pointing simplistically to song titles ("Now's the Time," "Freedom Now Suite") or to culling material from interviews in which musicians held forth on various social issues.[10]

In societies where all open contestation invited violent repression, acts of rebellion were necessarily hidden in all but the most extreme situations. These infinitesimal movements of hidden rebellion appeared as apparently inconsequential acts, as for example naming one's child after the Guadeloupean revolutionary hero Louis Delgrès (*IS* 187) or the fictionalized, hidden enactment of a slave's verbal revenge on his or her master in the songs and *contes* of the French Caribbean. The former slave-holding cultures of the Americas all have in common oral traditions whose necessity was exacerbated by limited access to a dominant written culture.

In light of these limitations, the "revolutionary" aspect of jazz so often evoked in *L'Isolé soleil* becomes clearer. Bebop, to take another practice Maximin addresses, was not simply a *musical* revolution but was equally an immanent critique of the society in which it appeared. This critique occurred, on a primary level, through a contestation of the aesthetic values operating in a segregated society, in a music whose sophistication at first made it nearly unplayable by more conservative musicians, both black and white. Its appearance provoked a violent racist response from the white custodians of jazz culture of the period at magazines such as *Downbeat*, and its message of aesthetic and technical self-sufficiency—though communicated in nonverbal form—was clearly perceived by its audience.

Maximin's blues historiography engages a vernacular reawakening of the past. At the same time, it uses poetic expression to avoid a purely documentary reproduction of social facts and historical events, always searching for the means to point beyond what has already existed. Jazz, in turn, is the critical, theoretical tool Maximin engages in this pursuit. The primary, fundamental relation of *L'Isolé soleil* to jazz is not thematic; rather, the mechanisms of social analysis developed by the historical musicians Maximin describes actually prefigure and inform the text's modes of understanding. Across the linguistic and cultural divisions that mark the Americas, a subterranean homology of practice occurs in the vernacular cultural products of music and Antillean literature. A methodological equivalency exists between Maximin's own poetic historiography and the musico-theoretical undertaking of Coleman Hawkins, the musician at the center of *L'Isolé soleil*. In order to demonstrate the novel's replication of the symbolic revolutions undertaken by jazz musicians such as Coleman Hawkins, I want to argue for the fundamental coherency between these two New World forms of social critique and creation.

Jazz: The Untold Story

To begin this process, I wish to examine an assertion one frequently comes across in African American letters, to explore some of the implications it might hold for a novel such as *L'Isolé soleil* that so intimately engages jazz in its thematic and formal structures. The point is a straightforward and seemingly obvious one: that an understanding of African American music is fundamental to our ability to understand African American culture in general. One comes across this sentiment in many different forms, and it is an axiomatic assertion in much of the greatest writing produced by black Americans this century. From Langston Hughes to Ralph Ellison and from W. E. B. DuBois's *The Souls of Black Folk* to Amiri Baraka's *Blues People*, to choose only a few canonical examples, countless writers have underlined this central aspect of African American culture. But it probably received its most direct, distilled formulation in the opening pages of James Baldwin's 1955 essay, "Many Thousands Gone": "It is only in his music, which Americans are able to admire because a protective sentimentality limits their understanding of it, that the Negro in America has been able to tell his story. It is a story which otherwise has yet to be told and which no American is prepared to hear" (65).

The attention devoted to jazz in literature, cultural criticism, and the media testifies to the fact that its centrality has remained far from unnoticed. And yet, in taking James Baldwin's assertion seriously, a whole range of problems open up that have only recently begun to be addressed in the field of jazz studies by writers such as Krin Gabbard, Ingrid Monson, Ronald Rodano and Bernard Gendron, problems which, I think, imply a fundamental shift in its mode of inquiry. For what Baldwin's statement claims is that African American music, and jazz in particular, is not merely a musical practice. It is also a vehicle of communication that tells a more than musical story in an encoded form, a story that is more than organized sound, one that instead contains within its material existence encryptions of the social reality out of which it arose.

Analysis of jazz has traditionally moved between the two poles of subjective, anecdotal commentary and analytic musicological inquiry. Despite their unquestionable importance, these methodologies largely abandon the problems of musical communication inherent in James Baldwin's claim. They submit to the immanence of the musical object as either pure immediate experience or abstract formal construction and tend to neglect its status as cultural product. Without there existing any clear musicological consensus regarding the status of music as historical signifier, the musical object's existence as a socially and historically inflected text is nonetheless a critical commonplace in the fields of cultural and African-American studies, once again succinctly summarized by Paul Gilroy: "The power of music in developing black struggles by communicating information, organizing consciousness, and testing out or deploying the forms of subjectivity which are required by political agency, whether individual or collective, defensive or transformational, demands attention to both the formal attributes of this expressive culture and its distinctive *moral* basis" (*Black Atlantic* 36).[11] Perception of what Ingrid Monson terms "the shaping of cultural meaning and human subjectivities" (211) via an analysis of musical processes themselves remains the exception in jazz studies.[12]

In fact, it is in the very nature of jazz to offer critical reactions and alternatives to social totality, whether we look at its often overt function as a music of protest, or within the actual structural modifications it has enacted upon American music. Anti-intellectual postulations of jazz's status as "just music" are one more form of the long-standing belief in the social autonomy of music, an ideology that forms the cultural capital of musicians, justifying their position within society through an insistence on their economic independence as "free artists."

Maximin's work upon his historical material, like that of the jazz improviser, proceeds in the manner of what Houston A. Baker has termed the "blues analysis." This practice spares no effort to confront history, yet its formal, poetic experimentation allows it imaginatively to transform the society it interrogates. As Baker eloquently states, "When [the blues analyst] is confronted with the 'break' constituted by the job of specifying a distinctive tradition in all its resonant fullness, he must know the vernacular or 'Native' level of the tradition and then be improvisationally nimble enough to advance both the tradition itself and its clearer understanding" (112). Indeed, the entire chapter of *L'Isolé soleil* entitled "Jonathon's Notebook" offers such a blues analysis of Guadeloupean history. The narrator Marie-Gabriel has taken the historical documents sent to her from Paris (and which we never read in their original form) and transformed them, basing that transformation upon her knowledge of what Maximin terms "our cultural identity" (*Lone Sun* xx). This identity is no simple essentialism but rather exists in dynamic relation with the consciousness of its incompletion; Marie-Gabriel, for example, comments on her inability to recreate Delgrès fictionally, a historical individual too far removed from her, by history, by documents, by his military, masculine personality (*IS* 107). Rather than unquestioningly accepting Delgrès as the hero of a revolutionary Guadeloupean past, Marie-Gabriel transforms this phallocentric and death-centered history via the author's productive imagination. She refuses to abandon history because of the role it plays in overcoming the alienation of a still-colonial culture. At the same time, she revindicates the aesthetic imagination; she recognizes both the epistemological impossibility of any full and unambiguous access to a historical referent; using the deterritorializing force of poetry in Caribbean culture Marie-Gabriel "will place the truth in the service of the imaginary and not the contrary" (18).

In passing through multiple discursive modalities, *L'Isolé soleil* demonstrates an intense preoccupation with the Guadeloupean history preserved in letters, folk tales, Afro-Caribbean syncretic religions, and the documents left as traces of colonialism. At the same time, the novel revindicates the imaginative freedom of a blues analyst who has processed those traces to improvise a new "break." This improvisation is based not on pure freedom, "anything goes," but rather on the freedom that comes through an intense familiarity with the constitutive elements of Guadeloupean identity, a critical creativity that breaks away from the inertial weight of those "facts" in an imaginative representation of the possible forms of a transformative social dynamic.

WE ARE NOW in a position to see that the usage of jazz in *L'Isolé soleil* entails far more than a ludic poetics of improvisation. As an example of what Henry Louis Gates Jr. has called signifyin(g), it also suggests a distinct relationship with historical source material: jazz reworks an original culturally dominant practice through the innovation that draws upon it, reproducing it with an essential difference.[13] This is evident in the creation of jazz as a syncretic practice, a syncretism Maximin dramatizes by the fictional character George's musical creativity, mixing European- and African-based musics into something new and unique in the years immediately preceding Delgrès's revolt: "George went to find his violin, and beneath the starlit night, to the rhythm of the gro-ka drums, he improvised melodies in unison with the voices of peasants" (34).

Many jazz musicians have, in highly articulate fashion, explored the historicity of jazz. Coleman Hawkins was, however, perhaps the first and certainly was one of the music's greatest structural "signifiers." The classic *Body and Soul* is in turn the standard he is most remembered for signifyin(g) upon. Appropriately, Hawkins's soloing on this composition is the thematic focus for Siméa's discussion of her Parisian jazz experience in *L'Isolé soleil*. Hawkins's playing on his famous 1939 recording of *Body and Soul* is signifyin(g) at its finest: the saxophonist never plays through the melody, instead referring to it ever more laconically. What Hawkins perfected in this improvisation was a system of signification upon standard tunes marked by their radical reharmonization in an improvised context.[14] The musician depended upon an informed listener to recognize the underlying melody and harmony even if, as with Hawkins and *Body and Soul*, he never actually played that melody to clue in less-informed listeners. Hawkins created elaborate new constructions in the improvised reharmonizations of *Body and Soul*, constructions whose formal distinction lay in his dynamic, arpeggio-based style.[15]

This stylistic trait is perhaps what motivated Maximin's choice of Hawkins in *L'Isolé soleil* rather than a less harmonically complex, more riff-based improviser of the period such as Lester Young or Ben Webster. For Maximin's own prose shows a certain affinity to Hawkins's playing, with its ornate, florid poetics. Moreover, a deeper homology lies in these two artists' resolutions of problems of form. Specifically, each addresses an African vernacular heritage (improvisation and the blues for Hawkins, Creole folk stories for Maximin) within forms taken from West European practice: the AABA song form and western instrumentation, or Maximin's troping of the postwar avant-garde French novel. Other musicians Maximin speaks of continued the critical practice begun by musicians like Coleman Hawkins in the 1920s and 1930s. Maximin's character Antoine evokes the musicians coming out of Chicago's Association for the Advancement of Creative Musicians (AACM) in a letter to Adrien: "Paris is becoming a reserve for 'Great Black Music'! I'm impatiently awaiting what you've promised to send me, especially Sunny Murray's *Hommage to Africa,* and the Art Ensemble of Chicago's record 'Ericka'" (267).[16] Although typically lumped in with lists of free jazz musicians, groups like The Art Ensemble of Chicago (whose slogan, "Great Black Music of the past and future," Adrien is referring to) have for nearly three decades evolved a syncretic music that looked as much to the eighty-year tradition of jazz and the various world musics as it did to the free jazz of the 1960s in its creation of a new music that was conversant with tradition yet refused to be constrained by it.

The musicians of the AACM, like Maximin himself, work as vernacular "blues analysts": "investigator[s] with both an interdisciplinary orientation *and* a tropologically active imagination—an imagination that ceaselessly compels the analyst to introduce tropes that effectively disrupt familiar conceptual determinations" (Baker 110). This involves the inclusion of multiple forms of African American expression in a highly sophisticated and open discourse, creating a music that simultaneously moves from a profound understanding and exploration of the past into the future.

Something more than the affinity of a Guadeloupean author for American jazz links Daniel Maximin and Coleman Hawkins. In fact, they are united by the two homological figures most typical of their discursive practices: the anagram (both in Maximin's title and those occurring throughout his narrative itself) and the arpeggio (Hawkins). While the anagram breaks the unity of a word into its constituent elements in a recombinitory gesture, so the arpeggio breaks up a unified sound image (the chord) into its individually articulated elements (notes). More than mere aesthetic indulgence, both the anagram and its musical corollary the arpeggio rework the antinomies of black Atlantic historical experience in the aesthetic constructions of Maximin and Hawkins.

Coleman Hawkins's music sustains the vernacular social critique of jazz, and this in ways that announce Maximin's own pan-American aesthetic practice. Like Duke Ellington during the same period, Hawkins offered technical solutions in his musical procedure to the more generalized existential problem confronting African Americans in this century: the divided subjectivity—or "double consciousness"—first theorized by W. E. B. Dubois, a subjectivity torn between a technocratic, racist culture and an oppositional, oral-based, organic blues culture (see chapter 2). Hawkins and Ellington, who on the surface shared a certain cultured aestheticism, each developed their practice as a means of surviving and flourishing in a hostile environment; both developed highly personalized means of uniting the two cultures that uneasily must find ways to coexist in a single subject. As Dubois famously put it, "One ever feels his two-ness,—an American, a Negro; two souls, two thoughts, two unreconciled strivings; two warring ideals in one dark body, whose dogged strength alone keeps it from being torn asunder" (45).

In Ellington's music, as René Ménil observes in his essay "On a Certain Ellingtonian Effect in Créolité," the vernacular blues legacy that Ménil calls "folklore" "is not an endpoint—the result of musical work—but the implicit point of departure for a music to be invented. [Ellington] incorporates a primary base of folklore in a construction (investigation of themes and rhythms, the organization of regular, syncopated, and silent time) that develops to the point of erudite symphonic composition—a practice that, in its development, utilizes all the technical resources at its disposal" (256). In so doing, Ellington created sound images of Dubois's "double consciousness," a "music of the *second degree [au second degré]*." Upon a sonorous matter and established rhythms, a *secondary* elaboration occurred in the modern industrial city that expressed a living modernity *[l'actualité de la vie]* and not regressive exoticisms of the primitive forest and sugar cane and cotton fields, [elements] that only took their place in these compositions as a foundation kept in the background" (255, emphasis added).

Similarly, Hawkins's improvisation in *Body and Soul* uses the tools of Western harmony to fashion an objective solution to this general existential conflict defining black experience throughout the Americas. He combines blues-based techniques of instrumental vocalization and improvisation with one of the most highly developed harmonic practices of arpeggiation of the period. Hawkins's improvisations strain the monophonic limitations of the saxophone against a wide-ranging harmonic sensibility. They place chord upon chord, break each into its constituent elements, reconstructing them in a series of musical anagrams. While maintaining this musical representation of social contradiction, Hawkins's flowing lines, as a crafted totality, construct an elegant, integrationist *modus vivendi* that uses music to resolve the conflict between the violence and normativity of American society and a traditional, oral-based African American culture.

By incorporating Coleman Hawkins into the narrative of a novel so intimately concerned with the development of French Caribbean identity, Maximin, a blues theorist himself, offers a further vernacular solution to a problem confronting African Americans throughout the New World. A specific form of Dubois's double consciousness can be said to exist in the French Caribbean struggle to mediate French and Caribbean, European and African cultures and histories in a neocolonial society. Hawkins's elegant fusing of blues and traditional Western harmonic practice has a clear affinity with Maximin's own Césaire-derived poetics, which combine a refined poetic surface with thematic material drawn from the black Atlantic world. Jazz and *L'Isolé soleil* both practice a form of vernacular historiography that explores the past with an eye to the future, "making poetry and history cohabit," using the tactics and techniques of an oral culture to point beyond neocolonial relations of dependency. Hawkins's integrationist resolution of social antinomy is structurally akin to Maximin's. Both artists refuse a revolutionary iconoclasm, searching instead for an elegant resolution to the social contradictions they objectify in their musical and poetic texts. Both build their solutions upon a mastery of their inherited historical material and a clear understanding of the specific social totality in which they participate. While not the "revolutionary restructuralism" (Anthony Braxton, qtd. in Lock, *Forces in Motion* 99) of a John Coltrane or Aimé Césaire, Hawkins's and Maximin's immanent critiques both invoke a resolution to a contradictory existence that avoids reification through the use of improvisation (for Hawkins) and (for Maximin) the affirmation of a poetic voice and a multiplicity of narrative subjects.

Master improvisers themselves, the multiple narrators of *L'Isolé soleil* depend on the audience to know the tune so that the latter can fully appreciate the narrators' improvisational flourishes. Their multiple articulations engage the masters of the past as they attempt to move beyond them. Maximin intimates a fluid French-Caribbean subject at home not only in the Americas of the Caribbean archipelago but in the entire black Atlantic world, marked by its multiple syncretic cultures. Music "is our first language; the others, such as English or Spanish or French, only came later" (*Lone Sun* xxi). Music provides both the theoretical and existential foundation upon which Maximin builds *L'Isolé soleil* and the imaginative, poetic vehicle that, through criticism and creativity, moves from the past into the future in a gesture that can be rightfully called an aesthetic and material restructuralism.

MAXIMIN'S 1995 novel, *L'Ile et une nuit,* continues the lyrical exploration of Guadeloupean experience begun in *L'Isolé soleil. L'Ile et une nuit* recounts the experiences of Maximin's protagonist, Marie-Gabriel, as she struggles against the forces of nature on the night in 1989 when hurricane Hugo unleashed its devastating force upon the island of Guadeloupe. The novel is divided into seven chapters that correspond to the temporal moments of the hurricane's passing: *première heure, deuxième heure,* etc. The most striking characteristic of the novel, which is principally a dialogue between Marie-Gabriel and Maximin's first-person narrator, is its sense of interiority and a lack of any references beyond the island of Guadeloupe or even the house itself in which Marie-Gabriel waits out the storm's passing. As the terrifying, raging forces of nature pound the island during the night, Marie-Gabriel retreats to her ancestral home, Les Flamboyants, on the flanks of Mount Matouba, beneath the volcano Soufrière, where "all the rooms have been barricaded shut" (22), as she attempts simply to survive through the night. This limiting of experience to mere self-preservation extends as well to the productivity of her imagination, in which the imperative of survival focuses the mind to reflect upon its own concrete sense data: "Outside, the hurricane had already begun blackening the house's facade. But there can be no question of imagining the exterior of our enclosed tomb. Amid the warmth of real history *[l'histoire vraie]*, our imagination itself must remain within the interior of this house. Above all not to become delirious. But to dream of the interior.... A tiny end of the world to be undergone without necessarily dying" (25).

Unlike *L'Isolé soleil*, whose narration roamed freely across time, space, and multiple subjectivities, *L'Ile et une nuit* is tightly focused and structured. It is tempting to read *L'Ile et une nuit* allegorically; by strictly reducing its narrative vision to seven hours of Marie-Gabriel's lived experience, the novel radically excises references to the external world—and to Guadeloupe's tortuous relations with its French colonizer in particular. It is only in a few laconic passages that there survive distant echoes of the critique of French colonialism and Antillean alienation inherited from Aimé Césaire and Frantz Fanon by authors such as Edouard Glissant, Maryse Condé, and, indeed, the Maximin of *L'Isolé soleil*. As Marie-Gabriel emerges to witness the hurricane's devastation, Maximin's narrator comments: "I leave, my imagined one [Maximin's narrator is speaking to Marie-Gabriel, the character he has created], in the company of a people who seem no more than an apparition, a mirage, an act of conjuring, a miracle at best, the masks of their obscure desire. I leave you a country without any famine other than the hunger for a life more dear than daily bread, without any epidemic other than the cancer of the soul of those sick in their healthy bodies" (155). Instead of the sustained critique of Antillean alienation of a novel such as Glissant's *Malemort* (to be discussed in the following chapter), the historical status of the DOMs remains entirely implicit; and, from a comprehensible historical process, the French colonization of the Antilles becomes instead an uncontrollable, sublime force of nature that devastates the island.

In this reading, the heroic resistance to colonization of the Haitian revolution and the 1802 Guadeloupean revolution of Louis Delgrès and Ignace are fast-fading memories; instead, *L'Ile et une nuit* describes a resistance of patient endurance in which "we shall let the catastrophe unfurl itself till it satiates its violence, and we shall mix dreams and nightmares without sleeping, to have a chance of reaching its end" (11). In the face of impending catastrophe, the narrator calls for a communitarian circling of the wagons: "Our island is a true shack [case], built by our great family of betrothed orphans" in which Guadeloupeans may "perish together if there is nothing left to do, [but] above all we must never ever go outside as long as the hurricane has not gone away" (13). In the all-enveloping interiority of a single night's endurance, consciousness is unable to reach beyond the mere immediate need for survival, and the overpowering, sublime forces of nature foreclose the possibility of comprehending the totality that determines the actual experience of the island's French, and now European, citizens.

To read *L'Ile et une nuit* as this allegory for political quietism, one that calls for the unprotesting and patient endurance of a long-suffering people, is perhaps overly facile; certainly, such a reading obscures a much more complex meditation on the relation between natural beauty and the second nature humans construct around themselves for survival, a narrative that itself undertakes the temporal construction of an autonomous, self-identical subjectivity in the battle to survive the ahistorical forces of nature. This book argues that French Caribbean colonial experience in its historical progress denies autonomous subjectivity, first in the dehumanization of slavery and then in the subtler undermining of productive economic autonomy called departmentalization. In response to this historical dilemma, *L'Ile et une nuit*, like all of Maximin's work, refers to a fundamental dimension of African diasporic experience that has remained relatively autonomous from the alienating effects of instrumental reason: music. As the eye of the hurricane passes over Guadeloupe, Marie-Gabriel emerges temporarily from her bunkered seclusion to witness the devastation of her world. Expecting to encounter a world frozen in death, she finds instead one still alive, in which the moonlight "illuminated on the contrary a luxuriance of crushed survivals, of broken trees and courageous underbrush, a rich regalia of resistances and fragile sufferings" (90).

Before retreating to her house, she stumbles upon her most prized possession, her father's box of jazz records that she had recovered from the debris of another disaster when his plane crashed in 1962. As the storm quickly returns to its full force, in a house with no electricity, Marie-Gabriel re-creates in her mind the sound world of those recordings, an imaginary *discothèque* whose resonances armor her resolve to survive through the night: "There was nothing human to preserve from the hurricane but the natural resistance of humans themselves" (93). This music she recalls is the blues of a patient endurance in the face of human possibilities foreclosed by social violence: the suffering of Lady Day, Billy Holiday, the tragedy of pianist Bud Powell beaten senseless by the police and gradually losing his motor skills (103). It is the music of invention that sounds out the contours of an experience beyond this suffering, the music of Ellington and Monk, "the two who enriched my scale with an eighth invented note: the note of silence" (108); the music of Abdullah Ibrahim and Albert Ayler and of Charlie Mingus, "who knew how to lend his ears to the other musicians, who improvised ruptures to harmonize the rage against all the segregations and all the divisions [partitions] of retarded pithecanthropes" (110).

More than any other, however, the music of John Coltrane stands at the center of this story of an embattled Antillean subjectivity, where art appears at the moment survival is most threatened. *A Love Supreme* ("by my Brother John, with his belief that his saxophone knew so much more than himself that he could hardly take it from his mouth amid a surfeit of measures as far as his breath could carry him," writes Maximin in a verbal mimicry of Coltrane's "sheets of sound") comes to represent sonically the project of *L'Ile et une nuit* itself (104). Not merely in its impassioned call for faith and transcendence of suffering but in its innermost procedures and constructions, *A Love Supreme* enacts the production of autonomous subjectivity at the heart of *L'Ile et une nuit*. From the opening notes of its first section "Acknowledgment," B to E and F♯ back to B, the interval of a fourth announces the dissolution of the stable social world as a hurricane of sound gathers force to wash over the listener.[17] This secure world of our daily experience takes in music the form of functional harmony, the regular, inevitable movement of tonics to dominants and back, the eminently analyzable functions of triadic harmony, where each chord fulfills its preassigned role. Instead, the quartal, fourth-based harmony of Coltrane's music from this period typically has no single fixed key center and freely moves among tonalities following only the logic of its own immanent cellular elements, transposed throughout the entirety of the sonic spectrum. This is not a music "free" of structure; instead, it generates the structural coordinates of its movement and development internally, immanently.

Like the wind blasting through Les Flamboyants to destroy the house by the night's end, Coltrane's saxophone devastates the world of sound and experience as we know it, and only a single foundation remains to guide us through the forty-eight-minute journey of *A Love Supreme:* Jimmy Garrison's rock-solid bass ostinatos anchored upon and circling around the root foundation note F, like the single point of Marie-Gabriel's subjectivity that must hang on through the night to emerge the next morning, transformed. Like the highly structured form of *L'Ile et une nuit* in which each hour marks the passing to another stage in the history of a natural devastation, each section of *A Love Supreme* follows a determinate path in the movement of the improvised composition through a cycle of tonic centers that survive amid the chromatic onslaught of Coltrane's improvisations. In fact, as Lewis Porter has demonstrated, the infinite explorations of *A Love Supreme* adhere rigorously to the logically possible recombinations of a single pentatonic scale—F, A♭, B♭, C, D♭—in a four-part movement that progressively turns and transposes this scalar material (236). From its first appearance (Pt. 1: "Acknowledgment") built upon a roof F, the most typical basic key of the blues, the scales moves down a whole step to E♭ (Pt. 2: "Resolution"), then returns up to the same position, but now shifted to take B♭ as its root, in a more complex and chromatic exploration of blues experience (the minor blues of Pt. 3, "Pursuance"), and then finally up a whole tone to the key of C (Pt. 4: "Psalm"), the home of triadic harmony it began by rejecting, a structure that has been won only by casting off any preimposed a priori model of experience by passing through a violent dissolution of the self, and yet surviving, perhaps stronger and more self-aware from having discovered and generated the parameters of self-same experience from within; that is to say, autonomously.

L'Ile et une nuit offers no image of an undamaged, presubjective Antillean natural beauty, nor, in the face of the historical devastation of multinational capitalism and colonialism, does it project a linguistic palimpsest of this lost wholeness. The natural beauty offered by Antillean exoticism is itself always already an image, a representation, mediated by both consciousness and society. In representing Antillean natural beauty as though it were undamaged and immediately accessible, whether to immediate sensuous experience or through language, that representation is itself contaminated by commodification, it is indeed commodification itself, only it hides this fact in an image of organic wholeness. *L'Ile et une nuit* instead describes the historicization of nature in which the most terrifying and uncontrollable of natural events is mastered through its subjection to a logical schema of understanding, the grid of hours that pass by—one, two, three, four—in which an endless cycle of devastation repeated every August becomes a unique historical event mediated through human understanding, capable of analysis: the hurricane consists of "winds that were going to blow at nearly three hundred kilometers an hour, an intensity never before recorded since the beginning of weather observation in Guadeloupe" (23). The undifferentiated flow of natural time is rationalized and quantified, to become the second nature that is our experience of commodified clock-time.

In its retreat into the most inward recesses of subjective experience, *L'Ile et une nuit* seeks to recover for the Antillean subject the possibility of an autonomous understanding by reducing experience to the most basic of sense data and to then master this nature through a poetic and musical quasi-logic in its struggle for self-preservation. African diasporic music objectifies this process insofar as it offers a noninstrumentalized model of self-same experience in which, as Kant put it, "the standing and lasting I . . . constitutes the correlate of all our representations" (*Critique of Pure Reason* 240). Music shows us how to stand as subjects, how to structure experience, not according to a priori models but following the imminent logic of our own experience, echoed and reworked in sound. Like the constant foundation and root that underlie Coltrane's *A Love Supreme*, music in *L'Ile et une nuit* carries Marie-Gabriel through the night, allowing her not only to preserve but to model her self as it persists in time. Maximin, in *L'Ile et une nuit*, turns to the music of John Coltrane as a historical model for this subjectivity in which, as in Deleuze and Guattari's description of a musical subject, "to stand on one's own, . . . this is quite simply the act through which the composite of created sensations conserves itself in itself" in which music forms a composed monument to autonomous experience, "a block of present sensations that owe their conservation only to themselves" (*Qu'est-ce que la philosophie* 155–58).

This musical plane of immanence points beyond itself to a transcendence of the given data of human experience; these material sound images thus offer a concrete image of the possible. These material sounds of possibility, as Deleuze and Guattari observe, "are neither virtual nor actual, they are possible, the possible as an aesthetic category, . . . the existence of the possible" (168). Music is not the eternal postponement of autonomy; it offers instead an imminent transcendence of unfreedom, it is the process of liberation itself, necessarily partial in an unfree world, only an incomplete semblance of transcendence, but it is nonetheless a material enactment of liberation and a spur that liberates creative potentiality, the constituent power from which unfree subjects construct their freedom. No other music of the twentieth century so aptly demonstrates this radical force of constituent, productive subjectivity as Coltranes's *A Love Supreme*.

As Marie-Gabriel constructs in her mind the sound images of the music she loves, her productive imagination reconstitutes the world music promises us can still be ours. Call to mind, as she does, the opening notes of Miles Davis's *Kind of Blue* (104). Miles shows up in the studio with a few notes sketched on a napkin, and a sound world is suddenly created. A musical image flashes into our memory, pointing toward an open, undetermined future where we can improvise the parameters of our world as our own active construction. We reenact as an inheritance this sound world of creative memory as a sound that is not merely for us but one that has awaited our appearance and that, for all its universality, can exist both for us and beyond the interiority of our experience in a community of listeners. Maximin's *L'Ile et une nuit* resonates with Proust's insight that we can only truly experience music through the laborious reconstructive act of remembering it. The image of beauty music presents to us, for Maximin no less than Proust, is not available in the immediacy of a "natural" listening experience; our experience of both society and nature itself is necessarily preconstructed by alienation and commodification, by colonialism and consumerism. Instead, our imaginative labor reconstructs an image of beauty as a materially constitutive force, as objectified memory, as the sounds and words that materialize for us strange concepts and impressions brought back from another world. As objects of aesthetic construction, musical sound offers a concretization of utopia at once real yet incomplete. "Swann was . . . not wrong to think that the . . . musical phrase really existed. Certainly, human from this point of view, it belonged nonetheless to an order of supernatural creatures that we have never seen, but whom despite that we recognize with delight when some explorer of the invisible manages to capture one, and to bring it, from the divine world to which he has access, to shine for a few moments above our own" (*Un Amour de Swann* 213–14). John Coltrane was one of these explorers of the invisible, and his music made visible and concrete an image of human possibility that, as Maximin's lyrical prose demonstrates, extends across time and space to stand as an uncoerced image of emancipated human subjectivity.

6 History, Totality, and Other Modernist Projects
Global Consciousness in the Writings of Edouard Glissant

> He who wishes to form a link must possess in some fashion a total comprehension of the universe.
> —Giordano Bruno

CRITICS OF Edouard Glissant's vast and diverse corpus of writings have generally agreed that Glissant's "poetics of relation" strikes out beyond the modernist aesthetics of Césaire and Fanon's negritude. In this view, Glissant enacts a Caribbean version of the poststructuralist displacement of the centered, Sartrian, patriarchal subject in favor of an increasingly postmodern, "rhizomatic" subjectivity of relation. In place of the putative binary logic of Hegelian dialectics, Glissant would articulate a differential thought of the "Tout-monde." J. Michael Dash, in his 1995 monograph on Glissant, succinctly articulates this view as it finds expression in *Poétique de la relation:* Glissant's "theory of *relation* . . . takes notions of *errance, métissage,* and creolisation to a new global level. . . . The old mechanisms of identity, the traditional process of recognition and delimitation, can no longer be maintained in a situation of cultural chaos. Identity is no longer stable and becomes threatened by otherness" (179).

Interpreters of the totality of Glissant's work have, however, debated other dimensions of its unity; Michael Dash perhaps typifies a school that finds in its development, in consonance with Glissant himself, a gradual deepening and enriching of themes present from his earliest work (175). Peter Hallward, on the other hand, makes a compelling case for a radical break in Glissant's work after *Le discours antillais* (1981), at which point the modernist aesthetics and nationalist politics of works such as *Malemort* and the *Discours* are gradually abandoned for an increasingly abstract, politically resigned postmodernism. In pointing to the continuity of the problem of totality for Glissant, Hallward nonetheless emphasizes the radical change in nature of this totality after 1981: from a dialectical, expressive totality reminiscent of Lukács's "class consciousness" and Fanon's rearticulation of that notion as "national consciousness" (Hallward 442),[1] Glissant comes to postulate a fully immediate, immanent totality, bypassing persistent social contradiction for what Hegel called a "bad [because abstract] infinity" and a logic of tautology (454).

Each of these views of Glissant's work marshals convincing evidence and argument. In what follows, I wish not to refute one or the other; indeed, I think that one possible measure of great writing is the amount of tension and contradiction it productively sustains in its lines. My contention is that the most visible strand of Glissant's recent work, what one might term a "postmodern" concern for immanence, immediacy, and the decentering of subjectivities, is in some sense superficial and in any case not its most interesting theoretical dimension. Instead, unlike both Dash and Hallward, I wish to argue for a stealthy, subterranean *continuity* of a *modernist* Glissant, through and including his most recent collection of essays, *Traité du tout-monde* (1997). My sense is that Glissant has sustained over fifty years a reflection on such "modernist" problems as historical experience, totality, dialectical thought (whether named as such or called "relation"), labor- and production-based subjectivity, and consciousness. In his most recent reworking of that quintessentially Sartrian concept of the "project" into a call to turn Martinique into the world's first "ecological nation," Glissant brilliantly unites a putatively *dépassé* philosophical modernism and a global consciousness of relation.

This "project" points beyond the nation-state in a concrete vision of just what a praxis of "tout-monde" might imply in a world of increasing globalization, an "Empire" (Hardt and Negri) in which both the suffering and the productivity of individuals (the "multitude") grow preponderant. As such, I wish to describe three moments of Glissant's thought, moments that find varying forms of expression across the whole of his writings: First, a discourse of immediacy, instantaneity, immanence, and identity; next a dialectics of consciousness, historical experience, social contradiction, and political engagement; and finally, what is less a resolution of these two moments than a means of productively sustaining their contradictions and antagonisms in a transformative, future-oriented project of global, ecological consciousness and politics.

NUMEROUS COMMENTATORS have drawn attention to Glissant's philosophical training. When he came to Paris after the end of the second world war, the Martinican studied philosophy, undergoing the same intensive preparation and intellectual formation for the *agrégation* Césaire had pursued before him, completing both a *licence* (1955) and *diplome d'études supérieures* (1956) in philosophy with Jean Wahl (see Mbom, Waldinger, and Fonkoua). Romuald Fonkoua describes the influence of Wahl, distinguished among academic Parisian philosophers since his 1929 reintroduction of Hegel's *Phenomenology* to France, upon the young Glissant. Fonkoua bases his analysis on the putative influence upon Glissant of Wahl's early (1920, republished in 1953) text, "On the role of the idea of the instant in the work of Descartes," rather than Wahl's subsequent (and better-known) vulgarizations of an existential Hegelianism, filtered through Kierkegaard, Heiddeger, and Jaspers. Wahl's earlier text finds in Descartes a notion of thought defined as "the idea [that] is in us in such a way that we are immediately conscious of it" (qtd. in Fonkoua 301). In basing his argument upon this text written more than three decades before Glissant met Wahl, Fonkoua can sustain the image of a Glissant whose early texts articulate an experiential immediacy: "I must grasp in an *instant,*" Glissant writes, "these enormous expanses of silence into which my history has wandered." The mirror ("Mirror, ... Immobile on the surface") in Fonkoua's reading offers Glissant a poetic trope of immediacy in poems such as *Un champ des îles* (1954) (qtd. in Fonkoua 305, 312).

While there is no doubt a certain validity to this argument, particularly if one focuses on Glissant's poetry, one could well argue that even the passages Fonkoua cites are marked decisively by the Hegelian problematic of labor and its relation to consciousness by a dialectical *refusal* of immediacy in its putative sufficiency for consciousness: "Let [poetry] accomplish through me its work *[travail]* to illustrate through it the work of my consciousness seizing me" (*Soleil de la conscience,* qtd. in Fonkoua 307). In any case, a surprisingly paternalist tone undercuts the author's argument in which Wahl's theories would have "permitted Glissant . . . to acquire the certitude of the existence of the possibility of thinking" (303). As Wahl is to Glissant, so, in Fonkoua's reading of *Les indes,* the absolutely "innocent" and defenseless slaves do not actively "invent" their new world (as do "the [European] navigators") but rather inhabit a magical time of immediacy and chaos that Fonkoua calls "original, primary, arisen from the abyss"(313).

More positively, in drawing our attention to Wahl's influence on Glissant, Fonkoua not only (unintentionally) illuminates one source of the dialectical strain of Glissant's thought (to which I will return in a moment) but also localizes the discourse of immanence that gradually grows preponderant in Glissant's more recent "postmodern" writings. Perhaps most important, Wahl's teachings on the preeminence of poetry as a means of overcoming the divide between subject and object, science and consciousness (*Essence et Phénomènes,* 307) doubtless influenced and confirmed Glissant's steadfast vision of poetry as "the movement, through which man displaces the relations among things, knows them and *totalizes* them" (*IP* 102). Though "we can accumulate studies and references, ... we will never finalize such an endeavor. ... We imagine [totality] instead in a poetics; this imaginary gives a full meaning to these various determinate materials" (*PR* 168).

Following Hallward's lead, one finds a Wahlian discourse of immediacy and instantaneity growing preponderant in the more facile dimensions of Glissant's writings on totality and immanence in the 1980s and 1990s (I will describe what I see as Glissant's more compelling, dialectical understanding of totality and "tout-monde" below). In this view, Glissant's gradual abandonment of a localized investigation into Antillean experiences of alienation and dependency, and his corresponding call for the construction of an independent national consciousness and politics, culminates after 1981 in the hollow aestheticization of global experience via an evocation of culinary tourism: "They navigate between two impossibilities, truly the salt of the world's diversity. There is no need for integration, no more than segregation, to live together in the world and to eat all the foods of the world in a country" (*TM* 274). "We ate *taro,* which resembles the Antillean *dachines,* and *ragout de cabri,* as you would say in Haiti. These comparisons from country to country, to which we are so often tempted by the course of the world, illustrate the permanent fragility of all our lives" (*S* 80). This aestheticization strips Glissant's writing of its political, critical dimension in a celebration of the "Chaos of beauty" (*TM* 55) in which "chaos is beautiful when one conceives of all its elements as equally necessary" (*IPD* 71).

In these recent texts, Glissant echoes the postmodern conviction that we now live in a situation of total immanence in which there no longer exists an outside ("transcendence," "metaphysics," "teleology," "utopia"): "Henceforth all the sites *[lieux]* of the world meet one another, up to and including sidereal [i.e., heavenly] spaces. No longer project into the beyond what cannot be mastered in your space. ... I tell you there is no longer either Here or There" (*TM* 29, 479). This tendency culminates in Glissant's hypostatization of a positive, actualized totality, through a correspondence of poetry and reality, in his 1996 collection of lectures *Introduction à une poétique du divers:* "It is only today, with the totality-world finally realized concretely and geographically, that this vision of the world, which formerly was 'prophetic' in literature, can deploy or exert itself by taking for its true object what was formerly its mere aim" (34). In a world in which suffering continues unabated, Glissant resigns himself to the thought that "to know the unpredictable is to enter into agreement with the present, with the present in which we live" (89).

The critical force of Glissant's earlier writing dissolves in these lectures into a weak voluntarism in which our salvation would depend on the mere decision to think and perceive the world as rhizomatic relation: "As long as we live with the idea of unique root-identities, there will be Bosnias, there will be Rwandas, there will be Burundis, and each time we'll find ourselves before the same impossibility. . . . The imaginary of the *Tout-monde*, . . . only this imaginary can allow us to overcome these fundamental limits that no one wishes to overcome" (90–91). In a world that we no longer can have any hope of changing, in which forces that lie beyond our control increasingly control us (as "unpredictability"), one can nonetheless change oneself and adapt to the way of the world: "A poetic vision allows us to live with the idea of unpredictability because it permits us to conceive of unpredictability not as a negative but as a positive, and it permits us to change our understanding of this matter when no [other] concept or conceptual system could accomplish this" (102). In this critical reading of Glissant's latest work, poetry becomes the symbolic Valium that allows us to survive and affirm a painful and violent world beyond our control.

IN CONTRAST to this euphoric acquiescence to the world's unjust course, Glissant's writing harbors a more critical dimension, up to and including his most recent work. I want to argue that this critique takes the form of a potent reworking of dialectical thought, inherited from Hegel and Marx, one that, like the "negative dialectics" of Adorno, Derrida's *différance,* or Lyotard's *différend,* freely adapts and reconstructs Hegelian insights. This is a thought that Glissant at times explicitly marks as "dialectical," but one that more frequently goes under the name of "relation." For all Glissant's reflexive dismissals of Hegel (*IP* 37), his critique of a "non-relational Reason" corresponds quite precisely with Hegel's undoing of a frozen, rigid *Verstand* in the *Phenomenology* (*IP* 38). One might understandably confuse Glissant's injunction (only a few pages after the dismissal of Hegel in *L'intention poétique)* that "we cannot stop with mere appearances, with the phenomenon, the mechanism; *we must enter into things themselves*" (98) with the very concept of experience at the heart of Hegelian thought.[2] Taken in terms of their content—Antillean postcolonial experience—such Glissantian notions as dialectical relation, totality, and possibility differ radically from Hegel's fetishization of the European *Weltgeist*. However, their underlying logic is identical; Glissant's work in fact demonstrates the actual universality of these Eurocentric Hegelian concepts precisely by refusing to limit their application to European culture. While many commentators have drawn attention to Glissant's exploration of the dilemmas of Antillean history, instead of rehearsing what has been thoughtfully described in other research, I wish to draw attention here to the close links between Glissant's critical reconstruction of Antillean historical experience and his notion of dialectical relation.[3] The prophetic historiography of French Caribbean literature, in which Antillean subjects begin to "undo a painful sense of time and suddenly to project it into our future," operates through what Glissant calls the domain of the "possible" (*DA* 438). The possible, this "prophetic vision," reworks in shorthand the concept of *Möglichkeit* (possibility) fundamental to thinkers such as Hegel, Ernst Bloch, Heidegger, Adorno, Lefebvre, and Antonio Negri. Jean-Godefroy Bidima's *Théorie critique et modernité africaine* demonstrates the centrality of this concept for postcolonial thought. Bidima's study challenges us to conceive of postcolonial thought as a participant in philosophical modernity; his iconoclastic deconstruction of the jargon of Afrocentricity places the philosophical notion of possibility, as developed by the Frankfurt School and Ernst Bloch, at the focal point of postcolonial (African) concerns.

Glissant's refractory Antillean reformulation of dialectical logic, left uninvestigated in Bidima's interrogation of African modernity, is complex; for the moment, let us unfold the configuration of a prophetic historiography it contains. While drawing upon multiple sources and influences, Glissant undertakes an explicit reappropriation and reconstruction of dialectical negation, Hegel's primary contribution to Western thought. In the section "Poétique de la relation" of *Discours antillais,* to take one example, Glissant describes a "multi-relation [in which] . . . the dialectic of Outside-Inside rejoins the assault of the Earth-Sea" (249). This revindication of dialectical thought remains a constant for Glissant notwithstanding his references to Deleuzian "rhizomatics" in "Poétique de la relation," where he continues to call for a "thought of *errance* and totality (relational, dialectical)" (30).

As poet, novelist, and social theorist, what Glissant offers us is not a "logic" of relation but its "poetics;" nowhere does he give an explicit theoretical genealogy of his concept of dialectical relation. For all its diverse modes of application, however, it is Hegel's analysis of dialectical mediation that informs the thought of such diverse thinkers as Marx, Sartre, Fanon, and Glissant. Hegel's *Logic* argues that an antagonistic present reality holds within itself the negation of its immediacy: it "contains . . . possibility" (qtd. in Marcuse 150). The actual constellation of present reality contains within itself its own determinate negation, and possibility exists immanently within present reality; what Hegel calls "real possibility *[die reale Möglichkeit]*" is not an abstract, ungrounded fantasy but rather "the totality of conditions" whose contradictory nature makes a given state of facts true only insofar as it will negate itself in its future determinations and transformations to become what it inherently might be (qtd. in Marcuse 152). Hegel's dialectic of freedom and necessity follows from this process: though history unfolds necessarily from the determinations of the present, within that necessity a self-consciousness that understands the law-like processes of nature (encompassing the self and its world) can act both spontaneously and teleologically.

Hegel's vision of a contradictory and differentiated dialectical totality thus forms an infinitely extensive network of relationships across both space and time. On the one hand, spatial objects exist only in their individual identity within relation, as negations of other objects; schematically, one might say that salt is not pepper because it is white and crystalline, *not* black and spicy, and so on, infinitely. Yet this identity of the object achieved through differentiation is contradictory not only in relation to other objects (salt *is* what it is because it is *not* pepper); in its determination the object is simultaneously the immanent negation of its own identity. The object is *one* thing ("salt") only insofar as it is constituted as a *multiplicity* of differentiations (white, crystalline, etc.); devoid of all plural determination whatsoever, the object simply *is:* what Hegel calls "*Being, pure Being,* without any further determination [that is to say,] *nothing*" (*Logic* 82).

The world of objects of our consciousness is thus a totality of contradictory spatial relations constituted through a force field of negations. "The 'thing,'" Marcuse comments, "turn[s] out to be a self-constituting unity in a diversity of relations to other things. . . . Thus, the qualitative determinants of a thing are reduced to relations that dissolve the thing into a totality of other things, so that it exists in a dimension of 'otherness'" (108, 132). In this field, objects are determined as the negation of other objects, while this process is itself in constant development since contradiction is inherent not only within this network of relations but within every object itself.

At the same time, dialectical negation implies a temporal, historical understanding of relation in which every being develops through the contradiction between its essence and its existence, through its nonidentity with its concept; its present determinations that give it its identity are precisely what prevent it from being identical with the objective possibility of its concept. Just as a seed must become a tree to become "true" to its objective possibility, all the more so must a slave become a self-conscious, autonomous human to realize his or her possibility. The social world itself, untrue insofar as humans are prevented by its present constitution from achieving their inherent potential, must therefore be transformed to become equal to the truth of what would otherwise remain an empty, abstract concept. The historical process of negation described in the introduction to this volume as the slave's self-externalization through labor can hence be understood not simply as the development of a single limited individual awareness but as the development of the totality of relations across both space (as the infinite movement between determination and negation of finite beings [*Logic* 136]) and time (as possibility).

Though Glissant conceives of relation primarily as a spatial redistribution of human experience, Hegel's analysis allows us to see the interpenetration of relation, Hegel's production-based model of consciousness, and a prophetic history.[4] Relation, Glissant writes, negates rigid, abstract, "monolithic" historicism, which he glosses as History (capital *H*): "The intrusion of (relativizing) relation in the heretofore absolute field of History has killed History" (*IP* 209). Within this global force field of spatial and temporal relations in which reified, static unities are transformed into infinite, future-oriented flows of becoming, Glissant underlines the special status of poetic creation: "To build a nation is today a matter first of all of thinking of systems of production, of profitable commercial exchange, the improvement of living standards, without which the nation would quickly become an illusion. But each day we discover in the world that we also require a sense of collective personality, of what is called dignity or specificity, without which the nation would be devoid of meaning. The work of artistic production, in the developing countries, in which the imperatives of technical decisions and productivity have not completely invaded that entire field of existence, remain indispensable" (*DA* 439).

This transformational force of aesthetic objectification first manifested in Césaire's notion of negritude in fact functions as a practical and ethical model for Antillean creation as a whole. In this view, the self-estrangement of colonized subjects within transformed aesthetic material generates an always-incomplete communal self-understanding and autonomy via an awareness of the constraints that impinge upon subjects and their possible (self-)transformation. This freedom, Glissant implies, arises precisely at the juncture of a prophetic historiography and the work of aesthetic production. Glissant's construction of such an aesthetics of Antillean experience takes the form of a critical representation of Martinican alienation from historical possibility, an investigation whose moments of greatest tension, specificity, and productivity occur in the roughly contemporary writing of *Malemort* (1974) and *Le discours antillais* (1981).

A HUNDRED and sixty pages into Edouard Glissant's magnificent and at times perplexing novel *Malemort,* an unnamed narrator describes in haunting terms the absence of memory at the heart of Antillean experience: "We lie in ambush from ourselves, enigmas of our so-called history, monsters of a mythology whose secret we never approach, mute effigies at the windows of our future . . .: we, pale and adrift, castrated of all sumptuosity but purified as well of those excesses of perdition through which a will to resistance becomes self-conscious; lifeless, we can only accept, since choice is no longer permitted of us" (161). Critics of Glissant have generally examined his analysis of memory in relation to his discussion of the traumas (of slavery, of successful colonialism) inhering in Martinican society and have focused on an *erasure* of Antillean memory understood as both individual and communal repression. In fact, I think that Glissant's analysis of memory is fundamentally informed by a different strand of his wide-ranging thought: the determinate problems he describes of dependency, commodification, and an absence of productive forces—from the economic to those of the imagination—in Martinican society. The problematic Antillean relation to memory Glissant describes is not fundamentally that of an erasure of a presence, of something already or once there, but rather a failure of representation, more specifically a failure of the *production* of memory by conscious subjects. A failure of representation underlies the Antillean blindness to global, dialectical relation; like Daniel Maximin's *L'Isolé Soleil,* Glissant's work is in this sense an ever-renewed attempt to represent to his readers that totality, both in its alienated absence in novels such as *Malemort* and in an intimation of its positive presence in more recent works such as *Tout-monde.*

Amid growing dependency and imbrication within French and global capitalism, Glissant's writings of the 1970s undertake a complex and compelling critique of Antillean self-estrangement and lack of historical autonomy, a project of ideology critique whose origins extend back at least as far as Kant's famous article "What is Enlightenment?" This continuity with the critical project of modernity implies that in its second, dialectical dimension, Glissant's work is postmodern only in the sense one can say a critic like Fredric Jameson is postmodern, that is to say in their undertaking a thorough critique of immanence understood as the historical alienation of possibility amid commodification and historical amnesia.

Glissant's analysis locates the Antillean historical dilemma in a crisis of production. *Malemort* describes a world in which people wander in search of work and find only *jobs,* in which "there is no more work at noon than at 6 AM" (63), in which useless factories lie abandoned and return to a state of nature: "the abandoned rum factory slept its tropical dream: crackled with unimaginable beasts, its tile roof opening its gaping jaws in the afternoon" (68). This departmentalized Martinique produces nothing of its own and is instead overrun with a bewildering display of imported commodities: "apples pears grapes stacked in the supermarket entrance boxes of Coca-Cola packages of imported cheese of champagne the cartons of Christmas trees twisted in their dull needles Christmas cakes and foies gras in boxes" (132). Tourism and folklore are mere semblances of production, and mental production is totally ineffectual. In *Malemort,* the mathematician Chadin reaches new heights of uselessness as he spends his time reducing passing license plate numbers to their primes, while the teachers Québec and Lannec produce endless streams of hollow French verbiage (158).

The only character in the novel who recognizes this crisis is, not surprisingly, insane. Standing on the side of the road, a man yells: "They shout in protest against the Metropolis ya but what do we make huh what do you do with your own two hands . . . it's the Metropolis that gives you a shirt . . . it's the Metropolis that gives you child support . . . it's the Metropolis your daddy your mama your nurse" (191), whereupon he tears off his clothes and runs amok in the crowd. At the root of both Glissant's critique of Antillean amnesia and the identitarian logic of "the One" lies the commodity structure itself, positing in every aspect of daily lived experience the false equivalency of necessarily nonidentical objects. In this Caribbean society of the spectacle, as one character in *Malemort* remarks, "the entire world has become a plantation" (149) bent on expropriating maximum surplus value from alienated individuals, where everyone is for sale and immediately replaceable.

In a narrative tour de force, a central chapter of *Malemort* flows through all of modern Martinican history in a single undivided sentence stretching out across nineteen pages, moving from the experience of maroon slaves in 1788 through Abolition, departmentalization, and into the narrative present of neocolonial consumer culture. This single sentence presents history not as the increasing articulation and determination of events, but as sheer, unmastered, immediate nature, its undivided linear progression flowing like some endless vine stretching across a tropical rainforest. This is indeed a linear history but one whose teleology leads only from the hold of the slave ship to the machine-gunning of strikers: "the banana workers asked for thirty-five francs per day they explained they asked no one heard is there a place in the world where they hear those who have no voice, once again the jeeps appeared then in a demonstration of the great advances of modernity the helicopters . . . already the cars who were following pressed them the gun butts went into action already some had fallen bullets flew a man walked without hesitation his machete in hand and got himself killed just like that beneath the wind of the surveillance helicopter" (133–34). The world of *Malemort* is one of utter confusion and wandering in which only the most cynical retain a measure of sanity (the mayor's assistant Lesprit) and others gradually subside into varying degrees of madness.

If Glissant subjects the logic of identity, of what he terms "the One," to such thorough critique, it thus is not to embrace absolute difference but rather to move toward this totality he calls relation, in which Antillean specificity is able to persist and yet takes its place within a larger totality. Texts as furtive, opaque, and multidimensional as *Antillean Discourse* or *Malemort*, by their very existence, posit subjects able to grasp their representations of a fragmented historical experience. Like the models of subjectivity elaborated by Blanchot and Levinas, this possible, ideal Glissantian subject finds its autonomy not in its own interiority but rather in the perception and cultivation of the autonomous subjectivity of those it encounters. This Antillean subject remains always yet-to-be-concretized, yet it is necessarily, logically, and, indeed, explicitly implied by Glissant's fragmented and nontotalized aesthetic constructions.

Malemort has generally been interpreted as Glissant's most pessimistic and opaque work, and indeed it is unrelenting in its refusal of stylistic compromise and its description of Antillean dereliction, whether experiential, linguistic, historical, economic, or political. As its stories grow clearer with re-reading, however, its narrative reveals an unparalleled rhythmic tension and brilliant construction, a razor-sharp vision of Antillean culture, and a bleak humor that is often penetratingly funny. In drawing such a despairing picture, Glissant simultaneously constructs a standpoint beyond this abjection, and this not only as the logical conclusion that, in order to represent such alienation, one must have already posited another point from which this representation can be enunciated; ours is quite concretely a standpoint that we as readers must reconstruct with every reading, producing *Malemort* anew as a totalized object of our understanding and representation.

Within *Malemort* itself, at certain moments, the text evokes, furtively, a self-consciousness that lies beyond Antillean alienation: "as though consciousness too heavy thick moored to its night gyrating through the night toward how many uprooted countries how many dreamed of countries in the end preferred to lose itself, softly to lose itself in sweet stupidity and renunciation in which each fell knowing that she is falling and preferring this stupid sweet clarity to the span of midnight that one would have had to agree to cross to know oneself truly" (169). "To know oneself truly": such flashes of historical self-consciousness interrupt the long chain of suffering Glissant presents. After the description of the massacres cited above, the text continues, "he went upright no longer toward forgetfulness but perhaps toward something that would finally begin to resemble knowledge and memory" (134).

In its exploration of a dialectical experience of relation, Glissant's work is no empty celebration of difference and deferral but rather their comprehensive critique. To extol this dimension of Glissant's work as a celebration of the difference Glissant terms *opacité* is to miss the forest because of the trees. Of course, Glissant criticizes the erasure of Antillean difference within the putative universalism of classical and late French colonialism, but he does so within the horizon of a greater totality: that of a self-conscious, globally engaged subject. To offer as he does a fragmentary, multi-faceted analysis of Antillean society in the throes of neocolonialist alienation is to posit silently, knowing subjects able to understand and see beyond this historical dilemma. Glissant maintains an unerring faith in the necessity of critical consciousness and enlightenment, from the early explorations of *Soleil de la conscience* to his affirmation in *Introduction à une poétique du divers* that "No solution, whether political, economic, military, or sociological will resolve [the problems confronting us] as long as the spirituality, mentality, and intellectuality of the human being has not changed" (30).

This consciousness has as its horizon an understanding and grasp of totality, an understanding, however, that has so far been blocked by the contradictions of society as we know it. In this experience of constantly blocked human possibility, actual experience is reduced to an enraged expression of suffering: "in the shanty towns and ghettos of . . . New York and Lagos . . . [or] the smallest cities, the same machinery is at work: the violence of misery and dirt, but also unconscious and desperate rage at not 'understanding' the world" (*PR* 155). Though it cannot eliminate suffering ("No imaginary can truly prevent misery" [197]), in this world poetry alone seems to offer a concrete intimation of a totality beyond the sublime terror that threatens every individual: "The world as totality, which is so dangerously close to the totalitarian. No science can procure for us truly global insight.... Writing, which leads us to unforeseen intuitions, leads us to discover the hidden continuities in the world's diversity" (*TTM* 119).

From this knowledge, we might gain unsuspected purchase upon possibility: "Our ready-made responses, if they are totally ineffective against the concrete oppressions that stupefy the world, are none the less capable of changing the imaginary of humanity: it is through the imaginary that we will fundamentally overcome these derelictions that strike us.... Without abandoning in any sense the questioning and struggle you undertake in your locality, we must extend our imagination through an infinite bursting outward" (*TTM* 18). As such, and despite Glissant's espousal of a discourse of sheer immanence at other moments in his writing, this notion of totality, in its evocation of differential, future-oriented possibility, places human consciousness over and against the world it perceives. Glissantian consciousness exists in a relationship not of abstract negation of the world but in a dialectical, temporal relation to that world, where first one's perceptual faculties and very identity are dissolved (as in the world of *Malemort*), only to return from that experience as the forces of critical cognition awaken. Glissant's *Tout-monde* is not the unbroken immanence of the world as it exists but rather "our universe as it changes and persists, and, at the same time, the 'vision' that we have of it" (*TTM* 176). As such, this project of human understanding is one of an infinite movement of increasing determination that, as an open and incomplete totality, bears an uncanny resemblance to Hegel's notion of the dialectical totality, in which "the whole is nothing other than the essence consummating itself through its development" (*Phenomenology* 11). "The definition of internal relationships is infinite.... [Relation] is only universal through the absolute and definite quantity of its particularities" (*PR* 183, 193).[5]

IN ITS attempt to recover a buried history, Glissant's fiction explores above all the repression and forgetting of suffering in Antillean society: "We don't even suspect how we can suffer so much," Mycéa observes in *Tout-monde* as she recalls the violent death of her son. "It seems that we've forgotten suffering, and that suffering exists" (349). Glissant's investigation of possibility is first of all that of the alienation of possibility, its systematic blockage embodied in the premature death of Glissant's friend and colleague Paul Niger (Albert Béville) as he returned to Martinique from political exile in France: "The disappearance [of Béville] in that catastrophic plane crash in 1962 in Guadeloupe left traces so deep that it was as though each one felt, even if it was unjust and incongruous, that she could mix her own sorrow with that one. As though this tragically inconceivable death had become for some, of whom Marie Celat was doubtless one, the concept itself, one of the factors in any case, of our most painful impossibilities" (*TM* 425). *Malemort* in particular describes both this suffering and the persistent intimation of a utopian space where its memory would be redeemed: "Is there a place? A place where everything is known. Everything that occurs on earth. A place where the smallest beings come to put down their story. Where no tear is forgotten. Is there? they said. Silacier, enraged, cried: there isn't, there never is" (150).

To recover this memory of suffering and lost possibility, something more than the simple archival retrieval of historical data is required. *Le quatrième siècle* describes the confrontation between Mathieu Béluse, a young Martinican intellectual in search of knowledge about his country, and Papa Longoué, whose memory stretches back in time to encompass the experiences of their enslaved and marooned ancestors. Glissant's early novel struggles to construct a poetic vehicle that would sustain the experiential plenitude that a merely intellectual historiography would erase: "Mathieu [attempted] to lead the old man to speak of . . . a knowledge . . . beyond words, that only Papa Longoué could grasp . . . ; yes, that speech that was so well suited to the thickness of the day, to the weight of the heat, to the inertia of memory, to clarify the past and, perhaps, to explain precisely that thirst for the past that was so inexplicable for Mathieu" (17).

This poetification of historical experience recovers the bodily, sensuous experience of pain and pleasure that the introduction found at the root of Baumgarten's conception of the aesthetic: "The rain washed [the slaves on board the ship], readied them for sale, absolved them. In the hold however the odor grew thick. The water carried down rotting stenches, excrement, rat cadavers. The *Rose-Marie*, finally washed of its vomit, was truly like a rose, but one which drew its sap from a living dung-heap" (25). This struggle toward a full experiential description of the past passes across the centuries, from the first ancestral Longoué to his descendant, carried within a language that somehow traverses body and intellect: "Long afterward, Longoué the ancestor knew that the ship's imperceptible exhalation was certainly as terrifying as the frightful reek of the hold; and he rediscovered in his memory, beyond the thick mass of rot and vermin from the voyage, that slight odor of death dispersed by the rainwater that had driven [one of the sailors] mad. He rediscovered it beneath the wood and roots [of the forest]. And that odor, he knew how to make his descendants smell it, from generation to generation, down to Papa Longoué" (28). Longoué passes this experiential memory on to Mathieu, in turn: "I'm telling you, Mathieu my son, you're lucky you have books to forget the details, but know what you're forgetting: the smell, for example, the night team, the dangers of the Senglis plantation, the terrain that changes everywhere, the trained dogs" (141). *Quatrième siècle* struggles to encompass the experiences of slavery that refuse to fit neatly into the words on a page: "One can never adequately describe the state of slavery (with that infinitesimal and irreducible given of reality that no description, no analysis will ever be able to include: a debilitated mind awakening to pain, at times in anguish at its existence, only to fall back into its daily routine, acceptance, which is more horrible yet than the spasms of damnation" (117).

This memorial experience, in its evocation of the suffering body, points beyond the archival relation to the past of historiographic inquiry, toward a life-based ethics; the experiences of Mycéa, most specifically in *La case du commandeur*, describe this aesthetic, corporal memory: "Mathieu produced with ideas or in words what Mycéa kept in the most unreachable recesses of her self" (159). A "register of torments," as a chapter of *Case du commandeur* puts it, describes a female slave's capture as "a volley of fire marked by white flashes, which floated before her in the pestilent night of the gangway, before they threw her into the hold with its odors of vomit and sea salt where she crouched for the duration of the voyage. And from that moment on, the sailors raped her, day after day and night after night, both of the women, one against the other" (130).

The description of such experiences, like the political engagement against French colonialism of *Discours antillais*, gradually becomes less pronounced in Glissant's work since *La case du commandeur* (1981). Were one to stop reading Glissant with *Introduction à une poétique du divers*, we could perhaps join Peter Hallward in detecting an increasing disengagement and aestheticism in Glissant's work. And yet, without returning to the violent engagement of *Discours antillais* and *Malemort*, I think that Glissant's surprising yet convincing call to turn Martinique into a biological nation in *Traité du tout-monde* (1997) not only recovers a political and ethical dimension seemingly lost in his later thought but is fully coherent with Glissant's lifelong project of enlightenment and striving for an intersubjective totalizing consciousness of the *Tout-monde*.

IN THE FINAL pages of *Traité du tout-monde*, Edouard Glissant articulates a humble yet impassioned appeal for a determinate "realizable utopia," to make of the French overseas departments a "biological land" *(terre biologique)*:

> Let us [in the Caribbean] unite as a single body to attempt a magnificent project. . . . Let us clean up our world, and let Martinique, for example, proclaim and maintain itself, as a single entity, a pristine ecological land. Let us stop believing in the production of unsellable, badly protected goods, whose destiny depends upon the whims of political decisions made elsewhere. Let us stop delaying, with readjustment plans and bankruptcies, aid packages and resignation. Let us seek in the elsewhere of the world *[dans l'ailleurs du monde]* the places where products that we will have desired, planned, and realized through a common will might be offered and accepted. In the world there is a place (of buyers, of determined amateurs, of those with a passion for exchanges) for all that might arise from a space of light, for all that might appear from a will to clean the waters and clouds, the Gardens and Sands. . . . Many others have struck out on this path. But for us, it is not too late. (226–27)

In a context of seemingly endless debates over protocol and terminology for any future transformation of the DOM, the corollary public manifesto of January 21, 2000, for a Martinican "biological nation," signed by Glissant, Patrick Chamoiseau, Gerard Delver, and Bertene Juminer, argues that such points of detail are secondary. Nominal and legal finery can make sense only within the framework of a social and ethical "project": "Every statute is a tool at the service of an intention, of a desire, of a projection into the world. The fight for a change in [the DOM's] statute is certainly legitimate. But this complex ensemble must arise from what one might call a project" (16). Statutory problems cannot be resolved, Glissant argues, before "independence of thought, decision, and enterprise" are attained (*TTM* 227). "It is the project that secretes the statute necessary [for its realization], and not the contrary" (*Manifeste* 16).

Such a call for an "ecological project" perfectly demonstrates Glissant's long-standing contention that imaginary production, the capacity to imagine the concrete, possible transformations of our world, must precede social transformations if they are to avoid simply repackaging the same problems in new guises. The force of Glissant's proposition is the result of an accretion of decades of reflection on the course of (post)modern and (post)colonial society and an intensive engagement for the future of Glissant's island. While the notion of an Antillean "ecological project" is readily comprehensible as a Caribbean localization of the turn to "green" politics in the late twentieth century, it receives its historical potency when understood more specifically as a development of Antillean colonial history. The ongoing process of regionalization begun with the election of François Mitterand in 1981 is rapidly transforming the long agony of Antillean colonization (Burton and Reno 32). To conceive of a postnational Antillean ecological community—a postcolonial, transnational ethical community that cultivates life, human and otherwise—is not to abandon the promise of decolonization. Instead, it is to perceive that actual decolonization must itself occur within the context of totality, encompassing (which is not to say erasing) all modern states and local communities; the instantiation of a "universal humanity," as Hegel observed, "constitutes through Nature a single nation" (*Phenomenology* 439). This is an idea that did not surge forth from an isolated originary consciousness, but instead Glissant's experience and expressive capacity dramatically focalized a preexisting planetary discussion. It is an idea whose seductive force, whose utter "rightness" as well as its deceptive simplicity, arise from its predetermination by a vast array of historical processes and one writer's synthetic insight into the course of the contemporary world. Glissant's proposition could be criticized for a certain abstraction and "idealism." It does not propose a series of concrete initiatives. I think instead that this is one of the virtues of this proposition; in refusing the narcissistic hubris of any number of intellectual manifestos, it demonstrates an intellectual and ethical coherency. Any proposal to refound our relations with the world around coexistence and the cultivation of biological life should perhaps begin by taking intellectual modesty as its norm.

Such a methodology extends the work of enlightenment. Rather than imposing upon the world a preestablished scholastic model to which it must be made to conform, Glissant here instead proposes norms and goals (a life-based ethics, relationality) while maintaining that the path to reach those goals must be invented and constructed in the world, in interaction with that world as it is given to us today. To declare the DOMs a biological nation will not solve all the world's problems, but it can form a localized project to start from the real strengths (a highly educated population at ease with novel forms of immaterial production, a developed infrastructure, unparalleled natural beauty, etc.) and weaknesses (existential alienation, economic and political dependency, etc.) of that region.

This "ecological project" need not amount to an imaginary resolution of the contemporary contradictions of Antillean culture. In fact, the term "ecological project" economically unites the competing strands of Glissant's thought that I have presented in this chapter, while extending them in novel, open-ended directions. An "ecological" vision implies the decentering of a dominant human subject who would master and transform the world, a subject whose totalitarian, instrumentalizing comportment culminated in the innumerable disasters of the twentieth century—genocidal, ecological, and experiential. Instead, what Verena Andermatt Conley has called an "ecological subjectivity" (10) can replace this domineering and controlling subject who kills to control. Such a transformation implies a move away from a binary logic of a subject who dominates a passive object, toward a relational logic of interpenetrating and interdependent subjectivities (98). And yet, if this book has been at all convincing, the reader will by now recognize that this much-disparaged "binary" logic is far from the equivalent of a putative "Hegelianism" but is rather what Hegel strove to replace with a relational understanding, the interdetermination and dependency of subject and object that he called dialectical totality.

That said, to speak of an ecological "project" forces us to confront another dimension of the world this book describes. For this ecological manifesto overtly and repeatedly describes itself using that quintessentially Sartrean concept of the project, the same Sartre whom Conley equates with a vilified "dialectics" that espouses a "regressive" vision of "progress and teleology" (13). Indeed, Sartre himself seems to supply us with no shortage of ammunition to turn against him: he repeatedly focuses narcissistically on the autonomous experience of a free (independent) subject. He writes not of the environment but, like the Heidegger of *Being and Time*, of "my environment," an instrumentalized world in which "to be free is to-be-free-to-change. Freedom implies therefore the existence of an environment to be changed: obstacles to be cleared, tools to be used" (*Being and Nothingness* 647, 650).

Sartre conceives of the "project" following not Hegel's relational understanding of totality but rather adopting Kojève's binary division between nature and human history that absolutizes Hegel and Marx's production-based logic of increasing consciousness, freedom, and relation. Sartre describes the project, "the free production of the end and of the known act to be realized" (581), in terms of the negative work-based activity that transforms the world as it exists: "Since human reality is act, it can be conceived only as being at its core a rupture with the given. It is the being which causes *there to be* a given by breaking with it and illuminating it in the light of the not-yet-existing" (736, 615, emphasis in original). The French tendency to filter Hegel through Kojève's simplifying (binary) lens has meant that too often in both France and the United States the complexities and productive difficulties of Hegel's rich and problematic thought have been simply chucked out in the call for new ideas, as a novel vocabulary needlessly reinvents ideas already worked through centuries before.

My argument in this book has been that we cannot simply discard the Hegelian insight into the transformative, enlightening potential of labor. Indeed, Verena Conley's call for an "ecological consciousness" implies that we must instead extend our understanding of production, a process whose full implications and potentials have remained blocked and unrealized. Not only Sartre's call for "an original project of *living*" (721) but more recent thought such as Deleuze and Guattari's espousal of "desiring machines" and Antonio Negri and Michael Hardt's conviction that "living labor is what constructs the passageway from the virtual to the real; it is the vehicle of possibility" (357) imply that we must reconceive our understanding of production. If to this day what have been produced are dead objects by deadened producers for deadened consumers, instead of simply making, we must *make live;* not a through a Frankenstein process that would bestow life on a passive object but through a relational behavior of interdependence that instead allows and encourages life to flourish. The political ecology implied by Glissant's manifesto is far more than a defense of natural resources. We must rethink political action as a movement toward totality, in which the world is no longer what Bruno Latour calls the "reservoir" and dumping ground of our projects but is the horizon and ground of relational consciousness and action. The cultivation of life can no more become an absolute than any other injunction. To cultivate life is not to conserve an imperfect world as it is, but rather to discover the means to make flourish the possibilities that are not yet, but of which we are able to conceive (Badiou 38). The construction of such a life-based ethics of possibility can offer nonregressive norms of comportment that address the actual dilemmas of globalizing, neocolonial societies caught up in what Glissant calls "Empire" (*TTM* 21).

TAKING GLISSANT'S cue, let me end these remarks by bringing his call for a Martinican biological country into dialogue with Michael Hardt and Antonio Negri's recent study *Empire*. Hardt and Negri's book is striking in its combination of a vision of globalization that extends the concept of imperialism to encompass the transformations of postmodern globalization while refusing a regressive retreat into localism. Following Marx's injunction that the only path leading beyond capitalism passes through the utmost development of the disbalanced logic of capital, Negri and Hardt argue that "the construction of Empire is a step forward to do away with any nostalgia for the power structures that preceded it . . . such as trying to resurrect the nation-state to protect against global capital. . . . Empire does away with the cruel regimes of modern power and also increases the potential for liberation.... We must push through Empire to come out the other side" (43, 206). Correspondingly, Glissant's "biological project" is neither a regressive Antillean nationalism nor an aesthetic withdrawal into a self-absorbed creole culture. Rather, it implies a developmental vision of the French Antilles that might realize the potential of that region in a global political economy.

Hardt and Negri's *Empire* throws light on Glissant's manifesto not only by placing its concerns within the larger processes of globalization but because this nearly-five-hundred-page text reproduces in diffraction and in a single volume the same contradictions I have argued inform the totality of Glissant's *oeuvre*. Like Glissant's work, *Empire* is divided, somewhat schizophrenically, I think, between a Spinozian discourse of unbroken immanence and one of dialectical enlightenment. On the one hand, Negri and Hardt reproduce the postmodern conviction that there is no longer any noumenal point beyond the immanent totality of the world: "There is no more outside," they intone, "no subjectivity is outside, and all places have been subsumed in a general 'non-place'" (186, 353). Such an assertion can only stand as an utter abstraction, like their invocations of a "multitude" who never become more determinate than the only slightly less abstract notion of "the poor" (156). Any such determination would necessarily reveal contradictions that might bring into question their abstract celebration of "our immanent labor" and the spontaneous capacity of the multitudes to determine its ends (396, 83). This tendency toward abstraction culminates in the book's odd call for a "material mythology" and "material religion" (396).

At the same time, *Empire* operates within a transformational logic of enlightenment that gives the book its inspiring intimation of historical dynamism. The authors see the unbounded creativity of human subjectivity, and not the reactive decisions of political powers, as the driving force to historical change (278). Amid their assertion of a world of total immanence, devoid of a vilified mediation and a "search for the outside" (78, 46), there is no explanation of how the book we are reading has obtained any explanatory purchase on the world it critiques. Indeed, one could hardly imagine a more typically Hegelian-Marxian project than a "critical approach... intended to bring to light the contradictions, cycles, and crises of the process" of Empire's construction (48). In fact, this lack of critical reflection on the act of critique itself leads Hardt and Negri to the problematically abstract conclusion that "we need to investigate specifically how the multitude can become a *political subject* in the context of Empire." Their espousal of a "prophetic function" that—notwithstanding any displacement onto "the prophetic powers of the multitude"—they as the authors of *Empire* have articulated could easily be read as a postmodern update of Lukács's Leninist investigations into the formation of an (imputed) "class consciousness" (394, 64). The problem with *Empire* is not its diagnosis of postmodern immanence (for surely this reveals a truth of what Jameson calls "the cultural logic of late capitalism"), nor the authors' hortatory call for greater enlightenment that would make globalization attain the possibility immanent in its concept, but rather Hardt and Negri's refusal to mediate these two categories in their reflection. Negri has consistently condemned all mediation as a "sordid game" (*Spinoza* 141), while nonetheless pursuing his critical project of enlightenment. The problem, in fact, is not mediation in itself, without which critique and understanding are impossible. Rather, it is the *alienation* and *appropriation* of mediation from individuals by the state that poses the problem to which Spinoza gives such a compelling response.[6]

The path beyond the "total" immanence of globalization lies in what Hegel, Glissant, and Hardt and Negri alike call "possibility." Hardt and Negri's evocation of a total plane of immanence, while perhaps (though it seems doubtful as well) a correct diagnosis of the world as it actually exists today, reflects the impoverishment of temporal experience that Glissant has striven so hard to counteract. Within the immanent relations of the world lies the virtual map of its future possibilities. In fact, the virtual, a concept Hardt and Negri borrow from Deleuze and Guattari's *Qu'est-ce que la philosophie?* is itself one more reworking of Hegel's *Möglichkeit* (357).[7] Glissant's attempt to recover a full temporal experience that would include not only abstract chronological events but the materiality and weight of sensuous experience finds its corollary in Hardt and Negri's final call to construct a world in which "time is reappropriated in the plane of immanence" (402). This time would not be lived for another, as alienation, but as a realization of an immanent intersubjective, nonexploitive global community.

Still, there remains something naggingly unsatisfying in such a vision; for all its celebration of our constructive potential, Hardt and Negri's productivist utopia in a sense turns the experiences and suffering of others into the means for our (at least no longer Sartre's "my") self-realization. In sympathy with Glissant's attention to a memorialization of the suffering of others, we might strive for an ecological consciousness that remains, as David Harvey urges, attentive to social inequity and the destruction of all species, including the human. As Glissant himself recognizes, an Antillean "ecological project" will surely fail if it remains focused on Martinican self-sufficiency and cultural interiority; it will of necessity have to join into relation the potentialities of the (over)developed DOMs with the differential potentialities of suffering nations such as Haiti or neighboring Dominica. In constructing the ecological consciousness of global relation Glissant and others rightly call for, we must simultaneously bear in mind the experiences of others, past, living, and not yet born, those lost and not-yet-realized potentialities that call out to us and await our determination to transmit them into the future, for others.

7 Voicing Memory
Maryse Condé, Edwidge Danticat

DANIEL MAXIMIN and Edouard Glissant's counter-models of subjective experience refuse Henri Christophe's suicidal annihilation of the particular in a postcolonial totalitarian Universal, without, on the other hand, recoiling from globalization into local particularism. Maximin and Glissant recover for Antillean subjects the dynamic process of their autoconstruction, culminating in Glissant's vision of a global, ecological consciousness and communal project. The writings of the Antillean authors Maryse Condé and Edwidge Danticat continue to give voice to this subjective and communal experience, while grappling with the materiality of history. Their voicing of memory finds its privileged vector within the realm of female subjectivity in a world in which, as Julia Kristeva has recently affirmed, "the arrival of women onto the forefront of the moral and social arena will result in the revalorization of sensible experience as an antidote to technical ratiocination" (*L'avenir d'une révolte* 17).

Maximin's own work, along with, to choose an obvious example, that of Proust, suggests a point of reflection informed by, yet not beholden to, the specificity of gender: that of subjectivity itself, Kristeva's *sujet en procès*, whose plasticity and capacity to overflow the limits and definitions of the symbolic order intimates a fully historicized experience filled with subjective affect.[1] In this sense, the writings of Condé and Danticat are no model of identity in which we might recognize the self-same individual we already know ourselves to be. Instead, they offer premonitions of what we might yet become, a call to possible subjectivities that would instantiate a transformative, dynamic, intersubjective experience, rendering a full expression of historical facticity mediated by the affect-charged resonance of the human voice.

Tracing Dystopia

The work of the Guadeloupean author Maryse Condé articulates both a constant concern for history in its concrete relation to French Antillean experience and a thorough critique of an illusory plenitude putatively to be recovered through writing. Her novels move between the dual registers of history and memory, engaging the concrete traces of human actions as they persist in the archives, while confronting the complex relation of members of the African diaspora with the past. Novels such as *Ségou* and, to a lesser extent, *Moi, Tituba, Socière* spring from the author's historical, archival investigations. *Ségou*, like Maximin's *L'Isolé soleil* and Vincent Placoly's *Frères volcans*, was originally conceived as a scholarly monograph; in this case, the massive French doctoral dissertation that formerly crowned years, often decades, of research: "I wanted to write a *thèse d'état* on certain Mandinka oral traditions. I went to Mali in 1976 to start my research. As I progressed, I realized that I had no desire to write a thesis with all these materials, and the idea of a novel began to germinate" (Pfaff 75).

Condé doesn't describe the exact nature of her dissatisfaction with her projected *thèse d'état*. It seems clear enough, though, that, like Maximin and the Césaire whose turn to poetry in the 1930s "disadapted" him for the *agrégation*, Condé's gesture was in part a refusal to submit her work to the anonymous "objectivity" of scholarly discourse. In so doing, she refuses a mimetic historiography, mimetic in the weak sense that so nauseated the Roland Barthes of *S/Z*. In such a concept of mimesis, the historical text serves as the supposedly transparent imitation of an external, objective world. In this mimetic practice of history, the historian dominates objective material through heroic encounters in the archive, appropriating this material and subsuming it within the universality of his discourse.[2] Condé, like Césaire before her, has repeatedly asserted a stubborn refusal to erase the particularity of French Antillean subjective experience within an abstract scholarly discourse. She consistently strives to overcome the petrification of historical experience as archival fossil. She thus provides an alternative mimetic practice, one more in keeping with the work of Theodor Adorno and Walter Benjamin in his articles "On the Mimetic Faculty" and "The Image of Proust." For these writers, mimesis is not simple imitation but rather the studied abandonment of the self to an other in which the expressive force of aesthetic objects is not consumed by instrumental reason, where one instead falls silent to let things speak in their own voice.[3]

Nor, however, does Condé retreat into a pure interiority of the subject, totally disengaged from the material, historical facticity that determined them as objects of a colonized Caribbean space. Drawing upon the terminology of Pierre Nora, Condé describes an encounter between history and memory, with the former gradually subordinated to the demands of the latter in her recent work. "History," Condé maintains, "must henceforth [following her historical novel *Ségou*] be subordinated to the work of familial or collective memory" (Pfaff 99). Her novel *Traversée de la mangrove* is emblematic of this exploration of French Antillean subjectivity as the staging site of memory. It recounts the reactions of a series of characters inhabiting *Rivière au Sel* in Guadeloupe to the death of Francis Sancher, a Cuban immigrant who had lived among them. Each chapter takes on the human voice of another inhabitant of *Rivière au Sel,* forming a polyphonic history of Sancher that avoids dissolving the particularity of each individual experience within the abstraction of a transcendent narrative.

The novel is a mystery with no solution. Condé creates a space in which concrete suffering finds expression in human voices, existing within the particularity of individual subjectivities like Césaire's poetic "zone d'incandescence," barricaded against the onslaught of history. After a shattering encounter with Sancher, one of these narrators states, "I hadn't realized that I was a scarecrow that sent men, love, and happiness fleeing. They will never again settle on my branches. I went home and I barricaded up my solitude and I cried every tear in my body, I cried like I hadn't cried in fifty years. I realized that my heart had remained a fragile onion, fragile, enveloped beneath layers of skin that I thought were thick, but which let through with no resistence the blade of the knife of suffering" (150). This is not suffering, but the memorial trace of suffering represented and projected in time and space to a community of readers. Condé's novel is antihierarchical, allowing the validity and autonomy of each textual subject to persist in its specificity, leading the reader to confront the subjective determinations of historical inquiry, an inquiry necessarily mediated through subjective experience of the phenomenal world in the form of discourse.

While rearticulating the notion of Antillean dependency she inherits from Glissant (see the introduction), Condé's text engages the recovery of subjective experience in the very process of describing its threatened erasure. Each chapter, bearing the name of the narrator whose voice animates it, reconstructs subjective experience through an individual voice. The content of each chapter registers in this manner the suffering and unfreedom of these subjects. Amid their despondency, these voices re-instantiate what colonial history had threatened to erase: an experience, immersed within history, that confronts the reader from within the fictional text as a model for a subjectivity yet-to-be-achieved.

In *Traversée de la mangrove* Condé fabricates a circular narrative structure, "a narrative that has no real beginning nor end" (Pfaff 107). The novel's form imitates that of the French Antillean wake, or *veillé,* in which members of the community speak of their life encounter with the deceased.

Condé's need to present a nonhierarchical plurality of experiences thus determines the novel's form, drawn from the resources of vernacular Caribbean culture. This decentered discourse supports the critique of history the novel engages. For all her ongoing engagement with black Atlantic history, Condé clearly subordinates a concern for the past to the need to live and act in the present. "One must live in the present, confront the problems of the present, and not live with one's gaze constantly turned back upon that which already was, toward a more or less mythological past" (Pfaff 140).

Traversée de la mangrove describes a Guadeloupe in which the revolutionaries Delgrès and Ignace are dead and gone and have too often served as mythologized distractions from the present. One of Condé's characters remarks polemically, "The Guadeloupe of yesterday has died its final death. Those who can't see that, those who think that the days of sugar cane will come back are crazy," while another cries, "Open your eyes! We're already European! Independence is a sleeping beauty that no Prince will come to awaken" (102, 218).

With biting irony, Condé, a Caribbean Flaubert, caricatures both herself and the earnest Antillean authors who mythologize Antillean culture, "dreaming of Alejo Carpentier and José Lezama Lima and already imagining [themselves] discussing style, narrative technique, and the use of orality in literature!" (219). In a parodic *mise-en-abyme*, Lucien Evariste, the self-declared writer in *Traversée de la mangrove*, abandons his stillborn project for a history of a maroon slave for dreams of a complex narrative totalization of Francis Sancher, one that we might, or might not, be reading. "Why not place back to back memories and recollections, eliminate the lies, reconstitute the trajectory and personality of the deceased? Of course, that idealist shorn of his ideals wouldn't make it easy for [Evariste]! He would need to overcome the vertiginous facility of clichés. Look into the eyes of dangerous truths. Risk offending. Shocking . . . He saw himself edited by a major publisher on the Rive Gauche, acclaimed by the Parisian press, confronting local critics" (227–28). In its mocking self-referentiality, *Traversée de la mangrove* describes the multiplicity of forces determining contemporary Antillean historical experience. The novel's array of narratives work to locate these subjects within a confluence of elements, including the forces of history, nature, and personality, that meet within a small island's topography.

If Condé's description of the writer Lucien Evariste ironizes the pretensions of a prototypical French Antillean novelist, the penultimate chapter of *Traversée de la mangrove* gently mocks the projects of Caribbean historians. Emile Etienne, "the historian," undertakes a modest, self-published study of a locality entitled "Speaking of Petit Bourg" that evokes only derision among "the intellectuals of Point-à-Pitre" (235). Evariste speaks in the earnest—yet clichéd—tones of the local historian: "I would like to write a history of this land that would be drawn only from the depths of people's memories, from the depths of their hearts" (237). Like his colleague Evariste, Etienne is plagued by a Proustian inability to concretize his grandiose plans: "Yes, tomorrow he would be sure to begin working" (237).

As a textualized, concrete exploration of history and memory, *Traversée de la mangrove* serves to refashion the "production-based subjectivity" at work in the poetry and theater of Aimé Césaire. For Condé, as for Daniel Maximin and Edouard Glissant, subjective experience is no longer articulated as the externalization of an autonomous, transcendent subject. Instead, writing serves to locate the multiplicity of Antillean experience within a confluence of individualities, each of which is able to maintain its particularity and difference within the confines of an isolated narrative topography at once taking its place within the novel's overall movement, yet highly complex and differentiated in its singular content. In a world in which individual experience has grown fractured and painful, the aesthetic recollection and representation of lived pain constructs a realm in which that full experience, which was never truly lived before its repression, can reappear: "Undamaged experience is produced only in memory," Adorno wrote of Proust, "far beyond immediacy. . . . Total remembrance is the response to total transience, and hope lies only in the strength to become aware of transience and preserve it in writing" (qtd. in Bernstein 114).

MARYSE CONDÉ'S recent memoir, *Le coeur à rire et à pleurer*, is itself written under the sign of Proust. It opens with a quotation from *Contre Sainte-Beuve:* "What reason [l'intelligence] presents us in the name of the past is not it" (9). As her reference implies, Condé here continues her exploration of memory, again reconstructing a textual space in which an autonomous subject might recover historical experience. The text is no mere erasure of history within the sheer subjectivity of individual recollection, however, but rather stages a series of encounters between history and memory. The title itself is emblematic of this confrontation: invoking the subjective affect of laughter and crying, its subtitle, *True Stories of My Childhood (Contes vrais de mon enfance)*, thrives on the ambiguity of the generic term *conte*: the *conte* is, according to the *Robert*, alternatively a "narrative of real facts. History" and a "narrative of imaginary facts destined to entertain." Though the author specifies that these are in fact *contes vrais,* her very need to reaffirm their objective status underlines to the reader the ambiguity of the genre she has chosen: is a *conte vrai* true in the same way an autobiography would have been? Measured by the standards of positivist historiography, the *conte* is an inferior representation of the past, but, as was the novel for the Proust Condé evokes, it serves here to construct a semblance of history more true in its aesthetic, mediated form than the passively lived events it represents.

Condé's mimetic relation to Proust implies a relation between subject and object in contrast to the referential "cannibalism" structuring the intellectual dynamic of Aimé Césaire (chapter 4). This intertextuality, signaled from the very first page, infiltrates Condé's text to a remarkable degree. The textualization of a narrator's memories of childhood passively invokes *Combray*, while a number of other moments more explicitly elicit this affiliation. Condé, as she had in *Traversée*, again rewrites Marcel's famous encounter with Gilberte's blue, or perhaps black, eyes from *Combray* from the perspective of a female subject. The young Condé is shocked to receive a *mot-doux* from her male admirer, the innocent "Gilbert," stating, "Beloved Maryse, for me, you are the most beautiful with your blue eyes" (54). This misrecognition of Condé's black eyes puts an end to their young love affair. "Gilbert"'s error was to have blindly erased both his and Condé's Antillean specificity and personality within the objectivity of the document: he had quite simply copied this stilted declaration from a French novel.

Other moments in the text evoke Proust, whether obliquely as stylistic trope, as in the phrase "Doubtless she had just remembered that I was only nine years old" (50)—recalling the innumerable "perhaps" that mark Proust's refusal to foreclose his lengthy explanations of human behavior —or the memory of a dessert taken from her: "Why, at a distance of over fifty years, does the image of this blue ramequin bordered with gold, filled with unctuous delights I was unable to taste, pass again and again before my eyes, a symbol of all I desired and never obtained?" (63).

Le coeur à rire et à pleurer returns again and again to the theme of Antillean alienation and reification, from Condé's parents' utter prostration before the values of metropolitan French culture to the narrator's own insight into her alienation as she reads Zobel's *Rue Cases-Nègres* for the first time, seeing herself as "without taste or fragrance, a bad copy of the French people I knew. I was 'Black skin/white mask,' it was for me that Frantz Fanon was going to write his book" (102). If Condé so forcefully describes this alienation of Antillean subjectivity, her text itself, in its mimetic relation to Proust, offers both an implicit counterimage to this alienation, while reproducing, mimetically, the problematic interiority fundamental to the Proustian artistic project.

The movement from Maryse Condé's *Traversèe de la mangrove* to *Le coeur à rire et à pleurer* is a passage from the aesthetic construction of multiple, heterogeneous voices, to that of the authorial subject herself. Here as well, Condé's novels mimic Proust. In similar fashion, albeit on a far grander scale, the *recherche du temps perdu* moves increasingly from the infinitely laborious and impossible task of representing the experience of others (Swann, Gilberte, Albertine) to a celebration of the textual representation of the authorial subject in its final pages. Proust, in *Le Temps retrouvé,* confronts this guilt of his artistic project: if the artwork comes to constitute for the narrator "true life" (300), he has in the process "used the suffering" of others for his novel, reducing their lives to the mere "materials" (304), the building blocks of his "construction" (480). His aesthetic "idealism" displaces an ethical concern for living beings to the "true life" of the aesthetic object.

Like Condè's text, Proust evokes the specter of reification—in which living, unique, and irreplaceable individuals are transformed into exchangeable commodities—through his repeated recourse to economic vocabulary in the final pages of *A la recherché:* "These beings who had revealed truths to me and who were no more, appeared to me as having lived a life that had only *profited* me, as though they had died for me" (308, emphasis added). Proust has no solution to this dilemma and can only conclude weakly, even cynically, "such is the lot of the dead" (309). If, as participants in a reifying social system, we are variously yet necessarily implicated in the guilt of that society, there may not be a choice of action that would unambiguously avoid that guilt, even in combating it. Merely to *represent* that guilt, or, conversely, to imagine a society in which all its members would realize their immanent potential, and to imagine that potential itself, are moments in our recovery of possibility, yet they are moments as guilty in their distance from practice as is the practice that always betrays its promise. Yet both advance beyond resignation.

If Proust is not alone in his guilt, we can still become conscious of our varying forms of implication in an unjust society, as I will argue more concretely in the next section on Edwidge Danticat. Unlike Danticat, yet similarly to Condé's shift in focus from *Mangrove* to *Le coeur à rire et à pleurer,* Proust avoids thematizing his own artistic guilt and the attempt to work through it. Proust subtly slides from the avowal that he has "used" the suffering of others to focus on his own suffering (311), a suffering that the *Recherche* might more realistically be understood to redeem: "my laziness . . . my work . . . my memory . . . my *oeuvre*" (482). Even here, however, the author can convincingly maintain his innocence: in using the first person, in reconstructing his own experiences over thousands of pages, he, like Condè, may instead be sacrificing himself for the reader's recovery of experience, despite his insistent use of the first person ("They would not be my readers, but the readers of themselves . . . my book, thanks to which I would give them the means to read themselves" [471]) and perhaps even, as Adorno poignantly thought of Proust, sacrificing himself for the possibility of happiness itself. Marcel would thus have turned his life into a reified object, a holder of value that might pay off the debt of his guilt by "enriching" the reader with his "treasure" by rendering his "egoism usable for another" (475).

If Condé's literary project is far more modest than that of Proust, it nonetheless mimics the *Recherche* in both its concern for the suffering of others and its turn to narrative interiority. *Le coeur à rire et à pleurer*, as critical *Bildungsroman*, hopes to invoke a free subject through the reconstitutive work of its reader. Condé's narrative subject undertakes a mimesis that would avoid subsuming the other, whether within the transcendent discourse of historiography or via the assimilationist French cultural model Condé explicitly critiques. Instead, Condé's mimetic relation with Proust implies a sympathetic immersion within the world he evokes, in which two narrative voices, those of Maryse Condé and Proust, are able to coexist in their nonidentity. While Proust furtively reappears throughout *Le coeur à rire et à pleurer*, Condé's prose is never dissolved within that Proustian model. Her text maintains the highly specific characteristics of a determinate human voice, that of the narrative subject Maryse Condé. As such, *Le coeur à rire et à pleurer* offers a countermodel both to Antillean assimilation within French culture and the cavalier objectivity of academic historiography. Instead, she articulates a site in which the subjective capacity for historical experience might be recovered.

MARYSE CONDÉ's play *En tan revolisyon*—like *Traversée de la mangrove*, also published in 1989—continues that novel's critique of historical experience in Antillean letters from yet another perspective, that of the theater. No celebratory recovery of the past, the play recalls the carnage that marks the revolutionary period in the Caribbean, pursuing the critique of the mystificatory glorification of Guadeloupe's heroic figures undertaken by Daniel Maximin. Revolution, in the words of the storyteller who presents and analyzes this "fresco" of events, "nourishes itself on fresh blood. It rubs its belly and licks its chops. And then, in the colorless early morning, it gives birth to monsters" (24).

In this play, the mocking, ironic laughter of a skeptical population challenges the actions and the text of Louis Delgrès, unconvinced as they are of the possibility of change in a world marked by the eternal recurrence of pointless suffering. The audience witnesses the demythification of Delgrès's hyperbolic, masculinist aura. The play's form contributes to this process; the storyteller (*conteur*) directly addresses the audience, mixing historical periods anachronistically in his presentation with no respect for a grand linear meta-narrative: "The conteur: When I was little, I had written on my notebooks: 'I want to be Victor Hugo or nothing.' . . . Can you imgine that? Me, a little black boy, those were my dreams. (Silence, then he breaks out laughing). You believed me? I really fooled you! . . . In my day, we didn't dream about poetry, literature, and all of those stupidities. We dreamed of liberty. Not like you who dream of BMW's and VCR's and vacations in Caracas" (32).

Each time a character risks glorifying or celebrating the autotelic agency of Ignace or Delgrès as autonomous agents of history, skeptical comments from a more sober character undermine this gesture (37). This demythification takes its most overt form when, after Ignace's inspiring exhortation of the crowd never to permit the reestablishment of slavery, an officer reads Delgrès's proclamation only to be shouted down by a crowd impatient with the elitist "français-français" of a proclamation incomprehensible to the majority of those it claims to represent (40).

In a series of violent illuminations that recall the shattered temporality and subjectivity of Buchner's *Woyzeck*, various historical and anonymous characters appear in flashes of light. The storyteller Zéphyr is the only character present through the whole of the play. Condé's "historical fresco" stages a confrontation between historical events and the subjects of that history. Condé incorporates raw historical documents into *An tan révolisyon* in a process of ironic pastiche. In a practice recalling Oruno Lara's history of Guadeloupe or Césaire's *Toussaint Louverture*, she inserts direct citations into her play from the *Abbé Siéyès*, extracts from the proceedings of the National Assembly, and the opening speeches from the *Etats-Généraux*. Her theatrical construction thus foregrounds the fabricated, representational nature of historical truth.

In this eminently historical play, this truth arises not from the historian's putatively transparent discourse but rather through a form that confronts historical facticity with the demands of Antillean subjects buffeted by the forces of a history that has systematically undermined their agency. History in the form of a constellation is objectified in the play's *mise-en-scène:* heterogeneous events surge forward out of the darkness, then quickly fall back into obscurity. Rather than enclosing her history within a totalized horizon of meaning, *An tan révolisyon* is a *mise-en-scène* of the nonidentical, in explicit contrast to the French government's celebratory recuperation of the Metropolian Revolution of 1789 in 1989. Though the *conteur* leads us through the events of Delgrès's later revolt, this is less to interpret them than to undermine our faith in their epistemological cohesion.

In the Antillean context of "successful colonization" and "disequilibrium," the recourse to an academic, putatively transparent historical discourse that integrates its documentation within a single transcendent narrative voice can become a mere academic *fantaisie,* in utter incongruity with the opaque, contradictory world it seeks to represent. In this sense, positivist Antillean historicism, for all its efficiency, fails to live up to its own criteria insofar as its search for truth terminates in a totality of seemingly true facts that fail to represent the exploded nature of Antillean experience. Clearly, Condé remains convinced of the efficacy of historical awareness: "To know one's past, to dominate it, to know it in its reality without making of it an object of backwards-looking veneration, is one of the conditions of freedom" (personal interview, 1997). Condé's *An tan révolisyon,* like Glissant's *Le discours antillais* or Richard Price's extraordinary study *The Convict and the Colonel,* however, critiques the past not only thematically but formally as well, forcefully portraying the disarticulation of Antillean culture through a structure that is itself an image of an exploded Caribbean historical experience.

If fidelity to the phenomenal world is the historian's credo, Maryse Condé cultivates instead an ironic sensibility, and her sarcasm condemns the events in question through narrative distantiation. Condé is a writer who works rigorously with historical material but whose sense of irony revolts against the bourgeois recuperation of history typified by the solemn annual deposition of flowers at Delgrès's memorial (chapter 1). History must function for Maryse Condé as "a prophetic vision of the past," thus Condé's remark, "I'm an optimist, in spite of the fact that I no longer believe in anything" (1997). Like Frantz Fanon before her, in the image of Antillean suffering and foreclosure of possibility she draws so forcefully, Maryse Condé holds out the promise of its determinate negation: "When all is said and done, I think we still must turn back to the past. I don't want to fetishize the past. I don't think that we need to mythify the past at all costs. But I'm convinced that we need to know that past, quite simply in order to master the present. If we continue to ponder an absence, trying to fill that absence with forms and events, I think it's a sign that we're not yet free" (Personal interview, 1997).[4] Maryse Condé refuses to represent a realm of mythified transcendence when people go on suffering. By evoking the catastrophe of history without ever becoming convinced of its necessity, she is able to point toward a utopia she refuses to name.

Condé's *conteur* Zéphyr, in closing the story he has presented to the audience, actively resists any mythification that could hide the fact that 1802 brought only death and suffering for an entire people: "What do you want me to say? You want me to invent a *happy end* like in an American film? This time will be like all the others. Death, never satisfied, will fill its belly and the lovers of liberty will fill the mass graves. Sometimes I think that if the earth of Guadeloupe is so red it's from the unending blood that's been spilled on it!" (41). Condé's narrator forcefully subverts the libidinal investment in Delgrès's exploit typical of a certain Antillean literary tradition in the name of the harsh reality of a revolt that ended, like so many others, in slaughter. This pessimism in turn reflects upon the historian herself, who has refused not only a mythological faith in a transcendent historical narrative but the hope that her own writing of history can offer any solid, ontologically grounded meaning: "We have to proceed as if what we were doing had some importance. I won't deny that in my heart I think that we're fighting a losing battle, but we keep fighting if only to avoid simply accepting defeat" (1997). As the metonymical representation of a recurring failure—the "impasse Delgrès"[5] that is the sign of a historical dereliction—the blood soaking the Place de la Victoire in Condé's *An tan révolisyon* remains faithful to human suffering in its betrayal of hope; Condé can only strive to provoke horror and disgust at history's onslaught, and in so doing she manages to recover the promise of a society where that suffering might finally be relegated to the past.

IN IMAGES of blood and fire, Edwidge Danticat salvages the scraps of life that persist amid terror and infuses them with the overwhelming semblance of subjectivity within vernacular poetic form. In a series of novels and short stories—*Breath, Eyes, Memory* (1994), *Krik? Krak!* (1995), and *The Farming of Bones* (1998), the Haitian-American writer describes the contents of Antillean historical experience from the radical displacement of exile, as political inertia, violence, and bloodshed continue in a land left behind by body if not spirit. The terrible reality of life extinguished amid senseless violence animates her work, imbuing it with an experiential content that is the mark of its authenticity. At the same time, the act of aesthetic representation draws her away from the immediacy of social and historical fact, calling into question her right to speak in place of others. The achievement of her undertaking lies in its persistent engagement with this contradiction and its obstinate working through of the sign of her project's fragility: guilt.

Danticat's texts are already guilty before one even reads them, guilty of their own popularity.[6] Applauded in *Elle* magazine and on *Oprah*, her writing is accessible in a way Glissant's *Malemort* or even Césaire's *Cahier* never will be. Like a bill of inspection, the sticker announcing the book's selection by Oprah's Book Club confronts the purchaser of *Breath, Eyes, Memory*, announcing that the book on the table before her at Border's is a commodity, chosen for her by someone else who has interposed her judgment to create a guaranteed best-seller. And yet Oprah's imprimatur tries to announce precisely that this book contains something more than commodified experience. In foregrounding its status as mere commodity, Oprah promises that this is one book that will not pass itself off as innocent in the general scandal. Instead, it will describe the damage wrought by that scandal and the hope that has survived it. To this end, Danticat's mastery of tone and her economy of means are stunning; in her best writing, her miniatures achieve a powerful simplicity through a construction as painstaking as the opaque modernist complexities of *Malemort*.

Danticat's work takes its place unavoidably in the guilt of a violent society even as it transforms the passivity of guilt through the act of aesthetic creation. She draws images that speak to a universal interpellation of the innocent in which one need never have shed blood or betrayed family or friend, to have always-already incurred a debt to others who have suffered more, if only by continuing to exist when they have disappeared. "You have never been able," she writes, "to escape the pounding of hearts that have outlived yours by thousands of years" *(Breath, Eyes, Memory* 224). She gives this pain a personal face; it haunts a mother and daughter's dreams, populating them with the threat of perpetuated life. In *Breath, Eyes, Memory*, she writes, "Some nights I woke up wondering if my mother's anxiety was somehow hereditary or if it was something that I had somehow 'caught' from living with her. Her nightmares had somehow become my own, so much so that I would wake up some mornings wondering if we hadn't both spent the night dreaming about the same thing: a man with no face, pounding a life into a helpless young girl" (193). Sophie Caco, the novel's narrator, bears her guilt in her very physical constitution: she resembles no one in her family, only the rapist whom her mother never saw. Unavoidably, she serves as the trace of a violence at once personal and systemic. Her predicament replicates that of her society, where innocence and sentiment are ineffectual when faced with the perpetuation of politicized terror.

In such a context, reproduction and heredity assume the form of traumatic compulsions. A woman clings to a dead child she has found, as it decays in her arms, another jumps from a sinking boat with her stillborn child, while Sophie's mother destroys herself and the child in her womb to still the voices she hears at night. Sex becomes an anguished humiliation, and the blood that flows through Danticat's prose marks the shame of a mother's testing to police a daughter's virginity or the ritual mutilation of a woman's body. In the feeling of guilt, the split subject turns against itself as it interiorizes its subjection to society in the form of the superego, and, in its extreme forms, the ego and superego paralyze the subject as they lock in combat (Freud, *Ego and the Id* 51). The mechanisms of guilt that society provides Sophie assure that the violence perpetuated upon her body will be internalized, consuming her innocence in a torment passed from mother to daughter. A woman's body becomes the grounds for systemic social violence in which the only escape from rivers of flowing blood is a becoming-flower or a becoming-butterfly with the help of the Vodou Lwa Erzulie, the goddess of love. This hoped-for immersion in nature, in an unconscious and cyclical time, figures the dreams of escape and the impossibility of achieving a social and historical experience free of violence that enter into conflict in Sophie Caco's experience.

And yet the body itself continues to hold forth the promise of an overcoming of the weight of history in its capacity for creation. Sophie Caco struggles to break the chain of violence with her daughter's generation, symbolically burning her mother's name and stating, "It was up to me to avoid my turn in the fire. It was up to me to make sure that my daughter never slept with ghosts, never lived with nightmares, and never had *her* name burnt in the flames" (203). She anxiously searches out the links she maintains with her mother, links that tie her to a land in which generations of women have survived and flourished. "I come from a place where breath, eyes, and memory are one, a place from which you carry your past like the hair on your head. Where women return to their children as butterflies or as tears in the eyes of the statues that their daughters pray to. My mother was as brave as the stars at dawn. She too was from this place. . . . Yes my mother was like me" (234).

The guilt of internalized social violence is compounded with that of another so typical of Antillean experience: the guilt of absence. The multiple displacements that have defined Haitian diasporic identity are localized in Danticat's work in the movement between Haiti and Brooklyn. She writes of a generation of "children of the sea," as the title of one of her most powerful stories would have it, driven from their homeland upon makeshift rafts, grasping at a salvation that retreats beyond the sea's horizon. The epistolary form of the story marks out the traumatic disjuncture and alienation of this process in which families are torn apart and those that never had a family to begin with have no voice and are lost at an undefined point somewhere between Port-au-Prince and Miami.

And yet these letters implicate the power of representation to preserve memory and to cultivate its capacity to serve as a receptacle for its other: life, the spirit that is snuffed out as a boat sinks into the ocean. Danticat's writing endeavors to work through the stifling sense of guilt and internalized violence of a society that has known centuries of suffering and bloodshed; the voices that populate her writing pursue the talking cure of a stricken community. Through language, she reignites the productivity of human subjectivity, but she does so not through the amnesic displacement of that violence by an ungrounded imaginary. Instead, she undertakes the transformation of guilt into a sense of conscious responsibility to a community extending across time and space. The constructed organic semblance of her language—in which it pretends to the humanity from which its rigid forms and structures are unavoidably alienated—becomes overwhelming in Danticat's poetic voice, and her lyricism manages to cultivate the fleeting illusion of the redemption of those for whom she speaks: "Behind these mountains are more mountains and more black butterflies still and a sea that is endless like my love for you" (*Krik? Krak!* 29).

Geographic displacement threatens to undermine Danticat's project, however, since, as an immigrant, the author must unavoidably remain an outsider not only to American society but also to the Haitian society she had left behind years before. This disjuncture would seem to call into question her very right to speak of a situation of which she can no longer have a direct, unmediated experience. Instead, her characters must work with the traces of dreams and memory:

> I only knew my mother from the picture on the nightstand by Tante Atie's pillow. She waved from inside the frame with a wide grin on her face and a large flower in her hair. . . . I sometimes saw my mother in my dreams. She would chase me through a field of wildflowers as tall as the sky. When she caught me, she would try to squeeze me into the small frame so I could be in the picture with her. I would scream and scream until my voice gave out, then Tante Atie would come and save me from her grasp. (*Breath, Eyes, Memory* 8)

This absence forms the very material of Danticat's prose; and, rather than turning away from the questions it raises, retreating into a fantasy of childhood or the exoticism of a direct interaction with an imagined Haitian culture, she marks out the process of disjuncture and reified displacement in the objects that populate Sophie Caco's world: photos, letters, and cassettes that carry the disembodied voice of an absent mother.

The guilt of this absence, where one flies off, leaving others behind to confront violence directly, invades Sophie's body and takes on a suitably first-world form: bulimia. Sophie's eating disorder registers a generalized subjection and unfreedom within a single body and the impossibility of an unproblematic relation to the natural world. Sophie has been violently separated from the realm of immediacy and immersion in a homeland, and bulimia marks the body's subsequent rejection of what is foreign in a movement of compulsion and guilt.

Danticat's writing describes the subjection to guilt of even the most innocent. If her fiction strives to work through and displace the weight of the past, that process is perhaps interminable. The suffering of past generations awaits the appearance of every new one and places upon us demands that exceed our ability to compose and produce ethical imperatives from within our own incomplete subjective experience. The totality of the social world, which structures our every thought, action, and feeling, is unavailable as such to our understanding. Knowledge of what we might be, and of the world's failure to correspond with its concept, cannot arise from comparison with any preexisting universal; Danticat's writing implies that any ethical imperative must itself arise from our reflection upon experience. While we can achieve no total insight into our implication in society, we can develop and extend our awareness of a responsibility to others. Only by turning toward the heterogeneous object world extending around us through time and space; by striving to know those objects as, instead, living subjects; and by addressing the claim their experience places upon those who live on after them can we begin to make amends for the damage progress has so far wrought as it extended the domain of human security. After all that has happened, no a priori universal—not even "autonomy," "possibility," or "life"—should turn suffering into an illustration of their truth, and yet to ban any universal concept that might orient ethics would itself create a far worse absolute and resignation to the course of the world. Only the full recollection of the experience of slavery, of prison-camps, of torture (itself, however, attainable only through the guilt of aesthetic illustration and critical inquiry into why and how these occurred) can begin to orient our ethical comportment: that these events should never happen again.[7] Danticat's writing transmits human voices in such an ethical reorientation of enlightenment toward individual experience.

Edwidge Danticat seizes upon the absence and distance of the Haitian diaspora from an immediate contact with violence and confronts this problem in the core of her work. The direct witness to violence, one who has never left the country and would seem to bear a privileged relation to the events unfolding there, can in fact be impeded by the burden of immediacy. Resurgent, atavistic violence strikes the witness with such force that little response may seem to remain but to fall silent and register its terror through the uncommenting gaze of, say, the documentary testimonial. In its submission to compulsion, the documentary response to suffering and loss gains its force through the immediate, preponderate facticity of violence. The putative transparency of the documentary is double-edged, however, for while it creates the traces in which memory may persist and live on beyond the moment when life is extinguished, in its immediacy the documentary can impoverish the utopian force of the imagination (see Huyssen 94). In speaking of the inhuman, the documenter can easily erase his or her critical distantiation from the event and can allow that same inhumanity to invade the future and live on beyond its allotted time.

Art provides a means of refusing violence without allowing its memory to be forgotten. The final guilt Danticat addresses is therefore that Proustian guilt produced ineluctably within the artistic object itself. For in speaking of suffering, in representing it aesthetically, the writer participates in a theft in which images are taken from the living and, perhaps worse still, from the dead, and merely represented.[8] If, as Adorno said, it is impossible to write poetry after Auschwitz, it is for this very reason: the poet takes from the dead their only possession, their memory among the living, and abrogates it to her own project. And yet in this aesthetic gesture lies the hope for overcoming the inhuman as the writer uses that same distance that threatened to undermine her project as a ruse in the struggle with violence. She turns the partial guilt of artistic representation back upon the total guilt of the midnight raid, the machine-gunning of women and children, and torture and summary execution, and presents to violence its own image as a reflection.[9] The geographic isolation of the diaspora spurs an aesthetic act of distantiation. The poetic image the artist offers to violence is not that of its simple, unmediated reflection but one in which it has been transmuted and called to account, where a human voice reappears and in which the semblance of life persists and calls forth the possibility of a transcendence of violence. Art thus invites violence to participate in the act of reflection and enlightenment. As the song says, "Haiti chérie, had to leave you to know you."

This then, is the locus of the Antillean writer's authenticity, for her project is to set the raw materials of a painful experience into motion, producing the forms of their overcoming not through a retreat from materiality but through a process of restructuration that manipulates memory to point beyond the present, through enlightenment. Danticat invokes this process via one of the primary tropes of Caribbean literature: education as the path to social mobility. *Breath, Eyes, Memory* describes the process by which thought begins, where reflection is called forth to overcome a state of servitude. Sophie's Tante Atie compels her niece to attend the school she never could: "At one time, I would have given anything to be in school. But not at my age. My time is gone. Cooking and cleaning, looking after others, that's my school now.... Cutting cane was the only thing for a young one to do when I was your age. That is why I never want to hear you complain about your school" (4). This pre-reflective realm Atie evokes is not simply one in which social ascension is impossible. More to the point, it serves to situate the violence Sophie must escape. In the novel's opening pages, the narrator recalls Atie's stories of the cane fields. "They saw people die there from sunstroke practically every day. Tante Atie said that, one day while they were all working together, her father—my grandfather—stopped to wipe his forehead, leaned forward, and died. My grandmother took the body in her arms and tried to scream the life back into it. They all kept screaming and hollering, as my grandmother's tears bathed the corpse's face" (4–5).

Sophie's mother also drives home this lesson: "Your schooling is the only thing that will make people respect you, [she tells Sophie]. You are going to work hard here, and no one is going to break your heart because you cannot read or write. You have a chance to become the kind of woman Atie and I always wanted to be. If you make something of yourself in life, we will all succeed. You can *raise our heads*" (43–44). The burden of guilt here becomes creative; the internalization of debt, as Nietzsche described it in *The Genealogy of Morals,* becomes guilt, then the artistic creativity of the ascetic ideal. The guilt Danticat portrays thus acts to redirect libidinal drives away from their simple reproduction and perpetuation in violence, in the cyclical return of the same, a natural, nonevolving existence here equated with the servitude of the cane fields. Instead, guilt sets into motion the thirst for truth amid a reality of contradiction and destruction and remains, in the form of responsibility, the silent partner of knowledge. "There is great responsibility that comes with knowledge," Sophie recalls her mother saying. "My great responsibility was to study hard. I spent six years doing nothing but that. School, home and prayer" (67).

Seven-year-old Guy, in the story "A Wall of Fire Rising," rehearses the lines he must recite in the school play where he has the role of Boukman:

"A wall of fire is rising and in the ashes, I see the bones of my people. Not only those people whose dark hollow faces I see daily in the fields, but all those souls who have gone ahead to haunt my dreams. At night I relive once more the last caresses from the hand of a loving father, a valiant love, a beloved friend" (*Krik? Krak!* 56). The narrator comments on the uncanny force of these stilted lines:

> It was obvious that this was a speech written by a European man, who gave the slave revolutionary Boukman the kind of European phrasing that might have sent the real Boukman turning in his grave. However, the speech made Lili and Guy stand on the tips of their toes from great pride. As their applause thundered in the small space of their shack that night, they felt as though for a moment they had been given the rare pleasure of hearing the voice of one of the forefathers of Haitian independence in the forced baritone of their only child. The experience left them both with a strange feeling that they could not explain. (56–57)

This "strange feeling" is the unsuspected gift of the artwork, achieved through its isolation as mere representation and semblance in a land of famine and torture. Its constructed nature, its status as a nonnatural, man-made object passes over into what it is not and, imitating the living, becomes productive, linking the present to both the past and an open future.

Danticat combines the experiential content of violent loss with the vernacular poetic forms of a communal historical experience. This vernacular poetry is made up of the tales handed down across generations or the scattered phrases that make up a daughter's love for her Haitian mother living and working in contemporary New York:

> My mother, who won't go out to dinner with anyone. "If they want to eat with me, let them come to my house, even if I boil water and give it to them." My mother, who makes jam with dried grapefruit peel and then puts in cinnamon bark that I always think is cockroaches in the jam..... My mother, who stuffs thimbles in her mouth, and then blows up her cheeks like Dizzy Gillespie while sewing yet another Raggedy Ann doll that she names Suzette after me. "I will have all these little Suzettes in case you never have any babies, which looks more and more like it is going to happen." (*Krik? Krak!* 148, 153)

These vernacular forms that structure Danticat's stories are a locus of both guilt, as they fabricate a mere representation of life, and its overcoming. The voicing of memory constitutes each story's otherness, its negation of the representational impulse toward the merely documentary. Narrative form is the receptacle for human voices, it gathers up immediate experiences and compels them to otherness, to become what they are not yet. In the forms she gives her work, Danticat reenacts the process of creation, fighting off the disintegration that recurs every time someone dies, starved or tortured. As Sophie accompanies her mother's coffin, her grandmother calls out the question that art presents across time and space to us who live on when others have died: "*Ou libéré?* Are you free?"

HISTORY IS the absent presence in Danticat's writing, where the memory of the past invades the subjective experience of those who have lived on and who struggle with writing to preserve the life that was stolen from others, erecting a small shrine in a corner of the temporal diaspora. Danticat's novel *The Farming of Bones*, more explicitly than her first two books, describes this experience of history, where the living bear witness to the loss of life. Inspired by Jacques Stephen Alexis's 1955 *Compère Général Soleil*, the book is itself literally framed by the terrifying deathly force of history: the inside front and back covers reproduce facsimiles of the letters of President Trujillo ordering the 1937 slaughter of Haitian migrant workers both novels describe. These letters serve as testimony to the author's immersion within both the documentary evidence of this event and its persistence within the memories of survivors and witnesses in Haiti and the Dominican Republic.

Danticat transforms the facts of history via a subjective, poetic voice that serves as that history's fictional articulation. The objectivity of these documents threatens to overwhelm subjective experience, as in the moment in which Trujillo's voice blares forth from the radio, interpellating Dominicans into the insanity of fascist xenophobia: "'You are independent and yours is the responsibility for carrying out justice,' the Generalissimo shrieked. . . . 'Tradition shows as a fatal fact . . . that under the protection of rivers, the enemies of peace, who are also the enemies of work and prosperity, found an ambush in which they might do their work, keeping the nation in fear and menacing stability.' The neighbors listened, nodding their heads in agreement as the Generalissimo's voice rose, charged with certainty and fervor" (97). As in Césaire's *Christophe,* the concrete autonomy of real individuals is here sacrificed to the police state, and the absolute freedom of Trujillo's abstraction of free will ("You are independent!") erases the subjectivity of both the automatized radio listeners and the lives of those Haitians who would soon die in Trujillo's fields.

Confronted by this abstract, depersonalized, deathly history, Danticat creates a field of interaction between history—as an ethical fidelity to the experience of those who have been killed—and a subjective, poetic voice that would recover something of the life that they lost. In the fields of the Dominican Republic, Haitian immigrants recall to each other their ties to an absent land rich in history and culture: "It was a way of being joined to your old life through the presence of another person. At times you could sit for a whole evening with such individuals, just listening to their existence unfold, from the house where they were born to the hill where they wanted to be buried. It was their way of returning home, with you as a witness or as someone to bring them back to the present. . . . This was how people left imprints of themselves in each other's memory" (73). In her project, the objective scraps of history take on the personal force of experience. Henri Christophe's citadel, from Césaire's perspective a monument to the terror of absolute freedom, becomes for Danticat's narrator Amabelle a refuge for her own subjectivity against the onslaught of history: "Each time I closed my eyes I saw the river and imagined Sebastien and Mimi drowning the way my mother and father and Odette had. To escape these thoughts, I envisioned Henry I's citadel as I had seen it again that afternoon, its closeness to the sky, its distance from the river. With my childhood visions of being inside of it, protected, I fell asleep" (227).

Trujillo's terror liquidated both lives and the autonomous experience of those who survived it. Amabelle's beloved friend Father Romain, tortured in prison following the massacre, has had his personality crushed and can only repeat the empty fascist jargon he must have grasped at to avoid losing his life altogether: "Our motherland is Spain; theirs is darkest Africa. . . . How can a country be ours if we are in smaller numbers than the outsiders?" (260). Destroyed by his encounter with fascist violence, his personality erased, Father Romain must be counted among the living-dead, or more precisely the dead-living, in whom torture echoes on in the present. Those who do live on are similarly haunted by the past and struggle to find a safe haven for their testimony: "The slaughter is the only thing that is mine enough to pass on. All I want to do is find a place to lay it down now and again, a safe nest where it will neither be scattered by the winds, nor remain forever buried beneath the sod" (266).

Proust thought that our "only painful memory is that of the dead" (272). We must question his assertion that only the artwork, composed "in the memory of an angel," in Alban Berg's loving words, can redeem the promise of a life cut short. The critical dimension of Antillean literature implies, in contrast, that death remains a painful memory and foreboding only because the world in which individuals fulfill their promise is blocked from them, from us, and, so far, from those who will come after us. "As subjects live less, death grows more precipitous, more terrifying"

(Adorno, *Negative Dialectics* 370, translation amended). Like life, death is a construction of human understanding, one that has no existence beyond that understanding. Death is no ultimate, ontological absolute. Even its apparent inevitability is itself historical; there is no reason to assume it is any more absolute than the plague or AIDS. We have glimpses beyond the "painful memory . . . of the dead" in loved ones who truly lived to fulfill some dimension of their potential and in the moments our own lives achieve fulfillment; then death is transformed, memory is sweet. Danticat's Proustian recourse to art is itself no absolute but an imperfect, unfortunate necessity that testifies to this blockage of life while it promises a world in which art would be unrecognizable.

Those still alive after the death of their beloved can continue to evoke freedom, striving to recover it in the face of its erasure. Insofar as they live not for themselves but for these cherished others who will never know freedom—that is to say in a voluntary unfreedom—they testify to the absence of those others and reanimate their life within language using the promise of freedom that is the aesthetic imagination:

> This past is more like flesh than air; our testimonials like the ones never heard . . . by the Generalissimo himself. His name is Sebastian Onius and his story is like a fish with no tail, a dress with no hem, a drop with no fall, a body in the sunlight with no shadow. His absence is my shadow; his breath my dreams . . . I wish at least that he was part of the air on this side of the river, a tiny morsel in the breeze that passes through my room in the night. I wish at least that some of the dust in his bones could trail me in the wind. (281)

It is here, in the haunting of the present by the past, in which subjects are enchained to their memories, that freedom might be recovered. To write of those who have been stripped of freedom and life itself does not yet free or redeem their premature disappearance but at least denies that their disappearance was absolute. The gift they left behind in others as they passed from this world can then express itself freely as the trace of life that animates our own encounter with the past.

Postscript

I AM NOT a native informer. Kant and Hegel are not native inhabitants of my world. Nor is Aimé Césaire. This book reflects my conviction that it is not enough for each of us to talk about ourselves, to define our subject positions, to rely on our immediate experience and the world we know, and then to leave things at that. Instead, a decade of research into Antillean society has only strengthened my certainty that the task confronting us now is to recreate the lived experience of others through all the resources of exchange, knowledge, and imagination available, such that that awareness inflects every level of our daily lives as members of multiple communities, global and local. To live as conscious global citizens is a Sisyphean task, as is the effort to understand our own lives, to say nothing of someone else's. The mirror we hold up to someone else will never correspond with that person's own self-awareness, nor will we ever fully understand our own implication in this act of reflection. Faced with this quandary, the isolationist temptation to turn that mirror back upon our own world can temporarily secure our fragile narcissism; but we are global citizens, nonidentical members of a universal community, and to lock others out is only to assure that they will either knock down the doors or, in their indifference to our plight, that we will suffocate in our hermetic fortress.

If we refuse the seductive call of regression that facilitated the genocides of the last century, the way out is not through an "immolation" and "sacrifice" of the ego, a "passive" subjectivity that would be "wholly an obedience" (Levinas). Instead, we must actively and ceaselessly strive to transform the conditions of society and experience that, as Levinas himself never tired of denouncing, reduce every Other to the Same; this we can do via reflection, a reflection of ourselves through others, in acts of auto-objectification and self-alienation that pass through the infinite world around us. The opening onto indeterminate possibility can be reached only through the work of determinate reflection. As an ethical practice, this can perhaps begin with the cultivation of what one could call modesty or reserve. To communicate with others without having known the answers in advance, to mold ourselves to another's experience, to actually learn something from an encounter instead of simply reinforcing our identity is more easily said than done. I have tried in these pages not to speak in the place of others but to speak with others and to bear witness to a critical process of reflection that preexisted us and will outlive us. Antillean intellectuals performed their own Copernican Revolution, making the West into an object of knowledge for the colonized; in so doing, they achieved insight into their own constitution as subjects of colonialism as well as concrete transformations of those conditions precisely through an active reflection of the self through the other.

To do justice to their thought as a call to critical (self-) understanding, however, it is not enough to echo their insights passively; we must instead work to extend and expand the process of enlightenment they began and handed down to us. We may do so with the confidence that ethical practice begins when we can overcome our self-centeredness to take the risk of mimetic experience. This mimetic risk, in turn, is not a matter of individual decision; it will be truly possible only when we cultivate the possibilities of every member of our life-world rather than simply accept the innumerable castrations and disempowerments that occur today. The local articulation of autonomous subjectivities is perhaps necessary prior to the creation of noncoercive relations of global dependency and ecological consciousness; if we hope in the future to become ethical subjects, we must cultivate the solidity of our self-awareness and of those around us as part of this intersubjective, differentiated totality so that we may take the risks of listening, questioning, thinking, speaking, acting, being wrong, and remaining silent. "If humanity announces itself not as a sort of undivided entity that will have to be reduced to *an essence* but as the deepened relation of the same to the other, of the diverse to the similar, it will be up to each individual to be a self, integral and integrated (but not assimilated to the other) in the totality" (*IP* 142).

Notes

Preface

1. Personal communication, Fort-de-France, 9 Nov. 2001.
2. I discuss this ecological project in chapter 6.
3. *Le Monde* 14 March 2000.
4. *Libération* 27–28 Nov. 1999. Chamoiseau continues: "A people who serve as machines of consumption. A people rendered irresponsible for their fate, fattened with subsidies, with protections, with decisions worked out thousands of kilometers away. A terrible (and silent) system in which the crotches of subjection resemble the arches of emancipation, of progress, and of modernity."
5. See Bongie, *Islands and Exiles* 13.

Introduction: Aesthetic Construction and Postcolonial Subjectivity

1. See Hardt and Negri 306 for a critique of the failure of decolonization as a preparation to postmodern "Empire."
2. See Gilroy's *Black Atlantic* for an argument presenting slavery as no aberration of modernity but concomitant with its historical expansion and success.
3. Though Oruno D. Lara describes a "willed oblivion, organized since 1848 by the French government and its accomplices: the colonial administration, the clergy, colonists, and the reactionary press" (10), we need not conclude that the French government had a conscious, articulated project to produce a culture divorced from its history; nonetheless, the reality of this erasure of memory, a structural effect of five hundred years of European colonization, remains compelling.
4. For variations of such an analysis, see Aubin, Bangou "L'Histoire," Drake, Jardel, Kyoore, Pizaroo, Rosello, Taylor, and Webb.
5. See, for example, the collection Hal Foster edited in 1981 under the title, *The Anti-Aesthetic: Essays on Postmodern Culture*. Foster concludes that the "criticality [of aesthetic representation] is now largely illusory (and so instrumental)" (xv). My argument here, to be developed below, owes much to works such as Terry Eagleton's *The Ideology of the Aesthetic,* Andreas Huyssen's "Twilight Memories" (1983: 85–101), and Robert Kaufman's suggestive essay "Red Kant, or The Persistence of the Third Critique* in Adorno and Jameson."

6. Etienne Balibar calls Locke the "founder of modern philosophy" (Locke 87). Balibar convincingly refutes the received wisdom that the invention of modern subjectivity occurs with Descartes, whose "philosophy of *Méditations* is not that of consciousness *(Bewusstsein)* but of certainty *(Gewisshet)* and of the necessary conditions for obtaining it" (32). In marked distinction to the immediacy of the Cartesian Ego (41), Locke's great innovation is to invent a temporal conception of consciousness, arguing for the first time in Western thought that the "identity of persons lies . . . in the memory and knowledge of one's past self and actions continued on under the consciousness of being the same person, whereby every man owns himself" (63). See also Paul Ricoeur's discussion of Locke's notion of the self in its relation to memory and temporal identity (*La mémoire, l'histoire, l'oubli* 123–31).

7. The interpretation of Delgrès's act has of course been the subject of much debate. Though the following chapter will trace this debate in the ensuing two centuries since Guadeloupe's revolt, it is important to stress here the mythological and misogynist character of much of the recent focalization on Delgrès. Moreover, Mireille Rosello has critiqued the fundamental contradiction between an Antillean drive for historical autonomy and the glorification of a sacrificial logic of suicide that reinforces "exactly the same law as that which the dominant power structures had wished to impose" (42).

8. See Oruno D. Lara (216–32) for a summary of the historical and political process of departmentalization. Despite their many differences, for the purposes of this study the islands of Martinique and Guadeloupe will often be referred to interchangeably. The validity of this gesture lies in the juridical, political, and economic identity the two islands enjoy thanks to their joint status as French overseas departments. Because of this shared structure and despite many dissimilarities—the continuing preponderance of a white, land-owning *béké* class in Martinique, for example—history has become a problem for both islands in precisely the same fashion, through the process of commodification to be described below. On the other hand, Haiti's historical development since 1804 has diverged sharply from that of Guadeloupe and Martinique. That being said, the shared colonial history of Martinique, Guadeloupe, and Haiti through 1804 allows one to consider these islands as a single region through the period of revolution and Haitian independence in the early nineteenth century. On the differences between the various DOMs, see Burton and Reno.

9. The citizens of the French DOMs enjoy political representation, (in theory) full rights of citizenship, and juridical equality as French and now European citizens. They produce no appreciable economic benefit for the métropole and receive their only "settlers" in the form of bureaucrats and tourists, all in contrast to pre-twentieth-century colonies. Rather than the raw and brutal "exploitation" of the plantation, a paracolonial world of dependency now ensures France's geopolitical presence in the Americas (Aldrich and Connell 289).

10. See Buffon, "Le système bancaire" 115.

11. Ibid. In this, the region is of course hardly unique. What distinguishes it from other postindustrial regions is the absence of accompanying autonomous production in areas ranging from basic agriculture to high technology.

12. Less than 20 percent of FIDOM expenditures actually support productive activities (Aldrich and Connell 146, 158).

13. That said, the DOMs' present dependency is in some senses no worse than that of "independent" neighboring islands beholden to former colonizers and the World Bank (see Hardt and Negri 174 for a general discussion of this dilemma).

14. Aldrich and Connell estimate that a mere 6 percent of tourist expenditure actually flows directly into the local economy (152). See Abenon 191–94 for a description of the long, drawn-out disappearance of the island's various agricultural industries. The Antillean tourist industry exploded in the 1960s, replacing dependency on a single cash crop with dependency on continuous flows of tourists.

15. This bill first appeared in 1954 and was modified in 1958 to the form depicted in figure 1. Copies of the bill printed until January 1, 1965, totaled 995,632 (Kolsky 208). See Buffon, "Le système bancaire" 81–82.

16. Like Bergson's intuition of a *"durée-qualité* . . . that consciousness attains immediately" (94), occurring at the level of a putative "fundamental self" (96), his spontaneous description of the reified world in which both objects and the self have become alienated, fungible commodities (101, 103, 174), for all its insight, remains a mystified, mandarin philosophical voluntarism: to overcome this alienation, we need only "break the bounds of language, . . . seizing our ideas themselves in their natural state, such as our consciousness, delivered from the obsession of space, perceives them" (100). Benjamin and Adorno each offer materialist critiques of Bergson along these lines. See Section II of Benjamin's "On Some Motifs in Baudelaire" (1978: 151) and Adorno, *Negative Dialectics* 8.

17. See Hanssen chapters 2 and 3 for a discussion of this aspect of Benjamin's thought.

18. Benjamin presumably fabricates this notion of allegory from Hegel's description of "analysis" as "the "break[ing] up of an idea into its . . . elements," an "activity of dissolution" that is "the tremendous power of the negative" or, in other words, "death. . . . The life of spirit . . . wins its truth only when, in utter dismemberment, it finds itself [by] tarrying with the negative" (*Phenomenology* 18–19).

19. See Corzani, "Poetry before Negritude," for a detailed description of the misogynist "doudouist" poetry in Guadeloupe and Martinique that preceded Aimé Césaire's invention of negritude. Corzani condemns this earlier poetry, of which he offers numerous examples, for its "dehumanization" of the objects of its lyricism in which "the doudous, reduced to their physical allure, to their birdlike twittering, or to their erotic potential, are subtly animalized" (474). On the complex functioning of Antillean folklore, see Glissant, *DA* 170.

20. Lukács's 1923 *History and Class Consciousness* is the classic text in which he elaborates his theory of reification.

21. Richard Price offers a memorable description of this situation in *The Convict and the Colonel* xi.

22. While "alienation" is perhaps, as Chris Bongie contends, a "highly ideological and extremely dubious concept" (*Islands and Exiles* 69), I hope my reference to it in this chapter will prove a critical and constructive refusal to let its theoretical taboo remain a mere abstraction.

23. Price describes this Antillean passivity as a generalized result of Martinican consumerism (xiii), evoking as well a more generalized relation between madness and

colonialism (157–61) equally visible in novels such as Glissant's *Malemort* and Tony Delsham's *Négropolitains et Euro-blacks*. See Dash, *Edouard Glissant,* and Bongie, *Islands and Exiles* chapter 4, for insightful summaries and analyses of Glissant's career and work. As an outsider to Antillean culture, I am convinced that in studying this experience in its local Antillean specificity, this investigation can illuminate a more general crisis of historical experience in modernity and postmodernity. Among the many difficulties of this project, perhaps the most fundamental is that I have set out to describe the experience of others; perhaps Glissant's assertion of historical alienation is only the "ideological error" (Bongie 143) of a "Martiniquan-who-knows-everything-about-Martinique-and-Martiniquans" (Jack Corzani, qtd. in Bongie, *Islands and Exiles* 143). I can only say that, though I am not Antillean or a descendant of slaves, I find myself not on the other side of this alienation looking back on it as a misguided relic of "ideological error" but rather interpellated by an experience that I recognize.

24. See Reinhart Koselleck's article "Le concept de l'histoire" in *L'expérience historique* for a comprehensive discussion of the development of the notion of history *(Geschichte)* in European thought.

25. Glissant studied philosophy as a university student in Paris in the 1950s with the Hegelian existentialist Jean Wahl (Fonkoua). The influence of Heidegger is explicit in Glissant's recurring references in his recent theoretical work (*Poétique de la relation, Introduction à une Poétique du Divers*) to the conflict between "l'être" and "l'étant," the two basic categories of Heidegger's thought rendered in English as "Being" and "beings." See Krzysztof Ziareck for a succinct and compelling defense of Heidegger's critique of history. See Bambach for a useful insertion of Heidegger's critique of history in *Being and Time* within the context of the crisis of historicism in German thought between 1880 and 1933. Beatrice Hanssen places *Being and Time* in the context of Walter Benjamin's reconceptualization of historical experience (19–23).

26. See Sloterdijk's chapter "Le 'On' ou: le sujet le plus réel du cynisme diffus moderne" in *Critique de la raison cynique* 255–73.

27. See Adorno's trenchant critique of Heidegger in *The Jargon of Authenticity* 99.

28. See Bidima 244 for a penetrating critique of this process in postcolonial African societies. I was struck by one example of this fabricated forgetfulness as I visited the Clément plantation in Martinique in November 2001. There, massive efforts have gone into memorializing George Bush and François Mitterand's meeting on its grounds after the Gulf War, but I was unable to find a single trace, written or visual, of the laboring, enslaved producers of the plantation's original wealth.

29. To address the vast literature theorizing human memory would exceed the project and scope of this volume. The first section of Paul Ricoeur's volume *La mémoire, l'histoire, l'oubli* offers a masterful overview of theories of memory from Plato and Aristotle through the writings of Bergson, Husserl, and Heidegger. Ricoeur's study, along with his earlier *Temps et récit*, is, for all its vast erudition, at times surprisingly unhistorical in its methodology. Ricoeur's analytical procedure often tends to ontologize memory, history, and forgetting into timeless constants of the human condition varying only quantitatively throughout human history, invoking a putative "natural memory" left unexplained in his 650-page study (80). On the importance of a future-oriented memory ("docta spes africana") for postcolonial thought, see Bidima 229–33.

30. Joan Dayan describes in the most powerful terms the dehumanization of Antillean slavery and its rationalization as human commodification in that document of distorted human reason, the Code Noir (199–258).

31. Arnold's description of the *Cahier* as a "contradictory . . . dialectical composition" that "bears the stamp of Hegel," as it "seeks to transform consciousness of the black experience from within" serves as the starting point for these comments as well as my more extensive analysis of the poem in chapter 2. His *Modernism and Negritude* remains the most thorough and balanced large-scale study of Cèsaire's complex aesthetic and theoretical relation to Western modernity. While Arnold sees Cèsaire's dialectic resulting in a Hegelian synthesis (164), my own analysis instead underscores a more Adornian persistence of contradiction in a poetic "negative dialectic."

32. See Adorno, *Prisms* 106. Sartre's endorsement of the process of aesthetic objectification in "Orphée noire" is in marked contrast to the pessimistic tenor of his other comments on objectification in which, as Fredric Jameson observes, "*all* action, *all* projects, involve a loss of self and an alienation of consciousness in objects and in the realization of work" (*Marxism and Form* 238). See also Jameson, *Late Marxism* 21, on Adorno's differentiation of objectification and alienation.

33. Since I will discuss the productive ambiguities and contradictions of Césaire's subject in chapter 2, and its historical and theoretical limitations in chapter 3, it is important for now simply to register the historical isomorphism existing between Kojève and Césaire's models of subjectivity.

34. Georg Lukács *(The Young Hegel)* argues convincingly that the notion of externalization is the key philosophical concept of the *Phenomenology,* clearly articulating its importance both within Hegel's intellectual development and its import for Marx in the *1844 Manuscripts.*

35. On Vico, see Jay's *Marxism & Totality* (32–37). See also Ernst Cassirer's discussion of Teten's *Philosophical Essays on Human Nature* (1777) as an Enlightenment forerunner to the Kantian notion of productive imagination (148).

36. See the articles by Bernasconi and Susan Buck-Morss for nuanced appraisals of such issues. As to the actual historical influence of Hegelian thought in French Caribbean letters, see chapter 4. For an overview of recent Caribbean postcolonial theory—which this study engages only in part, to describe instead its dialogue with European modernity—see chapter 2 of Chris Bongie's *Islands and Exiles.*

37. See Benhabib for a detailed description of the history of this idea in German critical thought from Kant to Habermas. Hardt and Negri's vast and at times contradictory study *Empire,* in addressing the transformation of labor to increasingly "immaterial" forms, draws attention to the increasing importance of both the heteronomous production and liberatory productivity of subjectivity: "Living labor is what constructs the passageway from the virtual to the real; it is the vehicle of possibility" (357).

38. Hegel goes on, however, to draw the opposite conclusion from Marx in light of this insight: the authoritarian state must be strengthened rather than transcended, he argues, in order to restrain the inherent anarchic tendencies of the social and economic order (Marcuse 105).

39. Lukács argues that "the awareness that life is based on contradictions is the fundamental problem faced by classical German literature and philosophy. . . . Hegel's

philosophical genius" was to see in contradiction not merely statements of particular aporetical experiences but rather "the dialectical nature of all life, of all being and thought" (*Young Hegel* 114, 105). See also Adorno's critique of the Cartesian norm of noncontradictoriness as the logical imposition of a formal presupposition upon material heterogeneous to subjectivity (*Negative Dialectics* 140–42).

40. While the conclusions Hegel draws from his analysis of labor increasingly sacrifice the individual to the dominant social order, that analysis itself remains unchanged even in the *Logic* (1812–16), though it grows increasingly abstract. The *Logic*'s model of purposive, teleological activity (work) is (formally) identical to that of the Jena *Logic* and the *Phenomenology* (the "end is the Notion that has come to itself in objectivity" [*Science of Logic* 741]), as is that of alienated labor (746, 750). Finally, Hegel's conclusion is likewise the same: confronted by his/her externalized "objectivity" (751), the slave must transform him or herself into an autonomous subject: "the truth of the means is . . . to become itself a real end" (752). For all its determinations, however, the world the absolute spirit has produced remains trapped within the tautological idealist realm of mere appearance Hegel has constructed, unable to reach and transform the "real" world-in-itself: "Spirit cognizes the Idea as its *absolute truth,*" Hegel concludes, "which is the *absolute knowledge of itself*" (760).

41. Glossing Adam Smith, Hegel also offers a proto-Marxian critical antithesis to his affirmative notion of "practical consciousness": in an industrial division of labor in which the worker never makes whole and complete objects but only performs partial, repetitive tasks, "the worker's consciousness is debased to the ultimate degree of brutishness" (*Le premier système* 105).

42. See Benhabib 47, 134 and, for comparison, Judith Butler's analysis of Hegelian self-consciousness in *Subjects of Desire* 29.

43. Ironically, given their abstract dismissals of Hegelian dialectics, Hegel's theory of "practical consciousness" operates, unacknowledged, throughout Hardt and Negri's revindication of "a humanity that is constructed productively" (350). Hardt and Negri's *Empire* at times tends to fetishize the liberatory potential of work. Instead, we might ask with Henri Lefebvre, "How do we pass from work to non-work?" (*La fin de l'histoire* 158). Marx, in the *Grundrisse,* recognized that not only labor but "free time . . . transform[s] its possessor into a different subject" (290). Adorno as well describes utopia as freedom from having to produce in the beautiful aphorism "Sur l'eau" in *Minima Moralia* 156.

44. See, for example, Césaire's critique of the ideological dimensions of negritude, a critique that nonetheless retains negritude, not as "cathedral," "tower," or "ideology," "an immense aggregate in which God alone will recognize his people," but rather as a radically historical "personal ethic" (qtd. in Depestre, *Bonjour* 144–45).

45. Benjamin and Adorno retain the basic Hegelian conception of experience as a transformative immersion in an object world, while bringing Hegel's notion into contact with the Marxian critique, described above, of the alienation, reification, and ensuing impoverishment of historical experience engendered by capitalist society. See, for example, Benjamin's reference to "self-immersion" in the fragment "Experience" (*Selected Writings* 553) and Adorno's article "Opinion Delusion Society" (*Critical Models* 110) as well as Bernstein's discussion of Adorno and Benjamin's concept of experience (111–20). See also Bongie, *Exotic Memories* 9–10.

46. See Reinhardt Koselleck's article "Mutation de l'expérience et changement de méthode" in *L'expérience de l'histoire*. Koselleck's historicization of the concept of *Erfahrung*, drawing upon an 1862 article by Jacob Grimm, inexplicably neglects to address Hegel's reformulation of the notion. Walter Benjamin outlines the subsequent development of the dialectical concepts of experience *(Erfahrung)* and lived experience *(Erlebnis)* in Dilthey, Klages, Jung, Bergson, Proust, and Freud in the first three sections of "On Some Motifs in Baudelaire" *(Illuminations)*.

47. "Experience rests on the synthetic unity of appearances, i.e., on a synthesis according to concepts of the object of appearances in general" (Kant, *Critique of Pure Reason* 282). While Paul Guyer and Allen Wood's introduction to the Cambridge edition of Kant's first *Critique* offers a lucid presentation of its history and basic argument, Adorno's 1959 lectures on the work form an immanent critique of it as a locus of philosophical contradictions that remains productive to this day.

48. Sartre's *L'Imaginaire: Psychologie phénoménologique de l'imagination* (1940) presents his appropriation and extension of Husserl's model of intentional conscious representation, a model that culminates in Sartre's disembodied notion of production and freedom abstracted from material social transformation: "The act of imagination is a magical one. It is an incantation destined to produce the object of one's thought, the thing one desires, in a manner that one can take possession of it" (qtd. in Butler 115). This Sartrian imagination indicates the capacity of an unfree individual to dream of freedom and to give that dream external objective form in an artwork. In other words, the heteronomous artist becomes the autonomous generator of representations of a nonexistent, utopian world (Butler 158).

49. Thesis # vii, qtd. in Löwy 55. Löwy cites the callousness of Victor Cousin as a corollary to Benjamin's reference to the reactionary historicism of Fustel de Coulanges: "I absolve victory as necessary and useful," writes Cousin; "I next strive to absolve it as just, in the strictest sense of the word; I attempt to demonstrate the morality of success" (qtd. in Löwy 57).

50. See Revel and Hunt for a broad sampling of the many tendencies of recent French historiography as well as Ricoeur, *L'histoire, la mémoire, l'oubli* 181–372).

51. Langlois and Seignobos's 1898 text *Introduction aux études historiques* outlines their conception of a "positive science" of history (qtd. in Carrard 4). Langlois and Seignobos enjoin the historian to remain "objective," avoiding opinions and subjective intrusions (Carrard 7).

52. To speak of a "voicing" of history and memory implies both an attention to the vernacular register of subjective experience fundamental to African diasporic communities and the structured organization of that experience—as in the process of "voicing" harmonic material in musical composition—that occurs in the act of aesthetic construction.

53. On the importance of Baumgarten's invention of a "scientific" aesthetics, see Eagleton 332 and Cassirer 275–346. Dominique Bouhours had earlier argued for the existence of an "aesthetic reason" in his *The Art of Criticism* from 1687 (Cassirer 29).

54. See Bernstein chapter 6 for an elaboration of this argument. Hume makes a similar argument for aesthetic indetermination in his essay "Of the standard of taste" (Cassirer 300).

55. Eagleton elegantly elaborates a similar argument in *The Ideology of the Aesthetic*, 97–100.

56. The concept of aesthetic construction carries a psychological dimension insofar as it elaborates a concrete response to the vicissitudes of the "collective memory" (Maurice Halbwachs) described by Glissant. In this sense, it redirects Freud's inherently aesthetic notion of "construction" in his 1937 article "Construction in Analysis." There, Freud describes how the analyst "constructs" a narrative description of the analysand's repressed memories that can either dislodge buried memories or represent to the analysand repressed memories that remain inaccessible in the patient's unconscious (see Laplanche and Pontalis 99).

57. Of the many studies of Adorno's aesthetic theory, those by Jameson *(Late Marxism)*, Nicholson, and Jay (*Adorno* and "Mimesis and Mimetology") are particularly useful, lucid expositions and analyses. A number of recent works of postcolonial studies, including Edward Said's *Culture and Imperialism*, Jean-Godefroy Bidima's *Théorie critique et modernité africaine*, and Asha Varadharajan's *Exotic Parodies*, have argued compellingly for the relevance of Adornian critical theory to the field of postcolonial studies; this study in turn takes that applicability as axiomatic. While Edward Said is perfectly right to observe that the Frankfurt School "is stunningly silent on racist theory, anti-imperialist resistance, and oppositional practice in the empire" (278), these works begin to remedy that blindness and to demonstrate the importance of a negative dialectics for postcolonial studies.

58. See also *Aesthetic Theory* 113.

59. Emmanuel Levinas, in his essay "Peace and Proximity," makes a similar point (165).

60. See Clément Mbom's article on Opacity and Relation in which the author concludes, unlike myself, that these two concepts are not in an antinomical relation but are distinct moments of Glissant's thought (250). On Glissantian "relation," see Britton 11–18 and her discussion of "opacity" on pages 18–25.

61. "Every outer perception therefore immediately proves something real in space, or rather is itself the real; to that extent, empirical realism is beyond doubt, i.e., to our outer intuitions there corresponds something real in space." Kant immediately adds the crucial proviso, though, reminding us that these "real" things are not things-in-themselves but mere appearances: "Of course space itself with all its appearances, as representations, is only in me; but in this space the real, or the material of all objects of outer intuition is nevertheless really given, independently of all invention" (429).

62. While Kant explicitly limits the noumenal to a negative "boundary concept" (362) that blocks the pretensions of reason to operate beyond the realm of experience, devoid of any positive being that would turn the noumenal into a determinate object of experience, Hegel remarks that "the thing-in-itself as such is nothing else but the empty abstraction from all determinateness[,] in so far as [these things] are thought devoid of all determination, as nothings" (*Logic* 488, 121). Hegel thus hypostatizes the noumenal (it *is* empty abstraction, they *are* thought) into a positive being.

63. As such, Hegel's argument gives a further twist to his fundamental insight that the determination of any limit necessarily and already effects the negation and transcendence of that limit.

64. See chapter 6's explication of Glissantian totality and relation as a development of Hegel's totality.

65. One might also understand this philosophical problem to underlie another dimension of postcolonial studies: the discourse of "exoticism" (see Bongie, *Exotic Memories* chapter 1).

66. Whether the "opacity" of many of these authors makes their texts, as putative "solutions" to the problems they address, unavailable to those who would most benefit from their critique is a problem I will return to in my final chapter.

67. Chris Bongie underlines this process of the aesthetic construction of historical experience in his analysis of Glissant's eminently historical novels *Quatrième siècle* and *Mahagony* in *Islands and Exiles* 167–86.

68. See Bernstein chapter 4 for a theoretical elaboration of such an ethics of the living, and Bidima (20) on the relevance of such an ethics to postcolonial thought. Here, I wish to emphasize that such an ethics must have a temporal dimension, directed as much to the past and future as to the present.

1. The Vicissitudes of Memory

1. It is important to remember that, unlike that of Martinique, Victor Hugues and the guillotine he brought to Guadeloupe during the Terror decimated Guadeloupe's white land-owning class. This difference in the overall makeup of the two islands' populations is at the root of the differences one sees persisting to the present, which one might render schematically as a stronger African cultural heritage in Guadeloupe and a more Francocentric Martinican culture.

2. Delgrès's text is reproduced in Saint-Ruf 107–9.

3. Abenon 92–97 and Adélaïde-Merlande offer concise summaries of these events.

4. Needless to say, this approach leaves unexplored many others; in particular, it would be interesting to pursue sociological research regarding social awareness patterns of Guadeloupean history, taking into account through what channels, whether the scholastic French school system, the oral tradition, or autodidacticism, this knowledge was encountered. This study is restricted to the analysis of a single field of investigation: the departmental archives at Bisdary, Guadeloupe.

5. This moment also signals their entrance into the circuits of metropolitan commodity culture as an embryonic consumer market, moving beyond an existence as (enslaved) producers. See Fallope 364–66.

6. See Fallope 178–79 for an overview of this literature.

7. Glissant's novel *Le Quatrième siècle* offers an imaginative recreation of this distribution of names in 1848. See also Glissant's discussion of this process in *Introduction à une Poétique du Divers* (86).

8. It was necessary to base calculations upon five-year sections of the population in order to avoid all possibility of ambiguity resulting from the less-than-exact attribution of an age to each former slave. In fact, ages are generally indicated in the 1848 *Etat-Civil* by the qualifier "d'environ," in a stock phrase of the type: "Louis, esclave agé d'environ 46 ans." The division of the analysis into five-year groupings helped to overcome the tendency of the officials to ascribe approximate ages to the former slaves. It was also necessary to take into account the relative number of individuals in

each age group who had survived until 1848. Assuming a relatively stable rate of birth, this factor increases the preponderance of older individuals (born between 1802 and 1810) who received the name "Louis."

9. See Sander L. Gilman on the origins of this discourse in thinkers such as Cuvier and Gobineau in the article "Black Bodies, White Bodies: Toward an Iconography of Female Sexuality in Late Nineteenth-Century Art, Medicine and Literature."

10. Chris Bongie's analysis of the monthly *Revue des colonies*—a paper published in Paris from 1834 to 1842 by the Martinican Cyrille Bissette—describes in contrast the rich historical material on the French Caribbean revolutionary past the paper presented to its readers (*Islands and Exiles* 266–87).

11. *Abolitionniste*, March-April 1844: 401.

12. Alain Buffon has emphasized that the author of *L'Histoire de la Guadeloupe* nonetheless remains tied to the values of his social class, as for example when he defends the gentle nature of a slave's life in the Antilles or when he reproduces stereotypes of blacks who are "naturellement indolents" ("Regard d'un historien créole" 14).

13. See Mary Louise Pratt's "Scratches on the Face of the Country; or, What Mr. Barrow Saw in the Land of the Bushmen" in Gates *"Race," Writing, and Difference* for a description of this exploratory colonial gaze as it functioned in late-nineteenth-century British and French discourse.

14. *Reveil social* 10 Sept. 1903.

15. It was only at the turn of the twentieth century that black politicians in Guadeloupe under the leadership of Légitimus achieved electoral victories at the expense of the mulatto class. (cf. Abenon 155–68).

16. *Le Socialiste* 20 July 1907.

17. René Arot, *Le Peuple* 4 Nov. 1899.

18. A. Fernand, *Le Peuple* 4 July 1900.

19. "Schoelcher, le grand Schoelcher, de qui tous les hommes politiques se réclament, trouva [l'esclavage] mauvais et inhumain. Il s'employa à la faire cesser et y parvint. C'était beau. C'était sublime, tout le monde exultait de joie. Hélas! Aujourd'hui, le mot patron a remplacé celui du maître" (A. Ducadosse, "Ouvrier forgeron," *Cri du peuple* 13 Feb. 1926.

20. *Cri du peuple* 7 Aug. 1926.

21. See also Bongie, *Islands and Exiles* 4.

22. *Etincelle* 17 May 1952.

23. The article is devoted to the question of Departmentalization versus Independence, and the paper, to argue its point, reminds readers with bureaucratic fervor that "les Communistes qui tiennent compte de la définition Stalinienne de la nation pour appliquer une politique salutaire à la Guadeloupe savent parfaitement que nous ne réalisons pas toutes les cinq conditions pour prétendre à l'indépendance rationale (Tarer, *L'Etincelle* 17 March 1956).

24. "La federation communiste de la Guadeloupe: 'la leçon de Delgrès,'" *L'Etincelle* 1 June 1957.

25. Henry Bangou, "Apercu d'histoire," *L'Etincelle* 21 March 1959.

26. *L'Etincelle* 21 March 1958.

27. *L'Etincelle* 23 June 1963.
28. *L'Etincelle* 30 May 1964.
29. *L'Etincelle* 8 Jan. 1966.
30. *L'Etincelle* 27 May 1967.
31. See Geyer and Hansen's description of the analogous situation of postwar German consumption of images of the Holocaust. Paul Gilroy provocatively and, to my mind, justifiably, explores such a comparison of the Holocaust and colonialism in *Against Race*.
32. "A la Guadeloupe et à la Martinique, c'est un fait que la mémoire est plus que raturée. On a complètement oblitéré tout ce qui rappelait l'action que les ancêtres avaient pu mener. . . . La situation de l'histoire des Antilles est déjà signée, entérinée, enterrée." ["In Guadeloupe and Martinique, it's a fact that memory has been more than erased. Everything that recalled the acts undertaken by our ancestors has been completely obliterated. . . . The situation of history in the Antilles is already signed, sealed, and buried"]. Personal interview 12 April 1997.
33. In his essays "The Storyteller" and "On Some Motifs in Baudelaire" (both collected in *Illuminations*). An interesting parallel could be drawn between Benjamin's evocation of the experiential plenitude of the "storyteller" and his or her championing in Antillean literature, most notably in the recent work of Chamoiseau and Confiant. See Bongie, *Islands and Exiles* 157.
34. *Illuminations* 159.
35. For a sociological overview of the function of the griot within traditional malinké society, see Camara. For a critical reevaluation of the postcolonial trope of *griotisme*, see Frindéthié.
36. Huyssen describes this process as a "return to history, the new confrontation of history and fiction, history and representation, history and myth that distinguishes contemporary aesthetic productions" (88).

2. Antinomies of Double Consciousness in Aimé Césaire's *Cahier d'un retour au pays natal*

1. This sublimation of powerlessness that fuels critique, for better and worse, is the process Nietzsche first described in the *Genealogy of Morals*. See also Bernstein 253.
2. Chris Bongie makes a similar point in *Islands and Exiles* 43.
3. See Roger Toumson and Simonne Henry-Valmore (part 1) for a comprehensive discussion of the intellectual and historical milieu in which Césaire composed the *Cahier*.
4. Commentators including A. James Arnold (*Modernism and Negritude*), Georges Ngal, and Daniel Delas describe in detail the vast range of the influences and references Césaire draws upon in his work, from Greek, Roman, and African civilizations through the French poets (Rimbaud, Lautréamont, Apollinaire) who are his most direct influences.
5. Abiola Irele describes the poem's subject as "multiple," "composite," and marked by "the burden of a double consciousness imposed by a situation that denies him a stable framework of reference for his sense of identity" (*Cahier* xlv–xlvi).
6. "Embrasse-moi jusqu'au nous furieux/ embrasse, embrasse NOUS."

7. André Breton presciently underlines this confrontation in his famous preface to the *Cahier,* "Un grand poète noir."

8. For Delas, the rejection of reason is the "decisive turning point," after which "a renaissance and new beginning can occur" (35), while Ngal insists that the poem presents a "revolt against a certain concept of Reason ... [in favor of] insanity, dementia, cannibalism, magic" (*Un homme à la recherche* 192). Victor Hountondji gives this praise of poetic irrationalism a materialist, Kojèvian twist: "A new race of blacks is born from revolt and revolution ... after the last bastion of domination, of alienation, that of reason which, according to the Surrealists, is the cruelest prison of all, the most horrible that can exist for man, will have been overcome" (33–34). Irele tempers Hountondji's equation of the abandonment of reason with the coming of utopia, offering a compelling refusal to view Césaire's critique of reason as a "regression." Instead, he sees it as "a movement from the passive state of a received condition to the positivity of refusal and self-affirmation, the transformation of an imposed negativity into a source of force and dynamic liberating action.... There is no need to cry primitivism to understand a process whose logical course the poet himself indicates. The refusal of responsibility is not a sign of a so-called regression, but a direct consequence of the slave's dependent consciousness and the unhappy consciousness of the culturally alienated" ("Les royaumes de colère" 83–84).

9. Raison, je te sacre vent du soir ...
   Parce que nous vous haïssons vous
   et votre raison nous nous réclamons
   de la démence précoce de la folie flamboyante
   du cannibalisme tenace.

10. Dévore vent ...
    et lie, lie-moi sans remords
    lie-moi de tes vastes bras à l'argile lumineuse
    lie-moi noire vibration au nombril même du monde
    lie, lie-moi, fraternité âpre
    puis, m'étranglant de ton lasso d'étoiles
    monte,
    Colombe
    monte
    monte
    monte

(*Poésie* 57)

11. Delas signals only a reversal of the "[prologue's] value-system, since for the demand for separation ('va-t-en') he substitutes a demand for connection ('lie-moi' repeated seven times)" (39). Dominique Combe underlines the sexual overtones of the passage, signaling "the erotic union of the Self and the world" (70). Irele tantalizingly evokes the passage's double nature but merely as two aspects of a single affirmation: "a double movement of the poet's imagination [occurs]: an elevation of body and soul in a scene of transfiguration that dramatizes its character as *anabasis,* an upward perspective of its imagery as well as a rising intensity of its rhythm, and a complementary descent that enacts a mystic rite of self-consecration." In an otherwise rich and insightful exegesis

of the poem, he offers no commentary on either the hortative "lie-moi" or the troubling present participle "m'étranglant" (*Cahier* xvii, 149). Bernard Zaourou sees in these lines "the marvelous, lyrical evocation of negritude [that] insists most particularly on the place of blacks in the world, on their unitary vocation among the other peoples of the world" (31). Zaourou is thus free to present the poem as effectively resolving immanent antinomy on a celestial scale: "The *Cahier* finishes in an expiatory revolution whose propitious outcome for the oppressed can alone explain the peaceful ascension of this dove of purity, universal symbol of a truly reconciled universe" (32). Keith L. Walker entirely divorces the troublesome verb from its context. "Spirit is 'bound' in fascination," he states, thus resolving the problems it might cause his celebratory reading: "Césaire's poetry is synonymous with liberation and revolution, with revelation, and above all with desire" ("Silence et solitude" 136).

12. Irele describes the polyvalency of this central image of the *Cahier.* Nonetheless, his defense of Césaire's use of blood imagery points to its undecidability; applied to an oppressed people, its use is salutary, while as a weapon of ideological terror, it becomes ethically suspect. (*Cahier* lxi).

13. Je serais un
   homme-juif
   un homme-cafre
   an homme-hindou-de-Calcutta
   un homme-de-Harlem-qui-ne-vote-pas
                                        (19)

See Irele, *Cahier* 59, 93.

14. Both Arnold and Fanon formulate a critique of the psychological stance of Césaire's poetry of this period ("1939 [to] the mid-fifties") in terms of the regression that other critics of Césaire so vehemently deny (*Modernism and Negritude* 260). Fanon critiques Césaire and Senghor's defense of the irrational in chapter 5 of *Peau noire masques blancs*. Fanon cites the *Cahier* in his condemnation of negritude's "regressive process," though he undertakes no sustained analysis of the poem itself (99).

15. Dash's study of Caribbean literature *The Other America* underscores the antinomical nature of the *Cahier*: "If we examine the end of Césaire's *Notebook of a Return to the Native Land* we find . . . a suggestion that modernization means leaving behind a closed, suffocating world and embracing a new realm of paradox" (136).

16. "Et nous sommes debout maintenant, mon pays et moi, les cheveux dans le vent, ma main petite maintenant dans son poing énorme et la force n'est pas en nous, mais au-dessus de nous, dans une voix qui vrille la nuit et l'audience comme la pénétrance d'une guêpe apocalyptique" (*Poésie* 51). See Gilroy, *Against Race* chapter 4 on Nazism, Reifenstahl, and racism.

17. Irele describes the affirmative thrust of Césaire's irrationalism as "a poetic statement of an alternative path to knowledge—that of an intuitive grasp of the reality of a living universe in intimate relation to human consciousness and sensibility" (*Cahier* 117). J. Michael Dash presents a probing critique of this "organicist dream of the union between man and nature" in his chapter "Orphic Explanations: Toward a Caribbean Heterocosm" (*Other America* 61–81). My point is not to refute the presence of this "monologic[al] . . . primacy of the transcendental subject" (61) in the project of

negritude but rather to argue that the poem's own immanent critical and aporetic nature explodes this regressive moment. An interesting parallel lies in Chris Bongie's examination of Pier Paulo Pasolino's "prehistoric" Third World humanism in chapter 6 of his *Exotic Memories*.

18. "A force de regarder les arbres je suis devenu un arbre . . . A force de penser au Congo je suis devenu Congo bruissant de forêts et fleuves" (*Poésie* 26).

19. "Cette ville inerte et ses au-delà de lèpres, de consomption, de famines, de peurs tapies dans les ravins, de peurs juchées dans les arbres, de peurs creusées dans le sol, de peurs en dérive dans le ciel, de peurs amoncelées et ses fumerolles d'angoisse" (*Poésie* 11).

20. In 1950 in the *Discours sur le colonialisme*, Césaire will deny the charge that he ever wished to regress to a pre-European golden age (21–22).

21. "Le rythme entendu dans un sens organique, irrationnel (ou du moins antérieur à la raison) est l'expression, la 'forme' d'un rapport immédiat à la réalité sensible" (74).

22. Cf. Combe 44. Irele argues persuasively that the poem develops "an aesthetic dictated by the principles of orality (*Cahier* lxv). If I maintain the terms "prose" and "verse" in speaking of the poem's rhythmic properties, they must, following Irele, be taken as thoroughly modulated from the traditional referents informing Césaire's practice, as they come to function within a "language of total performance" (lxvi).

23. J'accepte. J'accepte . . .
    six mois de caniche . . .
    et le pain
    le molasse
    le suicide
    la promiscuité
    le brodequin
    le cep
    le chevalet
    la cippe
    le frontal
        (*Poésie* 47)

24. I am here following Dominick La Capra's adaptation of the psychoanalytic concepts of "transference," "repetition," and "working-through" in *Representing the Holocaust: History, Theory, Trauma*.

25. And the nigger scum is on its feet
    standing
    and
    free
        (*Poetry* 81).

26. Polyrhythm refers to the simultaneous occurrence of two or more distinct rhythmic feels within a single musical texture.

27. "Duple" and "triple" meter patterns refer to the general organization of recurrent temporal patterns into groups of two or three pulses.

28. It seems, for example, to have singlehandedly convinced a skeptical André Breton that a poem could in fact be at once engaged and a work of art (Ménil 203–14).

3. Aimé Césaire, *Présence africaine*, and Black Atlantic Historical Experience

1. For example, though Césaire undoubtedly is forthright in his assertion that his entry into politics was a contingent "conjuncture," the Communist Party would never have sought him out for its ticket in 1945 if he had not acquired a reputation as a brilliant poet and orator, as both René Ménil and his students (Fanon, Glissant) have testified.

2. Cf. Sartre, *Questions* 86–87. In chapter 6 I discuss the implications of the Sartrian "project" in relation to Glissant's "project" to construct of Martinique an "ecological country."

3. On Sartre, see Bourdieu, *Les règles de l'art* 293–97. On Boulez's dominance of the postwar French musical milieu and his empowering mastery of diverse intellectual discourses, see Born 80.

4. Regarding Flaubert, see Bourdieu, *Les règles de l'art* 17–62. For a corollary discussion on Sartre's "sentiment d'élection," see Boschetti 157.

5. "Maintenir la poésie" from *Tropiques* Oct. 1943, reprinted in Delas 115.

6. "Poésie et connaissance" from *Tropiques* Jan. 1945; reproduced in Delas 122.

7. After having presented earlier versions of this analysis of *Présence africaine*, I heard Jim Arnold give a talk at Columbia University ("Misunderstandings: French Intellectuals and the Launching of *Présence africaine*") in which he describes similar contradictions of the French intellectual sponsorship of the journal's early issues.

8. For a description of the range of French intellectual journals from the 1930s and 1940s, see Boschetti. Despite its centrality to twentieth-century intellectual developments, *Présence africaine* is never mentioned in Boschetti's study, which limits its description to the texts in closest competition with *Les Temps modernes*.

9. Bernard Mouralis presents the appearance of *Présence africaine* within this field as a passive event rather than as a struggle for domination through the accumulation of symbolic capital (Mouralis, "Geography of an 'Ideology'" 4).

10. Cf. Sartre's famous liminal editorial in the journal's first issue in which he, as the prototypical total intellectual, asserts the authority to speak out on all issues concerning contemporary humanity through the methodology of a "synthetic anthropology" (14).

11. This orientation is explicitly developed by Diop in his introductory article to the journal's first issue, "Niam N'Goura ou les raisons d'être de *Présence Africaine*," reproduced in Grah Mel 313–21. It is interesting that Léon Damas explained his failure to participate in the journal's founding by precisely a misreading of this fundamental difference: "He would later explain that he had been under the impression that it was only another 'student journal'" (Toumson and Henry-Valmore 101).

12. For an evocation of Howlett's personal contributions to *Présence africaine*, see the testimony of Simone Howlett regarding the couple's close friendship with Alioune Diop in Mudimbe's *The Surreptitious Speech*.

13. Diop, in the journal's sixth issue, does criticize Césaire for what he describes as his "systematic defense of primitive societies" (6).

14. Feb. 1950 nos.8–9: 393–402.

15. None of the writers in Mudimbe's collective volume *The Surreptitious Speech: Présence Africaine and the Politics of Otherness*, in its five-hundred-some pages, mentions this change, nor does Mouralis (1984).

16. It should be pointed out, however, that Depestre later mounted a reasoned and insightful critique of Césaire, most particularly in *Bonjour et adieu à la negritude* from 1980.

17. *Présence africaine* 4, Oct.-Nov. 1955. This dominance will again be demonstrated at the September 1956 conference, when both the themes Césaire's speech addresses and the poet himself dominate the discussions transcribed in the conference proceedings.

18. As was shown in chapter 1, however, a certain discourse on Delgrès had already appeared within Antillean society; Césaire's poem thus appears as merely one further element in this process of anamnesis.

19. Ironically, though he had resigned from the P.C.F. five years before, Susan Suleiman points out that Césaire here takes up Stalin's notorious slogan for socialist realism from the 1930s.

20. See Boschetti 76 on Sartre's postwar reorientation within the French intellectual field.

21. See my article "African Music, Ideology, and Utopia," in which I describe the complex relationship between Guinean totalitarianism, utopianism, and cultural production in relation to the creation of Fodéba Keita's *Ballets nationaux*.

22. For all its substantive content and rhetorical force, however, Suret-Canale's article can only partially address the weaknesses that beset Diop's liminal article, since it speaks entirely of the past, not of the present independence and autonomy to which this issue of *Présence africaine* is dedicated. Even the author's book-length history of the West African independences is a primarily economic analysis, and one is forced to consult the few, often difficult-to-find studies of this crucial period—including Yves Bénot's rare, out-of-print 1969 study *Idéologies des indépendences africaines* and Frederick Cooper's masterful *Decolonization and African Society*—to learn the concrete details of the independences of Francophone West Africa.

4. Cannibalizing Hegel

1. John Heckman's introduction to Hyppolite's *Genesis and Structure of Hegel's Phenomenology* describes this historical milieu.

2. See Judith Butler's *Subjects of Desire*. The work of Raymond Queneau (editor of Kojève's *Introduction à la lecture de Hegel*), Raymond Aron, Michel Leiris, Maurice Merleau-Ponty, Claude Lévi-Strauss, Jacques Lacan, and Georges Bataille and Jean Hyppolite himself was influenced in dramatic and well-documented ways by their direct participation in Kojève's lectures at the Ecole des Hautes Etudes (Auffret 253–63), while Descombes goes so far as to describe Sartre's *Being and Nothingness* as merely an expansion of the "dualist ontology" at the heart of Kojève's reading of the *Phenomenology*.

3. Dates that correspond with Césaire's first tenure in Paris, as a *khagneux* at Lycée Henry-IV (1931–34) and then as *normalien* at the rue d'Ulm (1935–39).

4. "Au moment où la traduction de la *Phénoménologie de l'esprit* est sortie en France, je l'ai montrée à Senghor, et je lui ai dit 'Ecoute, Léopold, ce que dit Hegel: il

faut arriver à l'Universel par l'approfondissement du Particulier." Personal communication, Fort-de-France, 9 Nov. 2001.

5. This attention to the relation of western theoretical work and postcolonial cultural production is not merely a historical detail but confronts us daily as both global citizens and professional critics of cultural production: "From the work of Lukács, Fredric Jameson, Foucault, Derrida, Sartre, Adorno, and Benjamin—to mention only some of the obvious names—we have a vivid apprehension of the processes of regulation and force by which cultural hegemony reproduces itself, pressing even poetry and spirit into administration and the commodity form. Yet, in the main, the breach between these consequential metropolitan theorists and either the ongoing or the historical imperialist experience is truly vast.... We can and indeed must speculate as to why there has been a practice of self-confinement of the libertarian theoretical capital produced in the West and why, at the same time in the formerly colonial world, the prospect for a culture with strongly liberationist components has rarely seemed dimmer" (*Culture and Imperialism* 304).

6. One of the most concrete early benefits Césaire gained from the network of relationships he developed at the rue d'Ulm was his publishing contact for the first, 1939 edition of the *Cahier*: "Through the exertions of one of his professors at the rue d'Ulm, Pierre Petitbon, Césaire, who had encountered the refusals of numerous Parisian editors, acquired the agreement of the director of the journal *Volontés*, Georges Pellorson, to publish his manuscript" (Toumson and Henry-Valmore 68). See Boschetti 23 on the interwar domination of the E. N. S. in the formation of French cultural elites.

7. His article in *Tropiques* on Lautréamont and his 1956 speech "Culture et Colonisation," to be analyzed below, are obvious exceptions.

8. One of the few exceptions to this is Bouelet's study of the correspondences between Césaire's thought and Sartrian existentialism. While taking into account the thought of Hegel in this process, Bouelet limits its influence to the admittedly important master/slave dialectic of recognition.

9. See Descombes 9–54 for a summary of Kojève's philosophy and an analysis of the crucial role it played from the 1930s till the arrival of structuralism in the late 1950s.

10. Car il n'est point vrai que l'oeuvre de l'homme est finie
 que nous n'avons rien à faire au monde
 que nous parasitons le monde
 qu'il suffit que nous nous mettions au pas du monde
 mais
 l'oeuvre de l'homme vient seulement de commencer
 et il reste à l'homme à conquérir toute
 interdiction immobilisée aux coins de sa ferveur.

11. Je me lèverai un cri et si violent
 que tout entier j'éclabousserai le ciel
 et par mes branches déchiquetées
 et par le jet insolent de mon fût blessé et solennel
 je commanderai aux îles d'exister

12. The unconscious phallocentrism of this repeated reference to the "homme de culture" is obvious, notwithstanding any putative universalism of the French term. Richard Wright was the only speaker at the conference to have regretted the absence of women at such a historic event. Despite his lone request for a more equal representation, little change occurred at the 1959 Congress of Black Writers in Rome.

13. The text of Césaire's speech is reproduced in Ngal, *Lire* 121.

14. See Mouralis, *Littérature et développement* on the historical importance of this congress organized by Alioune Diop and *Présence africaine*. In describing Sartre's tactical accumulation of literary and intellectual references within *La Nausée*, Anna Boschetti could equally well be speaking of Césaire's speech: "No other French author, consecrated or new-comer, could rival this polyphonic virtuosity that destined every other success to appear incomplete, if not naïve and provincial" (56).

15. This "cultural cannibalism" of New World societies was first described in Oswald de Andrade's 1928 "Cannibalist Manifesto."

16. See Martin Jay's *Marxism and Totality* for an exhaustive investigation of concept of an "expressive" model of human subjectivity. Jay describes how Habermas's *Theory and Practice* in particular—written precisely in the period of the late 1950s and early 1960s when Césaire produced the texts under consideration in this chapter—maintains a faith in the possibility of an expressive recognition of subject-object identity that Lukács first articulated in *History and Class Consciousness* (469–77) and that we found at work in Césaire's forging of the concept of "negritude," discussed in the introduction.

17. Césaire's failure to pass the agrégation is in this respect of secondary importance; the primary elaboration of the disposition and ability to negotiate successfully the Parisian intellectual milieu, along with the network of personal relationships that make that process possible, generally occurs within the cadre of the E.N.S.: "The title of *normalien* underlies various practical solidarities . . .; As social capital of actual or potential relations, the fact of being a *'normalien'* exerts a multiplying effect upon all the social powers an individual possesses" (Bourdieu, *Homo academicus* 22, 116).

18. Jean-Pierre Lefebvre, who recently retranslated the *Phenomenology* into French, has observed that this is also true of the context in which Kojève and Hyppolite turned to Hegel in the 1930s and 1940s, amid a generalized breakdown of social structure and ensuing mass destruction (19).

19. Although the differentiation between Nature and History is present in the *Phenomenology* (most notably in the introduction to Section B, Part IV, "The Truth of Self-Certainty"), it was Kojève who developed Hegel's comments into a rigid dualist ontology rather than a dialectical process of the overcoming of one state by another. This distinction, in turn, has meant that the French poststructuralist rejection of Hegel is to an important degree a case of misrecognition.

20. A. James Arnold has underscored the relation between Ogun, as understood by Wole Soyinka, and Cèsaire's "Et les chiens se taisaient" (*Modernism and Negritude* 120–24). Rather than the historical aspect of Ogun I am underlining here, Arnold points to the Orisha's relevance, as a tragic, mythical figure, to Cèsaire's "modernist pseudo-myth," as Arnold quite rightly glosses Cèsaire's earlier poem (123).

21. See Frederick Ivor Case, "Sanga obo ko so" for a discussion of the role of Vodou in the play, as well as Pestre de Almeida.

22. For Hegel, this recognition is awakened via the appearance of a mediating being (Christ) who acts as a bridge uniting the physical and the spiritual, consciousness and self-consciousness, the subjective and the objective (416). For both Hegel and Kojève, the problematic status of this "religion of revelation" lies in the persistent separation between subject and object through an intermediary projection of the self onto another, as *representation* (Kojève 215).

23. "All these determinations have vanished in the loss suffered by the self in absolute freedom; its negation is the death that is without meaning, the sheer terror of the negative that contains nothing positive, nothing that fills it with a content" (*Phenomenology* 362).

24. Mireille Rosello offers a compelling critique of the suicidal logic of Antillean texts such as Césaire's *Et les chiens se taisaient*. Rosello argues that "by 'choosing' Death, the colonized subject plays doubly into the oppressor's hand; firstly, by adopting his ideology which makes of the soldier's death the moment of glory that will bestow upon the latter glorious distinction, while on the other hand, he chooses to annihilate himself as a rebellious subject (that is to say by inflicting upon his body in advance the treatment the master had reserved for him)" (51).

25. As I will argue in the last chapter of this study, the categories of modernist "elitism" and a contrasting writerly "accessibility" are not invalid, but are nonetheless foreign to this project. My focus lies elsewhere, with texts that seek to confront historical experience and the sacrifice of life to an abstract universal. In this light, and despite radically different means and voices, both Césaire and Delsham, Glissant and Condé are to my mind equally compelling.

5. Dreaming of the Masters

1. Although Maximin certainly undertakes a radical critique of the "piège de l'histoire glorieuse" (Zimra, "Je(ux) d'Histoire" 275), as Clarisse Zimra points out, the space he devotes to the elucidation of that same history clearly serves a heuristic, documentary function. These two tendencies exist in fruitful antagonism throughout Maximin's text.

2. "Lie-moi de tes vastes bras à l'argile lumineuse/ lie ma noire vibration au nombril même du monde" (Césaire, *Poésie* 57).

3. In addition to Bongie's *Islands and Exiles,* see in particular the insightful studies of *L'Isolé soleil* by Clarisse Zimra, John Erickson, Adlai Murdoch, and Ronnie Scharfman and Mireille Rosello's *Litérature et identité créole aux Antilles*.

4. For a detailed description of the cultural phenomena of Parisian negrophilia from the 1920s, see Gendron.

5. George Ngal, Aimé Césaire's first biographer, has elaborated a rudimentary analogical link between African and African-derived musics and Césaire's poetry ("Le tam-tam et le jazz: fondement d'une esthétique" [*Un Homme* 154–64]).

6. See Eagleton's *The Ideology of the Aesthetic* 107 for a summary of Schiller's defense of aesthetic play.

7. Interview with Daniel Maximin, Basse-Terre, Guadeloupe, 2 Dec. 1994.

8. Maximin's novel must be understood within the larger context of the phallocentric glorification of Delgrès described in chapter 1. More recent works such as

L'Epopee Delgrès by Germain Saint-Ruf and Léon Danquin's article "Delgrès: Figure du Tragique" continue to propose a veritable sacralization of the myth of Delgrès within the Guadeloupean community in explicitly mystical terms: "Delgres' proclamation deserves to be read and reread. Each Antillean should own it and conserve it with the same fervor as a Christian has for the Bible" (St. Ruf 110).

9. The examination of the social dimensions of music is a fundamental area of inquiry and debate in recent musicology. See my article "Sounding Autonomy: Adorno, Coltrane, and Jazz."

10. See also Gilroy's *Against Race* 296.

11. See Kofsky and Radano. Art Taylor's *Notes and Tones* is a wonderful series of interviews of socially aware musicians by another informed, articulate musician, forming a vernacular counterpart to these more analytical explorations of jazz and revolution.

12. Monson's *Saying Something* strikingly combines a personal familiarity with jazz music as a practice via the author's interviews with players and a theoretically sophisticated analysis of the ways in which "musical sound" comes to constitute social meaning.

13. See Gates's *Signifying Monkey* for a discussion of "signifyin(g)."

14. The emphasis here upon improvisation is essential, since the signifyin(g)' occurring in jazz is one that rejects Western European notational practices and instead affirms the oral-based culture from which jazz arose (see Sidrin chapter 1). An analogous process occurs in *L'Isolé soleil* as Maximin reaffirms the oral culture of Guadeloupe within the format of the French avant-garde novel.

15. An arpeggio breaks down a chord via the successive, rather than simultaneous, sounding of its notes. See Porter and Ullman 174 for a transcription of the first chorus of "Body and Soul" (1939), which illustrates Hawkins's restructural techniques.

16. See Radano chapter 3 for a description of the early years of the AACM.

17. See Lewis Porter's *John Coltrane: His Life and Music* 231–49 for an analysis of *A Love Supreme*.

6. History, Totality, and Other Modernist Projects

1. See Jay's *Marxism and Totality* on the notion of expressive totality (59–60) and my article "Négritude et imaginaire créatrice" on the relation between Fanon and Lukács's *History and Class Consciousness,* a relation first suggested by Edward Said.

2. See the introduction on Hegel's injunction that to be more than a mere schematic understanding, thought must "enter into the immanent content of the thing . . . [and] surrender to the life of the object" (*Phenomenology* 32).

3. On Glissant and history, see Bongie's *Islands and Exiles,* Celia Britton's *Edouard Glissant and Postcolonial Theory,* Bernadette Cailler's *Conquérants de la nuit nue,* and Dash's "Writing the Body."

4. Glissant mentions Deleuze and Guattari as a more recent philosophical influence for the concept of relation (PR 23), but the schematic definition of relation he offers there ("All identity extends itself in a relationship with the Other") is essentially the Hegelian one I am describing here.

5. *Phenomenology* 2. See Martin Jay's elegantly succinct presentation of Hegel's notion of totality in *Marxism and Form* (53–60).

6. See Negri's study of Spinoza, *The Savage Anomaly,* 136–43, for an analysis of this process that pits Spinoza against the theoreticians of this alienation and appropriation of mediation (principally Hobbes, Rousseau, and Hegel).

7. Michael Hardt's penetrating analysis of the nonidentity of the Deleuzian concept of the "virtual" and Hegelian "possibility" offers a compelling counterpoint to my argument (13–19). While an appreciation of the Spinoza-Bergson-Deleuze axis of philosophy surely holds important implications for postcolonial theory, this book hopes to prepare such an encounter by first investigating the Hegelian dialectical thought that more directly informs postcolonial Antillean culture.

7. Voicing Memory

1. For insightful analysis of the complex issues of gender, culture, and writing in the Antilles, see Françoise Lionnet's *Postcolonial Representations,* Suzanne Rinne and Joëlle Vitiello's *Elles écrivent des Antilles (Haïti, Guadeloupe, Martinique),* and Maryse Condé's *La parole des femmes: essai sur des romancières des Antilles de langue française* and Joan Dayan's remarkable study *Haiti, History, and the Gods.*

2. See Jay, "Mimesis and Mimetology": 29–30.

3. See chapter 4 of Shierry Weber Nicholson's *Exact Imagination, Late Work* for a description of Benjamin and Adorno's concept of mimesis.

4. In *Peau noire, masques blancs,* Fanon defends his method of negative critique as the only effective means to approach utopian social transformation without betraying that same goal in a positive *re*-presentation: "Toute critique de l'existant implique une solution, si tant est que qu'on puisse proposer une solution à son semblable, c'est à dire à une liberté" (50).

5. When the French government recently named a Paris street after the Martinican rebel, bureaucratic genius lighted upon the "impasse" as the appropriate site to commemorate his actions.

6. Thanks to Chris Bongie for urging me to address the issue of Danticat's popularity. One of the projects awaiting Francophone literature is a properly sociological investigation of its production and reception that refuses a facile criticism of either modernist "elitism" and "pomposity" or a populist literature of mere consumption and distraction. Instead, one must take into account, at the very least, the complex mediations each of these and other categories of judgment work upon one another.

7. Chapters 6 and 7 of Bernstein's *Adorno: Disenchantment and Ethics* develop aspects of this claim.

8. This guilt of aesthetic representation of the past remains unexamined in both Horkheimer's defense of Historiography as the "court of appeals" for the past suffering of humanity (Löwy 37) and Benjamin's messianic historicism, both of which implicitly glorify the critical historian as a "Messiah" who will redeem the suffering of past generations, turning the past into the mere means of a future redemption.

9. For the latest installment in this sad story as I write, see the testimony of a Haitian police officer in *Le Monde,* 12 Dec. 2001, p. 5: "In two months, I witnessed the execution of approximately fifty people."

Bibliography

Abenon, Lucien. *Petite histoire de la Guadeloupe*. Paris: L'Harmattan, 1992.
Adélaïde-Merlande, Jacques. *Delgrès, ou la Guadeloupe en 1802*. Paris: Editions Karthala, 1986.
Adorno, Theodor. *Aesthetic Theory*. Trans. Robert Hullot-Kentor. Minneapolis: U of Minnesota P, 1997.
———. *Critical Models: Interventions and Catchwords*. Trans. Henry W. Pickford. New York: Columbia UP, 1998.
———. *Hegel: Three Studies*. Cambridge: MIT Press, 1993.
———. *The Jargon of Authenticity*. Trans. Knut Tarnowski and Frederic Will. Evanston: Northwestern UP, 1973b.
———. *Kant's Critique of Pure Reason*. Trans. Rodney Livingstone. Stanford: Stanford UP, 2001.
———. *Metaphysics: Concepts and Problems*. Stanford: Stanford UP, 2000.
———. *Minima Moralia*. Trans. E. F. N. Jephcott. 9th ed. New York: Verso, 1996.
———. *Negative Dialectics*. Trans. E. B. Ashton. New York: Seabury Press, 1973.
———. *Negative Dialektik*. Frankfurt am Main: Suhrkamp, 1966.
———. *Prisms*. Trans. Samuel and Shierry Weber. Cambridge: MIT Press, 1967.
———. *Problems of Moral Philosophy*. Stanford: Stanford UP, 2000.
———. *Sound Figures*. Trans. Rodney B. Livingstone. Stanford: Stanford UP, 1999.
Adorno, Theodor W., and Walter Benjamin. *The Complete Correspondence: 1928–1940*. Ed. Henri Lonitz. Trans. Nicholas Walker. Cambridge: Harvard UP, 1999.
Adotevi, Stanislas Spero. *Négritude et négrologues*. Paris: Le Castor Astral, 1998.
Aimard, Gustave. *Le Chasseur de rats: Le commandant Delgrès*. Paris: E. Dentu, 1876.
Alexis, Jacques Stephen. *Compère Général soleil*. Paris: Gallimard, 1955.
Almeida, Lilian Pestre de. "Défense et illustration de l'anthropophagie: Le point de vue périphérique." *Césaire 70*. Ed. Georges Ngal and Martin Steins. Paris: Silex, 1984. 123–39.
Aldrich, Robert, and John Connell. *France's Overseas Frontier: Départements et Térritoires d'Outre Mer*. Cambridge: Cambridge UP, 1992.
Andrade, Oswald de. "Anthropophagite Manifesto." In *The Oxford Book of Latin American Essays*. Ed. Ilan Stavans. New York: Oxford UP, 1997. 96–99.

Antoine, Régis. "L'aloi et le remède des textes césariens." *Aimé Césaire ou l'athanor d'un alchimiste*. Paris: Editions Caribéennes, 1987. 311–20.

———. *La Littérature franco-antillaise: Haïti, Guadeloupe, et Martinique*. Paris: Karthala, 1992.

———. *La tragédie du roi Christophe de Aimé Césaire. Lectoguide Francophonie*. Paris: Bordas, 1984.

———. "Transe et régence dans 'La tragédie du roi Christophe.'" *Soleil Eclaté: Mélanges offerts à Aimé Césaire à l'occasion de son soixante-dixième anniversaire par une équipe internationale d'artistes et de chercheurs*. Ed. Jacqueline Leiner. Tübingen: Gunter Narr Verlag, 1984. 13–26.

Arendt, Hannah. *Imperialism*. New York: Harcourt, 1968.

Arnold, A. James. "D'Haiti à l'Afrique: La Tragédie du roi Christophe de Césaire." *Revue de Littérature Comparée* 60.2 (1986): 133–48.

———. "Les héritiers de Césaire aux Antilles." *Présence africaine* 151/152 (1995): 145–51.

———. "Misunderstandings: French Intellectuals and the Launching of *Présence Africaine*." Address at Columbia University, New York. Nov. 1997.

———. *Modernism and Negritude*. Cambridge: Harvard UP, 1981.

———. "Negritude: Then and Now." *A History of Literature in the Caribbean*. Ed. A. James Arnold, subed. J. Michael Dash. Vol. 1. Philadelphia: John Benjamins, 1994. 479–83.

———. "La récéption afro-américaine de Césaire: Un dialogue difficile aux Etats-Unis." *Césaire 70*. Ed. M. a M. Ngal and Martin Steins. Paris: Silex, 1984. 141–61.

Aubin, Danielle. "Aproche du roman historique antillais." *Présence africaine* 149.4 (1988): 30–44.

Auffret, Dominique. *Alexandre Kojève: La philosophie, l'état, la fin de l'histoire*. Paris: Bernard Grasset, 1990.

Badiou, Alain. *Ethics: An Essay on the Understanding of Evil*. Trans. Peter Hallward. London: Verso, 2001.

Bailey, Mariane. "Césaire: père du théâtre africain et fils de la tradition liturgique. Le rôle de l'hiérophante-metteur en scène." *Aimé Césaire ou l'athanor d'un alchimiste*. Paris: Editions Caribéennes, 1987. 239–50.

Baker, Houston A. *Blues, Ideology, and Afro-American Literature: A Vernacular Theory*. Chicago and London: U of Chicago P, 1984.

Baldwin, James. *The Price of the Ticket: Collected Nonfiction 1948–1985*. New York: St. Martin's, 1985.

Ballini, Jean-Marc Laleta, ed. *Le Code noir et la traite des negres*. Champigny-sue Marne: J. M. Laleta Ballini, 1998.

Bambach, Charles R. *Heidegger, Dilthey, and the Crisis of Historicism*. Ithaca: Cornell UP, 1995.

Bangou, Henri. *La Guadeloupe*. Aurillae: Editions du Centre, 1962.

———. "L'Histoire dans le Roman antillais." *Colloque Sur le Roman Antillais*. Paris: La Technique du Livre, 1967. 39–46.

———. *La révolution et l'esclavage à la Guadeloupe (1789–1802)*. Paris: Messidor/Editions sociales, 1989. 200.

Barnes, Sandra T. "Introduction: The Many Faces of Ogun." *Africa's Ogun: Old World and New.* Ed. Sandra T. Barnes. Bloomington: Indiana UP, 1989. 1–26.

Barnes, Sandra T., and Paula Girshick Ben-Amos. "Ogun, the Empire Builder." *Africa's Ogun: Old World and New.* Ed. Sandra T. Barnes. Bloomington: Indiana UP, 1989. 39–64.

Baudrillard, Jean. *Le miroir de la production* (1973). Paris: Galilée, 1985.

———. *Simulations.* New York: Semiotext(e), 1983.

Baumgarten, Alexander Gottlieb. *Reflections on Poetry.* Ed. Karl Aschenbrenner and William B. Holther. Berkeley: U of California P, 1954.

Benamou, Michel. "Entretien avec Aimé Césaire; Fort-de-France, 14 fevrier 1973." *Cahiers Césairiens* 1.1 (1974): 4–8.

Benelli, Graziano. "L'écriture des libertés." *Aimé Césaire ou l'athanor d'un alchimiste.* Paris: Editions Caribéennes, 1987. 23–32.

Benhabib, Seyla. *Critique, Norm, and Utopia: A Study of the Foundations of Critical Theory.* New York: Columbia UP, 1986.

Bénitez-Rojo, Antonio. *The Repeating Island: The Caribbean and the Postmodern Condition.* Trans. James Maraniss. Durham/London: Duke UP, 1992.

Benjamin, Walter. *Illuminations: Essays and Reflections.* Trans. Harry Zohn. Ed. Hannah Arendt. New York: Schocken, 1968.

———. *Selected Writings. Volume 2: 1927–1934.* Ed. Michael W. Jennings, Howard Eiland, and Gary Smith. Trans. Rodney Livingstone et al. Cambridge: Harvard UP, 1999.

Bergson, Henri. *Essai sur les données immédiates de la conscience 1888.* Paris: Presses Universitaires de France, 1927.

Bénot, Yves. *Idéologies des indépendances africaines.* Paris: François Maspéro, 1969.

Bernasconi, Robert. "Hegel at the Court of the Ashanti." *Hegel after Derrida.* Ed. Stuart Barnett. New York: Routledge, 1998. 41–63.

Bernstein, J. M. *Adorno: Disenchantment and Ethics.* New York: Cambridge UP, 2001.

Bidima, Jean-Godefroy. *Théorie critique et modernité africaine: de l'école de Francfort à la docta spes africana.* Paris: Publications de la Sorbonne, 1993.

Bjornson, Richard. "Alienation and Disalienation: Themes of Yesterday, Promises of Tomorrow." *The Surreptitious Speech: Présence Africaine and the Politics of Otherness 1947–1987.* Ed. V. Y. Mudimbe. Chicago: U of Chicago P, 1992. 147–56.

Bongie, Chris. *Exotic Memories: Literature, Colonialism, and the Fin de Siècle.* Stanford: Stanford UP, 1991.

———. *Islands and Exiles: The Creole Identities of Post/Colonial Literature.* Stanford: Stanford UP, 1998.

Born, Georgina. *Rationalizing Culture: IRCAM, Boulez, and the Institutionalization of the Musical Avant-Garde.* Berkeley: U of California P, 1995.

Boschetti, Anna. *Sartre et 'les Temps Modernes': une entreprise intellectuelle.* Paris: Editions de Minuit, 1985.

Bouelet, Remy Sylvestre. *Espace et dialectique du héros césairien.* Paris: Editions L'Harmattan, 1987.

Bouhours, Dominique. *La manière de bien penser dans les ouvrages de l'esprit.* Paris: Chez la veuve de Sebastien Mabre-Cramoisy, 1687.

Bourdé, Guy, and Hervé Martin. *Les écoles historiques*. Paris: Editions du Seuil, 1983.
Bourdieu, Pierre. *Homo academicus*. Second Augmented ed. Paris: Editions de Minuit, 1984b.
———. *Questions de sociologie*. Paris: Editions de Minuit, 1984a.
———. *Les règles de l'art: Genèse et structure du champ littéraire*. Paris: Editions du Seuil, 1992.
———. *The State Nobility: Elite Schools in the Field of Power*. Stanford: Stanford UP, 1996.
Boyer-Peyreleau, Eugène-Edouard. *Les Antilles françaises, particulièrement la Guadeloupe, depuis leur découverte jusqu'au premier novembre 1825*. Paris: Chez Ladvocat, Librairie, 1825.
Brathwaite, Edward Kamau. "The African Presence in Caribbean Literature." *Africa in Latin America: Essays on History, Culture, and Socialization*. Ed. Manuel Moreno Fraginals. New York, Paris: UNESCO, 1984. 103–44.
———. "Jazz and the West Indian Novel." Part I *BIM* XI (44) (1967): 275–84; Part II *BIM* XII (45) (1967): 39–51; Part III *BIM* XII (46) (1968): 115–26.
Breton, André. "Un grand poète noir." *Cahier d'un retour au pays natal*. Paris, Dakar: Présence Africaine, 1983. 77–87.
Britton, Celia M. *Edouard Glissant and Postcolonial Theory: Strategies of Language and Resistance*. Charlottesville: UP of Virginia, 1999.
Brown, Karen McCarthy. "Systematic Remembering, Systematic Forgetting: Ogou in Haiti." *Africa's Ogun: Old World and New*. Ed. Sandra T. Barnes. Bloomington: Indiana UP, 1989.
Bruno, Giordano. *Des liens*. Trans. Danielle Sonnier and Boris Donné. Paris: Allia, 2001.
Buck-Morss, Susan. "Hegel and Haiti." *Critical Inquiry* 26.4 (Summer 2000): 821–65.
Buffon, Alain. "Le système bancaire aux Antilles." *L'Historial Antillais*. Ed. Roland Suvelor. Vol. 6. Pointe-à-Pitre: Dajani Editions, 1981. 80–115.
———. "Regard d'un historien créole sur la Révolution: Auguste Lacour 1805–1869." Basse-Terre: 1994.
Burke, Edmund, ed. *A Philosophical Enquiry into the Origin of our Ideas of the Sublime and Beautiful*. New York: Oxford UP, 1990.
Burton, Richard D. E. "The French West Indies *à l'heure de l'Europe*: an overview." *French and West Indian: Martinique, Guadeloupe, and French Guiana Today*. Ed. Richard D. E. Burton and Fred Reno. Charlottesville: UP of Virginia, 1994. 1–19.
Burton, Richard D. E., and Fred Reno, eds. *French and West Indian: Martinique, Guadeloupe, and French Guiana Today*. New World Series. Charlottesville: UP of Virginia, 1995.
Butler, Judith. *Subjects of Desire: Hegelian Reflections in Twentieth Century France* (1987). New York: Columbia UP, 1999.
Cailler, Bernadette. *Conquérants de la nuit nue: Edouard Glissant et la l'H (h)istoire antillaise*. Tübingen: Gunter Nar Verlag, 1988.
———. *Proposition poétique: une lecture de l'oeuvre d'Aimé Césaire*. Sherbrooke: Naaman, 1976.
———. "*Totalité et infini, altérité et relation*: d'Eemanuel Lévinas à Edouard Glissant." *Poétiques d'Edouard Glissant*. Ed. Jacques Chevrier. Paris: Presses de l'Université de Paris-Sorbonne, 1999. 113–32.

Camara, Sory. *Gens de la parole: essai sur la condition et le rôle des griots dans la société malinké.* Paris: Karthala, 1992.

Carrard, Philippe. *Poetics of the New History: French Historical Discourse from Braudel to Chartier.* Baltimore: Johns Hopkins UP, 1992.

Case, Frederick Ivor. "Idéologie du discours esthétique césairien." *Aimé Césaire ou l'athanor d'un alchimiste.* Paris: Editions Caribéennes, 1987. 337–46.

———. "Sanga obo ko so: Les vodoun dans *La tragédie du roi Christophe.*" *Cahiers Césairiens* .2 (1975): 9–24.

Cassirer, Ernst. *La philosophie des Lumières.* Trans. Pierre Quillet. Paris: Fayard, 1966.

Certeau, Michel de. *The Writing of History.* Trans. Tom Conley. New York: Columbia UP, 1975.

Césaire, Aimé. "Aimé Césaire et les nègres sauvauges": interview with Aimé Césaire." *Afrique Action* (21 Nov. 1960): 23.

———. *The Collected Poetry.* Trans., with an introduction and notes by Clayton Eshleman and Annette Smith. Berkeley: U of California P, 1983.

———. *Discours à la maison du sport: 22 novembre 1956.* Parti Progressiste Martiniquais, 1981.

———. "Discours sur l'art africain (1966)." *Etudes Littéraires* 6.1 (1973): 99–109.

———. *Discours sur le colonialisme.* Paris: Présence Africaine, 1989.

———. *Oeuvres complètes.* 3 vols. Fort-de-France: Editions Désormeaux, 1976.

———. "Introduction." *Esclavage et colonisation.* By Victor Schoelcher. Paris: Presses Universitaires de France, 1948. 1–28.

———. "Mémorial à Louis Delgrès (Poem)." *Présence africaine* 23 (1959): 69–73.

———. "La pensée politique de Sékou Touré." *Présence africaine* 29 (1959): 65–74.

———. *La Poésie.* Paris: Editions du Seuil, 1994.

———. "Un poète politique: Aimé Césaire." Interview. *Magazine Littéraire* (Nov. 1969): 27–32.

———. "Préface." *L'Expérience Guinéenne de Sékou Touré.* Paris: Présence Africaine, 1959.

———. "Rapport présenté au congrès constitutif du Parti Progressiste Martiniquais le 22 mars 1958." *Oeuvres Complètes.* Vol. 3. Fort-de-France: Editions Désormeaux, 1976. 477–92.

———. *Une saison au Congo.* Paris: Editions du Seuil, 1973.

———. "Société et Littérature dans les Antilles." *Etudes Littéraires* 6.1 (1973): 9–20.

———. *Toussaint Louverture: la révolution française et le problème colonial; préface de Charles André Julien.* Paris: Présence Africaine, 1981.

———. *La tragédie du roi Christophe.* 1970 ed. Paris: Présence Africaine, 1963.

Chamoiseau, Patrick, Gerard Delver, Edouard Glissant, and Bertene Juminer. "Manifeste pour refonder les DOM." *Le Monde* (21 Jan. 2000): 16.

Chamoiseau, Patrick, and Raphaël Confiant. *Lettres créoles: Tracées antillaises et continentales de la littérature.* Paris: Hatier, 1991.

Chevrier, Jacques, ed. *Poétiques d'Edouard Glissant.* Paris: Presses de l'Université de Paris-Sorbonne, 1999.

Clark, Beatrice Smith. "IME Revisited: Lectures by Edouard Glissant on Socio-Cultural Realities in the Francophone Antilles." *World Literature Today* 63 (1989): 599–605.

Clark, VeVe A. "Haiti's Tragic Overtures: (Mis)Representations of the Haitian Revolution in World Drama (1796–1975)." *Representing the French Revolution: Literature, Historiography, and Art*. Ed. James A. W. Heffernan. Hanover: UP of New England for Dartmouth College, 1992. 237–60.

Combe, Dominique. *Aimé Césaire: Cahier d'un retour au pays natal. Etudes Littéraires*. Paris: Presses Universitaires de France, 1993.

Condé, Maryse. *An tan revolisyon: Elle court, elle court la liberté*. Basse-Terre: Le Conseil Régional de la Guadeloupe, 1989.

———. "Autour d''Antan Revolisyon.'" *Etudes Guadeloupéennes* 1.2/3 (1990): 164–71.

———. *Cahier d'un retour au pays natal: Césaire*. Collection *Profil d'une oeuvre* 63. Paris: Hatier, 1978.

———. *Le coeur à rire et à pleurer: Contes vrais de mon enfance*. Paris: Robert Laffont: 1999.

———. "Order, Disorder, Freedom, and the West Indian Writer." *Yale French Studies* 2.83 (1992): 121–36.

———. *La parole des femmes: essai sur des romancières des Antilles de langue française*. Paris: L'Harmattan, 1979.

———. Personal interview, Columbia University, 12 April 1997.

———. *Traversée de la mangrove*. Paris: Mercure de France, 1989.

Condé, Maryse, and Rita Dove. "An Interview with Maryse Condé and Rita Dove." *Callaloo* 14.2 (1991): 347–66.

Confiant, Raphaël. *Aimé Césaire: Une traversée paradoxale du siècle*. Paris: Stock, 1993.

———. *L'archet du colonel*. Paris: Mercure de France, 1998.

Conley, Verena Andermatt. *Ecopolitics: The Environment in Poststructuralist Thought*. London and New York: Routledge, 1997.

———. *L'archet du colonel*. Paris: Mercure de France, 1998.

Cooper, Frederick. *Decolonization and African Society: The Labor Question in French and British Africa*. Cambridge: Cambridge UP, 1996.

Corzani, Jack. "Césaire et la Caraïbe oubliée . . ." *Soleil Eclaté: Mélanges offerts à Aimé Césaire à l'occasion de son soixante-dixième anniversaire par une équipe internationale d'artistes et de chercheurs*. Ed. Jacqueline Leiner. Tübingen: Gunter Narr Verlag, 1984. 89–99.

———. *La littérature des Antilles-Guyane françaises*. 6 vols. Fort-de-France: Désormeaux, 1978.

———. "Poetry before Negritude." *A History of Literature in the Caribbean*. Ed. A. James Arnold, subed. J. Michael Dash. Vol. 1. Philadelphia: John Benjamins, 1994. 465–77.

Danquin, Léon R. *Contribution à une étude sur l'insurrection antiesclavagiste de mai 1802*. Basse-Terre: 1982.

———. "Delgrès Figure du Tragique." *Etudes Guadeloupéennes* 6 (April 1994): 67–130.

Danticat, Edwidge. "The Book of the Dead." *New Yorker* 21 June 1999: 194–99.

———. *Breath, Eyes, Memory*. New York: Soho, 1994.

———. *The Farming of Bones*. New York: Soho, 1998.

———. *Krik? Krak!* New York: Soho, 1995.

———. "Seven." *New Yorker* 1 Oct. 2001: 88–97.
David, Daniel, and Jean-François Persoud, Odile Le Fur. *L'Art du Billet: Billets de la Banque de France 1800–2000*. Paris: Editions des Musées/Banque de France, 2000.
Dash, Michael. "Le bateau ivre césairien et la quête de la connaissance." *Aimé Césaire ou l'athanor d'un alchimiste*. Paris: Editions Caribéennes, 1987. 157–64.
———. *Edouard Glissant*. New York: Cambridge UP, 1995.
———. "Exile and Recent Literature." *A History of Literature in the Caribbean*. Ed. A. James Arnold, subed. J. Michael Dash. Vol. 1. Philadelphia: John Benjamins, 1994. 451–61.
———. *The Other America: Caribbean Literature in a New World Context*. Charlottesville: UP of Virginia, 1998.
———. "Writing the Body: Edouard Glissant's Poetics of Re-membering." *L'Héritage de Caliban*. Ed. Maryse Condé. Pointe-à-Pitre: Editions Jasor, 1992. 75–83.
Dayan, Joan. *Haiti, History, and the Gods*. Berkeley: U California P, 1995.
Deberre, Jean-Christophe. *La Tragédie du roi Christophe d'Aimé Césaire: Etude Critique*. Paris: Fernand Nathan, 1984.
Delas, Daniel. *Aimé Césaire*. Paris: Hachette, 1991.
Deleuze, Gilles, and Félix Guattari. *Qu'est-ce que la philosophie?* Paris: Editions de Minuit, 1991.
———. *A Thousand Plateaus: Capitalism and Schizophrenia*. Trans. Brian Massumi. Minneapolis: U of Minnesota P, 1987.
Delsham, Tony. *Négropolitains et euro-blacks*. Schoelcher: Editions M.G.G., 2000.
Depestre, René. *Bonjour et adieu à la négritude*. Seghers, 1980.
———. "Le petit matin d'Aimé Césaire." *Présence africaine* 151/152 (1995): 152–60.
Derrida, Jacques. "'Eating Well,' or the Calculation of the Subject: An Interview with Jacques Derrida." *Who Comes after the Subject*. Ed. Edouardo Cadava, Peter Connor, and Jean-Luc Nancy. New York: Routledge, 1991. 96–119.
Descombes, Vincent. "Apropos of the 'Critique of the Subject' and the Critique of this Critique." *Who Comes after the Subject*. Ed. Edouardo Cadava, Peter Connor, and Jean-Luc Nancy. New York: Routledge, 1991. 120–34.
———. *Modern French Philosophy*. Trans. L. Scott-Fox and J. M. Harding. Cambridge: Cambridge UP, 1980.
Drake, Sandra Elizabeth. "The Uses of History in the Caribbean Novel." Diss. Stanford U, 1977.
Drury, Shadia B. *Alexandre Kojève: The Roots of Postmodern Politics*. New York: St. Martin's, 1994.
Dubois, Laurent. "Republic at Sea." *Transition* 8:3 (1999): 64–79.
Dubois, W. E. B. *The Souls of Black Folk* (1903). New York: Bantam, 1989.
Eagleton, Terry. *The Ideology of the Aesthetic*. Oxford: Blackwell, 1990.
Ellison, Ralph. *Shadow and Act*. New York: Vintage International, 1995.
Eluther, Jean-Paul. "Guadeloupean Consensus." *French and West Indian: Martinique, Guadeloupe, and French Guiana Today*. Eds. Richard D. E. Burton and Fred Reno. Charlottesville: UP of Virginia, 1994. 48–55.
Emeri, Claude, Jean-Pierre Sainton, Fred Reno, and Julien Mérion. *La question statutaire en Guadeloupe, en Guyane, et en Martinique*. Pointe-à-Pitre: Editions Jasor, 2000.

Erickson, John. "Le discours révolutionnaire dans *Les armes miraculeuses*." *Aimé Césaire ou l'athanor d'un alchimiste*. Paris: Editions Caribéennnes, 1987. 53–62.

———. "Maximin's *L'Isolé Soleil* and Caliban's Curse." *Callaloo* 15.1 (1992): 119–30.

Fallope, Josette. *Esclaves et Citoyens: Les noirs à la Guadeloupe au dix-neuvième Siècle Dans les processus de Résistance et d'Intégration (1802–1910)*. Basse-Terre: Société d'Histoire de la Guadeloupe, 1992.

Fanon, Frantz. *Les Damnés de la terre*. Paris: Gallimard, 1991.

———. *Peau noire, masques blancs*. Paris: Seuil, 1995.

Fonkoua, Romuald. "Jean Wahl et Edouard Glissant: philosophie, raison, et poésie." *Poétiques d'Edouard Glissant*. Ed. Jacques Chevrier. Paris: Presses de l'Université de Paris-Sorbonne, 1999. 299–316.

Foucault, Michel. *The Archeology of Knowledge and the Discourse on Language*. Trans. A. M. Sheridan Smith. New York: Pantheon Books, 1972.

———. "Nietzsche, Genealogy, History." Trans. Donald F. Bouchard and Sherry Simon. *Language, Counter-Memory, Practice: Selected Essays and Interviews by Michel Foucault*. Ed. Donald F. Bouchard. Ithaca: Cornell UP, 1977. 139–64.

"The Francophone Caribbean." *Journal of Caribbean History* 25.1–2 (1991): 1–183.

Freud, Sigmund. *Civilization and Its Discontents*. Trans. James Strachey. New York: Norton, 1961.

———. *The Ego and the Id*. Trans. Joan Riviere. New York: Norton, 1960.

Frindéthié, Kokroa Martial. "Trace, Ecart, Carte: Beyond the Exotic Nation." Diss. U of Minnesota, 1996.

Gabbard, Krin, ed. *Jazz among the Discourses*. Durham and London: Duke UP, 1995.

Gant-Britton, Lisbeth. "The Question of Power in *Monsieur Toussaint* and *The Tragedy of King Christopher*." *Paroles Gelées* 14.1 (1996): 43–62.

Gates, Henry Louis. "Editor's Introduction: Writing 'Race' and the Difference It Makes." *"Race," Writing, and Difference*. Chicago: U of Chicago P, 1986. 1–20.

———. *The Signifying Monkey: A Theory of African-American Literary Criticism*. New York: Oxford UP, 1988.

Gates, Henry Louis, ed. *"Race," Writing, and Difference*. Chicago: University of Chicago Press, 1986.

Gendron, Bernard. "Fetishes and Motorcars: Negrophilia in French Modernism." *Cultural Studies* 4.2 (1990).

Geyer, Michael and Miriam Hansen. "German-Jewish Memory and National Consciousness." *Holocaust Remembrance: The Shapes of Memory*. Ed. Geoffrey H. Hartman. Cambridge: Blackwell, 1994. 174–90.

Gilman, Sander L. "Black Bodies, White Bodies: Toward an Iconography of Female Sexuality in Late Nineteenth-Century Art, Medicine, and Literature." In *"Race," Writing, and Difference*. Ed. Henry Louis Gates Jr. Chicago: U of Chicago P, 1986.

Gilroy, Paul. *Against Race: Imagining Political Culture beyond the Color Line*. Cambridge: Harvard UP, 2000.

———. *The Black Atlantic: Modernity and Double Consciousness*. Cambridge: Harvard UP, 1993.

Glissant, Edouard. *La case du commandeur*. 1981. Paris: Gallimard, 1997.

———. *Le Discours Antillais*. Paris: Seuil, 1981.

——. *L'Intention poétique*. 1969. Paris, Gallimard: 1997.
——. *Introduction à une Poétique du Divers*. Paris: Gallimard, 1996.
——. *La Lézarde*. Paris: Editions du Seuil, 1958.
——. *Malemort*. 1975. Paris: Gallimard, 1997.
——. *Monsieur Toussaint. Version scénique*. Paris: Seuil, 1986.
——. *Poétique de la relation*. Paris: Gallimard, 1991.
——. *Le Quatrième siècle*. 1964. Paris: Gallimard, 1997.
——. *Sartorius: Le roman des Batoutos*. Paris: Gallimard, 1999.
——. *Soleil de la conscience*. 1956. Paris: Gallimard, 1997.
——. *Tout-monde*. Paris: Gallimard, 1993.
——. *Traité du tout-monde*. Paris: Gallimard, 1997.
Habermas, Jürgen. *Theory and Practice*. Trans. John Viertel. Boston: Beacon P, 1973.
Hale, Thomas A. "Césaire dans le monde blanc de l'Amérique du Nord." *Césaire 70*. Ed. George Ngal and Marin Steins. Paris: Silex, 1984. 109–21.
——. "Dramaturge et public: la nature interactive du théâtre d'Aimé Césaire." *Aimé Césaire ou l'athanor d'un alchimiste*. Paris: Editions Caribéennes, 1987. 195–200.
——. "Littérature orale: le discours comme arme de combat chez Aimé Césaire." *Soleil Eclaté: Mélanges offerts à Aimé Césaire à l'occasion de son soixante-dixième anniversaire par une équipe internationale d'artistes et de chercheurs*. Ed. Jacqueline Leiner. Tübingen: Gunter Narr Verlag, 1984. 173–86.
——. "Structural Dynamics in a Third World Classic: Aimé Césaire's *Cahier d'un retour au pays natal*." *Yale French Studies* 53 (1976): 163–74.
Halbwachs, Maurice. *La mémoire collective*. Edition critique établie par Gérard Namer. Paris: Albin Michel, 1997.
Hallward, Peter. "Edouard Glissant between the Singular and the Specific." *Yale Journal of Criticism: Interpretation in the Humanities* 11.2 (1998): 441–64.
Hanssen, Beatrice. *Walter Benjamin's Other History: Of Stones, Animals, Human Beings, and Angels*. Berkeley, Los Angeles, London: U of California P, 1998.
Hardt, Michael. *Gilles Deleuze: An Apprenticeship in Philosophy*. Minneapolis: U of Minnesota P, 1993.
Hardt, Michael, and Antonio Negri. *Empire*. Cambridge: Harvard UP, 2000.
Harvey, David. "What's Green and Makes the Environment Go Round?" In *The Cultures of Globalization*. Ed. Fredric Jameson and Masao Miyoshi. Durham: Duke UP, 1998. 327–55.
Hegel, G. W. F. *Hegel's Science of Logic*. Trans. A. V. Miller. Atlantic Highlands: Humanities Press International, 1969.
——. *Phénoménologie de l'esprit*. 2 vols. Trans. Jean Hyppolite. Paris: Aubier, 1941.
——. *Phenomenology of Spirit*. Trans. A. V. Miller. Oxford: Oxford UP, 1977.
——. *La philosophie de l'esprit de la Realphilosophie (1805)*. Trans. Guy Planty-Bonjour. Paris: Presses Universitaires de France, 1982.
——. *Le premier système: La philosophie de l'esprit (1803–4)*. Trans. Myriam Bienenstock. Paris: Presses Universitaires de France, 1999.
——. *Système de la vie éthique*. Trans. Jacques Taminiaux. Paris: Payot, 1992.
Heidegger, Martin. *Being and Time*. Trans. Joan Stambaugh. Albany: State U of New York P, 1996.

Herskovits, Melville J. *The Myth of the Negro Past; With a New Introduction by Sidney W. Mintz.* Boston: Beacon Press, 1990.

Hintjens, Helen. "Constitutional and Political Change in the French Caribbean." *French and West Indian: Martinique, Guadeloupe, and French Guiana Today.* Ed. Richard D. E. Burton and Fred Reno. Charlottesville: UP of Virginia, 1995. 20–33.

Hocquard, Jean-Jacques. "'Le temps de sang rouge': Interview with Aimé Césaire." *Le Point* (Jan. 1968): 30–31.

Hollier, Denis. *Les Dépossédés: Bataille, Caillois, Leiris, Malraux, Sartre.* Paris: Editions de Minuit, 1993.

Hommage à Alioune Diop. Rome: Editions des amis italiens de présence africaine, 1977.

Hountondji, Paulin. "Recapturing." In *The Surreptitious Speech: Présence Africaine and the Politics of Otherness.* Ed. V. Y. Mudimbe. Chicago: U of Chicago P, 1992.

Hountondji, Victor. "Les limites de la révolution césaireienne dans le cahier d'un retour au pays natal." *Peuples noirs/Peuples africains* 81, 1981.

Hunt, Lynn, and Jacques Revel, ed. *Histories: French Constructions of the Past.* New York: New Press, 1995.

Huyssen, Andreas. *Twilight Memories: Marking Time in a Culture of Amnesia.* New York: Routledge, 1995.

Hyppolite, Jean. *Genesis and Structure of Hegel's Phenomenology of Spirit.* Trans. Samual Cherniak and John Heckman. Evanston: Northwestern UP, 1974.

Iggers, Georg G., ed. *Leopold Von Ranke and the Shaping of the Historical Discipline.* Syracuse: Syracuse UP, 1990.

Irele, Abiola, ed. *Aimé Césaire: Cahier d'un retour au pays natal.* Ibadan: New Horn Press Limited, 1994.

———. "In Praise of Alienation." *The Surreptitious Speech: Présence Africaine and the Politics of Otherness 1947–1987.* Ed. V. Y. Mudimbe. Chicago: U of Chicago P, 1992. 201–24.

———. "'Les royaumes de colère' ou les voies de la révolte dans l'oeuvre poétique d'Aimé Césaire." *Aimé Césaire ou l'athanor d'un alchimiste.* Paris: Editions Caribbéennes, 1987. 63–86.

James, C. L. R. *The Black Jacobins; Toussaint Louverture and the Haitian revolution.* New York: Vintage Books, 1963.

Jameson, Fredric. *Late Marxism: Adorno, or, The Persistence of the Dialectic.* London, New York: Verso, 1990.

———. *Marxism and Form: Twentieth Century Dialectical Theories of Literature.* Princeton: Princeton UP, 1971.

———. *The Political Unconscious: Narrative as a Socially Symbolic Act.* Ithaca: Cornell UP, 1981.

———. *Postmodernism, or, the Cultural Logic of Late Capitalism.* Durham: Duke UP, 1991.

Jardel, Jean-Pierre. "Le Temps et l'histoire chez l'ecrivain: Afrique du Nord, Afrique Noire, Antilles." Ed. Jacqueline Bardoph et al. Paris: L'Harmattan, 1986. 114–23.

Jay, Martin. *Adorno.* Cambridge: Harvard UP, 1984.

———. *Marxism and Totality: The Adventures of a Concept from Lukács to Habermas.* Berkeley: U of California P, 1984.

———. "Mimesis and Mimetology: Adorno and Lacoue-Labarthe." *The Semblance of Subjectivity: Essays in Adorno's Aesthetic Theory.* Ed. Tom Huhn and Lambert Zuidervaart. Cambridge: MIT Press, 1997. 29–54.

Jos, Emmanuel. "The Declaration of the Treaty of Maastricht on the Ultra-peripheral Regions of the Community: An Assessment." In *French and West Indian: Martinique, Guadeloupe, and French Guiana Today.* Ed. Richard D. E. Burton and Fred Reno. Charlottesville: UP of Virginia, 1994. 86–97.

Joubert, Jean-Louis, et al. *Les littératures francophones depuis 1945.* Paris: Bordas, 1986.

Kant, Immanuel. *Critique of Pure Reason.* Trans. Paul Guyer and Allen W. Wood. New York: Cambridge UP, 1997.

———. *Critique of the Power of Judgement.* Trans. Paul Guyer and Eric Matthews. New York, Cambridge UP, 2000.

———. "What is Enlightenment?" *The Philosophy of Kant: Immanuel Kant's Moral and Political Writings.* Ed. Carl J. Friedrich. New York: Modern Library, 1949. 132–39.

Kaufman, Robert. "Negatively Capable Dialectics: Keats, Vendler, Adorno, and the Theory of the Avant-Garde." *Critical Inquiry* 27 (Winter 2001): 354–84.

———. "Red Kant, or, The Persistence of the Third *Critique* in Adorno and Jameson." *Critical Inquiry* 26 (Summer 2000): 682–724.

Kesteloot, Lilyan. *Aimé Césaire. Collection Poètes d'aujourd'hui.* Paris: Seghers, 1962.

———. "Alchimie d'un poème, *suivi de* Pourquoi toujours le surréalisme." *Aimé Césaire ou l'athanor d'un alchimiste.* Paris: Editions Caribéennes, 1987. 291–300.

———. *Comprendre le Cahier d'un Retour au Pays Natal d'Aimé Césaire. Les classiques africains.* Paris: Editions Saint Paul, 1982.

———. *Les écrivains noirs de langue française. Naissance d'une littérature.* Bruxelles: Université libre de Bruxelles, 1963.

Kesteloot, Lilyan, and Barthélémy Kotchy. *Aimé Césaire, l'homme et l'oeuvre.* Paris: Présence africaine, 1973.

Kofsky, Frank. *Black Nationalism and the Revolution in Music.* New York: Pathfinder, 1970.

Kolsky, Maurice. *Les Billets des DOM-TOM.* La Roche-Sur-Yon: L'Auréus, 1986.

Kojève, Alexandre. *Introduction à la lecture de Hegel.* Paris: Gallimard, 1947.

Koselleck, Reinhart. *L'Expérience de l'histoire.* Trans. Alexandre Escudier. *Collection Hautes Etudes.* Paris: Gallimard/Seuil, 1997.

Kristeva, Julia. *L'avenir d'une révolte.* Paris: Calmann-Lévy, 1998.

———. *Revolution in Poetic Language.* Trans. Margaret Waller. New York: Columbia UP, 1984.

Kyoore, Paschal. "The Francophone African and Caribbean Historical Novelist and the Quest for Cultural Identity." New York: Peter Lang, 1991.

LaCapra, Dominick. *History and Criticism.* Ithaca and London: Cornell UP 1985.

———. *History, Politics, and the Novel.* Ithaca and London: Cornell UP, 1987.

———. *Representing the Holocaust: History, Theory, Trauma.* Ithaca and London: Cornell UP, 1994.

Lacour, M. A. *Histoire de la Guadeloupe.* Basse-Terre: 1855.

Laplaine, Jean. "La Tragédie de l'histoire dans le théâtre d'Aimé Césaire." Doctorat du troisième cycle, Université de Toulouse-Mirail, 1975.

Laplanche, Jean, and J.B. Pontalis. *Vocabulaire de la psychanalyse*. Paris: Presses Universitaires de France, 1967.

Lara, Oruno. *La Guadeloupe Physique, Economique, Agricole, Commerciale, Financière, Politique, et Sociale: De la Découverte à nos jours (1492–1900)*. Paris: Nouvelle Librarie Universelle, 1922.

Lara, Oruno D. *De l'Oubli à l'Histoire. Espace et identité caraïbes: Guadeloupe, Guyane, Haïti, Martinique*. Paris: Maisonneuve et Larose, 1998.

Latour, Bruno. "Douze thèses pour sauver les Verts d'eux mêmes." *Le Monde* 7 Dec. 2001.

Lazzarato, Maurizio. "Immaterial Labor." In *Radical Thought in Italy*. Paolo Virno and Michael Hardt, eds. Minneapolis: U of Minnesota P, 1996.

Lefebvre, Georges. *Réflexions sur l'histoire*. Paris: François Maspero, 1978.

Lefebvre, Henri. *La fin de l'histoire*. Paris: Anthropos, 2001.

———. *La production de l'espace*. Paris: Anthropos, 2000.

Lefebvre, Jean-Pierre. "'L'oeuvre en mouvement': interview avec Jean-Pierre Lefebvre." *Magazine Littéraire* (Nov. 1991): 18–25.

Le Goff, Jacques. *Histoire et mémoire*. Paris: Gallimard, 1988.

Leiner, Jacqueline. *Aimé Césaire: le terreau primordial*. Tübingen: Gunter Narr Verlag Tübingen, 1993.

Lemoine, Lucien. *Douta Seck ou la tragédie du roi Christophe*. Paris: Présence Africaine, 1993.

Levinas, Emmanuel. *Basic Philosophical Writings*. Ed. Adrian T. Peperzak, Simon Critchley, and Robert Bernasconi. Bloomington: Indiana UP, 1996.

Lionnet, Françoise. *Postcolonial Representations: Women, Literature, Identity*. Ithaca: Cornell UP, 1995.

Lock, Graham. *Forces in Motion: The Music and Thoughts of Anthony Braxton*. New York: Da Capo, 1988.

Locke, John. *An Essay concerning Human Understanding. II, xxvii: "Identity and Difference."* Bilingual ed. Presentation, translation, and commentary by Etienne Balibar. Paris: Editions du Seuil, 1998.

Löwy, Michael. *Walter Benjamin: Avertissement d'incendie. Une lecture des thèses "Sur le concept d'histoire."* Paris; Presses Universitaires de France, 2001.

Lukács, Georg. *History and Class Consciousness: Studies in Marxist Dialectics*. Cambridge: MIT Press, 1971.

———. *The Theory of the Novel; A Historico-philosophical Essay on the Forms of Great Epic Literature*. Trans. Anna Bostock. Cambridge: MIT Press, 1971.

———. *The Young Hegel: Studies in the Relations between Dialectics and Economics*. London: Merlin Press, 1975.

Lyotard, Jean-François. *The Postmodern Condition*. Minneapolis: U of Minnesota P.

———. "Ticket to a New Décor." *Copyright* 1 (Fall 1987): 14–15.

Macherey, Pierre. "Kojève l'initiateur." *Magazine Littéraire* (Nov. 1991): 51–54.

Marcuse, Herbert. *Reason and Revolution: Hegel and the Rise of Social Theory*. 1941. Boston: Beacon Press, 1960.

Martin, Michel L., and Alain Yacou, eds. *De la Révolution française aux révolutions créoles et nègres*. Paris: Editions Caribbéennes, 1989.

———. *Mourir pour les Antilles: Indépendance nègre ou esclavage, 1802–1804*. Paris: Editions Caribéennes, 1991.

Marx, Karl. *The Marx-Engels Reader.* Ed. Robert C. Tucker. New York: Norton, 1978.

Maximin, Daniel. *L'Ile et une nuit.* Paris: Editions du Seuil, 1995.

———. *L'Isolé soleil.* Paris: Editions du Seuil, 1981.

———. *Lone Sun.* Charlottesville: UP of Virginia, 1989.

———. Personal interview, Basse-Terre, Guadeloupe, 2 Dec. 1994.

———. *Soufrières.* Paris: Editions du Seuil, 1987.

Mbom, Clément. "Edouard Glissant, De l'opacité à la relation." *Poétiques d'Edouard Glissant.* Ed. Jacques Chevrier. Paris: Presses de l'Université de Paris-Sorbonne, 1999. 245–54.

McAlister, Elizabeth. "A Sorcerer's Bottle: The Visual Art of Magic in Haiti." *Sacred Arts of Haitian Vodou.* Ed. Donald J. Consentino. Los Angeles: UCLA Fowler Museum of Cultural History, 1995. 304–21.

Mel, Frédéric Grah. *Alioune Diop: le bâtisseur inconnu du monde noir.* Abidjan: Presses universitaires de Côte d'Ivoire, 1995.

Ménil, René. *Antilles déjà jadis précédé de Tracées.* Paris: Jean Michel Place, 1999.

Métraux, Alfred. *Voodoo in Haiti.* New York: Schocken Books, 1972.

Miller, Christopher L. *Nationalists and Nomads: Essays on Francophone African Literature and Culture.* Chicago: U of Chicago P, 1998.

Monson, Ingrid. *Saying Something: Jazz Improvisation and Interaction.* Chicago: U of Chicago P, 1996.

Moudileno, Lydie. *L'écrivain antillais au miroir de sa littérature: Mises en scène et mise en abyme du roman antillais.* Paris: Editions Karthala, 1997.

Mouralis, Bernard. *Littérature et développement.* Paris: Silex, 1984.

———. "*Présence Africaine:* Geography of an 'Ideology.'" *The Surreptitious Speech: Présence Africaine and the Politics of Otherness 1947–1987.* Ed. V. Y. Mudimbe. Chicago: U of Chicago P, 1992. 3–13.

Mudimbe, V. Y., ed. *The Surreptitious Speech: Présence Africaine and the Politics of Otherness.* Chicago: U of Chicago P, 1992.

Murdoch, H. Adlai. *Creole Identity in the French Caribbean Novel.* Gainesville: UP of Florida, 2001.

Negre, Dr. Henri. *La Rébellion à la Guadeloupe (1801–1802).* Paris: Editions Caribbéennes, 1987.

Negri, Antonio. *The Savage Anomaly: The Power of Spinoza's Metaphysics and Politics.* Trans. Michael Hardt. Minneapolis: U of Minnesota P, 1991.

Nesbitt, F. Nick. "African Music, Ideology, and Utopia." *Research in African Literatures* (Spring 2001): 175–86.

———. "Negritude." *Encarta Africana.* Ed. Henry Louis Gates Jr. and Kwame Anthony Appiah. CD-ROM. Redmond, WA: Microsoft, 1999.

———. "Sujet producteur et autonomie postcoloniale." Forthcoming in *Rue Descartes,* Spring 2002.

———. "Sounding Autonomy: Adorno, Coltrane, and Jazz." *Telos* 116 (Spring 2000): 81–98.

———. "Le sujet de l'histoire: Mémoires troublées dans Traversée de la mangrove et Le cœur à rire et à pleurer." *Maryse Condé, Une nomade inconvenante: Mélanges offerts à Maryse Condé.* Ibis Rouge Editions: Guadeloupe, 2002. 113–19.

Ngal, Georges. "Aimé Césaire devant le 'grand public' Africain francophone." *Césaire 70.* Ed. George Ngal and Martin Steins. Paris: Silex, 1984. 163–202.

———. *Aimé Césaire: Un homme à la recherche d'une patrie.* 2nd ed. Paris: Présence Africaine, 1994.

———. *"Lire . . ." le Discours sur le Colonialisme d'Aimé Césaire.* Paris: Présence Africaine, 1994.

Nicholson, Shierry Weber. "Aesthetic Theory's Mimesis of Walter Benjamin." *The Semblance of Subjectivity: Essays in Adorno's Aesthetic Theory.* Ed. Tom Huhn and Lambert Zuidervaart. Cambridge: MIT Press, 1997. 55–92.

———. Exact Imagination, Late Work: On Adorno's Aesthetics. (Cambridge: MIT Press, 1997).

Nietzsche, Friedrich. *Human, All Too Human.* Trans. Marion Faber, with Stephen Lehmann. Lincoln and London: U of Nebraska P, 1984.

———. *On the Advantage and Disadvantage of History for Life.* Trans. Peter Preuss. Indianapolis: Hackett, 1980.

———. *On the Genealogy of Morals.* Trans. Walter Kaufmann. New York: Vintage, 1969.

———. *Par-delà le bien et le mal.* Paris: Unions Générales d'Editions, 1973.

Nora, Pierre. "Between Memory and History: Les lieux de Mémoire." *Representations* 26 (1989): 7–25.

Pardon, [Jean-Marie]. *La Guadeloupe depuis sa découverte jusqu'à nos jours.* Paris: Challamel, 1881.

Pestre de Almeida, Lilian. "Rire haïtian, rire africain (le comique dans La tragèdie du roi Christophe." *Prèsence francophone* 10 (Spring 1975): 59–71.

Pfaff, Françoise. *Entretiens avec Maryse Condé.* Paris: Karthala, 1993.

Pizaroo, Ana. "Reflections on the Historiography of Caribbean Literature." *Callaloo* 11.1 (1988): 173–85.

Porter, Lewis. *John Coltrane: His Life and Music.* Ann Arbor: U of Michigan P, 1998.

Placoly, Vincent. *Frères volcans.* Paris: La Brèche, 1983.

Porter, Lewis, and Michael Ullman. *Jazz from Its Origins to the Present.* Englewood Cliffs: Prentice Hall, 1993.

Price, Richard. *The Convict and the Colonel: A Story of Resistance in the Caribbean.* Boston: Beacon Press, 1998.

Price-Mars, Jean. *Ainsi parla l'oncle* (1928). Montreal: Lamèac, 1973.

Proust, Marcel. *A la recherché du temps perdu: Le Temps retrouvé.* Paris: Librairie Générale Française (Livre de Poche), 1993.

Ricoeur, Paul. *Temps et récit. Tome III: Le temps raconté.* Paris: Editions du Seuil, 1985.

———. *La mémoire, l'histoire, l'oubli.* Paris: Editions du Seuil, 2000.

Rinne, Suzanne, and Joëlle Vitiello. *Elles écrivent des Antilles (Haïti, Guadeloupe, Martinique).* Paris: L'Harmattan, 1997.

Rodano, Ronald M. *New Musical Figurations: Anthony Braxton's Cultural Critique.* Chicago: U of Chicago P, 1993.

Rosello, Mireille. *Littérature et identité créole aux Antilles.* Paris: Karthala, 1992.

Roth, Michael S. *Knowing and History: Appropriations of Hegel in Twentieth-Century France.* Ithaca and London: Cornell UP, 1988.

Said, Edward. *Culture and Imperialism.* New York: Vintage, 1993.

Saint-Ruf, Germain. *L'Epopée Delgrès: La Guadeloupe sous la révolution française (1789–1802)*. Paris: L'Harmatton, 1977.
Sartre, Jean-Paul. *Being and Nothingness*. Trans. Hazel E. Barnes. New York: Washington Square, 1954.
———. *L'imaginaire*. Paris: Gallimard, 1940.
———. "Orphée Noire." *Situations, III*. Paris: Gallimard, 1949. 227–86.
———. *Questions de méthode*. Paris: Gallimard, 1960.
Scharfman, Ronnie. "Rewriting the Césaire's: Daniel Maximin's Caribbean Discourse." *L'Héritage de Caliban*. Jasor, 1992. 233–46.
Schwarz-Bart, Simone and André. *Un Plat de porc aux bananes vertes*. Paris: Editions du Seuil, 1967.
Sekyi-Otu, Ato. *Fanon's Dialectic of Experience*. Cambridge: Harvard UP, 1996.
Senghor, Léopold Sédar. *Liberté I: Négritude et Humanisme*. Paris: Editions du Seuil, 1964.
Sheperd, Jon. *Music as Social Text*. Cambridge: Polity Press, 1991.
Shostakovitch, Dimitri. "Symphony No. 4, Opus 43." New York: Kalmus.
Sidrin, Ben. *Black Talk*. New York: Da Capo, 1971.
Sloterdijk, Peter. *Critique de la raison cynique*. Trans. Hans Hildenbrand. Christian Bourgois, 1987.
Songolo, Aliko. *Aimé Césaire, une poétique de la découverte*. Paris: L'Harmattan, 1985.
Spivak, Gayatri Chakravorty. *A Critique of Postcolonial Reason: Toward a History of the Vanishing Present*. Cambridge: Harvard UP, 1999.
Strauss, Jonathan. *Subjects of Terror: Nerval, Hegel, and the Modern Self*. Stanford: Stanford UP, 1998.
Suleiman, Susan Rubin. "Between the Street and the *Salon:* The Dilemma of Surrealist Politics in the 1930s." *Visualizing Theory: Selected Essays from V. A. R. 1990–1994*. Ed. Lucien Taylor. New York and London: Routledge, 1994. 143–58.
———. *Subversive Intent: Gender, Politics, and the Avant-Garde*. Cambridge: Harvard UP, 1990.
Suret-Canale, Jean. *Afrique noire occidentale et centrale (1961–63)*. 3 vols. Paris: Editions sociales, 1979.
Taruskin, Richard. "Public Lies and Unspeakable Truth Interpreting Shostakovich's Fifth Symphony." *Shostakovich Studies*. Ed. David Fanning. Cambridge: Cambridge UP, 1995. 17–56.
Taylor, Arthur. *Notes and Tones: Musician-to-Musician Interviews*. New York: Da Capo, 1993.
Taylor, Patrick David Michael. *The Narrative of Liberation: Perspectives on Afro-Caribbean Literature, Popular Culture, and Politics*. Ithaca: Cornell UP, 1989.
Toumson, Roger. "Une expérience des limites. L'épreuve du langage poétique chez Aimé Césaire. Le système métaphorique." *Aimé Césaire ou l'athanor d'un alchimiste*. Paris: Editions Caribéennes, 1987. 103–32.
Toumson, Roger, and Simonne Henry-Valmore. *Aimé Césaire: Le Nègre Inconsolé*. Paris: Syros, 1993.
Touré, Sékou. *L'Expérience Guinéenne*. Paris: Présence Africaine, 1959.
Varadharajan, Asha. *Exotic Parodies*. Minneapolis: U of Minnesota P, 1995.

Wahl, Jean. *Du rôle de l'idèe de l'instant dans la philosophie de Descartes.* Paris: J. Vrin, 1953.

———. *Essence et Phénomènes: La poésie comme source de philosophie.* "Les cours de la Sorbonne." Paris: Centre de documentation universitaire, 1958.

———. *Le Malheur de la conscience dans la philosophie de Hegel.* Paris: Rieder, 1929.

———. *La pensée de l'existence.* Paris: Flammarion, 1951.

Waldinger, Renée. "Edouard Glissant, professeur aux Etats-Unis." *Poétiques d'Edouard Glissant.* Ed. Jacques Chevrier. Paris: Presses de l'Université de Paris-Sorbonne, 1999. 255–64.

Walker, Keith L. *Countermodernism and Francophone Literary Culture: The Game of the Slipknot.* Durham: Duke UP, 1999.

———. "Silence et solitude brisés: Aimé Césaire et la révolution du langage." *Aimé Césaire ou l'athanor d'un alchimiste.* Paris: Editions Caribéennes, 1987. 133–44.

Webb, Barbara. *Myth and History in Caribbean Fiction.* Amherst: U of Massachusetts P, 1992.

Westphal, Merold. *History and Truth in Hegel's Phenomenology.* Bloomington: U of Indiana P, 1998 (1979).

White, Hayden. "Romantic Historiography." *A New History of French Literature.* Ed. Denis Hollier. Cambridge: Harvard UP, 1989a. 632–37.

Wilson, Elizabeth. "History and Memory." *Callaloo* 15.1 (1992): 179–89

Yerushalmi, Yosef Hayim. *Zakhor: histoire juive et mémoire juive.* Trans. Eric Vigne. Paris: Gallimard, 1984.

Yoder, Lauren W. "Developing Identity in the Caribbean: Writing about History in the Novels of Daniel Maximin." *Imagination, Emblems and Expressions: Essays on Latin American, Caribbean, and Continental Culture and Identity.* Ed. Helen Ryan-Ranson. Bowling Green: Bowling Green State University, 1993. 109–26.

Zaourou, Bernard Zadi. *Césaire entre deux cultures: problèmes théoriques de la littérature négro-africaine d'aujourd'hui.* Abidjan: Nouvelles Editions africaines, 1978.

Ziareck, Krzysztof. "The Ethos of History." *What Happens to History: The Renewal of Ethics in Contemporary Thought.* Ed. Howard Marchitello. New York: Routledge, 2001. 67–94.

Zimra, Clarisse. "Introduction to "Lone Sun." *Lone Sun.* Charlottesville: UP of Virginia, 1989.

———. "Je(ux) d'Histoire chez Daniel Maximin et Vincent Placoly." *L'Héritage de Caliban.* Ed. Maryse Condé. Pointe-à-Pitre: Editions Jasor, 1992. 265–87.

———. "Tracées césairiennes dans *L'isolé soleil.*" *Aimé Césaire ou l'athanor d'un alchimiste.* Paris: Editions Caribéennes, 1987. 347–68.

Index

Adelaïde-Merlande, Jacques, 72
Adorno, Theodor, 29; on aesthetic construction, 38–40; on death, 211; on poetry after Auswchitz, 207; on reification as forgetting, 17; in relation to postcolonial theory, 222 n. 57
aesthetic construction, 4, 36–40; in Antillean literature and art, 4, 40–2, 45, 74–75; Césaire's, 22–23, 28, 143–44; Glissant's, 183–84; and historical experience, 32–35; in relation to Freud, 222 n. 56
Afrocentrism, 151
Aimard, Gustave, 58–62
Alexis, Jacques Stephen, 210
alienation, 4, 20–21, 23–25, 27–28, 30–31, 45, 116, 217 n. 22–23; aesthetic representation of, 12–14; Henri Christophe's, 129, 132–33, 137, 139–40; as double-consciousness, 161; in Glissant's writing, 179–80, 181; in postwar DOMs, 71
anagram, 146–47, 161–62
anaphora, 90–91
Antillean literature, 33–35, 45–47
Antilles. *See* French Overseas Departments
Antoine, Régis, 135
Aragon, Louis, 106, 108
Aribot, Médard, 45
Arnold, A. James, 22, 82–83, 85, 108, 125, 219 n. 31
arpeggio, 161
assimilation, 6; Césaire's critique of, 122, 126; doudou as aesthetic representation of, 11–12
Auschwitz, 84, 207

autonomy, postcolonial, 1, 76–77; Antillean lack of, 8; of artwork, 39; Lukács on, 17

Baker, Houston A., 158
Balandier, Georges, 105
Baldwin, James, 157
Bangou, Henri, 66, 68, 72
Bataille, Georges, 84, 100–101
Baudrillard, Jean, 13, 72, 95
Baumgarten, Alexander, 36
bebop, 149, 156
Benelli, Graziano, 122
Benjamin, Walter, 29, 65; on dialectical and lived experience, 71–72; on memory, 18; and notion of collage, 38; and notion of constellation, 24; and notion of rememoration [*Eingedenken*] 40, 235 n. 8; on temporal experience and critique, 10; on triumphalist history, 34
Bergson, Henri: on temporal experience, 9–10, 16, 118, 217 n. 16
Bernabé, Jean, 35
Bidima, Jean-Godefroy, 46, 175
biological nation, 184–86, 188
blues, 154–55; and historiography, 156; analysis of, 158
Boisneuf, M., 63
Bongie, Chris, 148, 154
Boukman, 209
Boulez, Pierre, 97
Bourdieu, Pierre, 98
Boyer-Peyreleau, 54–56
Brathwaite, Edward Kamu, 153
Breton, André, 109
Brunschvig, Léon, 119

Buck-Morss, Susan, 130
Buffon, Alain, 9
Butler, Judith, 23

cannibalization, cultural, 126
Céline, Louis-Ferdinand, 89
Césaire, Aimé: biographical trajectory, 97–100, 120–22, 231 n. 8; concept of negritude, 21–24, 77; critical readings of, 122; critique of Antillean dependency in *Cahier*, 21; critique of racism, nazism, and totalitarianism by, 83–87; and death of subject, 95; and decolonization, xiii, 109; and departmentalization, 6; and dialectical history, 123–24; as engaged intellectual, 110–12, 118, 232 n. 14; and intellectual capital, 96; and *Phenomenology*, 120; and *Présence africaine*, 105; on reification and colonialism, 18–19. Works: *Cahier d'un retour au pays natal*, and Céline, 89; composition of, 78; contradictions of, 80–82, 88; historical importance of, 28–9; and nature, 89; originality of, 79–80; and rhythm, 90–92; and Shostakovich, 92–94. "Culture et colonisation," 125–27. "Letter to Maurice Thorez," 67. "The Political Thought of Sékou Touré," 112, 115–17. "Le verbe maronner," 108–9. *La tragédie du roi Christophe*, 127–44; dialectical historiography of, 130; and freedom, 128–29; and Hegel, 130–37, 139–42; historical importance of, 143–44; and Ogun, 137–39; role of Citadel in, 129–30
Césaire, Suzanne, 84
Chamoiseau, Patrick: on Antillean dependency, 8; on doudouist exoticism, 11, 35
Chirac, Jacques, relation to DOMs, 14
Christophe, Henri. *See* Césaire, Aimé
Citadel. *See* Césaire, Aimé
colonialism, 3; Antillean, 7; critique of, xii, 19–20, 76–77, 164; dependency and, 13; ideological defense of, 60–62
Coltrane, John, 166–69
commodification: aesthetic representation of, 9–13; and literature, 43, 203; of memory, 6, 69–75. *See also* reification
Condé, Maryse, 33, 71; relation to historiography, 193; relation to Proust, 197–99. Works: *Le Coeur à rire et à pleurer*, 196–99; *En tan revolisyon*, 199–202; *Traversée de la mangrove*, 194–96
Confiant, Raphaël: critique of Césaire, 99; on doudouist exoticism, 11, 35
Conley, Verena, 187
consciousness, and labor, 26–29, 30–31. *See also* double consciousness
construction. *See* aesthetic construction
contradiction: in Hegel, 26–27, 176; Césaire and, 80, 97
Creole (language), 20
Creole culture, 11
Créolité, 35, 161
Cri du Peuple, Le (newspaper), 63
Critique, (journal), 100–101

Damas, Léon-Gantran, 64, 76, 229 n. 11
Danticat, Edwidge, 202–12; and absence, 205–6; and death, 212; and freedom, 212; and guilt of the innocent, 206; and history, 210–12; and internalized guilt, 203; and representation, 205, 207, 209; and violence, 204
Dash, J. Michael, 170
Davis, Miles, 168
death: Danticat on, 212; Hegel and Césaire on, 140–41, 233 n. 24; Heidegger on, 16
decolonization, 1–3, 76–77; cultural prefigurations of, 106–8
Deleuze, Gilles, 168, 188, 235 n. 5
Delgrès, Louis: in Césaire's poetry, 109–10; colonialist memorialization of, 58–62; and the commodification of memory, 70–75; in *En tan revolysion*, 201–2; and events of 1802, 49–50; forgetting of, 51; in Guadeloupean historiography, 56–58; and Guadeloupean memory, 5–6, 216 n. 7; in *L'Isole soleil*, 154, 159; memorialization of, in Guadeloupean press, 62–63, 65–70; militarist memorialization of, 54–56; vernacular memories of, 51–54; and negritude, 64
departmentalization, 6; and commodification of memory, 70–71; as logical outgrowth of French centralization, 7
dependency, Antillean, 3, 6, 7–9, 18, 215 n. 4; and aesthetic construction, 46; and Antillean postmodernity, 13; Glissant on, 19–20, 178–79; resistance to, 4

Index

Depestre, René, 108–9, 144, 230 n. 16
Descartes, René, 216 n. 6
Descombes, Vincent, 119
Dialectic: Glissant and relational 175; Hegel's conception of, 43
Diop, Alioune, 100, 104–5
Diop, David, 76
DOM. *See* French Overseas Departments
double consciousness: and *Cahier d'un retour au pays natal*, 78, 79; and *L'Isolé soleil*, 161–62
doudou, aesthetic/ideological representation of, 11–13, 217 n. 19
Dualist Ontology. *See* Kojève, Alexandre
Dubois, W. E. B., 78, 161

Eagleton, Terry, 37
Ecole Normale Supérieure, 96, 97–98, 121, 232 n. 17
ecological consciousness, project of, 184–88, 190–91
Ellington, Duke, 161–62, 166
engagement (political commitment), 75–76; Césaire and, 94, 96–97, 99–100, 109–11
ethics, 46, 76; and *Cahier d'un retour au pays natal*, 80, 92, 211–12, 214
Etincelle, L' (newspaper), 65–70
Etudiant noir, L' (journal), 79, 101
Exoticism, aesthetic manifestations of, 11, 149, 167, 223 n. 65
experience, historical. *See* historical experience
externalization, Hegel's concept of, 24–28, 177

Fallope, Josette, 52
Fanon, Frantz, 20, 26, 31–33, 76, 201
fascism, and *Cahier d'un retour au pays natal*, 82–87, 87, 93–94
Fonkoua, Romuald, 172
Foucault, Michel, 119
France: and assimilation of colonized, 11; as concept, 46; and Maximin, 165; motivations for departmentalization of, 6–7
French Overseas Departments (DOM), xvi, 6, 216 n. 8–9; disappearance of memory in, 70–75; as ecological nation, 184–88, 190–91; monetary system of, 9; structural characteristics of, 7–8
Freud, Sigmund, 204, 222 n. 56

Gide, André, 102–4
Gilroy, Paul, 24, 79, 148; on African diasporic music, 144, 151, 220
Girard, Rosan, 66
Glissant, Edouard: on Antillean alienation, 146; on Antillean dependency, 7, 8, 19, 20; on Antillean ecological nation, 184–88; on Antilleans and Europe, 14; on concepts of relation and opacity, 43–45, 175, 177; critical interpretations of, 170–71; on erasure of Antillean memory, 51, 74, 182–84; philosophical training and influences, 171–73, 218 n. 25; on possibility, 175. Works: *Malemort*, 178–81; *Le Quatrième siècle*, 183–84; *Traité du tout-monde*, 184–85
globalization, 1; and colonialism, 3, 13, 69
Guadeloupe, 3; difference from Martinique, 223 n. 1; and historical memory, 5–6, 50–54, 70–75; in nineteenth century, 54–63; and tourism, 9; in twentieth century, 63–70. *See also* French Overseas Departments
guilt: of aesthetic production, 46, 203, 235 n. 8; of critical reflection, 76; nature of, 204–10
Guinea, 112–17

Habermas, Jurgen, 232 n. 16
Haiti, 56; in *Tragédie du roi Christophe*, 127–39; in relation to Martinique and Guadeloupe, 216 n. 8
Haitian Revolution, xii, 21, 128
Hallward, Peter, 170–71
Hardt, Michael, 106, 188–91, 220 n. 43
Harvey, David, 190
Hawkins, Coleman, 160–63
Hegel, G. W. F., 125; on aesthetic, 37; concept of experience *(Erfahrung)*, 29–33; concept of externalization *(Entaüsserung)*, 23–28, 220 n. 40; importance for postcolonial thought, xiv, 74, 116, 118–22, 123; Kojève's interpretation of, 23, 78; relation to Glissant, 174–78, 186, 187–88; relation to Kant, 42–44; relation to Marx, 37–38; and *Tragédie du roi Christophe*, 129–38, 139–44
Heidegger, Martin, 15–17, 218 n. 25
historical experience: aesthetic representation of, 12, 20–21; in Antillean literature, 33–35, 45–47; Césaire and, 28–29,

historical experience (*continued*)
123–24; and colonialism, 3; definition of, xi, 4, 221 n. 46; Fanon's critique of, 31–33; Glissant on, 14, 176–77, 178–80, 182–84; Hegel's conception of, 27–28, 29–31; Heidegger on, 15–17; and jazz, 151–52, 155, 156–61; Ménil on, 14; in postwar Guadeloupe, 70–75; reification and, 17–19, 18, 220 n. 45

historiography: and Antillean literature, 34–35; Césaire and, 127–28, 141–44; and Delgrès, 50–51, 54–58; Maryse Condé and, 193–94, 195, 200–201; nineteenth-century French, 60; postwar Guadeloupean, 72–75

history: in the Antilles, 14, 15, 28, 33–34, 45–47; jazz and, 148, 151–52, 155–56, 158, 162, 186, 194, 204, 214; and postmodernity, 2–4. *See also* Césaire, Aimé; Glissant, Edouard; historical experience; historiography; Heidegger, Martin; Lukács, Georg

Holocaust, and postcolonial experience, 71
Horkheimer, Max, 34, 235 n. 8
Howlett, J., 105
Huyssen, Andreas, 2, 4
Hwalbachs, Maurice, 18
Hyppolite, Jean, 119

identity, 15; and negritude, 22; politics of, 151. *See also* commodification; subjectivity

Ignace (revolutionary), 50, 164, 200; revindication of, 64, 67; vilification of, 56

imperialism, xi
improvisation, 153. *See also* Baker, Houston A.
intellectuals. See *engagement*

Jameson, Fredric, 3, 74; on Adorno, 39
jazz, and Antillean literature, 147–63

Kant, Immanuel: notion of aesthetic cognition, 36, 150; notion of experience, 30; notion of thing-in-itself (noumenal), 42–43, 222 nn. 61–62; racism of, 24; and subjectivity, 168; and *Tragédie du roi Christophe*, 132

Kaufman, Robert, 36–37
Kojève, Alexandre, 23, 78, 118–19, 232 n. 19; and Césaire, 123–24; importance of,

for postwar French thought, 230 n. 2; and Sartre, 123, 187; and *Tragédie du roi Christophe*, 130–35, 138–39, 142, 186. *See also* Hegel, G. W. F.

Kristeva, Julia, 81, 192

LaCapra, Dominick, 92
Lacour, Auguste, 56–58
Lacrosse, General, 49
Langlois, Charles-Victoire, 35
language, 29, 39, 44–45, 81, 135, 143, 217 n. 16. *See also* neologism
Lara, Oruno D., 51, 64, 200
Latour, Bruno, 188
Leclerc, General, 49
Légitime Défense (journal), 79
Légitimus (politician), 62
Le Goff, Jacques, 35
Levinas, Emmanuel, 213, 222 n. 59
Locke, John: on temporal conception of subjectivity, 4, 216 n. 6
Louverture, Toussaint, in *Cahier d'un retour au pays natal*, 28
Love Supreme, A (Coltrane), 166–67
Lukács, Georg, 26, 171; concept of reification, 12, 190

Marcuse, Herbert, 25–26, 176
Martinique. *See* French Overseas Departments
Marx, Karl, 17, 25, 26; and aesthetic experience, 37; critique of Hegel, 31–32; and production, 28
Maximin, Daniel: and Antillean postmodernity, 145–47, 163–65; critique of phallocentric historiography, 154–55, 233 n. 8; and gendered voice, 192; and jazz, 147–63, 165–69. Works: *L'Ile et une nuit*, 163–69; *L'Isolé soleil*, 145–63

memory, 18, 211–12, 218 n. 29; disappearance of, 13, 14, 51, 56, 58, 62, 70–75, 178, 182–84, 215 n. 3, 218 n. 28; as inherently aesthetic, 4; and postmodernity, 2–4. *See also* alienation; commodification; French Overseas Departments; history

Ménil, René, 14, 82, 85; on Antillean historical experience, 18; on double consciousness, 75; on jazz, 150, 152, 161–62; on *Tragédie du roi Christophe*, 127

métissage, cultural, 126
Métraux, Alfred, 138
mimesis, 193, 197–99
Mingus, Charles, 152, 166
modernity, and the Antilles, xii, xiii, xvi–xvii, 3, 14, 24, 71–72, 231 n. 5
modesty, 186, 214
Monson, Ingrid, 158
montage, 19, 91
Mukhina, Vera, 86
music: and *Cahier d'un retour au pays natal*, 92–94; and resistance, 52. *See also* jazz

nature, 9, 10, 23, 123, 164, 167; alienation from, 88–89; and the irrational, 82; mythical, 10–13, 146, 164–65, 169; in *Tragédie du roi Christophe*, 130, 131, 134–35, 138, 157, 158, 159, 162, 163, 177, 186, 207
Nausée, La (Sartre), 149
Negri, Antonio, 106, 188–91, 220 n. 43, 235 n. 7
negritude, 21–24, 28–29, 77, 81, 92, 122, 137; and fascism, 82–88, 90, 130; prefigurations of, 63–64, 73
neologism, 21–24
Nietzsche, Friedrich, 4, 208, 225 n. 1; and slave morality, 29
Nora, Pierre, 193
normalien. *See* Ecole normale supérieure
noumenal, the. *See* Kant, Immanuel
Nouvelle Critique, La (journal), 100–101

objectification. *See* externalization, Hegel's concept of
Ogun (Haitian god), 40. *See also under* Césaire, Aimé: *La tragédie du roi Christophe*
opacity, 42–45

Pardon, Jean-Marie, 58–62
Peuple, Le (newspaper), 62
Placoly, Vincent, 35
play, aesthetic, 146–47, 153
Porter, Lewis, 167
possibility, 190, 214, 234 n. 4; and Antillean literature, 35, 46, 168; and Glissant, 175–78, 181–82, 183; and Hegel, 25, 28; and Heidegger, 15
postcolonial theory: relation to European theory, 24–25, 30; and theorization of "other," 42

postmodernism: and colonialism, 3, 6; and Glissant, 170, 171, 173, 178; and *L'Isolé soleil*, 145–46, 148; and memory, 2; and notion of immanence, 189; relation to Heidegger, 15
Poughéon, Eugène, 9–13
Présence africaine (journal), 100–109, 112–17
Price, Richard, 24, 58; on economic dependency, 8; on postcolonial memory, 3, 72
production: absence of, in DOMs, 7–8, 146, 173, 175, 176, 178–79, 185–86. *See also* aesthetic construction; subjectivity: production-based
project, teleological, 42; and Glissant, 171, 185–88; Sartrean, 96
Proust, Marcel, 38, 169, 192, 211–12; and Maryse Condé, 197–99

reification, 17–19; aesthetic representation of, 11–13, 146–47. *See also* alienation; externalization
relation, 42–45, 174–78, 181–82
representation, 27, 43; aesthetic, 33, 45, 62, 68, 94, 113, 144, 145–47, 177, 178, 196, 198, 202, 205, 207, 209
responsibility: as overcoming of guilt, 205
Réveil Social, Le (newspaper), 62
rhythm, 90, 93
Ricoeur, Paul, 35, 218 n. 29
Riefenstahl, Leni, 85
Rosello, Mireille, 73, 154, 233 n. 24
Rousseau, Jean-Jacques, 133

Said, Edward, xi, 22, 106, 121, 231 n. 5
Saint-Ruf, Germain, 69
Sartre, Jean Paul, 22; comparison with Césaire, 97, 118, 120–21, 142; concept of project, 187–88; domination of postwar French intellectual field, 100–105, 232 n. 14; *La Nausée*, 149
Schoelcher, Victor, 62–63, 67, 68, 99
Schwarz-Bart, Simone and André, 20–21
Sekyi-Otu, Ato, 120
Senghor, Léopold, 83, 84, 120
Shostakovich, Dmitri, 92–94
signifyin(g), 159–60, 234 n. 14
Socialiste, Le (newspaper), 62
St. Jean (Haitian *bòkò*), 40–42, 45
subjectivity, 213; "death of," 95–96; ecological, 187; gendered, 192;

subjectivity (*continued*)
  production-based, 21–28, 29–33, 37, 110, 126, 129, 132, 134, 196, 232 n. 16; reified, 12–13, 17–18, 20, 71, 137; relation to aesthetic construction, xiii, 33, 39, 40, 80, 86, 88, 135, 144, 145, 146–47, 165–66, 168–69, 180, 194, 202, 205, 221 n. 48; temporal definition of, 4, 216 n. 6. *See also* double consciousness
Suret-Canale, Jean, 114–15, 230 n. 22

Temps modernes, Les (journal): position in postwar intellectual field, 100–101; relation to *Présence africaine*, 101–5
terror, 90. *See also* Césaire, Aimé: *La tragédie du roi Christophe*
Thierry, Augustin, 60

thing-in-itself (Kantian). *See* Kant, Immanuel
Touré, Sékou, 112–17
Toussaint Louverture. *See* Louverture, Toussaint
Tropiques (journal), 83–85, 99

Valentino, M., 63
Vilar, Paul, 35
Vodou, 137–39

Wahl, Jean, 119, 172
Westphal, Merold, 139
work. *See* aesthetic construction; production; reification
Worker and Collective Farm Girl (Mukhina), 86

New World Studies

New World Studies publishes interdisciplinary research that seeks to redefine the cultural map of the Americas and to propose particularly stimulating points of departure for an emerging field. Encompassing the Caribbean as well as continental North, Central, and South America, books in this series examine cultural processes within the hemisphere, taking into account the economic, demographic, and historical phenomena that shape them. Given the increasing diversity and richness of the linguistic and cultural traditions in the Americas, the need for research that privileges neither the English-speaking United States nor Spanish-speaking Latin America has never been greater. The series is designed to bring the best of this new research into an identifiable forum and to channel its results to the rapidly evolving audience for cultural studies.

Vera M. Kutzinski
Sugar's Secrets: Race and the Erotics of Cuban Nationalism

Richard D. E. Burton and Fred Reno, editors
French and West Indian: Martinique, Guadeloupe, and French Guiana Today

A. James Arnold, editor
Monsters, Tricksters, and Sacred Cows: Animal Tales and American Identities

J. Michael Dash
The Other America: Caribbean Literature in a New World Context

Isabel Alvarez Borland
Cuban-American Literature of Exile: From Person to Persona

Belinda J. Edmondson, editor
Caribbean Romances: The Politics of Regional Representation

Steven V. Hunsaker
Autobiography and National Identity in the Americas

Celia M. Britton
Edouard Glissant and Postcolonial Theory: Strategies of Language and Resistance

Mary Peabody Mann
Juanita: A Romance of Real Life in Cuba Fifty Years Ago
Edited and with an introduction by Patricia M. Ard

George B. Handley
Postslavery Literatures in the Americas: Family Portraits in Black and White

Faith Smith
Creole Recitations: John Jacob Thomas and Colonial Formation in the Late Nineteenth-Century Caribbean

Ian Gregory Strachan
Paradise and Plantation: Tourism and Culture in the Anglophone Caribbean

Nick Nesbitt
Voicing Memory: History and Subjectivity in French Caribbean Literature

www.ingramcontent.com/pod-product-compliance
Lightning Source LLC
Chambersburg PA
CBHW021852230426
43671CB00006B/355